designing web sites that work

USABILITY
FOR THE WEB

Usability for the Web:
Designing Web Sites that Work
Tom Brinck, Darren Gergle, and Scott D. Wood

Usability Engineering:
Scenario-Based Development
of Human-Computer Interaction
Mary Beth Rosson and John M. Carroll

Your Wish Is My Command:
Programming by Example
Edited by Henry Lieberman

THE MORGAN KAUFMANN SERIES IN INTERACTIVE TECHNOLOGIES

Series Editors:

Stuart Card
Xerox PARC

Jonathan Grudin
Microsoft

Jakob Nielsen
Nielsen Norman Group

Tim Skelly
Design Happy

GUI Bloopers: Don'ts and Dos for Software
Developers and Web Designers
Jeff Johnson

Information Visualization:
Perception for Design
Colin Ware

Robots for Kids: Exploring New
Technologies for Learning
Edited by Allison Druin and James Hendler

Information Appliances and Beyond:
Interaction Design for Consumer Products
Edited by Eric Bergman

Readings in Information Visualization:
Using Vision to Think
Written and edited by Stuart K. Card,
Jock D. Mackinlay, and Ben Shneiderman

The Design of Children's Technology
Edited by Allison Druin

The Usability Engineering Lifecycle:
A Practitioner's Handbook
for User Interface Design
Deborah J. Mayhew

Contextual Design: Defining
Customer-Centered Systems
Hugh Beyer and Karen Holtzblatt

Human-Computer Interface Design:
Success Stories, Emerging Methods,
and Real World Context
Edited by Marianne Rudisill, Clayton Lewis,
Peter P. Polson, and Timothy D. McKay

designing web sites that work

USABILITY FOR THE WEB

tom brinck
DIAMOND BULLET DESIGN

darren gergle
CARNEGIE MELLON
UNIVERSITY

scott d. wood
SOAR TECHNOLOGY

MORGAN KAUFMANN PUBLISHERS
AN IMPRINT OF ACADEMIC PRESS
A Division of Harcourt, Inc.
SAN FRANCISCO SAN DIEGO NEW YORK BOSTON
LONDON SYDNEY TOKYO

Morgan Kaufmann Publishers
340 Pine Street, Sixth Floor
San Francisco, CA 94104-3205 USA
http://www.mkp.com

ACADEMIC PRESS
A Division of Harcourt, Inc.
525 B Street, Suite 1900
San Diego, CA 92101-4495 USA
http://www.academicpress.com

Academic Press
Harcourt Place
32 Jamestown Road
London, NW1 7BY United Kingdom
http://www.academicpress.com

Executive Editor Diane D. Cerra
Publishing Services Manager Scott Norton
Senior Production Editor Cheri Palmer
Assistant Editor Belinda Breyer
Editorial Assistant Mona Buehler
Project Editor Jacqueline Volin
Cover/Text Design Chen Design Associates
Cover Image Photonica
Composition/Technical Illustration Chen Design Associates
Copyeditor Carol Leyba
Proofreader Ann Wood
Indexer Ty Koontz
Printer Courier Corporation

06 05 04 03 02   5 4 3 2 1

Library of Congress Control Number: 2001095449

ISBN 1-55860-658-0

This book is printed on acid-free paper.

Designations used by companies to distinguish their products
are often claimed as trademarks or registered trademarks. In
all instances in which Morgan Kaufmann Publishers is aware
of a claim, the product names appear in initial capital or all
capital letters. Readers, however, should contact the appropriate companies for more complete information regarding trademarks and registration.

CONTENTS

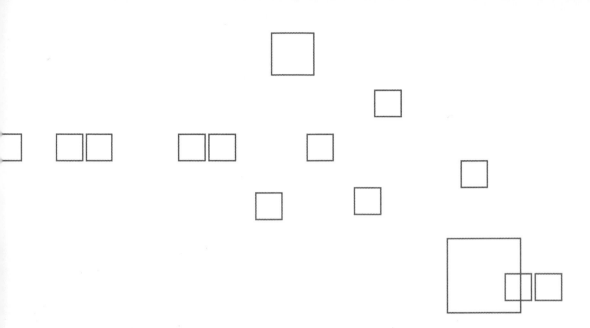

List of Forms   *xi*

Preface   *xii*

Introduction   *1*
- What Is Usability? 2 ▪ Why Is Usability Important for Web Sites? 3 ▪ Web Usability Problems 4

PERVASIVE USABILITY

Chapter 1.   ***Usability throughout the Design Process***   **12**
- Web Sites for People 14 ▪ Usability Methods 14 ▪ The Design Process 15 ▪ Project Management 20 ▪ Resources: Budget, Staff, and Schedule 21 ▪ How to Succeed at Project Management 29 ▪ Comparing Usability Methods 30 ▪ Pervasive Usability 35

REQUIREMENTS ANALYSIS

Chapter 2. **Target Audience and Target Platforms** **36**

■ Understanding Your Audience 38 ■ Scenarios 39
■ Design for Diversity 42 ■ Individual Differences 45
■ Differences in User Preference Settings 49
■ International Differences 51 ■ Hardware and Software
Differences 55 ■ Walking in Someone Else's Shoes 61

Chapter 3. **User Needs Analysis** **62**

■ The Objectives of User Needs Analysis 64 ■ Setting
Your Objectives 65 ■ Background Research 72
■ Surveys 72 ■ Competitive Analysis 83 ■ Interviews
and Focus Groups 85 ■ Informed Project Objectives 93

CONCEPTUAL DESIGN

Chapter 4. **Task Analysis** **94**

■ What Is Task Analysis? 96 ■ Task Analysis for Web
Site Design 99 ■ Use Cases 99 ■ Hierarchical Task
Analysis 101 ■ A Hybrid Approach to Task Analysis 108
■ Performance Improvements 110 ■ Human-Error-
Tolerant Design 115

Chapter 5. **Information Architecture** **118**

■ What Is Information Architecture? 120 ■ How People
Navigate 120 ■ The Process of Developing an
Architecture 130 ■ Maintenance and Expansion 142
■ Organization Schemes 146 ■ Ways to Present
Navigation to the User 155 ■ Labeling and Orientation
Cues 164 ■ Search Techniques and Search Engine
Design 169 ■ Embedding Your Site within the Framework
of the Rest of the Web 175 ■ Conceptual Design 177

MOCKUPS AND PROTOTYPES

Chapter 6. ***Page Layout*** **178**

■ The Goals of Your Layout 180 ■ Page Components and Basic Page Layout 182 ■ Some Common Page Structures 183 ■ Page Layout Techniques 184 ■ Page Layout Constraints, Common Pitfalls, and Solutions 197 ■ How Does Page Layout Affect Usability? 210

Chapter 7. ***Envisioning Design*** **212**

■ The Goals of Envisioning Design 214 ■ The Fidelity of Mockups and Prototypes 216 ■ Mockups 216 ■ The Mockup Creation Process 220 ■ The Mockup Review Process 232 ■ Prototypes 238

PRODUCTION

Chapter 8. ***Writing for the Web*** **244**

■ Writing to Communicate 246 ■ How People Read 256 ■ What to Write About 264 ■ Writing Style 276 ■ How Writing for the Web Differs from Writing for Print 281 ■ Text Formatting 294 ■ Getting Your Message Across 301

Chapter 9. ***Design Elements*** **302**

■ Goals of Graphic Design for the Web 304 ■ Establishing the Design Parameters 305 ■ Color 309 ■ Typography as a Design Technique 310 ■ Icon Design 314 ■ Designing Online Forms 318 ■ Navigation 325 ■ Interactivity and Multimedia 334 ■ Effectively Integrating Visual Design Elements 337

Chapter 10. **Usability in Software Development**   *338*

  ▪ Usability Problems 340 ▪ Web Site Engineering
  Techniques 343 ▪ Engineering Web Site Components
  353 ▪ Usability of Web Technologies 361 ▪ Principled
  Software Development 364

LAUNCH

Chapter 11. **Pre-Launch and Post-Launch**   *366*

  ▪ In the Months before the Launch 368
  ▪ The Challenge of Quality Assurance Testing 369
  ▪ Quality Assurance Testing before the Site Is Launched
  373 ▪ The Final Hurdles before Going Live 383
  ▪ Taking the Site Up 387 ▪ Immediately after the Site
  Is Up 388 ▪ Post-Launch Testing and Analysis 393
  ▪ Launch as a Process 402

EVALUATION

Chapter 12. **Usability Evaluation**   *404*

  ▪ Types of Evaluation 406 ▪ Usability Inspection 408
  ▪ Group Walkthroughs 419 ▪ User Testing 423
  ▪ Evaluation throughout the Design Process 441

Appendix   ▪ Usability Inspection of *www.whitehouse.gov*   *442*
References   *451*
Index   *459*
About the Authors   *482*

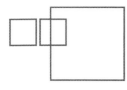

FORMS

Form 3-1	Client Interview/Web Site Information Worksheet	66
Form 3-2	Goals Checklist	68
Form 3-3	Web Site Survey	76
Form 3-4	Focus Group Preparation Worksheet	90
Form 5-1	Architecture Review Checklist	144
Form 7-1	Mockup Checklist	231
Form 7-2	Sample Mockup Development Schedule	233
Form 7-3	Mockup Style Review Form	236
Form 8-1	Writing Guidelines Checklist	257
Form 9-1	Web Site Materials Request Form	306
Form 9-2	Form for Brainstorming Icons	316
Form 9-3	Form for Testing Whether an Icon Is Recognizable	319
Form 9-4	Form for Testing Whether a Set of Icons Maps Uniquely to a Set of Concepts	320
Form 11-1	Problem Report and Resolution Form	381
Form 11-2	Problem Summary Report	382
Form 11-3	Postproduction Checklist	384
Form 11-4	Web Site Final Approval Form	386
Form 11-5	Minimal Maintenance Checklist	392
Form 12-1	A Detailed, General-Purpose Checklist	412
Form 12-2	User Testing Preparation Worksheet	424
Form 12-3	Typical Testing Script	429
Form 12-4	Consent Form	431

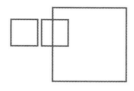

PREFACE

A fundamental truth in business is that sales are only successful if both the buyer and the seller benefit from the transaction. It's the same way with a web site: both the provider and the consumer (the customer or user) must benefit or the web site fails. From this perspective, user-centered design is just plain business sense. Usability is all about solving this equation: How do you help your users succeed within the context of achieving your own business or organizational goals?

And while usability is good business, we also firmly believe that it's the most humane, ethical, and responsible approach to design. Making a better user experience is about making the world a better place.

You can find other books that will tell you *what* to design. Having designed web sites from the beginnings of the Web, we've found that this isn't enough; in fact, it's hardly even a beginning. While some common principles are useful—simplicity, consistency, aesthetics, and so forth—there's inevitably a debate when we get down to the details.

This book is therefore about *how* to design. We'll give you plenty of design principles, but they're couched within an overall process and a set of methods that enable you to get the information you need to settle design decisions. In our experience, systematic processes not only produce better-quality work, they *simplify* your job, shortening the overall time to get to the desired result.

These methods are also largely developed around the idea that design should be rational, based on a careful allocation of development resources, thoughtful decision making when choosing among tradeoffs, and decisions based as much as possible on actual data about your users as opposed to opinions about users. We believe web site design is most fun when it's done well and you've made a difference for people.

Who This Book Is For

This book is for people who want to design web sites well. It will be extremely useful for

- managers of and within web site design organizations

- web site designers and developers themselves

- usability specialists and information architects

- those who hire a web developer and want to understand what's going on

- those who want to enter a career in web design and development

The book assumes you have some in-depth experience browsing the Web (if you don't, well, get out there and start browsing). We periodically discuss the code for web sites, but it's not necessary for understanding the majority of the book.

Acknowledgments

We all began our web usability adventure at Diamond Bullet Design, and our friends and colleagues there have taught us, encouraged us, challenged us, and provoked us. All of the staff there deserve our thanks. Equally so, our clients made it all possible and grounded this work in business reality. Diamond Bullet staff who specifically contributed to or influenced this book include Stephen Markel, Karsten Nielsen, Mike Monan, Chris Weatherford, Frank Levy, Alfred Speredelozzi, Elle Piekny, Heather Bradley, Jason Withrow, Kathy Withrow, Juliane Morian, Rod Lowe, Seunghee Ha, Katrina Brehob, Erik Zempel, Nick Pritula, Aric Watson, and Bryce Erwin. In addition, Soar Technologies generously supported Scott Wood during his work on this book.

We also all passed through the human-computer interaction (HCI) discipline at the University of Michigan, where our advisers have had a lasting influence on our perspectives, leaving a firm imprint on this work. In particular, we'd like to thank Judy Olson, Gary Olson, David Kieras, David Meyer, and George Furnas for their longtime guidance and support.

Our editors at Morgan Kaufmann, Diane Cerra and Belinda Breyer, provided us with gentle nudging, tolerance, and faith. Deborah Mayhew and our anonymous reviewers provided invaluable suggestions and insights in refining this work.

Of course nothing could have been possible without the support we got in our personal lives by Demet Wood and Tracy Zawaski.

INTRODUCTION

What is a highly usable web site? Highly usable web sites are intuitive. They are transparent. They support the users and allow users to accomplish their goals quickly, efficiently, and easily. In contrast, poor usability means that people using your web site cannot efficiently perform the tasks you intended. Poor usability can come from overly complex web sites, can lead to large numbers of user errors, or can mean that people just don't like using your system. For example, one aspect of usability is that users should know what to do next. They should either be given explicit instructions or the web site should follow some known interaction pattern. If the next steps are not obvious, users will spend precious time trying to figure them out. They may make mistakes or may just leave your web site with a bad feeling (see Figure I-1).

Figure I-1.

An Example of Poor Usability.

It isn't clear what's going on. Is something loading? Is the user supposed to click on one of the links? Where are we? Why is the screen mostly blank? Is my browser compatible?

WHAT IS USABILITY?

Usability is defined as the degree to which people (users) can perform a set of required tasks. It is the product of several, sometimes conflicting, design goals:

- Functionally correct: The primary criterion for usability is that the system correctly performs the functions that the user needs. Software that does not allow users to perform their tasks is not usable.

- Efficient to use: Efficiency can be a measure of the time or actions required to perform a task. In general, procedures that are faster tend to be more efficient.

- Easy to learn: Ease of learning determines how quickly new users can learn to accurately perform a task procedure. In general, the fewer steps a procedure contains, the easier it is to learn.

- Easy to remember: The degree to which a system taxes human memory determines how easy it is for users to remember. Systems that compel users to paste memory aids on their display screens are not easy to remember.

- Error tolerant: Error tolerance is determined by how well errors are prevented, how easily they are detected and identified when they occur, and how easily they are corrected once they are identified. Error-tolerant systems can also prevent catastrophic results if all other measures fail.

- Subjectively pleasing: In the end, usability is often determined by how users feel about using the system. Although nonfunctional graphics and other interface elements can skew a user's perception of usability, user satisfaction is probably a combination of all these criteria.

Because the goals of usability can conflict with one another, the context of the design will determine the priority with which each goal is applied. For example, a kiosk system that assumes no prior training would probably have ease of learning as a primary usability goal. A safety-critical system, such as a nuclear power plant, would have error tolerance as its primary usability goal. On the other hand, a video game would have to be fun to use (subjectively pleasing) in order to succeed in the marketplace. Furthermore, video game designers often depend on human error to make their designs more compelling, so conditions for human error are purposely built into games.

Only by attending to the myriad details does usability emerge as a dominant property. To ensure high usability on our own web projects, we defined a development process that incorporates proven techniques from software and usability engineering, graphic design, project management, and other disciplines. The process had to be practical and lean. It had to allow us to work on multiple projects of varying sizes with fixed budgets. It had to help us keep track of the details that can kill usability and destroy profitability. This book is about that process.

WHY IS USABILITY IMPORTANT FOR WEB SITES?

Web browsers have become a de facto standard for interbusiness communication and commerce in the new e-business paradigm. We are in the midst of a massive shift from diverse technology structures within business organizations, to a model in which business units have access to the most up-to-date information available, data is only entered once, and changes propagate instantly. Legacy information systems have been given new life as businesses use the Web to provide stored corporate knowledge to those who need it, both inside and outside an organization. Web-based applications have become a standard, cross-platform, nonproprietary means for businesses to communicate with each other and with consumers.

Businesses are continuing to increase their productivity, with information technology playing a critical role. Increased productivity is becoming an essential element for achieving or retaining a competitive edge. It may even be the key to survival for some businesses. However, we have seen in the past that technology alone cannot achieve increased productivity. In fact, there is ample evidence that technology can decrease productivity if poorly applied. High usability is a key factor in achieving maximum return on information technology investments.

WEB USABILITY PROBLEMS

Although the Web is based on a relatively simple interface consisting of links, buttons, menus, text fields, text, and graphics, severe usability problems are common. This chapter discusses four broad areas that contribute to these problems: human perception, navigation, human memory, and database integration. We will discuss these areas in detail and provide examples for the types of usability problems they can include. While there are certainly other areas that can be troublesome, this discussion should provide a convincing argument for integrating usability into web design.

Human Perception Problems

Perceptual issues can arise when pages are designed according to how the underlying information is physically stored (e.g., in a database), rather than how the information can best meet the needs of the user. This strategy may make page delivery and maintenance efficient, but it can also make the user's task slow and error prone. Figure I-2 (*www.cbsmarketwatch.com*) shows a table made for financial users to look up the stock symbols of publicly traded companies. The stock symbol is shown in the left column, the exchange where the stock is traded is shown in the center column, and the company name is shown in the right column. To find a symbol, the user must scan the right column to find the company name, then look across to the left column to find the corresponding symbol. In addition, the page uses black text on a gray background, and the tight line-spacing makes it easy to confuse which symbol corresponds to which company. By changing the layout, contrast, and typography, the designers could substantially eliminate unnecessary confusion and improve usability.

Other perceptual problems can arise when artistic style is considered before usability. Figure I-3 (*www.firstunion.com*) shows a portion of the home page for a bank web site. The colors used in this graphic are dark green text on a medium green background (on the left side), and dark purple text on a medium

AMBI	NASD	A M B I INC
AEN	AMEX	A M C ENTERTAINMENT INC
DIST	NASD	A M C O N DISTRIBUTING CO
AMEDE	NASD	A M E D I S Y S INC
UHAL	NASD	A M E R C O
PIN	NYSE	A M F BOWLING INC
AMLJ	NASD	A M L COMMUNICATIONS INC
AMXI	NASD	A M N E X INC
AMP	NYSE	A M P INC PENNSYLVANIA
AMR	NYSE	A M R CORP
AMXX	NASD	A M X CORP
ANBC	NASD	A N B CORP
ANSS	NASD	A N S Y S INC
TNT	NYSE	A O TATNEFT
APAC	NASD	A P A C TELESERVICES INC
APAT	NASD	A P A OPTICS INC
ATS	NYSE	A P T SATELLITE HLDGS LTD
ATT	AMEX	A R C INTERNATIONAL CORP
ARIA	NASD	A R I NETWORK SVC INC

Figure I-2.

Perceptual Problems.

In this lookup table, the contrast, column layout, and typography make this site difficult to use.

↔ Products and services overview		↔ Corporate and institutional overview	
Accounts, cards, loans, and more		Capital markets	Institutional services
Choose a product or service ⬦	Go	Cash management	International
		Commercial banking	Merchant services
↔ Financial planning overview		Commercial cards	Economic information
News and advice for your financial life.		↔ Small business overview	
☑ Investing	☑ Women's finances	Solutions center	Resource center
☑ Home	☑ Managing your money	Online advisor	Information center
☑ Retirement	☑ College		

Figure I-3.

Hard-to-Read Design.

Poor contrast and layout contribute to perceptual usability problems.

purple background (on the right). Although the First Union home page is somewhat visually appealing, the weak contrast makes the menu items difficult to read. Furthermore, the poor organization of items also hurts navigation. Although the items are separated into four main groups, it is not clear where to look first. Since there is no apparent ordering of the items, users need to read the entire list before determining that what they seek is not there.

Navigation

Navigation disorientation is among the biggest frustrations for web users. Three common questions users ask themselves while navigating on the Web are, Where am I now? How do I get where I want to go? and Where does this go? To find a navigation path, users must predict what will happen if a particular link is pressed and determine whether it takes them closer to their goal.

Navigation design issues include whether there is a logical architecture to the information in a site, whether there are sufficient indicators to give the user's current location, and whether the language and the organization of the navigation system match the user's expectations and needs for the task.

One navigation problem comes from the use of ambiguous links that may cause the user to go to the wrong page. For example, Figure I-4 (*www.direct banking.com/homebanking/index.html*) shows how links can be misused. What does "click here" mean? Reading the sentence, it is not clear if the links refer to *directbanking.com* and SalemFive accounts, checking accounts and

Figure I-4.

Problems with Link Labels.

Ambiguous language, poor use of
hypertext, and poor visual contrast
make navigation unpredictable for
the user.

> **Here's the next step!**
>
> If you'd like to add PC HomeBanking to an existing
> directbanking.com or SalemFive account, please click here or click
> here for more information about your checking account and
> HomeBanking options, or to apply online or by mail. Questions?
> Click on Most Popular Destinations or call

Homebanking options, applying online, or applying by mail. In addition, the bright yellow background color is tiring on the eyes, and the orange link colors do not provide sufficient contrast.

A second navigation flaw can be seen in the United States Information Agency web site (Figure I-5, *www.usia.gov*). The main problem with this page is that it uses nonstandard navigation elements. Instead of making the text items on the right function as links, as would be standard, the diamond-shaped graphics on the left of the text items function as the links. Not only does this provide a very small target for pointing and clicking, but there is no indication that pressing the graphics will have any effect. Standard techniques for indicating that a graphic is also a link include giving it a 3D, raised appearance (similar to a real button), providing redundant textual labels with the graphic, or providing an animated or other visual cue when the mouse cursor is moved over the graphic. None of these techniques, or any other ways of indicating links, were used on any of the links. To further complicate matters, a raised 3D effect was used for two of the other graphics (Public Diplomacy Forum and the "New" graphic in the upper left-hand corner of the screen), which are not links. These design flaws make navigating the site slow and error prone.

Figure I-6 (*www.congress.gov*) shows another misuse of graphical navigation elements. The core problem here is that users are not provided with any navigational context. There is no "You are here" indicator. The text-based links provide navigation to subpages, but the only other navigation elements are

Figure I-5.

Hidden Links.

On this navigation page, the diamonds
next to each line are links, but nothing about their appearance suggests
that they are buttons.

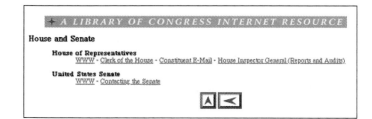

Figure I-6.

Where Are We?

The use of the arrow graphics for navigation can create confusion for users. Here, the navigation tells neither where the user currently is, nor where the icons will lead.

the arrow graphics at the bottom. There is no universal standard as to what arrows mean, but most commonly an up arrow navigates to the top of a page and a left arrow takes the user back to the previous page or across to a sibling page. However, if the user arrives at the site from somewhere other than where the designers have assumed (i.e., from a search engine site, such as *yahoo.com*), this "back" arrow will take the user to someplace unexpected. In this case, it will always take the user to the parent page. Although the parent page is a reasonable destination, the graphic does not convey the destination, possibly confusing users. There are times when arrows work but, because of the lack of context, this is not one of them.

Other problems can be created by not accurately indicating the user's current location. The title of the page in Figure I-7 (*www.congress.gov*) suggests that it is the home page of the United States Congress. In fact, it is the home page for the Government Printing Office (the office responsible for congressional printing). Consider also the links at the bottom of the figure. If you were looking for transcripts from someone that appeared before Congress, would you click on Congressional Committee Prints, Congressional Documents, or Congressional Hearings? The links are similar enough that additional descriptive information is necessary.

Human Memory

There are three primary human memory issues to consider when designing for the Web. First, if too many items must be remembered, it is likely that something will be forgotten. Second, the longer the time frame that items must be remembered, the more likely they are to be forgotten. Third, the greater the similarity among the remembered items, the more likely they are to be confused with one another. Web sites that require users to remember items from one page to the next are likely to cause problems.

Online financial services represent a task domain where human memory problems are prevalent. One web site that illustrates how human memory issues can affect usability is the Fidelity Investments online trading site

Figure I-7.

Poor Site Identification.

The title of this page suggests a different level in the hierarchy than it actually represents, and the links at the bottom are ambiguous.

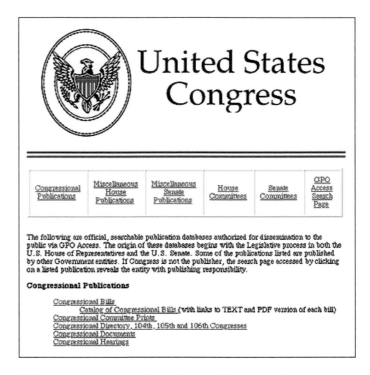

(*www.fidelity.com*). Figure I-8a shows the Portfolio screen for the system. Here, the user has access to all investment holdings (also called *positions*) within a single Fidelity account. To sell some or all of a holding, the user must press the Trade button in the holding's Description column, which brings up the Trade Stocks screen.

The Trade Stocks screen is shown in Figure I-8b (*www.fidelity.com*). It contains fields for the user to enter all the information necessary to buy or sell a stock or mutual fund. The problem is that the system does not automatically fill in the symbol or the quantity fields (or show the available quantity), so the user must go back to the Portfolio screen to get that information. From personal experience we know that such backtracking happens often. Even for users who are aware of this flaw, the task still requires that they remember the symbol (a possibly non-mnemonic string of three to five characters) and the quantity (e.g., 523.156). The stress under which many people manage their finances, the similarity of symbols and digits, and the potential network delays can combine to overload working memory. The result is that errors are very likely. Since many erroneous values can still be considered a valid trade, the error may not be caught until much later (e.g., while reviewing a monthly report). Depending on when the error is caught, such confusions can be slightly costly (lost time reexecuting the trade), moderately costly (paying transaction fees to undo the erroneous trade), or very costly (loss due to lost opportunity or unalterable trade).

Database Integration

As Web technology has matured, database systems have become a central tool for building web-based software applications. Although this approach is very powerful and can vastly streamline ongoing system maintenance, issues with integrating database technologies can create severe usability problems for the end user. A common problem is that information that the user sees gets out of sync with information in the serving database. That is, what the user sees is not what the database contains. Figure I-9 (Northwest Airlines, *www.nwa.com*) shows how information can change even in the middle of a short transaction. Sites that do not check for such changes can cause even greater user confusion.

(a)

(b)

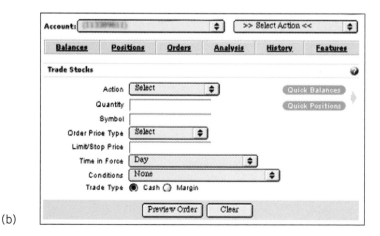

Figure I-8.

Memory Problem.

(a) This page shows portfolio information for an individual. To trade a current holding, the user clicks on the Trade button (text intentionally blurred). (b) After clicking on the Trade button, this page is presented to the user. The problem is that the user needs information (symbol and quantity) from the previous page. Even if the user remembers to get the information, page load-time can cause the user to forget or misremember the items needed.

Figure I-9.

Database Integration Problem.

Changing information can cause the user's assumptions to become invalid.

Price Changed

Please review the information below and confirm your decision. If you wish to proceed, click the **Accept New Price** button at the bottom of the page. If you click **Cancel Reservation**, the price for this flight will still be updated, but no purchase will be made. Your reservation will be saved so that you can purchase it later or cancel it.

The price of this flight has changed from US $208.00 to US $205.00.

Do you still want to proceed?

ACCEPT NEW PRICE   CANCEL RESERVATION

Figure I-10.

A Weak Solution.

Many systems explicitly instruct users to periodically reload pages where the displayed information may change.

[Follow Ups] [Post Followup]

[Post Message] [Search Messages] [Reload Message List]

Because of problems with database integration, some sites ask users to reload a page when information has changed. But it is easy to forget to do so. This can occur in many situations, such as with online message systems. These systems allow users to post, read, and search for messages on various topics. Figure I-10 shows the menu choices for such a message system. Here, the user must periodically reload the message list to find new messages that others may have posted. If the user never reloads, the message list will never change, and the user will not know when new information is available. This can cost the user time and cause the user to post multiple requests for information.

Similarly, users can continue to send information requests and transaction responses while the server is still processing prior transactions. If a user re-presses a transaction button or reloads a page at the wrong time (say, while waiting for the server to respond), the original transaction may be duplicated. For instance, instead of purchasing one airline ticket as intended, the system could sell you two. Many sites, such as the Northwest Airlines site (Figure I-11, *www.nwa.com*) warn users of this possibility and its consequences, but having the server identify unique transactions can actually prevent the problem.

Figure I-11.

Unintended Consequences.

If users accidentally double-click on the Purchase button, they can purchase two tickets instead of one.

When you are ready to make your purchase, please click the **Purchase** button **only once**. Purchases may take a few minutes. A blank screen may appear while you wait. This is normal. If there is no response after 5 minutes or an error occurs, please verify that your purchase has been completed with the following steps:

1. Click **Cancel** to return to your itinerary.
2. Click the **Update!** button on the itinerary screen.
3. If your purchase is confirmed, the flight will be marked as ticketed in your itinerary.

PURCHASE   CANCEL

Today's Schedule | This Week | Future Schedules
Debates | Hearings | Press Conferences | Special Events
Today on FEDNET
Please press the Reload (or Refresh) Button each time you come to this page!

Figure I-12.

Placing the Burden on the User.

This is another example of a site that asks the user to reload pages periodically, but it's not unusual for a user to forget to do so.

Another usability issue stemming from web technology involves the caching systems in most web browsers. Applications cache web pages to improve performance. When users return to a page, especially shortly after an initial visit, the page is likely to be loaded from the client-side cache. New information is not seen by the user unless the page is reloaded from the server. To help prevent problems with cached pages, some sites remind users to reload pages (Figure I-12, from *www.fednet.net*), but users often forget to do this.

These examples show just a few of the many ways that usability problems can surface in web sites. Their causes range from inaccurate requirements, to bad design, to bad implementation, to poor choice of technologies, to poor deployment and maintenance. To combat the pervasive problems of poor usability, we have defined a development process that addresses usability issues throughout the development lifecycle. We call it *Pervasive Usability*.

01

PERVASIVE USABILITY

USABILITY THROUGHOUT THE DESIGN PROCESS

WEB SITES FOR PEOPLE

Users need to be considered early and often. Usability needs to be a part of *every* step of the design process. Our approach is *pervasive usability*—integrating usability into everything we do. Our philosophy is that usability should not be an add-on, but that everyday processes should be modified to be user-centered.

Make usability part of everything you do. Make it a lifestyle.

People shouldn't be an afterthought in design. Testing and fixing a web site *after* it's built is inefficient and unlikely to produce a good design. Information about users should come as early as possible in the design process, and bad designs need to be weeded out long before you've overcommitted to them. Building web sites for people happens from the start.

Our view of how usability must be achieved parallels the modern view of quality assurance. A hundred years ago, creating a quality product was achieved by hiring a master craftsman and relying on expertise. As more and more production became automated, quality control shifted to a perspective of testing a product to verify its high quality, a procedure that did not require as much expertise. But testing is an expensive technique because it can mean that a large number of low-quality products are being produced before being filtered out at the end. To achieve quality at a reasonable cost, we need to push quality assurance back to the earliest point in the production process.

Today, total quality management (TQM) programs look at every step of the process to ensure that quality isn't compromised along the way. This is achieved with appropriate planning, process management, documentation, and verification. From our perspective, quality assurance is a subset of the overall usability goal (after all, a web site isn't usable if it isn't working).

Our goal in this chapter is to examine how usability can be achieved, with a focus on planning, process management, documentation, and verification (what we call *evaluation*). Design *process* is at least as important as design *principles*. Planning and method are the only reliable, effective means to achieving usability within other design constraints.

USABILITY METHODS

A usability method is any technique you use to create a design from a user-centered perspective. This starts from the outset of a project, where you begin by defining who your target audience is and then try to understand what that audience wants and how they want to work. The idea is that, no matter what you're doing, there's a user-centered way of doing it, and at the core, that means having the user on your conscience even when there are no users nearby.

Two broad categories of usability methods exist: those that gather data about the behavior of actual users and those that can be applied even without users present.

Real Data from Real Users

Traditional design training has emphasized mastering principles of good design and gaining experience to create excellent designs, but this is not enough! Skilled designers will usually create better designs than nondesigners, but no matter how experienced you are, you're bound to make some mistakes and have some false expectations about the users. The only way to be sure is to gather information from actual users, and this can be accomplished by various means, such as focus groups, interviews, and usability testing. We'll cover these techniques throughout the book.

In the User's Absence

Why wouldn't you gather information from users for every design decision? In very small web projects, you may not have the budget to do usability testing, and on some projects, you'll find it's incredibly difficult to arrange to meet your target audience. Even on projects where you can do some user testing, it's never possible to test every single design decision that you make.

In these circumstances, you'll have to estimate how usable your design is, based on previous experience, models of user behavior, and widely agreed upon design principles. Even when you can reach users, you'll find that talking to them is much more constructive when you've done some planning ahead of time, based on what you expect might be an appropriate design for them. Various paper-and-pencil techniques can help you work out designs from a user-centered perspective, and we'll cover these throughout the book as well.

THE DESIGN PROCESS

Our general design process is illustrated in Figure 1-1. We call this the Pervasive Usability Process. This process is relevant to design in almost any domain whatsoever. In the figure, evaluation appears below, on its own, to indicate that similar types of evaluation can occur at different stages of design. Evaluation helps to ensure that the design is on track to satisfy the goals of the design. Evaluation may include usability evaluation, client review of the design, quality assurance, or technical feasibility evaluation. Evaluation is part of what makes usability pervasive, but usability is also fully integrated into every stage of the process.

Figure 1-1.

The Pervasive Usability Process.

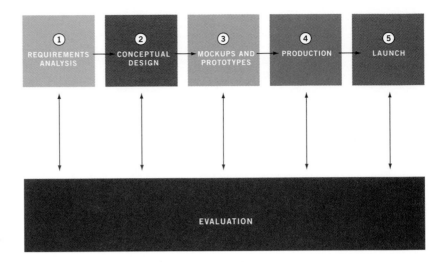

This process is meant as a paradigm that any actual project should take as an ideal model, but it is not meant to be a rigid prescription forced onto a project. For instance, the model is drawn as a linear sequence from Requirements Analysis to Launch. This emphasizes the practical reality that projects must move forward on a sequential schedule, but at the same time it's common, and perfectly reasonable, for a later step, such as Mockups and Prototypes, to provide information that causes an earlier step, such as Requirements Analysis, to be refined. Some feedback is perfectly natural.

This process handles multiple activities occurring in parallel. Layout, content development, and technical proof-of-concept designs need to be explored simultaneously as you proceed in the process. They may follow separate timetables in larger projects, but the same overall process applies.

Iterative Design

Our design approach is to progressively refine the design through low-cost evaluation at early stages of design, building up to successively more usable designs at each stage. The most expensive stage is Production, where the final web site is produced. We want the final design to be as usable as possible so that only minimal changes will be needed at completion. At each stage, we want to cycle between refining our design and evaluating our latest refinement, iterating until we've achieved a level of usability that we're satisfied with before continuing to the next stage. Evaluation at each stage enables us to incorporate user and client feedback loops to optimize the design.

At each evaluation, we determine whether our design is adequate for continuing on. We do this by establishing *benchmarks,* or target usability goals. For example, we might say that before accepting a page layout, we would like at least 80 percent of the people who see the design to rate it at least a 6 on a 7-point scale from *very obscure* to *very obvious.*

The difficulty with the iterative design approach is that budgets and deadlines are typically set *before* the process, and thus, we may not be able to afford to iterate until we meet our final criteria. Instead, we may only be able to iterate until our budget has been exhausted, which could be well before our goals are met. Of course, the critical questions to ask are, If we haven't met our benchmarks, will the project be successful? And if not, should we extend the budget and deadline or should we cancel the project?

So how do we iterate appropriately given these constraints? We must (1) plan which types of evaluation to do and how many cycles of iteration will be allotted for each step; and (2) leave some slack time in our original schedule to allow for unexpected iterations.

Stages of the Process

The following describes each segment of the Pervasive Usability Process, including the Evaluation component, which can take place throughout the process.

Stage 1. Requirements Analysis

This is the stage at which you formulate the design problem. At this stage, you determine the target audience and target platforms, user goals, business goals, technical requirements, and so forth. This is where user needs and target usability requirements are determined. Evaluation at this stage usually involves evaluating prior art—previous versions of the product being designed, competitive products, or how people have achieved the same goal without software. Common evaluation methods at this stage are competitive analysis, user interviews, and surveys. This is the most important step in the process because if you incorrectly identify the goals and parameters of the project, then everything you do after this stage is wasted. Requirements Analysis is covered in Chapter 2, "Target Audience and Target Platforms," and in Chapter 3, "User Needs Analysis."

Stage 2. Conceptual Design

At the Conceptual Design stage, the functionality of the product is worked out. The design is sketched out at an abstract level of specification that avoids committing to any specific layout or implementation. Typical design methods include use cases, task analyses, and information architecture (working out flowcharts and outlines of the system). Task analysis is covered in Chapter 4. Information architecture is covered in Chapter 5.

Stage 3. Mockups and Prototypes

At this stage, visual representations (mockups) or interactive representations (prototypes) of the final design are created and refined. The sole purpose of creating these mockups is to get a chance to evaluate the design early, before the final system is produced. The goal is to produce these mockups rapidly and evaluate them efficiently so that they can be refined, elaborated, and reevaluated before you produce the final product. This can save tremendous time and money by avoiding expensive changes later in the process. Common evaluation methods at this stage include user testing and focus groups. Specific page layout concepts are covered in Chapter 6. Mockup and prototyping techniques are covered in Chapter 7.

Stage 4. Production

At the Production stage, the final product is created. Final text and graphic content must be developed, and the site must be coded. Common evaluation methods include quality assurance, user testing, and field testing. Production issues are covered in Chapter 8, "Writing for the Web," in Chapter 9, "Design Elements," and in Chapter 10, "Usability in Software Development."

Stage 5. Launch

Finally, the product is launched and made available to the public. Just before launch, a final quality testing phase must assure that everything is ready to go online; immediately after launch, the correctness of the site must again be verified. Later, a web site will continue to be maintained and refined, and the design process is repeated again from step 1. Pre-launch and post-launch activities are covered in Chapter 11.

Evaluation

At every stage of development, some type of feedback system is necessary. We want to identify as quickly as possible when the design process veers off track. Are we failing to meet critical usability or business requirements? We'll address these evaluation issues throughout the book, with descriptions of user studies, client feedback forms, and design checklists that help spot problems. Finally, Chapter 12, "Usability Evaluation," provides in-depth information about the processes of evaluating our sites with checklists or through user testing.

The Project Schedule

In Figure 1-2, a typical project schedule for a relatively small project illustrates how the abstract design process is achieved in terms of concrete project milestones and client checkpoints. Typically each milestone is associated with a specific planned date. The top of the diagram represents milestones for the development team, and the bottom of the diagram represents checkpoints with the client.

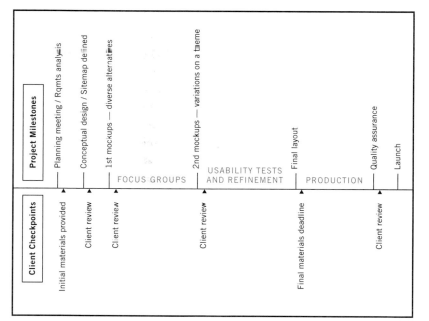

Figure 1-2.

An Example Project Schedule

While this diagram illustrates the abstract process, each project will need to choose specific methods and milestones and lay out a schedule.

As a relatively small project, this example has allotted iterations for the mock-up stage but no significant iterations for other stages. A typical project of this size generally can't be done in fewer than six to eight weeks. An even smaller project would likely need to limit mockup iteration as well. With larger projects, this kind of diagram doesn't work very well because of the large number of activities and milestones, and project management software can display these timelines in more convenient Gantt charts and PERT charts. Larger projects will need to show the parallel development of the content, layout, and back-end software (databases, e-commerce engines, etc.).

While this diagram is not to scale, it is relevant to point out that actually *building* the front end of the web site (the Production stage—creating final text, graphics, and HTML code) is commonly a relatively small piece of the overall process.

PROJECT MANAGEMENT

Effective project management is crucial to seeing a user-centered design approach succeed. Why? Without good project management, usability is unlikely to be factored into the process as problems arise. Effective project management responsibly makes tradeoffs to ensure a rational decision-making process. The key is to remain accountable to your own usability goals. When a project runs into trouble, a common solution is to remove usability processes from the project. However, project managers who keep the big picture in mind can see the real cost of removing usability reviews, user testing, and so forth, and can therefore effectively optimize project activities.

Table 1-1 shows the elements that effective project management needs to incorporate.

Table 1-1.

The Elements of Effective Project Management.

Inputs	Resources	Process
Client needs	Budget	Planning and communication
User needs	Materials	Documentation
Other stakeholder needs	Schedule	Efficiency and repeatability
Competitive environment	Personnel	Quality assurance
Market factors	Technologies	Deliverables

Tradeoffs

A total project plan must satisfy needs beyond usability, such as profit requirements, technology limitations, and workforce satisfaction. The most important project principle is that design is a process of resolving tradeoffs. You shouldn't get tied up on one principle at the expense of every other concern. Remember that *every* design has to make certain sacrifices because of limited time and budget. It's okay to take shortcuts and make compromises, as long as they're thoughtfully considered.

Throughout this book we'll be covering several design tradeoffs. Effective tradeoff analysis involves listing the pros and cons of each alternative, weighing their relevance in your design situation, and then making a decision appropriate to the context of your problem. There are few design guidelines that can be viewed as absolutes. Instead, an appropriate rationale needs to be developed for each application of the guidelines in each circumstance.

The following are some key principles for making effective tradeoffs.

The 80/20 rule: This is a principle for setting priorities. The idea is that users will spend 80 percent of their time using 20 percent of the web site, so you should put

PERVASIVE USABILITY

80 percent of your design effort into that same 20 percent of the web site. In other words, determine what's most important, and put your effort into getting those things right.

Design for manufacture: This is a common principle of industrial design, which says that design must take production needs into account, including the capabilities of the production tools, the skills of the production staff, delivery limitations, and the cost of materials.

Design for evolution: Design also needs to take into account the likelihood that the web site you're developing will grow and evolve over a long period of time. Long-term maintenance means that you'll need to make the navigation flexible and facilitate adding information with minimal coding.

Stakeholders

Design is a team effort, drawing from many different areas of expertise. Numerous people have a stake in any design decision. While we put users first in importance, any design that doesn't account for the other stakeholders is likely to fail. Common stakeholders include the users, your client, your management, your design and development team, your marketing team, the press who will review your work, the customer support team, the shipping department, the system administrators, and so on. All of these people have an interest in and are affected by any design decision and must be considered.

One of the most difficult aspects of resolving tradeoffs is being accountable to all stakeholders. Many of the stakeholders may not have usability as a top priority. As a designer, you have the responsibility to educate the teams you work with to ensure that usability is factored appropriately into the decision process.

RESOURCES: BUDGET, STAFF, AND SCHEDULE

The three critical resources of any project are money, people, and time.

Budget

Everyone wants more than they can pay for. That's human nature. We all dream of doing just a little more than our resources permit. A good budget plan is an effective tool for controlling our own and our clients' expectations.

Staffing is likely to be your highest cost, so that will be our focus in this discussion. However, make sure you plan for the other costs. Typical capital equipment costs include office equipment, computers, printers, web servers, scanners, and digital cameras. Typical operating expenses include standard business overhead, such as rent and office supplies, as well as specific web development costs, such as ISP and hosting fees, clip art and fonts, web reference books and magazines, software, and storage media.

A spreadsheet is a good place to start with budget planning, and even a very simplified budget, like the one in Figure 1-3, is very helpful.

While the numbers in this spreadsheet are hypothetical, they're also quite realistic for a web site of a certain scale (that is, with a couple of relatively straightforward databases). The amount of time you allocate to any specific task can vary, and should vary, based on the exact scope of your project, such as how many pages the site contains, how many users are brought in for testing, when testing occurs, and so forth.

This part of the budget is for the web site design and development team. A broader view needs to incorporate other aspects of the business for which the web site is being developed. During development, there may be legal expenses, such as trademark registration or privacy policy review. At release, marketing the web site may incur substantial marketing costs. During main-

Figure 1-3.

Planning Your Budget.

A sample worksheet for analyzing a budget and developing project priorities.

DEVELOPMENT PROCESS	CYCLES	HOURS/ CYCLE	HOURS	COST/ HOUR	COST
Requirements Analysis	1	30	30	$100	$3,000
Conceptual Design	1	16	16	100	1,600
Mockups	3	30	90	100	9,000
Production:					
Graphics	1	10	10	100	1,000
Writing	1	60	60	100	6,000
HTML	1	30	30	100	3,000
Database Development	2	40	80	150	12,000
Software Development	0	n/a	n/a	150	n/a
Project Management (10%)			31.6	150	4,740
Slack Time (10%)			31.6	100	3,160
EVALUATION					
Surveys	0	60	0	150	0
Focus Groups	1	40	40	150	6,000
Interviews	0	40	0	150	6,000
User testing	1	40	40	150	6,000
Quality Assurance	2	8	16	100	1,600

Total hours 475.2   Total cost $57,100

PERVASIVE USABILITY

tenance, the business may have a variety of operational costs to support the activity generated by the web site: customer support, order processing, shipping, and so forth.

Iterations and Slack Time

The Cycles column in the sample budget represents the number of times you plan to iterate at any given project stage. If you need additional, unpredicted iterations, the slack time included in the spreadsheet (the last row in the Development Process) should accommodate that need. This spreadsheet sets slack time as 10 percent of the design and development time, although as much as 20 percent could reasonably be allocated for smaller jobs, and considerably more for larger jobs. You could incorporate the slack time into the estimates at individual stages, but leaving it as a separate line item is a more flexible way of handling the possibility that an entire stage may need to be repeated if it doesn't perform well in evaluation.

How Much Time It Takes

The Hours/Cycle column takes into account the project scope and web site features (on large projects, we will often compute this on the basis of days instead of hours). For example, 40 hours of user testing is appropriate for running ten users on a working web site (1 hour for each user, plus time for planning, recruiting, analysis, and fixing the design), but substantially less time is needed if you do informal user testing on web site mockups. Software development is marked as n/a (not applicable) because this is a small project. Making an estimate for substantial software development will require breaking that process down at a much finer level of detail, perhaps in a separate spreadsheet. The Hours column here simply multiplies the number of cycles by the number of hours at that stage based on Cycles and Hours/Cycle columns.

Cost

The Cost/Hour column is the hourly rate at which each type of activity is typically billed. These numbers reflect the fact that you may have different rates for the different skill sets that are dominant during each project stage. The last column indicates the cost of each project stage.

Evaluation

You can see from this budget that the evaluation steps account for about a quarter of the overall cost, and that's quite reasonable, although of course it ought to vary based on the needs of the project. Often, however, when project costs are being trimmed, usability evaluation gets shorted. Just as you wouldn't want your doctor to give you a prescription without making a reliable diagnosis, it's a bit silly to move a project forward without having put some time into checking that your ongoing design is workable.

We can't stress enough how important it is to let nonessential features be omitted from a product so that you can cover the costs of user testing to ensure that the core product features are usable. It's better to reduce the scope of your project than the usability of your product.

Projections

Once you've got your budget put together, you can start adjusting it to see the impact of different project emphases. What if I add this feature? Where can I cut back my cost while still achieving optimal results? What will be the best investment: an early user survey at the requirements stage or user testing at the production stage? These types of projections and what-if scenarios are exactly what spreadsheets are designed to facilitate.

Beyond Design and Production

Make sure the client plans a budget that includes all relevant business costs beyond designing and building the web site. Two large costs that are commonly overlooked are site promotion and long-term site maintenance. People frequently underestimate the support costs of a web site and take the attitude, "if we build it, they will come" and treating their web site as a marketing engine without understanding that it needs to be marketed through traditional marketing channels.

Staff

There are three key staffing challenges: (1) finding people with the right skills; (2) having those people available when you need them; and (3) forming successful teams of people who work together well.

Design Is a Team Effort

To begin dealing with these challenges, list the skills you need for your project, including staff on the design team and staff on the client team. From the budget you should be able to determine how much time you need from each person. Make a list of the people involved, including their contact information, and use this to work out communication channels with your client. Typical skills you need are as follows:

Design Team	Client Team
project management	project management
interaction design	division management
information architecture	marketing
usability evaluation	technical support
HTML	customer support
system administration	writing
database development	graphic design
quality assurance	
writing	
graphic design	
audio and video design	

Some skill sets may be represented on either or both sides, such as writing. The Client Team may be writing domain-specific content, such as marketing materials, while the Design Team produces web-specific content, such as help pages or error pages. Frequently one person will take more than one of the roles listed. Still, it's worth listing these separately; while a given usability specialist may do interaction design, information architecture, and usability evaluation, others may have strength in one area and not in others.

Learning on the Job

With technologies and the competitive landscape changing rapidly, you need to allocate resources for learning new skills as a regular part of the web design process. When you don't have people with the exact skills you need, you must hire them, train them, or contract the work out. It's rare to have a team that is expert at everything, so at the minimum, learning on the job is absolutely necessary. Adjust for this in the budget. Adjustment for missing skill sets usually involves additional project management time.

As an example of allocating time for learning, your usability specialists may be experts at conducting surveys but have little experience in running focus groups. If this is the case, you should allow extra time for focus group planning and analysis, because your staff is learning as they go. You should also allow for an extra focus group in case one doesn't work out. For instance, someone conducting a focus group for the first time may forget to ask certain questions, or may forget to record certain results. Thus you would need another opportunity to gather the missed data. A project manager will also want to follow the task of the focus group carefully to stop or repair the task when it isn't working out.

Cross-Disciplinary Interaction

To get teams to work successfully together, people from different disciplines need to communicate effectively. Mutual respect is essential. We find that people with cross-disciplinary training work well at this. We believe it's good to create intimate teams of people with varied backgrounds rather than discipline-specific groups, which require, for example, tossing designs over a wall from the Design Department to the Development Department.

Each specialty needs to have respect for every other specialty, knowing when to defer to better-developed skills, and knowing when to question decisions. Software developers are more effective when they have some sense of design and know how designers need to work. Designers are more effective when they understand technical capabilities and limitations.

Schedule

Scheduling is an extraordinarily dynamic process. You can plan ahead, but project delays outside of your control are common. So prepare for change.

Scheduling Terminology

The following are some common concepts used in scheduling.

Milestones: *Transition points between stages of the project, often corresponding to the completion of deliverables and client approvals of the work completed at that point.*

Critical path: *The shortest possible path to completion, dictated by situations that require one task to wait for another to complete. When something goes wrong along your critical path, your whole project gets delayed.*

Bottleneck: *A task along the critical path that is the most time-consuming of several tasks that can be done in parallel.*

Slack time: *Extra time available in your schedule in case a task along the critical path is delayed. Build slack time into every project. Something along the line will always be delayed! This is the cushion you need. Slack time is always the first to go when people want to push deadlines as early as possible, but removing slack time substantially increases the risk of failure within a project. It's generally better to reduce the scope of your project in order to succeed at a more aggressive schedule.*

Dead time: *Time in the project when one team can't do any work until something else is completed. When a task along the critical path delays, other tasks may experience dead time in which they may be unproductive unless their efforts can be applied to other projects or to noncritical project activities.*

Scheduling Staffing by Project Stage

Different specialties will be needed at different stages of design. The graph in Figure 1-4 indicates a typical example of how work is distributed among different skill sets. This is a stacked area chart, which shows you how much each individual specialty is involved at each stage as well as which stages will take the most time. It's useful to compare this against your budget to make sure the assumptions are consistent.

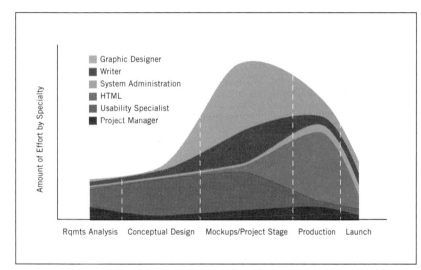

Figure 1-4.

Staffing by Project Stage.

This diagram illustrates the relative proportions of work that must be done by different personnel at each stage. The exact values are hypothetical and depend on the scope and functionality of the web site. This graph can be used to see where each type of skill set will be needed most on a project, enabling more effective staff allocation.

Because the graph shows when one specialty will be especially busy during the project, it can help avoid the problem of, for instance, having a programmer put in 160 hours in a single week to get the job done. It also makes clear when it's reasonable for a person to take on more than one role in the same project. The usability specialist and the writer are busy at roughly the same times, so combining those duties would result in an overwhelming workload for a single person at certain points. On the other hand, the usability specialist and HTML programmer are busy at very different times. Of course, you don't want to force someone into multiple roles when he or she is good at one role but not the other.

One caution: It may be more appropriate for you to break down the project into a greater level of detail. For instance, if we break out the evaluation steps within the Mockups stage, we see that the graphic designer and usability specialist have less overlap than seen here, since mockup generation and user testing don't necessarily overlap in time.

Multiple Projects

The representation in Figure 1-4 is also particularly useful when you have more than one project going on at the same time, a condition that holds true for almost everyone today. There are always at least three or four things going on, and you want to make sure that at a critical point in your process, you don't have a single person extremely busy on multiple projects. From this diagram, we see that the HTML programmer is especially busy during the production process, so we want to make sure the scheduled time for the production process is set for a different time for each project, allowing us to spread our human resources across projects effectively.

Figure 1-5 illustrates a simple approach to anticipating conflicts among multiple projects. A bar for each project is shown with milestones marked, and each project stage is identified in a separate color. This is another way of looking at how your human resources may overlap. This provides a nice overview of projects, and it's useful to mark milestones on this global map of projects (marked by small triangles on this diagram). You'll want to watch out for milestones for different projects all falling on the same day.

Figure 1-5.

Project Schedules across Multiple Projects.

By laying out the phases, it's possible to see where staffing conflicts might occur. Milestones (▲) help identify possible days of congestion. The presence of too many overlapping bars suggests personnel limits might be exceeded.

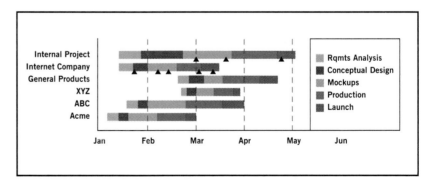

PERVASIVE USABILITY

HOW TO SUCCEED AT PROJECT MANAGEMENT

Three basic techniques of project management will help facilitate a smooth, efficient, and reliable process: standardize your process, communicate, and document.

Standardize Your Process

Your goal is to develop a clear and efficient process, along the lines of the process sketched out in this chapter. Realize that no process is meant to be rigid, but always needs to adapt to your circumstances. When the process is well defined, you'll know at every step what comes next and you can plan for and anticipate upcoming activities. Problems can be spotted early because the process makes clear what accomplishments are expected at any time.

A well-documented process can usually help overcome difficulties inherent in such tasks as keeping a project on budget and on schedule; replanning a project when materials are delayed, technical problems are encountered, or usability criteria aren't met; maintaining high quality standards and usability standards; and helping to focus a client organization that disagrees internally or vacillates.

Communicate

Effective communication among the members of the project team, the clients, and the users must be achieved. Clear communication helps avoid all sorts of problems, including diverging expectations and falling off track with the design. For example, good communication can usually solve such problems as clients and external vendors delaying a project by delivering materials late; the production team and the clients having different ideas about what deliverables will be created; the client being caught by surprise when a deadline is missed; and clients not understanding the magnitude of a change.

Regular meetings should be scheduled with all project stakeholders. You should tell them everything as early as possible. Explain dependencies and bottlenecks in the schedule. Educate the clients regarding usability principles and the design process. Because time is usually limited for doing so, communication needs to focus on the most common problems and confusions. Use project graphs and forms to help spell out what has been done and to get feedback from the clients. Be sure to explain to clients how design decisions will get made and that user testing may provide design input that modifies their initial design preferences.

Document

All milestones in the process should be matched with clear deliverables. You should record all client communications and all promises made to any of the stakeholders. Take meeting minutes. Record all design decisions, so you don't end up repeating your decision process. Organize and record files, fonts, colors, and all project requirements. When documentation is created, make sure the project manager gets copies of everything, so that the project manager is aware of all design decisions and client communications and can route appropriate information to the client and other team members as needed.

Good documentation can often help solve problems. Common problems that occur include clients adding extra work beyond the scope of a project, team members forgetting previous design decisions and specifications, team planners adding time-consuming redundancy in planning and preparation, and a critical person leaving the project in midstream.

Documentation may include such items as requirements, client communications, client approvals, design decisions, user data, work processes and results, design parameters, style guidelines, and schedules.

Combine These Approaches with Effective Forms

To facilitate these techniques, we use a series of forms that are introduced throughout the book. The design process itself is encoded into these forms. They enable the process by helping the development team to remember the steps involved in any activity and what information needs to be recorded. They make the process more efficient and help encode organizational memory so that newcomers can be trained easily.

COMPARING USABILITY METHODS

The intent of this chapter has been to show how usability can be factored in throughout the design process. Usability needs to be part of every task in the design and production process. In this book we'll be walking through every task and explaining the usability aspects of each. However, as we do so, we're covering a number of methods that won't be used in every project. How do you choose among them? How do you decide which methods are relevant to a given project? This will be answered as we address each method in the book. In this section, we introduce the framework for making these decisions.

Conceptually, it all boils down to a cost analysis. The argument for usability will pivot on what *value* the method provides and at what *cost*. Methods may achieve value in the form of improved profitability, marketing, employee retention, and humanitarian benefits. Value is limited by various risk factors. How reliable is a method? How confident can we be in the design guidelines the method suggests? In addition, cost is not just the amount of time and materials involved in performing the method, but also the cost of training and the impact on the development schedule.

Method Selection Criteria

Table 1-1 shows some of the primary criteria for selecting among various usability methods. These methods are just some of the more representative methods for each stage. Each method can be implemented in a number of ways, so instead of listing explicit times, we've simply distinguished between long and short time frames; the detailed information in the following chapters should help in pinning down more exact estimates. For another point of view on comparing methods, see Olson and Moran (1995).

Required Tasks

Certain tasks need to be performed at some level no matter how you develop a web site. All sites, for example, require you to develop the information architecture, one way or another, whether it's deliberately and thoughtfully or not. You can choose to skip the step of quality assurance, but skipping it will practically guarantee a malfunctioning product. Similarly, you can ignore user complaints and avoid tracking user problems, but it's highly unproductive to do so, especially as it costs relatively little (although the cost might be high if your design is awful, but that's all the more reason to take care of it).

Time to Perform the Method

We haven't set out exactly how long each usability method takes because this depends on the variables of your project. However, a short task like reviewing usability checklists can take as little as 10 or 15 minutes. A medium-length task such as user testing typically takes anywhere from a few hours to a couple of weeks. A long task such as running field observations or user surveys can be completed in a couple of days up to several months.

Costs

A variety of costs can apply, although most techniques, marked in Table 1-2 by dashes, can be easily performed with the equipment sitting around a typical office: paper, pencil, email, and computers with standard software suites. A common cost is recruiting and paying users, which often becomes more expensive as you choose a more specific and more narrow, hard-to-find target population. In the case of surveys, you may need to pay for mailing lists as well as the cost of mailing. For quality assurance, you'll need to reproduce and maintain all the target computing platforms, with the associated costs.

Table 1-2.

Framework for Contrasting
Usability Methods.

Usability Methods	Required?	Time to Perform
Requirements Analysis		
Requirements Specification	yes	short
User Interviews	no	medium
User Surveys	no	long
Competitive Analysis	no	short
Conceptual Design		
Idea Generation	yes	short–medium
Information Architecture	yes	short–medium
Card Sorting	no	short
Task Analysis	no	varies
Mockups and Prototypes		
Mockup Generation	yes	medium–long
Focus Groups	no	short
User Testing	no	short
Production		
Usability Checklists	no	short
User Testing	no	medium
Launch		
Quality Assurance	yes	short–medium
Field Observations	no	long
User Problem Tracking	yes	short

Learning Time

How long does it take to learn how to perform each method? Most methods are relatively straightforward, and learning the useful minimum can be achieved in a matter of hours. Practice is necessary in every case, though, so the first time you try a new method, plan extra time to run through a few practice trials to get out the kinks.

Confidence Level

Each method will suggest changes to your design. How confident can you be in those suggested design changes? How valid is each method? You don't want to spend a lot of money making design changes that you can't rely on.

Costs	Learning Time	Confidence Level	Impact on Final Design
—	short	low	high
recruiting	medium	medium	high
mailings	medium–long	high	medium
—	short	low	low
—	short	low	high
—	medium	low	high
recruiting	short	high	medium
—	medium	medium	high
—	long	low	high
recruiting	medium	high	medium
recruiting	medium	medium	medium
—	short	low	medium
recruiting	medium	high	medium
platforms	medium	high	medium
varies	medium–long	medium	low
—	short	low	low

Probably the least reliable method is to rely on intuition, although an experienced designer's intuition may be somewhat better than average. For the most part, you can have greater confidence in methods that obtain information from actual users, and then greater confidence still the more users you deal with (in some methods, statistical tests may be able to give you a much better measure of confidence level).

Low-confidence methods do not necessarily give you bad information, but you must weigh the risks against the costs of other, more reliable methods. In almost every case, any of these usability methods will help you create a better design, but all of them will occasionally provide misleading information that can undermine the design to some degree.

Impact on Final Design

In general, methods applied later in the process will have less impact on your final design than methods applied earlier. It's usually too costly to revisit old design decisions or make radical changes in design as you get further along in a project.

How to Decide Which Methods to Use

You want fast, low-cost, easy-to-learn, high-confidence, and high-impact methods. For each method ask yourself: To what extent is this going to save you redesign time later in the process? To what extent is this going to save money on the product and save money and time for the user? Does that justify the cost?

For example, in the requirements stage, should you conduct user interviews or user surveys? Both will be useful if the budget can handle it, but if your budget is limited, interviews will be better. Why? Because they usually take less time than surveys, and because they provide more detailed insights into what the project requirements should be. Even though surveys provide input from more users, the types of questions that can be successfully answered are much more limited. Should you also perform a competitive analysis? It doesn't cost much to do, but on the other hand, the information you receive is often much less useful than that from other types of requirements analysis, and its usability insights are much less reliable. So, competitive analysis is usually worth doing (because of the low cost), but needs to be supplemented with other information if possible.

Types of Usability

The exact way you conduct your user studies depends on what you want to learn from them. Three common approaches are as follows:

Mining for problems

The approach to user testing explained in Chapter 12, "Usability Evaluation," is a common test used to identify problems in a design. The primary concern of such a test is finding out what problems the user encounters.

Criterion testing

In a criterion test, your concern is, Does this site meet the explicit goals we set for it? Ideally, at the beginning of the project, you've defined some usability objectives, things like "most users will be able to complete a product purchase in three minutes or less" or "users will give an average usability rating of 2 or better on a scale of easy (1) to hard (5)." In this type of test, your focus is on the measurements. If you've met your objectives, you can safely end the design cycle. However, if you don't, you'll need to have recorded the problems in order to keep improving the design.

Comparison testing

In a comparison, you are trying to see which of two or more designs is better. You'll want to measure usability in more than one way to guide your decision. How much time does each task take? How many mistakes does the user make? How do users rate the site? If one design is better on all these dimensions, your decision is an easy one. If not, you may be able to identify a compromise design that integrates the best features of each alternative.

PERVASIVE USABILITY

Usability needs to be a pervasive element of your entire work process to achieve the most usable web site possible. By formalizing your design process and adopting appropriate documentation, these methods will save you time in the long run. By establishing clear usability goals at the outset of your projects, establishing user needs, and continually refining and evaluating designs, you'll save considerable time in production and after launch by avoiding the high cost of fixing a failed design. Pervasive usability is about making usability matter in all aspects of design.

02

REQUIREMENTS ANALYSIS

TARGET AUDIENCE AND TARGET PLATFORMS

UNDERSTANDING YOUR AUDIENCE

To start your entire web design process, begin by defining your audience. Who do you hope and expect to be visiting your web site? Define this as precisely as possible. This audience specification can be used for recruiting potential users for surveys and user testing, so the demographics should be clear enough to reproduce accurately. Define age, gender, income, education, occupation, computer experience, and anything else that would affect who you would recruit and how they would use your web site.

After your first brush at defining your audience, you need to do research on what your audience is really like and what they need. You can find statistics about your users from a wide variety of marketing resources including the Census Bureau, industry analyses, and online surveys. If the information is not available, you'll want to conduct your own surveys and user interviews. Even when information is available, you'll often need to develop a more detailed understanding of your users. This is especially true when you have a very specific target audience with specialized skills or interests, such as when you're developing intranet or extranet applications.

Why is it so important to talk to users at this stage? After all, we'll be conducting user testing later on. Early discussions with users are helpful because it's common to learn at this point that your assumptions about your users are wrong. You may learn that you've targeted the wrong market. You may learn that users are or are not worried about their security and anonymity, significantly affecting the entire structure of your application. Perhaps they're prepared for one payment model but absolutely reject another. The types of information you learn may radically alter your plan. Learning this information at a later stage can involve substantial and costly reengineering to fix, if it's even possible to backtrack at that point.

In this chapter, we look at defining *who your users are*. In Chapter 3, "User Needs Analysis," we look at *what they want and need*. In understanding your target audience, you not only need to understand specific personal attributes, you also must understand what types of computers and software they're using—that is, the *target platform*. Therefore, in this chapter we'll specifically discuss the ways people vary. Market segment, disabilities, education, and experience are examples of individual differences that can have an effect on user needs. There are differences in user preference settings, and international differences. Beyond differences in people, there are hardware and software differences in the areas of operating systems, monitors, browsers, and networks.

A good way to get started is to write down specifically who you believe your target audience is. A *scenario* is an approach for clarifying exactly who these people are.

SCENARIOS

Your web site needs to work for *somebody* if it's going to work for *anybody*. The goal of a scenario (see Figure 2-1) is to make sure the site is not merely theoretically usable, but that it actually serves the needs of specific people in real life. You do this by describing how your web site will be used by *specific* individuals in *specific* circumstances. This helps make sure you've considered the small details necessary for actually accomplishing real tasks with your system. It also ensures that you've considered the design in context, in the way that it relates to the lifestyle and work environment of your users. For example, by carefully considering the needs of a home user who may want to buy a product from your site, you realize that the home user is not likely to call an 800 number to order the product because the user probably has only one phone line, which is currently being used to access the Internet.

A scenario brings out additional functional requirements and ideas for the user interface that are driven by user profiles and context—ideas you wouldn't have thought of from an abstract consideration of the design. A scenario also provides a rationale for design decisions that can be useful in presenting designs to the development team or to decision makers. Keeping scenarios posted on your wall during web site development helps ground your work by holding the development in focus and personalizing the design as you grapple with how your decisions will impact specific people. It's convenient during a design debate to be able to say, "You know, I think Bryce would prefer if the web site worked like this."

Typically you need three to four scenarios as a good starting point to cover the standard users of a web site, though many more may be needed if your site has a diverse audience with very different needs. For instance, the post office might not need very many scenarios because the number of common tasks on such a site is relatively limited; by contrast, a federal government portal would require numerous scenarios to cover a wide variety of needs. Whenever possible, you should validate the scenarios by asking the users they represent to review each scenario.

Figure 2-1.

Example Scenario.

This example scenario for a film and video news web site is 100 percent fact about a living, breathing person (with his permission, and with his income hidden to protect the innocent), which provides realistic and specific information for design. For this scenario process to be reasonably complete, however, it would need similar descriptions for at least two or three additional users.

PROJECT: Film and Video News Web Site

NAME:	Bryce
AGE:	29
GENDER	Male
LOCATION:	Southeast Michigan, USA
EDUCATION:	BS Film
FAMILY:	Married, no kids
HOBBIES:	Church, mountain biking, making short films, UFOs, paranormal phenomena
OCCUPATION:	Graphic designer
INCOME:	Paid in Ding-Dongs and beer
WORK HOURS:	10 a.m.–6 p.m.
DISABILITIES:	Wears glasses
COMPUTER:	High-end Macintosh (work) consumer PC (home)
MONITOR:	1024 x 768 (both)
NETWORK:	T1 at work, 28.8 at home
TECH SKILL:	Power user, Web savvy, film and video expert
FAVORITE MOVIE:	*Close Encounters of the Third Kind*

TYPICAL SCHEDULE

9:15 a.m.   Bryce wakes up and prepares for work. He lives in the boonies, so he has a long commute.

10:30 a.m.   He gets to work. He's got our site bookmarked with a few other favorites of his, and he checks it out first thing in the morning to see if there's anything new. He'll check it out for 10 or 15 minutes to review the production status of various movies, to see what new projects are starting, and to download trailers. Morning. Bryce may leave a browser window open with our site or another favorite site, and will follow interesting links whenever he gets a break. His boss will occasionally wander by, but the boss doesn't mind because he sees our cool web site and figures it's good for Bryce's creativity.

(Continued)

1 p.m.	Lunch. He got caught up with a cool project he's working on and almost forgot lunch, so he's eating late. He slips some leftovers in the microwave, then comes back to his desk and checks out some other sites.
5 p.m.	When work is over, Bryce may shoot off an email to an old film buddy. Not for the first time, his sysadmin complains when he tries emailing 60-megabyte movie files.
6:30 p.m.	Bryce goes home.
Evening	Bryce has a computer at home and may check out a site occasionally. He regularly rents DVDs to watch in the evenings.
EXCEPTIONS/ INFREQUENT EVENTS	
	When he sees a trailer in the theaters that he hasn't seen online, he will sometimes come to download it.
	Occasionally he'll look into TV show information, though he mostly sticks with film.
	Evenings and weekends, Bryce will sometimes shoot his own film projects.

Three Parts of a Scenario

The typical scenario has three parts: a profile of the user, a schedule and interaction episode, and a sketch or photo of the user in the setting in which the web site is used (see Figure 2-1).

In profiling the user, it is best to describe a specific person. You can base this profile on an actual user you've encountered during interviews (but protect his or her confidentiality if the profile will be shared outside the design team). Give the person a name. Describe all of the demographics: age, occupation, gender, education, family, hobbies, disabilities, type of computer and network used. If you're basing this on discussions with a real user, include information about his or her browser settings, feelings about online privacy, and design tastes. This user profile is also sometimes called a *persona*.

The schedule and interaction episode describes how your users work each day. What are their work hours? Do they carpool? When do they use their computers? How do interactions with friends, family, and co-workers influence their use of the web site? Describe what they do with the web site and why it's important to them. *If you can't think of a compelling reason why they would use your web site versus engaging in some other activity, then they probably wouldn't.* This part of the scenario addresses the users' motivations, and real-life problems that determine their priorities. In addition to working out a typical day, you should include some relevant exceptions: infrequent events, emergencies, special times that involve using the web site, or special problems that may occur on the site (such as dealing with a rejected credit card).

A sketch or photo of the user in the setting in which the web site is used can be helpful. While not strictly necessary, a sketch of the person in context helps remind you of factors you may otherwise overlook. You can draw this by hand, compose it with clip art, use a photograph of an actual user you've visited, or use a photo clipped from a magazine. Don't worry about a well-drawn picture, just get a rough sketch that captures the type of person and his or her work environment. Is the user's desk cluttered? Are other people around? Is it a noisy environment? What type of lighting is available? Are the user's hands busy with work tasks that make keyboard use difficult? What tools does this person use?

When to Use Scenarios

Scenarios are a relatively inexpensive technique. They are most useful when grounded in actual data about real users based on surveys, interviews, focus groups, or observations of work environments. Their utility is limited when your user population is extremely diverse and you don't have the time to generate enough scenarios to have good coverage. They are most useful when the user's work environment will have a big impact on the use of the web site—which will be true, for example, in many business-to-business transactional systems. They will be less useful for simple marketing sites and whenever the context is unlikely to be a major factor, which may be true for many generic applications such as search engines, although it's difficult to know that context is a minimal factor until after the scenarios have been developed.

DESIGN FOR DIVERSITY

One of the biggest challenges in web design is developing for the wide diversity of users, user preferences settings, hardware and software platforms, browsers, and network speeds. While it's impossible to create an optimal design for everyone, you'll need to decide how well you want your site to work for each segment of the target population.

When designing for diversity, several options are available that make trade-offs between cost and the quality of the design for various user segments (see Table 2-1).

Our compatibility philosophy is that we want our designs to work great for *most* people and effectively, if not ideally, for most of the remaining people.

▪□□□□ **REQUIREMENTS ANALYSIS**

We recognize that some small segment of the target population is bound to have a less-than-satisfactory experience, but we want to keep that to as small a percentage as possible. Perhaps less than 2 percent is a realistic goal, but this cutoff will depend on the scope of your project and budget and the impact of failing to serve a given target population. When you've decided who you're *not* going to please, that needs to be part of the documentation of your target audience. Choose this group carefully: for what group of users is it okay for them to say, "Your site just doesn't work for me"?

For some markets, you may have a sufficiently well-defined and homogeneous target population that you don't need to worry about significant variation. For instance, when developing intranet applications, you not only know exactly who your target users are, but you may be able to require that they use a certain platform, enabling you to rely on a wide range of assumptions that considerably simplify design.

In considering each type of variability—computer users, hardware and software platforms, browsers, and network speeds—it's a good idea to keep track of the latest available statistics. Unfortunately, no single source of statistics produces good data on all these factors, so you'll need to seek out multiple sources. Up through 1998, one of the best online surveys was the GVU survey (GVU 1998), which has unfortunately been discontinued. You can also track some types of stats, such as browser types and operating systems, using your own server logs.

2 + 2 Is More Than 2

Suppose you decide that your site doesn't need to work for browsers having 2 percent market share or less. That doesn't mean that your site will work for 98 percent of browsers. Rather, it probably means your site will work for fewer than 95 percent of browsers, because several different browsers have less than 2 percent market share. Then perhaps you decide it doesn't need to work for visually impaired users (3.5%) or for non-English speakers (say, another 5%) or for people with small screens (640 x 480 or less, which is, say, another 10%).

In each case, it seems that very few users are being excluded, but when you add them all together, you'll soon find that your site doesn't work for 15 percent of your potential customers. Excluding so many people from your web site is as arbitrary as excluding people from your brick-and-mortar store because they aren't driving expensive cars. ("Dear customer: If your car is more than three years old, please upgrade it at your local auto dealer and come back when you're done.") It makes for fewer sales and bad customer service.

Table 2-1.

Designing for Diverse Audiences:
Four Alternatives.

	Examples	
Design Alternatives	**Linguistic Diversity**	**Browser Compatibility**
1. General-purpose design Create a general-purpose (lowest common denominator) web site for everyone.	*Globalization* Create an international web site by using well-known international icons and a simplified subset of English that is easily understood by nonnative speakers.	*Platform independence* Create a web site that works in every browser by writing in a limited subset of standard HTML that works in even the oldest browsers.
2. Optimization Create a single design for a narrow target group, and neglect broader audiences.	*Language optimization* Create your web site only in Japanese, relying on Japanese idiom, because you know you are solely concerned with a Japanese audience.	*Platform optimization* Create a web site for internal use by your company that heavily depends on a version of Java that only runs in one browser but provides you with far greater functionality and lower development time than cross-platform development would allow.
3. Proliferation of alternatives Create individual web sites for each target group.	*Localization* Create a web site in English and another web site in Spanish, so that each site is optimized for each language.	*Platform-specific alternatives* Create a version of your web site for common browsers on desktop computers and an alternate text version that is optimized for viewing on small displays, such as PDAs.

Design Alternatives	Linguistic Diversity	Browser Compatibility
4. Multipurpose design Create a single design with different parts of the page for each target group.	*Multilingual design* Create a web site with both English and French labels side by side, as is fairly common for Canadian web sites.	*Cross-platform compatibility, with browser-specific enhancements* Take advantage of new browser features in your web page, but use them in such a way that older browsers will ignore unrecognized tags, and include text content and text links so that even if users can't view a plug-in, they can still understand and explore the site.

INDIVIDUAL DIFFERENCES

To develop a user profile, you need to find statistics on what your users are like and how they vary. A survey is particularly effective at developing this kind of demographic information. Some of the common ways people vary include

Market segment: Age, gender, education, occupation, hobby, or income

Disabilities: Visual, hearing, movement, or cognitive impairments

Experience level: Computing, internet culture, subject domain

These different types of audiences will influence the selection of content and functionality for your site, the way text is worded, the appearance of your site, and the level of simplicity of your design (see Figure 2-2). These choices will be based both on the preferences and interests of your target audience and their needs and abilities. A straightforward example is designing for children: a heavier emphasis is needed for imagery over words, simplified language is needed, the complexity of the screen layout should be reduced (with a real-ization that an unbalanced display may easily pull a child's attention in one direction or another), and the topics must address issues interesting to kids (who really don't want to hear about retirement planning).

Disabilities

Around 22 percent of the U.S. population has some kind of disability (see sidebar "How Many People Have Disabilities?"). Addressing the accessibility of your site potentially expands your audience significantly, increases user satisfaction, helps to comply with legal regulations regarding accessibility, and avoids unnecessary discrimination. The dominant standards for accessibility in web design are currently established by the W3C (*www.w3.org/WAI*). Several tools are available for evaluating your web site in terms of access for users with disabilities. For instance, Bobby is a web tool that provides detailed suggestions for improving your site (*www.cast.org/bobby*), and RetroAccess is a commercial product that identifies accessibility problems and helps guide you through their repair (*www.retroaccess.com*).

Figure 2-2.

Web Sites with Different Target Audiences.

Age: Kids (*ctw.org*) versus retired folks (*aarp.org*)

Gender: Men (*gq.com*) versus women (*oxygen.com*)

Language: English (*theatlantic.com*) versus Japanese (*lovelife.org*)

Some Typical Guidelines

Most current accessibility guidelines are focused on the concerns of people with visual impairments and those with motor difficulties that affect their ability to type or position a mouse pointer precisely. Among the guidelines are the following:

- Avoid using color to make meaningful distinctions between items because of the prevalence of color blindness, especially red-green color blindness (8% of men and 0.5% of women in Europe and North America are color-blind).

- Use high contrast and highly legible fonts to help those with even minor visual impairments. Allow the user to control fonts and font sizes for optimal reading.

- Make sure all graphics and other multimedia elements have text equivalents so that people who are blind can hear descriptions of them with a screen reader.

- Don't rely on spatial relationships to make the text sensible. For instance, don't refer to "the column to the right" or "the button below."

- Avoid uses of DHTML or Java, such as rollovers and nonstandard pop-up menus, that make it difficult for screen readers to interpret where the buttons are or what text is displayed.

- Avoid using small graphics as buttons and make sure small buttons are spaced well. Young children and people with arthritis will often have difficulty targeting small regions and may hit the wrong button if buttons are too close together.

- Avoid requiring typing when selecting a button or link will do. Avoid requiring the user to switch frequently between clicking and typing.

- When you are using audio or video, provide closed captions or other text equivalents of the audio for the hearing impaired.

- For the cognitively impaired, minimize the need to remember items between screens. Use simple, direct, concrete language. Expose the document structure as much as possible.

Accessibility Helps Everyone

Some types of disabilities are so extraordinarily common that most people do not classify them as such, despite the fact that they have an enormous impact on design. While relatively few people are blind, an enormous number of people have imperfect eyesight and benefit from larger graphics and higher contrast.

Data from GVU's Tenth WWW User Survey (GVU 1998) represents self-reported disabilities of those who responded to their online survey (see below). Some types of disabilities are likely to be underrepresented because of the difficulty of accessing and responding to the survey.

Type of Disability	% of Responses
Vision	3.5
Hearing	1.7
Motor	2.0
Cognitive	0.5
Not impaired	90.8
No response	1.5

A report from the U.S. Census tabulates the distribution of disabilities among people 16 years and older (see below). Notice that nearly 22 percent of all people report some type of disability.

Type of Disability	Number in Thousands	% of Population
Any disability	45,416	21.8
Difficulty walking	9,209	4.4
Vision problems	7,310	3.5
Hearing problems	6,961	3.3
Difficulty using hands	6,272	3.0
Learning disability	2,945	1.4
Total population (16 years and older)	208,783	

Source: Survey on Income and Program Participation, research data file (August–November 1999, Wave 11), U.S. Census Bureau, U.S. Department of Commerce.

And while relatively few people have severe motor impairments, clicking small buttons and navigating multilevel menus can be difficult for small children and for those with arthritis.

Many people also suffer occasional temporary disabilities (a broken wrist, a swollen eye) during which accessibility is much appreciated. Similarly, users may encounter *situational disabilities* in their everyday experience. Situational disabilities are those challenges caused by imperfect situational factors, such as having to reach around a desk awkwardly to control the mouse when standing up, giving a presentation in an unfamiliar room, or being in too much of a hurry or having other problems on your mind that make it difficult to concentrate. In each of these cases, people appreciate the fact that fonts can be made larger, buttons are large enough to press easily and difficult to press by mistake, pages load fast, and the interface doesn't require a lot of mental overhead. In addition, noises in the workplace or silence in the workplace (such as a library) may mean that people can't use any audio, and alternatives to audio are helpful.

Accessibility Standards Are Only a Starting Point

Many typical guidelines for accessibility stress the use of standard technologies or recommend providing standardized fallbacks when using nonstandard technologies. In particular, most advise following HTML standards strictly. Unfortunately, the real world is rather messy, and most web browsers do not follow HTML standards exactly, making strict adherence to the standards sometimes *less* accessible in practice. The only certain way to ensure accessibility is to follow the recommendations as well as possible and then test the site with users with disabilities.

DIFFERENCES IN USER PREFERENCE SETTINGS

Users may set their browser preferences to all sorts of odd settings, which can baffle the designer. Fortunately, most users never change their preferences at all, so it's fairly safe to do the majority of your testing with the default browser settings. However, a few settings are changed quite often. Some of these settings may be dictated by corporate requirements for convenient system administration or security standards, so users may not be able to change them to your preferred settings even if they want to. Preferences that can be changed by users include the following.

Fonts: *While the typeface itself isn't changed often, the font size varies widely among users and platforms. Available typefaces will depend on platform and which typefaces users have installed.*

Link colors: *Fortunately it doesn't happen often, but users can change the default colors of links and can turn off the underlining of links.*

Image-loading: *Users with slow connection speeds will often avoid loading images.*

Plug-ins: *While the percentage of users with standard plug-ins like Flash, Acrobat Reader (for PDF files), RealAudio, and Quicktime is increasing, many still don't download them in order to avoid lengthy download times or bloating their systems.*

Enabled features: *Users may turn off Java, JavaScript, cookies, and other features for security, speed, or personal preference.*

Web sites that require users to have specific plug-ins can create a system administration burden for them, since they must monitor plug-in versions and maintain and replace them as they upgrade their system or move from one system to another. Try to minimize reliance on plug-ins; when you do use them, strive for compatibility with multiple versions, to minimize the burden on your users.

Similarly, it makes little sense to tell users to change their browser settings to conform to your site. This places the burden of ease of use on the user, which is hardly user friendly. The site in Figure 2-3, for instance, presumes to ask you to use Netscape and a 10-point Times Roman font. Are you supposed to quit Explorer just to use it? What value do you get from the settings they recommend? In fact, the settings the site suggests don't even work very well, since 10-point Times Roman is very difficult to read in italics (this screen shot was taken with 14-point Times New Roman because 10 point was too small to read).

Figure 2-3.

*Adapt to the Users—
Don't Make Them Adapt to You.*

A robust design should be created for and tested on multiple platforms and at many user-preference settings. When it's not, it often adds more work for the user with little perceived benefit (*www.usernomics.com*).

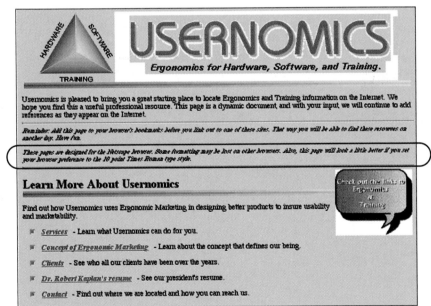

REQUIREMENTS ANALYSIS

INTERNATIONAL DIFFERENCES

While users from the United States represent a large proportion of users on the Internet, this is changing over time, and even from the beginning, the Web has been international. Sites that do not even intend to cross national boundaries will find by examining their hit logs that they have quite a few international users.

Different countries and cultures use different languages, different units, different symbols, different currency, and different conventions for all sorts of things. Even countries that share a common language can have differences in dialects and differences in standard practices that can cause confusion.

What Country Is This?

Since users may be coming from absolutely anywhere, be clear when you are targeting a specific local market (Figure 2-4). If you have no interest in users outside your geographical region, or if you know you aren't interested in a certain audience, you need to indicate to such users that this site is not for them. This is usually as simple as making your location or target market highly visible at the top of each page.

Include the country in your address, and include international codes in the phone number. For example, a U.S. phone number should include a +1 as the country code, as in +1 (734) 665–9307. An exception to this rule is U.S. 800 numbers, which are not available internationally, so should not include the country code. If you are expecting many international visitors, be sure to comment that the 800 number is "(U.S. only)."

Language

You may choose to write only in your native language, provide access to multiple-language translations of your site, or provide your site in a common international language, such as English or Spanish. Writing direct and simple text, without too much idiom, slang, or metaphor, will help nonnative speakers read your text.

When offering multiple languages, avoid using national flags to identify each language. Some languages are spoken in a variety of countries, and many countries have several different languages. Thus, flags can be ambiguous about which language they represent. Also, when a language is spoken in multiple countries, you face the daunting challenge of deciding which country's flag is the most appropriate to represent that language without making other countries feel excluded. In general, rather than using flags (as the Disneyland site in Figure 2-5 does), you're much safer to simply state the name of each language in its native tongue: "English—Français—Español—Nihongo."

Figure 2-4.

Identify Your Location.

The people at the Bank of Holland (*www.bankofholland.com*) may not confuse any of their customers in Holland, Michigan (USA), when they advertise locally, but online they've been careful to specify their location to avoid confusion. Including their contact address (right under their logo) serves the dual role of providing contact information and implicitly distinguishing them from any banks in the country of Holland.

Units

Use metric units when it makes sense, but for many common uses, especially when targeting the U.S., a local unit needs to be used, as in Figure 2-6. Provide metric equivalents when you can, but if your primary target audience uses local units, at least provide a link to a table of conversions. When the unit is ambiguous, be sure to specify the relevant measuring system—certain units, such as a pint, can represent different amounts in different measuring systems.

Currencies

Be sure to include currency units on prices. The same currency symbol, such as the dollar sign ($), may be used in multiple countries, so it's a good idea to provide a country indicator to clarify which currency you're intending (e.g., "US$").

Remember that exchange rates change quickly, so you're best off leaving conversions to the user rather than computing them on your site (unless you have live access to the latest rates in your back-end system). Give the user a link to a current rate chart if you expect it to be needed (as in Figure 2-7).

Symbols

Use religious and political symbols only after very careful research into their
appropriate usage. Symbols of any kind are culture specific. Even color represents different meanings in different cultures. For instance, white is a color
for weddings in some cultures and for funerals in others. Red is a color of cel-
ebration in some cultures and violence in others. So avoid using color as a
symbol, and avoid using color as a specific differentiator of categories. Also
avoid using human facial expressions or hand signs as icons. Hand signs, in
particular, have many different interpretations throughout the world.

Date and Time

Date formats vary throughout the world. For instance, September 10, 2001,
may be written as "10 September 2001," "9/10/01," "10/9/01," or "01/09/10,"
among other variations, and that's considering only the variations of order,
not of punctuation. To clarify dates, a good approach is to spell out the month
and use a four-digit year, as in "10 September 2001."

It is extremely problematic to specify a particular time to people in multiple
time zones. If you must do so, be sure to include the time zone, although
many people will not recognize time zones (and giving the offset from GMT

Figure 2-6.

Units Used in Cooking.

This web page has readers from all over the world. However, while Tom's Recipes (*www.scifaiku.com/tom/misc /recipe.html*) contains a link to international conversions, measurement remains extremely difficult across countries. Conversions are inconvenient, and they still don't address all needs. Concepts that are obvious within the U.S., like "a stick of butter," mean nothing in countries where butter never comes in sticks, and where different standard stick sizes may be used. Worse yet, no conversion table will ever list the conversions for "sticks." In many countries, there's no such thing as a "bag of chocolate chips." Egg sizes differ. Cooking time varies by altitude. It's a sheer miracle if anyone can make these cookies (though the apple cookies are especially delicious).

Figure 2-7.

Exchange Rates.

The *x-rates.com* web site provides a quick way to interpret currency conversions. (Note that not even *x-rates.com* guarantees the accuracy of its data.)

REQUIREMENTS ANALYSIS

is a lot of work to decipher even for those people who understand it). Include an "a.m." or "p.m." if the hour is 12 or less, realizing that 24-hour time will confuse many U.S. readers, and 12-hour time will confuse many people who expect 24-hour time. Times are best avoided entirely, but can be unavoidable when scheduling some events. When possible, a reasonable solution is to dynamically provide the time in terms of an offset from the current time, as in "The live broadcast will begin in 2 hours and 45 minutes."

HARDWARE AND SOFTWARE DIFFERENCES

Users' hardware and software configurations vary widely. Despite noble attempts at making web technologies transparently cross-platform, platform differences still play a significant role. Hardware and software configurations need to be carefully sampled and tested. Hardware may be one of the easiest things to control for when designing *intranet* applications, but even then, be sure to verify your assumptions by visiting actual user sites to see if they have the hardware and software settings you expect.

Identify all platforms you need to work well on, and test them thoroughly. Consider even relatively small populations, and make sure your site works adequately, if not elegantly, on less pervasive platforms.

A common surprise is with screen resolution. While many users own machines that are capable of higher-resolution display, they often leave their computer configured at a lower resolution because either they don't know how to change it or they actually prefer the larger, easier-to-read fonts. Chapter 6, "Page Layout" provides a detailed discussion of screen size issues.

Why Don't They Upgrade?

From a developer's point of view, an ideal situation would be one where every user has the same hardware and software and the most advanced possible versions. This reduces testing and enables the developer to rely on the latest technological capabilities. However, that simply isn't realistic.

The Problem: Users Actually Are Using Systems and Settings That the Designers Consider Non-Optimal

We often get asked: Do any users actually have 640 × 480 monitors? Do they still turn images off? Is it realistic to think that users turn off cookies (after all, if they did, they wouldn't be able to use many sites on the Web)? The answer is yes, yes, yes. Are such people just extreme examples? No. They're everyday normal people who have valid reasons for their situations. Hasn't everyone loaded all the plug-ins? No. Lots of people haven't.

The Solution: You Can't Change the Users, so Understand Them and Design for Them

Don't rely on your intuition for information about users' platforms. Find the current data. If only 40 percent of potential users have the plug-in you need, then they probably don't want to use up their hard disk space or destabilize their computer system, or maybe they just aren't interested. Are they wrong or just stupid? Probably not, but even if they've made the wrong choice, are you going to start a lonely crusade to upgrade all the hardware and software used throughout the world? Hopefully not. Watch the trends, and design for the level of adoption you expect to be valid when your web site is launched.

You've Learned Everything, but Newbies Abound

We get asked: Isn't such-and-such technique a web convention? After all, the Web has been around for over five years. Isn't everyone familiar with these yet? Actually, something may be a convention, but at best that might mean that 5 or 10 percent of web sites are applying the convention. Furthermore, most people online are relative novices. Why? Exponential growth—the number of people online is still growing at an exponential rate, and as long as that remains true, many new people who don't know how the Web works will continue to come online.

Low-End Use Is Counterintuitive to High-End Users

For those of us who have been online for what seems like our whole lives and who buy all the latest hardware and software, the practices of low-end users can sometimes be hard to believe. Designers and developers need user studies precisely because they're too expert to form reasonable assumptions of what the users are like.

Hardware and Operating Systems

While the Windows PC is the most common platform, consider which other platforms play a significant role in your target population. While certain industries may have very little Mac usage, Macs have a higher market share than average among home users, and in markets such as education, graphic design, and video. Unix and Linux users are relatively uncommon, but they should be considered when targeting technical audiences, such as IT workers and web developers. As you're testing these platforms, be sure to consider earlier versions of the operating systems, as a large fraction of users will not have upgraded to the latest version. For instance, when testing for Windows, you should test Windows 95, 98, NT, ME, and 2000. Unfortunately, the same browser often works differently on each platform, so every combination needs to be tested.

Common differences between PCs, Macs, and Linux/Unix include default font-size differences (and differing interpretations of font specs), color calibration, level of support for plug-ins, minor variations in browser implementations, and differences in how form elements and other widgets work (e.g., if you spawn a new window, make sure all the window controls, such as a close box, work as expected on all platforms). See Figure 2-8 for an example of how a single site can differ on different platforms.

Other platforms to pay attention to include Palm OS, WebTV, and mobile phones. Most of these individually represent a very small target population, but internet appliances and mobile devices are becoming increasingly popular, and for some domains may represent a highly desirable target audience. In most circumstances, no single platform among these can justify the cost of a custom site design, nor are they sufficiently standardized to give detailed design suggestions that will work for all of them.

Generally, to work well across a broad set of devices, you should design according to well-established standards, avoid novel technologies, depend primarily on text, keep the content as concise as possible, and avoid altering defaults such as fonts and background colors (or use style sheets to do so, but realize that many users won't know how to override a style sheet they don't like). Where you intend to target a specific platform, such as WebTV, specific design standards are sometimes available from the manufacturer (e.g., see WebTV guidelines at *developer.webtv.net/design/*).

Monitors

Monitor sizes vary dramatically and can create significant design difficulties (see Figure 2-9). We cover the tradeoffs in designing for different screen resolutions in Chapter 6, "Page Layout." Monitors vary in resolution (common standards are 640 × 480, 800 × 600, and 1024 × 768, but the resolutions are getting much higher) and in color depth (from black and white to grayscale, and from 8-bit to 32-bit color). Don't rely on users having the latest high-resolution system. At the same time, it's nice to give users with a high-resolution screen the ability to take full advantage of their systems. We'd hope that users with two-page displays would use the extra space for a second browser window or another application, but users quite often maximize their windows and grow frustrated if the design, created for a smaller screen, fills up only a fraction of their screen.

Figure 2-8.

Platform Differences.

The same web site (*www.macro media.com*) on Linux, Mac, and PC demonstrates several accidental differences due to differing window sizes and font-size settings. Notice that part of the page is broken in Linux (the right navbar) and that fonts are somewhat less optimized on the Mac (the right navbar has a special font that is used on PC but not on Mac). Differences in screen resolutions and available plug-ins are also showing up.

Linux

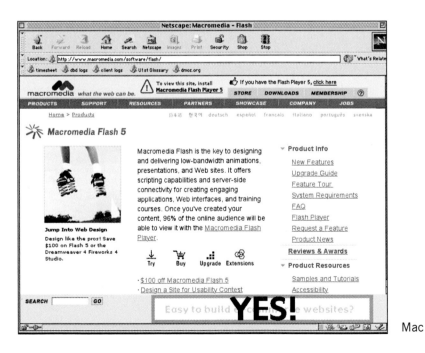

Mac

REQUIREMENTS ANALYSIS

PC

Users with 8-bit color monitors will get a different set of 256 colors depending on their platform. Therefore, pages can be designed using only the colors in the web-safe color palette, a subset of 216 colors that displays fairly reliably on all 8-bit platforms, without dithering the colors or mapping them to unexpected colors. Web-safe colors were previously a critical design criterion for web designers but are becoming relatively unimportant as the number of users with 8-bit color is dwindling, and because using non-web-safe colors compromises visual quality but rarely interferes with usability (except when legibility of text is compromised because of dithering).

Browser Differences

Browser variation is extraordinarily hard to keep up with. While the vast majority of the browser market is held by Internet Explorer and Netscape Navigator, the variations among versions of these browsers demand lengthy testing. When writing HTML, you need to consider backward compatibility with older versions of HTML, but you also need to consider how HTML standards are likely to evolve in order to avoid writing code that won't work in future browser releases. In addition, while you can write to fit the formal specifications of these browsers, you also need to work around lesser-known browser bugs.

Testing is essential or you're likely to build a site that fails in unexpected ways (as in Figure 2-10). When testing your code in different browsers, write down

Figure 2-9.

Squeezed to the Point of Breaking.

A common mistake is to create a design like this that won't lay out properly on smaller monitors or in a smaller window (notice how the two leftmost columns overlap). Even on larger monitors, some users will use smaller windows so that they can view two browser windows or multiple applications side by side (*www.microsoft.com*).

the name of the browser, the operating system, and the browser version, as well as any nonstandard user settings. This way, when a problem comes up later, you can check whether it should have been spotted in the version you tested, or whether you should have been testing a configuration you weren't. For instance, during testing, write down the browsers tested in a quick short-hand like

NT: E4.0, E5.0, N4.1, Opera3.0

Mac: N4.7, E5.0, iCab(beta)

Browsers often vary in how they handle aspects such as proprietary tags, horizontal rules, margins, link colors (especially visited links), and table formatting. And while conventions exist for how tags such as `<blockquote>` or `<strong>` are implemented, individual browsers may display them in a unique way or allow users to set their own format. So, although `<blockquote>` is normally used to indent a paragraph, an old version of Explorer displayed block quotes in italics. The only way to rely on how the tags will be interpreted is to test in all relevant browsers. The only way to ensure that new browser releases will interpret the tags in the way expected is to conform to the standards specifications as closely as possible. Don't depend on any display characteristics that aren't spelled out in the standards. Even so, the standards may not be implemented correctly, and testing remains the only way to verify compatibility.

REQUIREMENTS ANALYSIS

Figure 2-10.

*Watch Out for Browser
Incompatibilities.*

This site (*www.sitesandsounds.com*)
recommends Internet Explorer.
In fact, they've apparently forgotten
to test their site in Navigator.
In Explorer, you can easily scroll
through their long pages of text.
In Navigator, as shown here, the
scroll bars are missing!

Network Differences

Slow download time is one of the most frequent usability complaints. Slow
pages will drive users away. Users may have 28.8–56K modems, ISDN, DSL,
cable modems, T1 lines, or other broadband services. Low-bandwidth modems
are still common, in homes and in small businesses, so optimize your site for
slower modems, and test from home rather than in a high-bandwidth development environment to get a feel for the user experience.

WALKING IN SOMEONE ELSE'S SHOES

User-centered design must begin with knowing who your users are. Thus,
we've identified the target audience and started the process of understanding
what they're like. A fundamental theme is diversity—even with a narrowly
defined audience we're likely to encounter quite a bit of variety in the people,
their preferences, and their technology. To move forward, we need to step
into their shoes to see the world from their perspective. In Chapter 3 we'll
uncover what our users want, and why.

03

REQUIREMENTS ANALYSIS

USER NEEDS ANALYSIS

User needs analysis sets the groundwork for the entire design process. The principal purpose of this stage of design is to define design goals and constraints and develop an understanding of your audience and what they do. This chapter covers the basic process of setting goals and objectives, and then discusses the methods of background research necessary to elaborate and clarify these goals: surveys, competitive analysis, interviews, and focus groups.

Four primary activities are involved in user needs analysis:

Investigation: Do the background research to understand your audience and business needs.

Analysis: Analyze this information to understand the priorities.

Specification: Specify your objectives, assumptions, and design constraints.

Documentation: Document all of your lessons learned, goals, and design decisions.

THE OBJECTIVES OF USER NEEDS ANALYSIS

At the end of the process, your goal is to emerge with clear statements about the following issues, informed as much as possible by objective data from your target users:

Define your audience: Who are the users (see Chapter 2)?

Identify user goals: What do your users want and need? How do they solve their problems now?

Define your business goals: What do the users need to do in order for this web site to be a viable investment?

Set usability objectives: To what extent does the site need to satisfy both user and business goals? How do we measure success?

Identify the design constraints: Define the budget, the time line, and the project team. Investigate target platforms and their technical limitations. Identify which platforms will not be targeted and possible constraints that will not apply.

Define functional specifications: Based on all of your goals and design constraints, specify the detailed functionality of the web site.

Spelling out this information early in the design process avoids costly redesign and repair later in the process and focuses all future work toward these goals.

Many web design firms use a form like Form 3-1 to help identify the project goals during an initial client interview. (Download from *http://www.mkp.com/uew/*.) This worksheet can be a useful shortcut when in-depth user research is not possible.

SETTING YOUR OBJECTIVES

After defining your audience (see Chapter 2), you need to define the goals for the web site. Why are you creating a web site? Who is it for and what do they need to do on the site?

A form like Form 3-2 can be used to help you clarify the stakeholders, business goals, user goals, and usability objectives for the site. (Download from *http://www.mkp.com/uew/*.) Feel free to expand on it if it isn't quite the right list for your site.

The Stakeholders

Who will be affected by the existence of your web site, and why do they care? Your clients. Your design team. The end users. For an e-commerce site, the stakeholders include the vendors, the distributors, the shipping company, business partners, advertisers, investors, all departments within the e-commerce company (marketing, purchasing, billing, shipping, customer support), the customers, the person they're buying for, the customers' spouses who get ignored while the customers are using the computer, and their friends who are trying to call while they're monopolizing the phone line.

You've got to factor in the concerns of all these people in a complex set of design tradeoffs. If you ignore some stakeholders, someday they're going to walk in and play their trump card, and an otherwise careful design will be shot full of holes. If you've never bothered to consider what information the shipping company wants, and you don't have what they want, then you may find yourself with hundreds of orders (or worse yet, millions) with no way to fulfill them. For instance, you may have assumed a flat shipping rate or a rate scaled to the purchase quantity, but your shipping department may surprise you with extra charges for fragile items, hazardous chemicals, or biological waste.

Stakeholders who are affected by your site design but don't actually use it themselves are sometimes called *indirect users*. Excellent usability means working for the indirect users as well as the direct users.

Client Interview/Web Site Information Worksheet

Project Name _____ **Date** _____

Client Contacts

Name	*Role*	*Phone*	*Fax*	*Email*
	Principal Contact			

Project Team

Name	*Role*	*Phone*	*Fax*	*Email*
	Account Rep			
	Project Manager			
	Lead Designer			
	Lead Developer			

Project Schedule and Milestones

Date	*Milestone*
_____	Initial Meeting
_____	1st Mockups Delivered
_____	Feedback from Mockups
_____	2nd Mockups Delivered
_____	Focus Groups
_____	Final Mockup Approval
_____	User Testing
_____	Final QA
_____	Launch
_____	

Description of Business/Organization (Current web site address, primary market, primary products/services, competitive advantages)

_____

_____

_____

Competitors (Web site addresses, why they're good or bad, differentiators)

_____

_____

_____

Other Web Sites You Like (Web site addresses, why you like them)

_____

_____

_____

Web Site Goals (Primary reasons for and goals of this project, and how you will measure success)

_____

_____

Target Audience (Business or consumer, narrow or mass audience, age range, computer skills, platform considerations, screen sizes, accessibility concerns)

_____

Development Considerations (Hosting platform and software, plans for maintenance)

_____

Design Considerations
What is your logo? _____

What fonts do you use? _____

What colors do you use? (Pantone, RGB, etc.) _____

What other elements constitute your design identity?
(Slogans, bylines, illustrations, etc.) _____

Sections of Your Site (e.g., Home, About, Products/Services, Contact, Privacy Policy, Help, Site Map)

Page   _Requirements_

_____   _____

_____   _____

_____   _____

_____   _____

_____   _____

Goals Checklist

Identify the Stakeholders

Stakeholder   *Needs*

_____

_____

_____

Business Goals of the Site

☐ Brand image marketing   ☐ Sales

☐ Customer support   ☐ Lead development

☐ Interactive service   ☐ Persuasion: alter ideas or behavior

☐ Provide a free community   ☐ Sell advertising
   service: information,
   entertainment, etc.   ☐ Other_____

User Goals

☐ Have fun   ☐ Find information

☐ Purchase something   ☐ Ask a question

☐ Meet people   ☐ Get a job done

☐ Other_____

Usability Objectives

Primary task   *Time to do it*   *Number of mistakes users can make*

_____

_____

_____

How long it takes to learn the system _____

Subjective Impressions

How well should the average user rate the web site on each of these dimensions?

Easy to use	1 2 3 4 5 6 7	Hard to use
Attractive	1 2 3 4 5 6 7	Unattractive
Useful	1 2 3 4 5 6 7	Waste of time
Efficient	1 2 3 4 5 6 7	Tedious
Well organized	1 2 3 4 5 6 7	Haphazard
Entertaining	1 2 3 4 5 6 7	Boring
Valuable information	1 2 3 4 5 6 7	No information
Responsive	1 2 3 4 5 6 7	Slow

Business Goals

What are the business reasons for this web site? What's the value proposition? How is the business going to determine whether the site was a success? For some sites, the evaluation is simply, "How much money did we make from customers of the web site?" In the large number of marketing web sites, the value is assessed based on indirect effects on purchasing, lead generation, and company reputation and valuation.

For many first-time sites, the criterion for success is that the business gains a better understanding of the role the Internet can play in its business. In redesigning or expanding an existing web site (or developing a large initial web site), a cost justification is in order, without which the site is destined for failure. Business goals have to be factored into consideration with user goals. For example, if usability goals aren't tempered by business goals, the most usable e-commerce site is one where users get everything for free (it's not only cheaper, it's also a lot simpler)!

User Goals

Why will users come to your site? To be entertained or to get work done? To learn something or to create something? To interact with other people or to avoid having to talk to one of your salespeople? Set up your initial expectations and refine them as you learn more about the users.

If you can't think of a reason users would come, then they probably won't. Some web sites try to lure users by providing portals or news, but if you can't think of a reason users would *prefer* your portal or news service over another source, then they probably still won't come. So consider how your service can be more useful—for example, greater relevance (e.g., local news), more up-to-date information, or easier use. Try adding value to your core services rather than throwing in unrelated extras.

Define Usability Objectives

Determine how well the site needs to work for users. Consider how often they're likely to come to your site and how much time they can spend there. Based on that, how much time can they afford to spend learning how to use your system? How many times can they afford to make mistakes? If they get confused, will they simply leave your site and never return? How impressed do the users need to be? What activities do they need to perform? How often do they need to come back? These questions will be elaborated as you learn more about your users. Table 3-1 shows some common types of usability objectives that may apply to your site.

Table 3-1.

Example Usability Objectives.

Category	Examples of Specific Objectives
Learning time/task time	Users will be able to use this site the first time without any training.
	First-time users will be able to find their topic of interest within two minutes of visiting the site; expert users (5 or more visits) will be able to find a topic within 30 seconds.
Number of errors	Users will not visit more than three incorrect pages (on average) in completing a task.
	Users will make no fatal errors at least 99 percent of the time (such as entering an incorrect credit card or shipping address).
Subjective impressions	On a scale of 1 (really appealing) to 7 (really unappealing), users will rate the site at least a 2.5.
Accomplished tasks	At least 75 percent of users who add an item to a shopping cart will complete a purchase.
	At least 95 percent of users who complete their credit card information will complete a purchase.
Revisits	At least 50 percent of registered users will return to the site at least once per month.

Don't be overly simplistic or unrealistic in setting these objectives. A three-click rule is a popular target ("the user should be able to get to any page within three clicks"), but it's not a realistic objective for large sites. It's good to minimize the number of clicks users have to make to get something done, but it's more important to consider how long it takes them and how many mistakes they may make than to worry about the specific number of clicks. Similarly, it's good to aim for fast downloading of pages, but you should be realistic about how fast they can possibly be.

Define Functional Specifications

While functionality is sometimes considered outside the domain of the usability specialist, it's clear that if users simply *can't* do something they need to do, then the system isn't usable. As such, much of the work done in user studies during user needs analysis is focused on uncovering the capabilities and functionality that the users will need.

A traditional requirements document in software engineering focuses on functional specifications, or specs. These list each subsystem of the software and all functional requirements within each subsystem. This document is revised throughout the requirements analysis phase, and additional functional requirements may be added during development as the functionality is understood more intimately or as usability studies reveal that a feature needs to be added or removed. Later changes are reviewed carefully to understand their impact on schedule and budget. Functional requirements are explicitly prioritized and desired features are scheduled for later releases of the web site.

The functional specs are referenced throughout design and production of the site to verify that the system being produced corresponds to the necessary functionality. In addition, the quality assurance team uses the functional specs as the basis for the majority of its testing.

A large site will have hundreds, thousands, or even more functional requirements specified. Some example functional requirements for the site visitor include the following:

• Site contains a help system that can be brought up from any screen.

• Site contains links to contact information on every screen.

• Error pages include a customer service phone number.

• Searches that return zero matches include suggested products to view.

• Product listings include product name, description, size, and weight.

• Site sends email to buyers when orders are back-ordered, and when back-ordered products are received.

• Site emails a welcome message to users when they register.

Many sites need an administrative interface for those who must update the site content or process orders. Don't forget to plan the features for these users also. Some example functional requirements for the administrative (or back-end) portion of the web site include the following:

• Ability to add, modify, and delete product listings on the site.

• Ability to add, modify, or delete banner ads posted throughout the site.

• Notification system that emails copies of all orders to the shipping department and to the site administrator.

• Nightly transaction reports listing all orders through the site.

- Reports upon request for

  - money made per period—by ads and by orders

  - user demographics by product category

  - products sold by user category

  - banner ad hit counts by company purchasing banner ads

- Ability to tell if the system is down and send an alert to the system administrator and to the manager responsible for the site.

BACKGROUND RESEARCH

Several forms of background research are used to uncover user needs: surveys, scenarios, competitive analysis, interviews, and focus groups. These give us a better idea of our true user profile, user needs, and user preferences. Most of these methods are also very good at generating conceptual design ideas. Designers don't have to rely on their own ingenuity to solve design problems but can use background research to elicit the considerable knowledge and domain expertise of the target users.

With most of these methods, you'll want to work closely with the marketing department, because of the large overlap of interests between usability concerns and marketing. You'll also find that there are some distinct interests: whereas marketing is interested in how much people are willing to pay, what magazines they read, and how they make purchasing decisions, the usability specialist is more interested in their disabilities, computer skills, and work practices. As a result, while many of these techniques are also part of traditional marketing practice, such as competitive analysis, you'll see that the way we carry them out is somewhat different than the traditional methods, stressing usability concerns.

SURVEYS

The first method of background research that we'll discuss is conducting a user survey. Since most people have answered a marketing survey at one time or another, this method is likely to be the most familiar.

What to Ask About

What kinds of information are surveys particularly good at collecting? Surveys work well for issues that are clear cut and easy to categorize, such as basic demographics. They should also focus on questions that directly resolve design dilemmas, helping to guide your design decisions.

Demographics

Surveys are a good way to collect the demographics of your users, especially to help uncover the breadth of diversity. A quick questionnaire can determine the target population's general age, gender, profession, education, computer skill, type of computer, and nationality. The first use of demographics is to verify that you have properly sampled your target population. The second use is to find out basic data about your audience's skills, experience, and lifestyle. For instance, if you are building a gaming site for young men, you can first check to make sure that your responses are actually from young men, and then you want to find out what those young men are like: what computers do they use, what games do they play, what types of game controllers do they have, what is their reading (or education) level, and how much time do they spend on internet gaming sites?

Needs and Preferences

Surveys explore people's preferences with questions such as "What kinds of products would you like to buy online?" Surveys explore the problems people have with web sites by asking questions such as "Which of these issues would you consider to be the *worst* aspect of browsing the Web: __ download speed, __ browser incompatibility, __ getting lost." And surveys also explore the problems users have with the job task for which they are using the Web by asking questions such as "What are the most common problems you have with tracking inventory today?"

Design Impact

In crafting your survey, choose questions that will have a direct impact on your design. If you can't decide how an answer would affect your design, then delete the question.

For instance, if your design wouldn't be affected by gender, don't bother asking users to specify their gender. And definitely do not depend on stereotypes of how gender should influence the design. Your stereotypes may be wrong, so *rely on user data*. If you think men prefer black backgrounds on their web sites, you're much better off asking "What background color do you prefer on web sites?" than asking their gender. Similarly, don't assume technical people want a design with elaborate technical wizardry or that children prefer talking animals before you've actually asked them.

While it may be interesting to ask about gender and find out how gender correlates with other responses, this is mostly useful if you're trying to do long-term research rather than practical design. For solving the design problem at hand, keep the survey short and to the point, skipping questions you won't apply directly, and design your web site to work across the spectrum of responses you get. Occasionally, it may be useful to ask general questions to look at how users' backgrounds may affect their responses. This may lead you to broaden your survey sample if the pattern of responses suggests you had a biased sample. Form 3-3 is a sample survey template that can be modified according to the kind of information that is needed. (Download from *http://www.mkp.com/uew/.*)

How to Structure the Survey Responses

The type of response you allow—checkbox, multiple choice, free response—is guided by several concerns: keeping the survey short and making the responses fast; enabling straightforward analysis with statistical tools; encouraging accurate and complete responses; and encouraging new information that you could not have anticipated.

Free Response

A free response option asks an open question and lets respondents enter any response they like. Since this takes more effort than most types of questions, free response questions tend to get the fewest responses. In addition, because the responses can be in any form the respondent chooses, it can be difficult to tally up the answers and compare them. You may be able to categorize typical responses, but exceptional cases that don't fit categories well are quite likely.

Free response questions can include those that encourage specific answers, such as asking for specific quantities. These are obviously easier to tally and compare.

Use free response questions at the end of your survey to see if respondents have any other comments that go beyond what you were looking for. Make sure there is some place for respondents to write in concerns about your survey: how it will be used, ways in which they chose to interpret your questions, and response options you may have left out.

Free response items can be a very useful way to get ideas from potential users at a very low cost. Use these responses as directions to explore as you investigate more deeply with other methods: interviews, focus groups, user testing, and so forth.

Checkboxes and Checklists

Checkboxes and checklists allow the respondent to quickly answer a large number of questions, keeping writing to a minimum. A checklist might, for instance, list products that a respondent owns or would be interested in purchasing through your site. A checklist can list possible problems people have in doing their jobs. A checklist could ask users what features they'd like on your web site.

While no other response is quite as fast, respondents often skip reading long checklists or overlook checklist options. It's very difficult to tell whether an unchecked box was explicitly left unchecked or was simply ignored. For this reason, in counting up the number of people who responded to a particular checklist item, you should view the total as a likely underestimate of what might have been the actual interest in that item. A checkbox can usually be replaced with a Yes/No response, which eliminates the problem of interpreting whether the item was skipped but may still have a relatively low response rate.

Multiple Choice

Multiple choice responses enable you to restrict the response set to easily understood categories, making analysis of responses more straightforward than with free response questions. Providing choices requires that you anticipate what responses are possible. When you believe you may be missing important alternatives, leave an option to choose "Other" and space to write in a response.

For online surveys, make sure all multiple choice items, typically displayed as radio buttons, default to a "No Response" option or have none of the radio buttons selected.

Likert scales are multiple choice responses like "strongly disagree 1 2 3 4 5 6 7 strongly agree," which have a numerical range of choices with typically five or seven options in a range. You can label each option, omitting the numbers (e.g., "strongly disagree   disagree   neutral   agree   strongly agree"). This is most useful when you have an uncommon response dimension (e.g., "cool" versus "uncool," which is not recommended) or where the intermediate levels could be interpreted differently by each respondent. It's most accurate to include a neutral or middle option, but in some types of surveys you may find respondents will tend to gravitate toward a "no opinion" stance (out of politeness, for instance). When you omit the middle option (leaving four or six options), you can draw out small preferences. Because of their numerical interpretation, Likert scales enable you to take an average of the responses.

Web Site Survey

This survey is designed to gather information about the users and potential users of our web site in order to make sure we serve your needs as well as possible.

Please answer the questions as completely as you can. Do not include your name—your participation in this survey is anonymous.

About You

Your job title _____

Your age   under 18   18–29   30–39   40–49   50 or over

Gender   female   male

Highest level of education
   high school   some college   bachelor's degree   graduate work

Your Experience

How long have you used computers?
   under 1 year   1–3 years   more than 3 years

Which computer systems have you used regularly?
   DOS   Windows   Mac   Unix   Other _____

Which browsers have you used regularly?
   Internet Explorer   Netscape Navigator   Other _____

Our Web Site

The following questions are about your experiences of our web site at *www.examplewebsite.com*.

How many times have you visited our web site? _____

List any other sites you have used that are similar

_____

_____

_____

_____

_____

Please rate our site on the following dimensions

Easy to use	1 2 3 4 5 6 7	Hard to use
Attractive	1 2 3 4 5 6 7	Unattractive
Useful	1 2 3 4 5 6 7	Waste of time
Efficient	1 2 3 4 5 6 7	Tedious
Well organized	1 2 3 4 5 6 7	Haphazard
Entertaining	1 2 3 4 5 6 7	Boring
Valuable information	1 2 3 4 5 6 7	No information
Responsive	1 2 3 4 5 6 7	Slow

What do you consider the most valuable aspect of the web site?

_____

_____

What is the biggest problem with the site?

_____

_____

Which features would you like us to add to this site?

☐ Ability to purchase products online

☐ Online discussion boards

☐ An announcements mailing list

☐ Additional online help

☐ Ability to place classified ads on our site

☐ A jobs board

Do you have any other comments about our web site you would like to offer?

_____

_____

_____

Thank you for participating in our survey.

Interpreting Responses

When analyzing responses to your survey, you'll generally look for the average or most common response. You can count the total number of responses to a checked item. Low response to an individual question may indicate that the question is unclear and the responses should be interpreted cautiously. Surveys can provide extremely useful data, but remember to document the limitations to the data, such as a low response rate, sampling problems, or biases, discussed below.

Exceptional responses should not be ignored. You're not simply looking for an average response. While it's useful to know how an "average" person responds, it's also very useful to understand the spectrum of responses. How much do people vary in their responses? You may want to create a design that serves two or more divergent audiences. Also, some outlier populations may be extremely important to your site design. For instance, 2 percent of your users may be millionaires, but they may buy your most expensive products and account for far more than a 2 percent portion of your profits. And some small populations may require extra attention to serve more challenging needs, such as providing an accessible design for people with disabilities.

Sampling

How many survey responses do you need to collect? Even a small number of responses can be useful. Designing from *any* information is better than designing with *none,* so long as you're careful not to be overconfident in a limited sample. If you're trying to achieve statistical significance, the degree of significance will depend on both your sample size and the range of responses you get to each question. You'll need to consult with a statistician to work out a good number for your case. A helpful rule of thumb is that fewer than 10 returned surveys is not likely to be useful, and 50 returned surveys is a good target. Solid scientific research may in some cases require more surveys, but 50 should be more than adequate for most practical design situations.

Return Rate

To get 50 surveys back, you'll need to send out quite a few more than that. Online surveys can expect as few as 1 to 2 percent of site visitors actually to respond. Email and snail mail surveys typically are returned at a rate of 5 to 10 percent, meaning that you need to send out as many as 1,000 to get 50 returned. People who are highly motivated to be involved in the design will return the surveys at a much higher rate. It's not unusual to get 100 percent return rate when surveying within a small organization that will be using your web site in daily work.

REQUIREMENTS ANALYSIS

You can improve the rate of return in several ways:

- Offer a small gift or prize drawing for those who return it.

- Include a small gift with the survey, whether or not they return it.

- Make sure the survey does not look like junk mail: address envelopes by hand, lick stamps rather than using a machine, sign cover letters by hand (or even write the cover letters by hand), personally address the cover letter to the recipient. For email surveys, make sure each email is personally addressed rather than sent to a list.

- Use unusual paper and envelopes to make the survey stand out in the mail.

- Include a referral letter in cases where you are contacting members of a specific organization. For instance, surveys going out to employees of a company should include a letter from a relevant manager.

- Keep the survey short and say how long it is likely to take to fill out.

- Include a self-addressed stamped envelope (SASE).

- Emphasize that responses will be kept confidential.

- Emphasize the benefits to users of having a web site design reflecting their needs and interests.

- Specify a date by which you'd like the survey returned. Otherwise, respondents may procrastinate.

- Follow up the initial survey with a query to those who haven't responded, encouraging them to participate.

Selecting Survey Recipients

When dealing with a small number of customers or a small number of users, as with an intranet, you can send the survey to everyone; your only limiting factor is the cost of distributing the survey and analyzing the responses. If the survey can be created online, the cost of distributing the survey and collecting the data is minimized, and development time is your only significant cost.

It is trickier when you're targeting a mass market, an ill-defined group, or prospective customers. You may not have an appropriate mailing list to start out with. Here are some ideas for getting started. Advertise the survey on your current site or on another web site in the industry. If there are appropriate mailing lists or newsgroups, send your survey to them. Make sure this is within the usage policy of the list; identify yourself and your purposes clearly at the beginning of the message; keep the message short; and post only once. Go where your users congregate. If it's a local site, hand out surveys on a street corner. If it's an industry site, visit an industry convention. Use the *snowball* technique: ask each respondent to suggest another appropriate recipient (gathering respondents like a snowball accumulates snow rolling down a hill).

For email surveys, ask respondents to forward surveys to their friends and colleagues. In email, be sure to specify by what date the survey needs to be returned, or you may end up getting surveys coming to you for years as they circulate around the Internet. While you should avoid *looking like* junk mail, you also need to avoid *being* junk mail. Be careful not to abuse mailing lists that were clearly not intended for the purpose of your survey. Ask permission of organization leaders before sending it to members of their group. Make sure that your company has decided that it's okay to send surveys to customers before the surveys go out, and include appropriate cover letters from account representatives.

Self-Selection

You usually can't control who responds to your survey, so the people who take the time to fill it out are the people who *choose* to do so. These motivated people may be exactly the people who are sufficiently interested in your web site that they'll be your regular users, but there are many reasons for not returning a survey. For instance, people who have been dissatisfied with your web site may not want to waste their time providing you with information, but you especially want to know what problems caused their dissatisfaction. People who are motivated to provide feedback may have significantly different usage behavior than other users.

Self-selection should be a concern, and you want to minimize it, but don't view it as a reason not to conduct a survey. Any user study will have some limitations, and sampling problems are a common one. Carefully document which target groups did and did not receive the survey, and write down the reasons you think people may not have responded. Include this information in your survey results, and factor these limitations into your design recommendations based on the survey. You will often find that you can have fairly high confidence in your results despite self-selection problems.

Avoiding Bias

Survey questions need to be carefully worded to avoid biasing the responses. Respondents will actively try to understand and interpret the purpose of your questions and will often try to determine what answers you're expecting and

REQUIREMENTS ANALYSIS

how they think you'll use those answers. Often, the way they respond will not correspond to the question you were hoping to ask.

Pretest the survey to identify questions that are misleading, ambiguous, insulting, or just plain nonsense. The pretest will identify questions that are always skipped and answers that are always the same. The pretesters will often give you insights into how to fix the questions. Below are some tips for minimizing these biases.

Question Skipping

People have a tendency to skip questions in surveys, because they don't understand the questions, don't consider them relevant, can't figure out an appropriate answer, or are just bored with a long questionnaire. As a result, surveys need to be kept short and relevant to maximize the quality of responses. In addition, asking respondents to answer every question can increase the completeness of their responses.

Response Order

Put response options in their natural order, say from lowest to highest value. Or, if there is no natural order, scramble them. You will have the tendency to place possible responses in the order that you think of them, and because of this, you'll want to rearrange the responses to avoid implying that some responses are "better" than others. Respondents may also have a tendency to choose either the first or last item, so watch for this in pretesting or rearrange the order on different versions of the survey. Don't rearrange the order between questions if some of the questions involve negatives, or respondents will likely become very confused.

Rote Answers

One problem with arranging all answers in a consistent order is that respondents may fall into a pattern of marking all low or high responses in a series, without thinking through each question. Without confusing the respondent, vary the responses. To keep people thinking, switch often between types of responses: multiple choice, free response, checklist.

Negative Questions

Avoid all uses of negatives, such as "Which of the following is not a problem in using our web site?" If you have to use a negative term, emphasize it as "NOT." Watch out for subtle implied negatives, such as "Which of the following are you least likely to consider your most delightful fantasy: ice cream, world peace, or pots of gold?" Among such great alternatives, the word "least" can easily be missed.

Leading Questions

Nobody loves a *terrorist,* but *freedom fighters* can be pretty popular. Your choice of words may imply a certain response that is the opposite you'd get by phrasing it differently.

Ambiguity

The same question or response may mean different things to different people. Make your responses as specific and concrete as possible. If you choose to imitate the phrasing of an older questionnaire (one you dug out of a book, for instance), make sure that the language is contemporary and that words haven't shifted meaning. A common example is the use of the word "fair" as a response option: some people feel that "fair" is a positive term and others feel it's a negative term.

Range Bias

If you ask, "How many times per week do you use the Internet?" you've already implied that the respondent uses the Internet at least once a week. Instead ask, "How often do you use the Internet?" If your response options are "15 hrs/day or more; 10–15 hrs/day; 5–10 hrs/day; and less than 5 hrs/day," you'll arrive at more frequent use than if your options are "at least once per day; 1–5 times per week; 1–5 times per month; and less than once per month." Requiring a write-in response may minimize the bias but will reduce the comparability of responses, frustrating your analysis. This bias can't be avoided entirely, but be sure to choose sensible ranges and pretest to make certain you get an effective range of responses.

When to Use Surveys

Surveys can be an inexpensive way to gather large amounts of data from potential users. Because you can get a large sample size, a good survey can provide you with the most reliable demographics possible. Surveys are especially useful before a project starts, and once the web site has gone live they can be used to inexpensively gather feedback online. They are less successful when you have trouble identifying who the target users will be or when the target users have a very low motivation to return the survey. Surveys often come back with very incomplete data. By contrast, direct user contact in interviews and focus groups can provide both more complete feedback and more in-depth, thoughtful responses. However, the complete anonymity of a survey can give you personal information that wouldn't come across in a face-to-face interview.

COMPETITIVE ANALYSIS

A competitive analysis can be one of the fastest ways to hone in on a workable design paradigm for your product. If you are designing a portal, take a look at Yahoo. If you're designing a shopping site, look at Amazon. If you're building an auction system, look at eBay. One caveat: Yahoo, Amazon, and eBay are all multimillion-dollar systems, so you may find some excellent features on their sites that are not possible within your budget.

Traditional competitive analysis will focus on the market niche being targeted, the price of the product, and the unique selling point being promoted. In analyzing for usability, we're looking for user interface ideas. What categories, labels, icons, processes, and features are they using? What audience are they targeting, and what user goals are they trying to serve? We want to steal their good ideas and apply them to our design. This can be as simple as visiting competitors' sites and listing all the features they support as a first step to writing a functional specification for your site.

Stealing ideas from your competitors is a time-honored technique for innovation, but it needs to be done with a cautious respect for intellectual property. Copyright law protects the way web sites express their look and feel—the creative aspects of their design, such as their exact words or images and the way they've chosen to combine them. Don't copy text or images directly, although it's usually safe to copy an individual label, and it's okay to show a dog if another site has shown a dog, even the very same dog. You just can't use the same picture of the dog. If it's the same dog (or a similar one), watch out for trademarks. Similarly, if you copy a label, make sure it's not a label that is trademarked, such as a brand name or service mark. Don't assume it's safe to copy just because there's no copyright notice: copyright and trademarks don't have to be explicitly declared to be protected. If there's only one *optimal* way to do something, copyright law would not protect it, because there's no creativity involved in choosing the *unique* optimal solution. However, in this case, patent law may apply. Someone may have patented a specific process that enables users to perform a task or a specific way of computing results. If you have any doubts about which, if any, intellectual property laws apply, you'll need to consult with your lawyer.

Competitive analysis techniques apply to your competitors' sites, to other sites with similar functionality (whether they compete with you or not), and to previous versions of your own site. In addition to simply listing things your competitors have done, you can evaluate them for usability, through user

Figure 3-1.

Comparing Two Bookstore Web Sites.

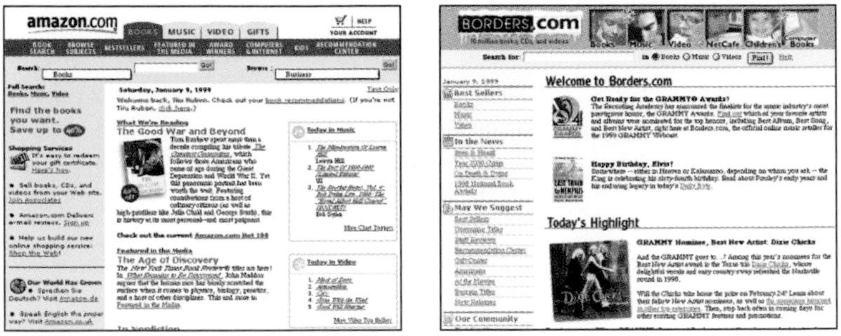

Amazon.com

Pros
- Two-tiered menu at top shows structure hierarchy
- Search toward top of page
- Text-only option at top

Cons
- Too cluttered
- Layout unclear, not sure where to look
- Help not available if no images

Usability Issues
- Typography contributes to confusing layout

Borders.com

Pros
- Browsable navigation on side
- Good visual hierarchy
- Search toward top of page

Cons
- Icons are difficult to interpret
- Music dominates top of fold

Usability Issues
- Top navbar different from text navbar at bottom
- Light-brown links

testing or usability inspections (covered in Chapter 12, "Usability Evaluation"), or by asking people to respond to the sites in interviews and focus groups. Evaluating the usability of competitors' sites identifies problems you should avoid and establishes a benchmark for comparing the ease of use of your own site.

A competitive analysis is a fast, easy way to establish a starting point in design, but don't give too much credit to competitors. You don't know if your competitors have tested their site or what hidden influences may have played a role in their design. Their site may look great, but they may be getting customer complaints left and right. More than anything, competitive analysis should be used for idea generation, but ideas you develop will need to be corroborated with feedback from users.

As a brief example, we compare the home pages of the Amazon and Borders web sites in Figure 3-1. Both are attempting to target mass-audience sales of books and other media. The Borders home page has a heavy emphasis on music, suggesting that this is a relatively high priority for them. In this comparison, we identify the main techniques, both good and bad, used on the pages. In a more complete analysis, we'd want to examine the site architectures and the steps necessary to find a product and complete a purchase.

A competitive analysis is most useful in the following circumstances:

- When you're designing a product from scratch. (When you're building a revision of your current system, feedback from your users will play a larger role.)

- When you have little experience in the target domain and need a source of good ideas.

- When you're developing a transactional system, as opposed to a purely marketing site. In both cases, some competitive analysis is useful, but transactional systems are more likely to have evolved in response to user demands and have unexpected features.

- When the application is complex, so that good shortcuts and simplifying metaphors are crucial to discover.

INTERVIEWS AND FOCUS GROUPS

Interviews and focus groups are useful for getting subjective reactions to your designs and for finding out how people live and work and solve their problems. The main difference between the two methods is that interviews entail speaking to one individual at a time while focus groups gather a group of people together to discuss issues that you raise.

The main advantage of an individual interview is that the individual is not biased by other people in the group. The advantage of a focus group is that if one person raises an idea, then another person can develop that idea, and you can delve into far greater detail on some issues by following up lines of thought that the interviewer might not have even known to pursue. On the other hand, you need to watch out for *groupthink* in focus groups, where people tend to conform to one another's views and are reluctant to disagree with the consensus view. A group can get sidetracked on a particular topic or point of view because it is easy or interesting to discuss rather than because it is an important topic. Table 3-2 summarizes the advantages of each method.

Conducting the Interview or Focus Group

Interviews and focus groups are best started by getting to know the interviewees. Many interviewees are nervous, and simple introductions can help

Table 3-2.

Interviews versus Focus Groups.

Advantages of Interviews	Advantages of Focus Groups
Interviewees do not influence one another's responses (no groupthink).	Group members can react to one another's ideas and can be prompted by another group member into considering an issue that the interviewer could not have anticipated.
For the same level of confidence in the results, fewer people are required to sample a broad range of viewpoints.	For the same number of interviewees, the time and cost are much smaller.
In-depth exploration of individual tasks and problems is possible.	Incorrect facts (that the interviewer may not know) can be corrected quickly.
Each interview can refine the questions for following interviews.	Noncontroversial issues are quickly resolved, and controversial issues are quickly identified.

encourage them to speak more freely. You should wear a name tag so that the interviewees don't need to learn your name. At the beginning of a focus group, ask everyone to introduce themselves, which will help to get participants accustomed to participating in the discussion.

When interviewing people in a corporate setting, where they might feel their views could affect their job stability, it's a good idea to let people know that their participation will be anonymous and that they can review your notes if they are worried about what you may tell their boss.

Including a Survey

You may want to begin or end the discussion with a written survey that addresses basic information such as demographics and simple facts and preferences that won't affect the interview. A survey at the beginning is helpful if the interview might be interrupted prematurely. Usually, in a reasonably structured session, a survey is a good way to signal the end of the interview, and putting it at the end avoids biasing the interviewee about the intent of your interview.

Structured versus Unstructured Interviews

A structured interview is one that follows a fixed list of questions—essentially a survey conducted conversationally. An unstructured interview opens the floor to almost any kind of relevant discussion. The interviewer asks open-ended questions and follows them up by asking for more detail as such detail seems important. Most interviews fall somewhere between the two extremes. The structured interview gathers more consistent responses, permitting easier analysis, while the unstructured interview allows issues to be explored that could not have been anticipated by the interviewer.

User Needs and Functionality

Focus groups and interviews are really good for eliciting user needs and functionality ideas. Ask people what they want from your web site and why they would go there. Ask them how it fits into their lifestyle, and when and how they'd like to use it. Ask them what features they'd like and what they'd use; provide them with suggestions if they don't come up with anything on their own. While people can give you very accurate descriptions of how they currently do their work, hypotheticals are another story, and you should not rely too heavily on them. People are very poor at saying how likely they would be to use a feature that doesn't exist. However, their ideas for such features are a gold mine of possibilities you may not have considered.

Reviewing Mockups

Focus groups and interviews are also very good for exploring preferences, opinions, and subjective reactions. If you already have a web site online or you have mockups available, ask people to look at the designs and tell you what they think. Reviewing alternative mockups with a set of users is a much more valid approach to choosing a design direction than reviewing them with management. A nice trick is to take your competitors' designs, brand them with your logo, and ask people which design they like best for your site. If your own design is among them, then you can verify whether your design is more effective than your competitors', and you can find out what aspects of your competitors' sites they like, while avoiding the bias of having them try to favor your own design.

As you review mockup alternatives and competitors' sites, ask people to respond to the layout, color, ease of use, and appeal of the site. If you've determined a specific feel that you want, ask them how well your designs fit your intention. For instance, you may want a site that is professional (vs. personal), traditional (vs. futuristic), objective (vs. subjective), and conservative (vs. daring). Your business has a certain image it wants to project, and you can ask whether that image makes sense and how well you've achieved it.

Walkthroughs

If you already have a web site or you've worked through the design so that you have several screens or a storyboard to review, you can also walk people through the design, asking them for their reactions as they go, performing an informal kind of user testing. This helps identify labeling and placement problems early on. And unlike most user testing, you'll more easily get feedback on the look and the concept of the site. People may comment on text or layouts they don't like, inefficient tasks, concerns about privacy, and their own design tastes. This type of feedback is easier to get in an interview than in user testing, where you'll often miss out on more global issues because the users are focused on problem-solving and they're not as likely to mention odd aspects of the interface as long as they're able to get their task completed.

Recordings

Audio recordings can capture what transpired in an interview and help you to fill in the holes from your notes when you fall behind. Get permission from anyone you're interviewing before recording them. Most people are quite comfortable with audio recordings if you keep them inconspicuous, but prepare for a mix of both recorded and nonrecorded sessions (when interviewees don't agree to being recorded).

Videotaping is typically so conspicuous that it makes people self-conscious about what they're saying, and rarely offers enough value to be worth the trouble. In focus groups, video cameras can be hidden in a corner or behind a mirror, which typically works out well. Video is useful for capturing gestures or drawings (which are rarely an important part of a focus group), for filling in your notes on what was said (but audio recordings are usually sufficient), or for presenting video clips later to the design team or the client. However, it is usually quite time-consuming to do the video editing.

Organizations

When developing intranet or extranet applications, the interview is an especially appropriate technique for uncovering complex organizational roles and relationships and understanding work processes (workflow). As an interviewer, you'll need to be especially sensitive to the politics of the situation and develop an empathy with each interviewee without appearing to take sides. In these settings, many people are concerned with how your work will affect theirs: Will the new system create more work for them or threaten to eliminate their job role? Save sensitive questions until the end of an interview in order to develop as much empathy as possible before addressing them. Your letter of introduction may seem to ally you with a particular perspective, and, when possible, you may want to stress your status as an outside observer.

Look for where work practices vary from officially documented processes and explore why these exceptions take place. Do your best to discuss each job role with the person who fills that role rather than getting that information secondhand. Management will often have a different mental model of how work gets done than the people actually doing the work.

Preparing for an Interview or Focus Group

Most of the same issues apply in recruiting interviewees as in getting a sample for your survey or recruiting users for user testing. Do your best to choose a representative sample of users. Selection is especially important because you can't get the quantity you would in surveys, and the types of opinions you collect require representative users. If you talk to people who aren't in the target market, you are likely to get uninformed and misleading ideas that are no more useful than guessing at the answers yourself.

Prepare all of your questions and materials ahead of time, even if you are planning an unstructured interview (see Form 3-4; download from *http://www.mkp.com/uew*). Rehearse the interview or focus group with some of your colleagues, ensuring that your questions can be answered in a reasonable amount of time and that you're able to encourage a constructive dialogue. Practice taking notes and work out a shorthand so you can take notes quickly and inconspicuously during the conversation. When possible, conduct team interviews with a primary interviewer and a note-taker, so that the primary interviewer can focus on the conversation and the note-taker can focus on capturing everything said.

A typical note-taking approach follows these guidelines. (1) Mark every page of notes with the interviewer's name, the date, the project, and any other context that will help you remember the situation (location, interviewee code, etc.). (2) Write down exact quotes in double quotes, write down paraphrases in single quotes, and write general conversation topics and opinions without any special marking. (3) If you have any design ideas that derived from the conversation, but that weren't explicitly discussed, write them down in square brackets. (4) Put an asterisk (*) next to important issues you'll want to make sure you don't miss in analysis. (5) In focus groups you may want to number each participant on a seating chart and number each comment you write down accordingly. (6) Type up your notes as soon as possible after the interview so that you remember as much as possible.

Focus Group Preparation Worksheet

Project _____

Dates and times _____

Location _____

Facilitator and other observers _____

Required demographic _____

Number of groups _____

Number of people (per group) _____

Payment (per person) _____

Food and refreshments _____

Videotaping and audiotaping: video / audio / none

Recruiting ad   *Where to place it?* _____

                 Wording _____

                 _____

Questions to ask:

_____

_____

_____

Materials
Check that you have each of the following, as needed, for your focus group.

☐ Consent form
☐ Demographic questionnaire
☐ Debriefing sheet
☐ Mockups
☐ Observer notes sheets
☐ List of participants
☐ Name tags
☐ Payment checks
☐ Audio and videotape
☐ Seating chart

Focus Groups

Focus groups have some additional considerations not required for interviews. They are concerned primarily with deciding how to select and organize groups of people. Groups are more difficult to coordinate, and a facilitator is needed to help manage interpersonal interactions.

Facilities

While interviews can easily be conducted on the street or in someone's office, focus groups need a good meeting place with a quiet, undistracting atmosphere, a way to display mockups to the participants (which can be mounted on boards and passed around or displayed on an overhead screen), a central table for participants to sit around, and an appropriate place for observers to sit. Many focus group facilities have an observation room behind a one-way mirror for sets of observers to watch. If people are being surreptitiously observed, you need to tell them about it in advance, and usually it's not a problem. However, we usually find it's just as easy to have up to three observers sitting in the room who are introduced as assistants.

The Facilitator

The primary person conducting the focus group is known as the *facilitator*. You can hire professional facilitators who are expert at encouraging discussion and getting everyone to participate. One of the goals of a focus group is to get people to respond to one another's input, and so you may even want to foster arguments—these lead to a lot of information about why people feel the ways they do and reveal the controversial issues. Of course, you'll want to prevent arguments from getting out of hand and hurting people's feelings. Generally, the idea is that one person's ideas can generate deeper analysis by a second person. The facilitator also encourages each person to participate, so no viewpoints get lost.

Number of People per Group

Since not everyone shows up as scheduled, it's usually best to invite about two more people than your optimal number of participants. A focus group generally works well with six to twelve participants. We typically invite about ten people, expecting anywhere from eight to ten. Ask people to show up ten minutes early so you can start on time. Bring drinks (coffee, water, soft drinks) and possibly some simple snacks, and prepare for a break in the middle if you go over an hour. A good way to handle a break is to give participants a questionnaire or some other individual activity in the middle of the session. However, the risk in taking a break is that some people may never return from it, especially if you're conducting your session during work hours or in their workplace.

Number of Groups

You'll want to conduct more than one focus group, typically three to five. A single focus group may be heavily biased by the mix of people involved, and you would never even know there was a problem unless you'd conducted a second group. Two groups is a bare minimum to get a sense of how opinions vary, but optimally you'll continue recruiting groups until additional groups provide no substantial new information.

Composition of Groups

What's a good mix of people in the group? In heterogeneous groups, you select a diverse set of people. Each group then contains a reasonably representative sample of your target audience. This is usually the preferred approach if you have a small number of groups. However, heterogeneous groups may comprise too wide a sample, bringing together people who have little in common and thus have little to respond to in what others say. In homogeneous groups, people of common demographics are selected, and you make sure each group samples a different demographic. This may lead to easier conversation, but each group tends more toward a single viewpoint so that more groups are necessary to sample a diversity of demographics.

When to Conduct Interviews and Focus Groups

Interviews and focus groups are a good way to understand work practices and obtain subjective reactions to your web site. They're appropriate at almost any stage of design. Conducting them earlier will enable lessons learned to have a bigger impact on the final design. Conducting them later enables the interviewees to react in a more specific and concrete way to actual designs. As such, if you can only do them once, an optimal time is usually early in the design process when some mockups have already been created. They are sometimes not practical to conduct with highly inaccessible user populations, such as high-paid, busy professionals and business executives (doctors and movie producers). Focus groups are difficult to conduct for users who are geographically isolated and for highly specialized fields where the target population is small (ambassadors and arctic explorers). These may be problems that can be solved: seek conferences they all attend and consider conducting online interviews.

INFORMED PROJECT OBJECTIVES

It's all too common for internet businesses to be founded on *presumed* user needs and *presumed* market demand, only to discover that false assumptions about users won't support the financial needs of a business. These steps of user inquiry—surveys, interviews, and focus groups—involve nontrivial time and cost, but the information they provide aims a project in the right direction so that the web site can actually fulfill real needs. Many of the steps taken at this stage, such as listing functional requirements or analyzing competitive sites, are undertaken for the sake of being methodical and complete. These steps establish the groundwork upon which the design is laid out.

04

CONCEPTUAL DESIGN

TASK ANALYSIS

Once you've determined the initial requirements for your web site, you need a way to analyze and optimize the procedures your users will follow while using your site. This forms a crucial part of the specifications for the web site. From your requirements analysis, you should be able to build a profile of who your users are, what knowledge and abilities they come with, and the general goals you'd like them to be able to achieve while at your site. As a designer, you want to provide an efficient means for your users to achieve those goals. Task analysis is meant to specify how the information and functionality found in the requirements analysis will be used. In addition to codifying user procedures, task analysis can also be used as a design tool.

A *task* is the sequence of steps a user will follow to achieve a specific goal. Whether you're using web technologies to automate a company's processes or you're providing information about your grandmother's favorite cookie recipes, there is always a set of goals in mind and a set of tasks for achieving those goals, even if they are somewhat implicit. The purpose of this chapter is to provide you with some simple, practical techniques for analyzing the tasks that will make your site development more efficient and make the user experience dramatically simpler. We describe the components of a task analysis, how it can be used in different situations, and how you can combine use cases with hierarchical task analysis within the web site development process.

WHAT IS TASK ANALYSIS?

Task analysis refers to a family of techniques for describing various aspects of how people work. This can include procedural analysis, job analysis, workflow analysis, and error analysis. Procedural analysis is a set of techniques to analyze the procedures people perform for an individual task. Job analysis is the set of all tasks a person performs as part of a job or to achieve some overall goals. Workflow analysis examines the flow of information and control that is necessary to complete a process that may include multiple people and multiple tasks. Error analysis determines where, when, and under what circumstances errors will occur.

The most crucial component of task analysis is gaining a deep understanding of the goals people are trying to achieve. You can apply various task analytical techniques within your web site development process to clarify and formalize the information from requirements gathering, and to design a process within your web site that allows people to efficiently achieve their goals.

To illustrate how a task analysis might be used, consider the flowchart in Figure 4-1, which maps out a sequence of screens a user might go through while purchasing a stuffed giraffe. Each thumbnail represents a screen in the buying process. The arrowed lines connecting the screens on the left represent a normal sequence of events. For instance, the user starts at the home page, goes to the Products page, goes to the Giraffe page, completes the billing information, verifies that he or she really wants to make the purchase, and receives a confirmation by the system that the stuffed giraffe has been ordered.

The lettered lines on the right side of the figure represent possible optimizations that can be found through a task analysis. For example, if the task analysis revealed that a significant number of users came to the site to buy giraffes, the company might place a giraffe link on the home page that would take users directly to the Giraffe page (line A). This could save users a significant amount of time by bypassing the Products page. As indicated by line B, the company could also place a Buy Giraffe button on the home page that would take users directly to the Billing page, bypassing two unnecessary screens. If the company had customer billing and shipping information stored from a previous visit, it could also bypass the Billing page, saving customers even more time (line C). Likewise, there are other optimizations that could occur within the process, such as placing Buy links on the Products page to bypass individual product pages (line D). In addition, there may be ways to eliminate screens, perhaps by combining the purchase confirmation with another page, thus saving the user even more time and effort. There are many different optimizations that might be made, and making the process explicit through a task analysis allows designers to make rational choices regarding them.

Task analysis can help improve the consistency and coherence of the procedures required to use your web site. Because it makes explicit the procedural knowledge expected from your users, it also clarifies learning requirements and can provide the basis for training materials. Furthermore, since the procedures are clearly spelled out, a task analysis can be used to provide a context-based help system for your users. Task analysis is critical to providing a system that is efficient to use and easy to learn while not exceeding human limitations. In addition, the high-level goals specified in the task analysis make explicit the functionality that you are building into the system. Thus, there is little confusion about the intended purpose of the site.

Figure 4-1.

Example Flowchart:
Buying a Stuffed Giraffe.

This flowchart illustrates a standard e-commerce purchase process. By making the steps of the process explicit, it's easy to see how the task can be improved, as illustrated by the labeled shortcuts on the right.

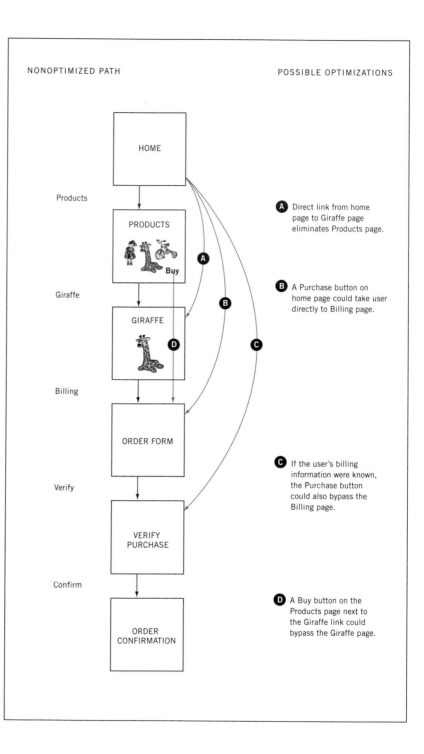

NONOPTIMIZED PATH

POSSIBLE OPTIMIZATIONS

HOME

Products

PRODUCTS

Buy

A Direct link from home page to Giraffe page eliminates Products page.

Giraffe

GIRAFFE

B A Purchase button on home page could take user directly to Billing page.

Billing

ORDER FORM

C If the user's billing information were known, the Purchase button could also bypass the Billing page.

Verify

VERIFY PURCHASE

Confirm

ORDER CONFIRMATION

D A Buy button on the Products page next to the Giraffe link could bypass the Giraffe page.

Task analysis is used throughout the design process because it acts as a road map for the entire design team. In each portion of the design, the task analysis is used as a guide to answer the question, Does this design support the task? For example, an information architecture is only useful if it supports the task. The same goes for writing and graphic design. No stage of design can be done in a vacuum. Likewise, when performing quality assurance and user testing, the task analysis tells the team what to focus on, how important each element is, and how to determine whether the overall design is successful.

TASK ANALYSIS FOR WEB SITE DESIGN

If we only look at a single web page, the procedures for using it are typically trivial. So why go to the extra effort of conducting a task analysis? The answer, of course, is that web sites are not made up of just one page, and the interactions between users and web pages is not necessarily trivial. We need to consider at least three distinct levels when conducting a task analysis.

1. We need to look at the big picture. Who are the user groups that will be using the site, and how do they interact with other users of the site in the course of their overall job responsibilities?

2. We need to consider the pages that a single user will navigate to accomplish his or her goals.

3. We need to address the procedures that a user will utilize within each of the pages.

If we address only one of the levels, we may make the procedures within each of the pages very simple, but might neglect the possibility that some of the pages may be altogether unnecessary. We may also fail to see additional improvements that could be made to the overall workflow.

One way to specify the necessary information at each of the levels is to combine *use case analysis* with *hierarchical task analysis*. Use cases document the interactions between different user groups and are used as a first pass at high-level design. The following sections describe use cases, hierarchical task analysis, and their combination into a powerful analysis technique.

USE CASES

Use cases were developed by Ivar Jacobson as a way to analyze software development from the perspective of how a user would typically interact with the system. Use cases combine a simple way of capturing user scenarios (i.e., instances of how a user might perform a procedure) in a text document and diagramming how different user groups interact while using the system. They start with the users or *actors* of a system and describe the activities the actors engage in while using the system. Actors can be users, databases, other companies, or anything else that interacts with your system. A scenario is the set of steps or actions that an actor must accomplish to achieve a particular goal. Use cases include the typical, or primary, scenario that the user will go through to accomplish a particular goal and can also include a set of alternative scenarios that the user may go through in atypical situations. An example use case is shown in Figure 4-2.

Figure 4-2.

An Example Use Case Specification.

This use case shows how a customer would use the system to buy a book. The specification identifies the name and description of the use case, the actors involved, and the step-by-step process. In addition, exceptional circumstances, such as Alternative 1, can be spelled out.

Use Case: "Buy a Book"
Description: Customer orders a book using the book's ISBN
Actors: Customer, System
Additional Use Cases Needed: "Complete Order" use case

1. Customer locates the search field.
2. Customer enters the ISBN into the search field.
3. Customer presses the Search button.
4. System displays the Description page for the book.
5. Customer verifies that the book is correct and presses the Order button.
6. Customer completes the order (follow a "Complete Order" use case).

Alternative 1: ISBN incorrectly entered
At step 5 the customer realizes that the book displayed is not the desired book.
5a. Customer sees wrong book displayed.
5b. Customer locates search field and returns to step 2.

Use cases are easy to work with because most of the necessary information for building a system can be specified in a standard format. The interaction between different actors in a system can then be captured using use case diagrams. Use case diagrams provide a standard means for viewing an entire transaction in a single view. See Figure 4-3 for an example.

Although use cases are a very powerful tool for system development, they have some weaknesses in the design of usable systems. For instance, a use case won't necessarily tell us if a procedure (scenario) is inefficient. It also won't tell us whether our procedures are within the possibilities of human performance or how much training would be required for a person to perform them. These weaknesses exist because use cases were developed as a software development tool. They are not rooted in human psychology, nor are they intended for that purpose. For many projects, such attention to detail may not be necessary. For mission-critical or safety-critical tasks, ensuring efficient,

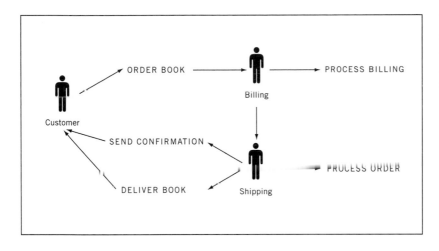

Figure 4-3.

An Example Use Case Diagram.

This diagram shows the actors and use cases involved in a simplified process for selling a book to a customer.

error-free performance becomes much more important. For these types of tasks, we turn to hierarchical task analysis.

HIERARCHICAL TASK ANALYSIS

Hierarchical task analysis is a means of systematically defining a task from the user's perspective. We can look at task procedures on three levels: user level, platform level, and application level.

User-Level Goals and Procedures

At the top level, task procedures are generic descriptions of the goals users will accomplish, like buying a book. These descriptions can be viewed as generic because we can accomplish the goal of buying a book through many means, both electronic and physical.

Platform-Level Goals and Procedures

At the bottom level, task procedures are those imposed by the interface. If we are buying books online, we will probably be using a web browser and will be utilizing common web browser interaction techniques such as pointing, clicking, and using pull-down menus and text-edit fields. Alternatively, if we are buying our book from the local bookstore, we will probably employ different interaction techniques, which might include driving a car, searching bookshelves, and completing a transaction with a clerk. This level is also generic in that many different high-level goals can be accomplished using various combinations of low-level procedures.

Application-Level Goals and Procedures

In between the high and low levels, task procedures at the middle level specify how users will accomplish their top-level goals using the low-level interface procedures required by your system's platform. This is the level where, as designers, we can often have the greatest impact. High-level goals are driven by user needs and marketing decisions that are often a fixed requirement given to the design team. Likewise, low-level procedures are often determined by the underlying hardware and software, and also cannot be changed. What we can easily change is how the low-level procedures are used to accomplish the higher-level goals. We can affect how many and what kind of steps the users must perform. We can determine what information is shown on their screens, and we can determine how many pages they have to navigate. This is true of noncomputer interaction as well. For instance, we could change the procedure by which customers bought books in our bookstore example by having employees personally find books for customers and suggest related books for them. This would minimize the time customers spend searching for books, but doing this for every customer would be very expensive and might have undesired side effects like reducing impulse buying.

Understanding the Tasks and Their Context

The biggest challenge in performing a task analysis is accurately capturing the essence of the user's job. Simply asking users how they do what they do is not enough because users don't think about the steps they go through. A typical response to "How do you do this?" is "I don't know. I've been doing it this way for 20 years and it's the only way I know." Describing procedural knowledge is notoriously difficult for many people. The most direct method is to start by finding any written documentation on how users are supposed to be doing their job, and observing them in action to see how their behavior differs from the "official" instructions. If no written procedures exist, then analysts must observe users as they perform typical task scenarios. Formal methods exist for understanding the context of people's tasks, such as *contextual inquiry*. For a comprehensive treatment of contextual inquiry and contextual design, see Beyer and Holtzblatt (1997). Use cases provide a good starting point for organizing this information. For other techniques, see the sidebar "Techniques for Understanding Tasks."

A potential pitfall when interviewing users is putting too much emphasis on their design suggestions. Although user participation is critical in the design process, caution should be exercised because users don't always know how to

CONCEPTUAL DESIGN

design what they want or need. For instance, it is common for some users to assume that an aesthetically pleasing site is more productive. Likewise when considering task performance time, users' perceptions of their productivity do not always reflect their actual efficiency. Their opinions about interface quality are always valuable, but they are not always correct.

Hierarchical Task Analysis for Web Site Design

Applying hierarchical task analysis to web site design is a direct and systematic approach to characterizing the knowledge required by a typical person to use your site. As the name implies, it involves organizing the tasks in a hierarchy and decomposing the procedures to an adequate level. The process of decomposing the user's tasks is iterative and involves the following steps:

1. Identify the primary user goals.

2. List the steps that a user must perform to accomplish the goals.

3. Optimize the procedure.

After the task is described at a sufficient level of detail, the procedures can then be optimized to minimize the number of steps, improve consistency among similar procedures, reduce user errors, or make any other adjustments that may be critical to your site's goals.

Often, as a procedure is listed, it will be revealed that the steps to accomplish a goal are actually a collection of other, smaller subgoals. For instance, filling out a form involves filling out a series of text fields, radio buttons, checkboxes, and so forth. Instead of listing out each individual action for each form element, we can just say "Complete the address text field" or "Select a country from the pop-up menu." Each of those steps is actually a low-level interface goal involving a number of user actions. For example, to accomplish the goal "Select a country from the pop-up menu," the user must

1. Locate the pop-up menu named "Country."

2. Move the cursor to the menu.

3. Press the mouse button.

4. Locate the appropriate country from the list.

5. Move the cursor to the country name.

6. Press the mouse button.

TECHNIQUES FOR UNDERSTANDING TASKS

In developing web-based tasks, we'd like to understand how people currently perform their tasks without the Web. This is especially useful when building web sites that will support people's job tasks. Gathering task data is a natural extension to techniques such as interviews and observations, discussed in Chapter 3. We need to understand how domain experts currently do their jobs, how they think about the tasks that are necessary to their jobs, and consider how their lives might be improved by optimizing those tasks and creating better user interfaces to support them. There are several techniques to start collecting such data. Typically, they are used in combination.

Training Materials

Existing training materials illustrate how the designers of a system think the job should be done. Such materials are often a good place to start, because they help to build an initial framework for the roles and tasks involved in the job.

Standard Operating Procedures

Manuals of standard operating procedures specify how management expects tasks to be performed. Manuals can clarify the interaction between roles, establish responsibilities for individuals, establish performance criteria, and identify risks inherent to the tasks.

Observation

Users can be observed or videotaped while performing the task of interest. This is a relatively unobtrusive way to get information about people's observable actions. However, it's not possible to observe how decisions are made or how thought processes unfold.

Interviews and Focus Groups

Interviews and focus groups can be conducted in conjunction with other techniques (such as observation) to uncover the thought processes behind people's actions. However, inaccurate recollection, groupthink, and other limitations of interviews apply here as well.

Think-Aloud Protocol

In the think-aloud protocol, users explain their actions as they perform their tasks. It is more obtrusive than observation and thus has a greater likelihood of changing how the task is performed. For example, talking through the task as they perform it may help people recall certain things they need to remember for the task, or it may make them forget. Despite this caveat, the think-aloud protocol is, in general, helpful for determining why users behave in the manner observed. It's especially helpful when users act in unexpected ways.

Instrumented Browsers

Certain browsers can be used that record users' actions as they browse. Collecting keystrokes, mouse clicks, and other user actions automatically is an unobtrusive way to collect accurate data on user behavior. On the downside, it suffers from the same disadvantages as observation. These browsers can also provide a massive amount of data that may be difficult to decipher.

Contextual Inquiry

The goal of this technique is to understand the context in which a task is being performed. In contextual inquiry, the usability specialist actually becomes involved in the users' tasks, experiencing them in the same manner, under the same risks and performance criteria, as the users themselves. A successful way of conducting such a study is to establish a master/apprentice relationship with a domain expert. In this way, the domain expert (master) teaches the usability specialist (apprentice) how to do the job. Such studies can be time-consuming and expensive, but they are effective when the cost can be justified.

This type of generic procedure may be used many times in an interface by just changing the name of the menu and the menu item to be selected. Do we need to list this out every time? No, it is only necessary to specify it once, knowing that it is simply a generic procedure, much like a computer program. Change the input data (e.g., the menu name) and the same procedure can apply anywhere there is a pop-up menu. Furthermore, there is an additional incentive to optimize such routines, because if you optimize one generic routine, the benefits are seen every time the routine is used, potentially a much greater payoff than optimizing a procedure that is only used once.

How Far Down Should You Decompose a Procedure?

Tasks should only be decomposed to a granularity that you have any control over or that will affect your decisions on interface design choices. The point is that task decomposition should only be done as long as there is a potential gain from the analysis. For example, it may not be necessary to list out the steps to select an item from a pop-up menu because there may be nothing you can do to change it. If the system dictates that only a limited set of interface elements can be used, then a deeper analysis is pointless. However, if you need to choose between two interface elements that can produce the same result, it may be useful to see what is required from the user's point of view.

A typical stopping point for decomposition is the level of observable user actions, such as keystrokes and mouse movements. However, designers should not neglect the mental effort that users must exert while performing a task. For example, each new screen presented to the user will require at least several seconds to understand (i.e., time to establish a gestalt). It is also important to consider items that users must remember between screens and complex decisions that users must make, as these are a prime source for errors. For guidelines on how to assess the mental actions that users must perform during a task, see Kieras's "A Guide to GOMS Model Usability Evaluation Using NGOMSL" (1997) or Raskin's *The Humane Interface* (2000).

A good benchmark for determining an appropriate stopping point is whether a person can perform the task properly using your procedures. The task procedures should be general enough to apply to any set of input data, but include enough specific information that a person could perform the task. For more information on this type of task analysis, see the "GOMS Analysis" sidebar.

GOMS ANALYSIS

A powerful, formal technique for conducting a task analysis is GOMS analysis. GOMS is a family of techniques developed by Card, Moran, and Newell (1983), for modeling and describing human task performance. GOMS is an acronym that stands for Goals, Operators, Methods, and Selection Rules, the components of which are used as the building blocks for a GOMS model. Goals represent the goals that a user is trying to accomplish, usually specified in a hierarchical manner. Operators are the set of atomic-level operations with which a user composes a solution to a goal. Methods represent sequences of operators, grouped together to accomplish a single goal. Selection Rules are used to decide which method to use for solving a goal when several are applicable. One reason GOMS is so powerful is that it is rooted in cognitive psychology. This makes it relatively straightforward to optimize procedures, check for consistency, and detect procedures that users may have difficulty performing.

Uses of GOMS

From a research standpoint, GOMS provides a framework for modeling aspects of human performance and cognition. From an applied perspective, GOMS provides a rich set of techniques for evaluating human performance on any system where people interact with machines. GOMS analysis can provide much insight into a system's usability, such as task execution time, task learning time, operator sequencing, functional coverage, functional consistency, and aspects of error tolerance. Some type of GOMS analysis can be conducted at almost any stage of system development, from design and allocation of function to prototype design, detailed design, and training and documentation for operation and maintenance. Such analysis is possible for both new designs and redesigns of existing systems.

For More Information

Bonnie John's article "Why GOMS" (1995) provides a very nice introduction to GOMS. "Using GOMS for User Interface Design and Evaluation: Which Technique?" (John and Kieras 1996a) provides guidance for choosing a GOMS technique using a series of case studies for illustration. "The GOMS Family of User Interface Analysis Techniques: Comparison and Contrast" (John and Kieras 1996b) compares and contrasts the predominant GOMS techniques according to their basic assumptions and constraints. It uses a single task example as a comparison vehicle. *GOMSmodel.org* provides more information, links to different techniques, tools for automating GOMS analysis, and a bibliography to abstracts and references for over 140 GOMS-related publications.

A HYBRID APPROACH TO TASK ANALYSIS

We favor a hybrid approach to task analysis that combines both the high-level interactions of users and other actors with the depth and psychological grounding of hierarchical procedure decomposition. The general steps are (1) start with use cases, (2) decompose tasks hierarchically, and (3) determine appropriate technologies.

Start with Use Cases

Determine the actors by asking who will be using the system and what parts of the system they will be interacting with. For example, in a simple business-to-business commerce web site, actors might include a set of office personnel from each department responsible for keeping office supplies in stock. Also from the customer's company, purchasing agents might need to negotiate prices and confirm orders over a certain dollar value. Users from accounts payable would need to review monthly bills from the seller and issue checks. Actors from the seller's side might include customer account representatives who would need to see customer buying patterns, credit representatives who would need to approve high-value orders, and shipping agents who would handle customer deliveries.

Next, build user profiles by determining the background of the users, their knowledge, skill level, motivation, and any other relevant background information. Obviously the backgrounds of the actors described will vary greatly from financial experts to office administrative staff to delivery staff. Their possible motivations will be likewise varied. For instance, the motivation of the office staff might be to make sure no one in their department runs out of essential supplies. Users from the purchasing department, on the other hand, might be tasked with ensuring that departments don't go over budget. The seller's account representatives would be motivated by sales amounts and would instead try to maximize sales.

The next step is to develop typical scenarios by asking, What are the users' goals? What are the typical things they will try to accomplish? Do this for each user group identified. For instance, one scenario for the customer's office staff might describe placing a regular monthly order for pens, paper, and printer cartridges. Another scenario might describe someone from the customer's company purchasing a special onetime item like a microwave oven.

From your scenarios and user profiles, determine the necessary functionality by asking what additional functionality the system must provide to support the users. In the first example scenario just described, the customer needs a way to see the previous month's order for office supplies and modify it for the current month. Upon placing the order, the customer would need to complete the transaction and verify any billing information required. In the second example, the customer would need a means for quickly performing a keyword search from an online catalog, comparing costs and features for all of the microwaves sold, and seeing which models were available. As in the first case, the users in this example would also need to complete the transaction.

Finally, you need to organize the scenarios. Based on common functionality within user groups, what are the high-level tasks? In both of the examples given, the users needed to place orders, confirm transactions, and verify billing information. Although not specified, they also probably needed to log in at the beginning and obtain written confirmation at the end. Each of these subgoals requires a specific task procedure that will allow users to accomplish their goals and complete their tasks.

Decompose Tasks Hierarchically

In this phase, your first task is to prioritize and determine the frequency of tasks. Start with high-priority, high-frequency tasks. After looking at all of the scenarios for all of the actors, the designer in our example might determine that the monthly purchase task would occur with the highest frequency and would be classified as such. Given the importance of the task—the dollar value of the combined instances in any given month and the potential cost of making mistakes within an entire month's purchases—it might also be classified as high priority, perhaps warranting additional analysis and testing.

Next, decompose the high-level tasks down to page- or mid-level procedures. For example, the monthly purchase task might be decomposed into the following subtasks: (1) log in, (2) view previous month's order, (3) modify previous order with current needs, (4) confirm order, and (5) get receipt.

Evaluate at each level of decomposition and repeat the process as necessary. For example, if we saw that several of the high-frequency tasks also included the login task, we would know that logging in was a high-frequency subtask that warranted additional optimization. If it was also known that users operated from secure computers, some or all of the login information could be stored on their computers. This would allow the login procedure to be simplified by requiring the user to enter less information during login.

Determine Appropriate Technologies

This phase begins with mapping out server requests and data flow. For example, the monthly purchase task might translate to these steps: (1) get customer ID from login, (2) determine the department, (3) access the account, (4) get the previous month's purchase, (5) look up item descriptions from item numbers on the purchase, (6) generate a new order form, and (7) format and display for the customer.

Next, create low-level, generic system procedures. For instance, looking up item descriptions could become a generic, building-block procedure that could be used in the monthly purchase task, and any other task that required the information.

Finally, map these into the application level. Combinations of system procedures can then be formed into application-level user tasks. For example, getting the customer ID, department, and account information could be combined into an Account view for the customer.

PERFORMANCE IMPROVEMENTS

The goal of a task analysis is to improve the user's performance, productivity, and, ultimately, his or her experience. Used in conjunction with other design techniques, task analysis can be a very powerful tool that can improve procedure consistency and clarity, reduce task execution and learning time, and reduce the number and types of errors that can occur.

Consistency

Interface consistency means that a system behaves in ways users expect. It means that users can transfer the knowledge they gained in some previous experience to the current situation, and that their prior experience will in some way enhance their current performance. That is, if users have already learned one method for doing something, their performance will be better if they don't have to learn another means for doing the same thing with your system. For example, nonstandard use of blue or underlined text that is not a link often confuses users and results in increased errors and slower performance time.

Consistency also applies to the design of procedures. Although there are times when consistency itself can be confusing, such as when users mistake one procedure for another, it is generally a good idea to make procedures as consistent as possible. An example of inconsistent procedures can be seen in the JC Penney web site shown in Figure 4-4. Here there are two paths by which a person can purchase the sweater featured on the home page. By clicking on the thumbnail image, the user is presented with the screen shown in Figure 4-5. There is a numbered sequence of steps that leads the user through selecting size, color, and quantity. If instead, the user enters the catalog number for the sweater in the field at the top of Figure 4-4, the user is presented

Figure 4-4.

A Problem with Task Consistency.

The JC Penney site (*www.jcpenney.com*) allows two ways to purchase products. Customers can either click on a product shown or enter the catalog item number in the text entry field at the top. Although both actions allow the user to purchase a sweater, there are separate procedures for selecting size, color, and quantity. See Figures 4-5 and 4-6 for detail.

with a different method for selecting the desired sweater (Figure 4-6). In this case, all of the colors and sizes are listed in a single pull-down menu at the bottom of the page.

Both procedures seem to be adequate for selecting a sweater, but why are they different? At first glance it might seem that the designers went to extra effort just to make the procedures inconsistent. In reality, there is probably a technological or business-related reason for it: perhaps the two business functions of selling catalog items via the Internet and selling promotional items on the company web site were designed by different development teams. But users don't care why. It may not even bother users enough that they would consciously notice that the procedures were different. But it might add a few extra seconds of confusion, and it might make users misremember where they bought a previous item if the procedure is not the same. Furthermore, it might leave them with a feeling that things just aren't right. In general, you should strive to be consistent unless there is a good reason not to be. Technological issues alone should not dictate your users' experiences.

Brevity and Clarity

Task analysis can also help to clarify and shorten your procedures. What may seem like an acceptable process for users to perform can sometimes prove much more convoluted when seen on paper. Task analysis makes your user interface procedures visible, showing both their good and bad aspects. It is the best way to find problems prior to user testing. There are two rules of thumb when considering procedure clarity. First, procedures should be relatively short, no more than 15 to 20 steps, although 10 to 15 is better. People have trouble with long procedures unless there are memory aids provided on paper or by the system. The second rule of thumb is that if a procedure is difficult to describe on paper, it is probably difficult for users to perform.

Combined Functionality and Fewer Server Requests

Another goal of task analysis should be to combine functionality when possible. Each screen a user must view probably adds at least 30 seconds to a procedure (very complex pages can add significantly more time). Combining functionality means minimizing the amount of effort users must exert to accomplish the same goal, commonly by minimizing the screens users must navigate. A task analysis can be used to determine where such combined functionality might make sense. For instance, when the analysis shows that users do the same task multiple times, it might make sense to allow them to make multiple entries at the same time.

Figure 4-5.

One Form of the Sweater Selection Task.

Clicking the image link takes the user through a series of numbered steps (and screens) for selecting the size and color of a sweater.

Figure 4-6.

Another Form of the Sweater Selection Task.

If instead the user enters the catalog item number, a different procedure for selecting size and color is required. In this case, the user selects sweater style from a single pull-down menu that combines size and color based on what's available.

The catalog ordering system seen at the JC Penney web site (Figure 4-4) is an example of where such combined functionality might be useful. The site is designed to allow customers to order only one item at a time. However, the paper catalog on which the web site was based contains an order form that allows multiple items to be ordered at once. This encourages customers to purchase multiple items per order. Since the web site design doesn't duplicate the functionality of the old paper-based system, ordering multiple items online is painfully slow. Purchasing multiple items per visit is therefore discouraged by the design. When designing technological replacements for manual systems, the new process should always be at least as good as the old process.

Example: Inefficient Tasks

Another suitable occasion to combine functionality is where little new information is given on a new screen. For example, a pattern that has emerged in some web applications, especially those driven by database requests, is that of Search-List-Detail. Search denotes the screen on which some database query is generated, List is the set of items returned by the search, and Detail is the item from the list that contains the necessary information for the task. This pattern is common because development tools support it easily. However, it sometimes results in tasks with extraneous and nonfunctional steps that the user must perform. In many cases, screens can be combined to reduce number of server requests, the number of screens, and, as a result, the overall task time.

Consider, for example, the train schedule shown in Figure 4-7a (*www.amtrak.com*). It shows the normal schedule for all trains from Chicago to Ann Arbor. To find the current status of a particular train, the user must select that train by clicking on a radio button, and then pressing the Show Train Status button.

The system responds to the status request with the Train Arrival page shown in Figure 4-7b. One way to optimize this procedure would be to replace the "Choice" buttons on the Schedule page with links or graphic buttons. This would eliminate the need for the Show Train Status button and save the user a couple of actions. A more fundamental change could be made by adding the status information to the Schedule page. This would eliminate both the selection actions and the need to load another page. Such systems are often designed in this way because the information sources are held in different databases (and possibly in different physical locations). To simplify the database queries for the web-application programmers, only one query is made per page. However, this type of technology-driven design is often inconvenient for the end user.

CONCEPTUAL DESIGN

(a)

(b)

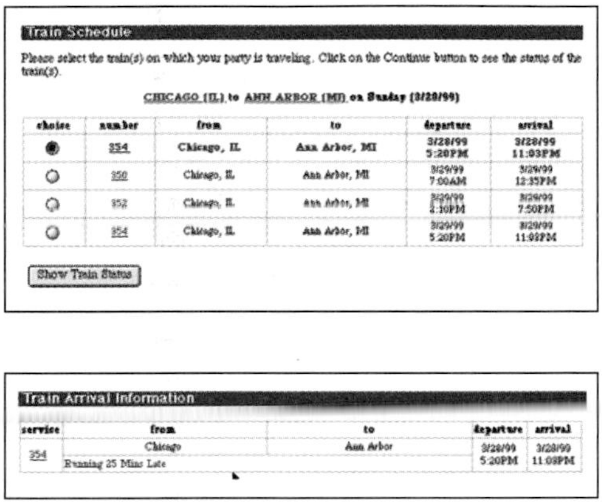

Figure 4-7.

Example of an Inefficient Task.

(a) The Schedule page shows the published schedules for each train on a route. To get the true status for a train, the user must select a train and press the button at the bottom of the page. (b) The Status page adds actual status to the schedule for each train. The user's task could be optimized by including the status information on the Schedule page.

HUMAN-ERROR-TOLERANT DESIGN

Designing systems that are tolerant of human error becomes crucial when any task has potentially dangerous and costly consequences, or when the outcome is not easily reversible. Financial and medical web applications are prime examples of sites where reducing human error is especially important. A central theme in designing for human error is to build a multilayered defense. Designing for human error effectively requires addressing several aspects of error management, including the following:

Prevention: *Eliminate the potential for error to occur by changing key features of the task or interface. This is always the preferred method for error management and also the most effective.*

Reduction: *Reduce the likelihood that the user will get into an error state when prevention is not possible by ensuring the user is aware of action consequences and by training users on both normal and error-recovery procedures.*

Detection and identification: *Ensure that if the user does err, the system makes it easy for the user to detect and identify the error.*

Recovery: *Following error detection and identification, ensure that the system facilitates rapid correction, task resumption, and movement to a stable system state.*

Mitigation: *Minimize the damage or consequences of errors if they cannot be recovered from. Even when all other error management steps have been taken, errors will still be made, so systems should be designed such that catastrophic outcomes from human error are not possible.*

Example: Error Recovery

The issues for error recovery are detection, identification, correction, and resumption. For the user the questions are simple: What happened? What do I do now? Electronic commerce is a prime domain for error-recovery design flaws that can adversely affect usability. Consider, for example, the order form in Figure 4-8a (slightly modified from *www.netopia.com*). Here, the form indicates that certain asterisked fields are required. The credit card selection menu is not indicated as a required field and is easy to miss (the card type is not really necessary and can be derived from the card number). Also note the instructions at the bottom of the form telling the user not to use the Stop or Back buttons. These instructions help prevent users from accidentally performing multiple transactions or from mistakenly believing that a transaction was canceled when it was not. The problem is that this error management measure hinders recovery from other error types. If the user forgets to select the credit card type from the pull-down menu, the commerce server indicates an error by displaying the screen shown in Figure 4-8b.

Figure 4-8.

An Error Prevention and Recovery Problem.

(a) The form indicates that asterisked fields are required. It does not indicate that selecting the credit card type from the pull-down menu is also required. (b) The error page indicates that an error has happened, but doesn't clearly identify the error. It also doesn't provide the user with adequate navigation instructions to correct the error.

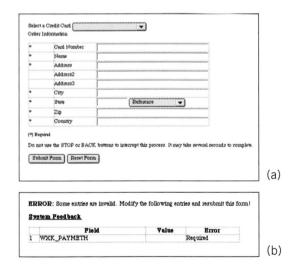

(a)

(b)

The user detects that an error has occurred from the message heading. The system even identifies the error as an invalid entry in "WXK_PAYMETH" field. Unfortunately, that field name is only clear to the system and its programmers. Most users would not know from this that the problem is an incorrect entry for the payment method. In fact, the credit card menu is not strictly a field and does not really reflect an entry as the message suggests. This would likely cause more confusion. Even if the error is deduced by the

CONCEPTUAL DESIGN

user, correction is hindered by the message on the original order form that said, "Do not use the STOP or BACK button." There is no other navigation on the error page, so using the Back button is, in fact, the only option.

A better way to handle incorrect data entries is to return the user to a facsimile of the order form, with the missing or erroneous data fields highlighted in red (or indicated in some other salient way). Examples of correct entries can also be helpful. Minimally, error pages should identify errors in a way that users can understand and provide clear recovery paths when possible.

Simple, practical techniques, applied consistently, can dramatically improve the web site development process. More significantly, these fundamental task analysis methodologies please the ultimate critic: the user.

05

CONCEPTUAL DESIGN

INFORMATION
ARCHITECTURE

WHAT IS INFORMATION ARCHITECTURE?

Information architecture refers to the structure or organization of your web site, especially how the different pages of the site relate to one another. It involves such issues as content analysis and planning, organization of the pages, providing cues to help users orient themselves, labeling, search techniques, and navigation design. The main principles are rooted in database design and information retrieval, with strong influences from the fields of human-computer interaction, library science, technical writing, and psychology (specifically, how people organize concepts and categories). This chapter covers how people navigate, the process of developing an architecture, site maintenance and expansion, organization schemes, ways to present the navigation to the user, labeling and orientation cues, search techniques and search engine design, and embedding your site within the framework of the rest of the Web.

There are many possible ways to organize a site. As ever, the core theme of this book is to choose an organization that best supports how the user will use the site. Organize your available information to support the user's tasks.

Does information have its own inherent structure? Can we simply explore and organize our information in its most logical form and present that structure? The answer is both yes and no. Yes, we should spend considerable time exploring and understanding the information we'll be organizing, identifying patterns and relationships. But no, there is rarely a *single* logical organization, and even when there is one, this still may not be the best organization for the user. The same information may have many different reasonable structures depending on how people think of it, talk about it, or use it. Psychological or "use-based" organization recognizes human limitations such as memory span and the need for absorbing information in sequential, well-defined chunks. With this in mind, our first topic considers how people actually navigate through information spaces.

HOW PEOPLE NAVIGATE

Consider this scenario: you've just opened up your browser and you hope to send some flowers to your mom for Mother's Day. Where do you begin? You might just guess and type in *flowers.com,* hoping to find a flower site. Maybe you already know a popular flower service, and type in its URL. Perhaps you go to a search engine and type "mother's day flowers." You might use a bookmark or go to a friend's hotlist. While it seems there are a lot of possibilities, the common approaches are relatively few and can be enumerated and analyzed.

CONCEPTUAL DESIGN

So now you've come to a flowers web site. What next? You need to find some Mother's Day flower options. You look around the screen for something that suggests Mother's Day or something that suggests viewing flowers; on many sites, you may just look for a generic "Products" or "Buy stuff" link. A basic information analysis can explain much of what happens in this scenario: at each point, users look for anything on the screen that provides a cue to where they are and how they can get closer to their goal.

Navigation Style Depends on Task

People determine the way they'll navigate by what they're trying to accomplish. In information-seeking activities, users want to find something, so they directly follow links until they find it. However, when they don't have a clear idea of what they're looking for, they tend to explore more. When users are trying to study a topic, they may spend less time navigating and more time dwelling on the specific topic, perhaps taking a linear path through a site and making sure they read every page. When they're simply trying to understand what a site is about, they may sample a lot of pages but spend little time on each one. As we discuss how people navigate, we'll ground each idea in a certain type of task, but the specifics will vary based on the type of task.

Models of Human Navigation

If users were omniscient, they would know the entire structure of your site and would follow the shortest, simplest path to their goal. This optimal path forms a good point of comparison when evaluating how well your users are actually doing.

A slightly more realistic model of how people navigate is the *optimal rationality model*. In this approach, users determine the probability that each link goes to their destination and then follow the highest-probability path, remembering everything they see and backtracking as soon as a trail they left behind has a higher probability of taking them to their goal than the trail they're on. They estimate the probability based on the *information scent* in the link label (see sidebar "Information Scent"). If you watch people navigate, you will sometimes see behavior that looks similar to this approach, but you're likely to see people forget alternatives and persevere on unpromising paths.

A more realistic view is a *satisficing model*. Satisficing is an approach that emphasizes that people tend to behave in a way that minimizes mental effort. They remember as little as needed and avoid complicated planning. Figure 5-1 describes how someone would look for information from a satisficing approach. As they browse, at each page they make their best decision based on the information available on that page.

Figure 5-1.

A Satisficing Model of Navigation.

In the satisficing approach, rather
than remembering or planning,
users simply look at a page, and
if it doesn't have what they're looking
for, they scan the navigation bar and
choose a promising link to follow.

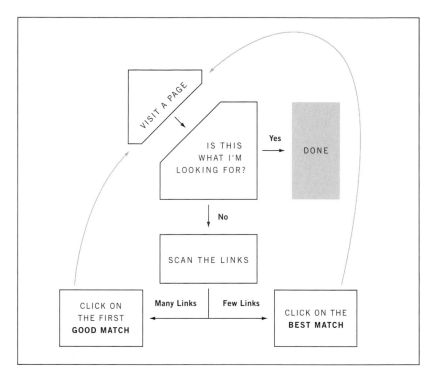

A typical user goal might be "I want to find a specific piece of information." The first step the user might take is to visit a page. Then the user would follow the visual hierarchy of the page to identify where to start. If it's a content page and it has what the user is looking for, then the task is done. If it's a routing page or the content is not relevant or sufficient, the user will scan the options. In a given navbar, he or she will scan the links from top to bottom or from bottom to top. From here there are two options. The first is to find the first good match (especially in long lists). For each link, the user will evaluate the likelihood that it contains the target content. If it does, the user will follow it, without reading the remainder of the list. In the second option, the user finds the best match (especially in short lists) by scanning all links and following the link to the best match.

This model of navigation has some immediate implications for how you design your site. It suggests that the page title and a brief summary of the page content be immediately visible, and important navigation elements should be visually salient in a quick scan of the page. It also suggests that frequently used links should be toward the top or bottom of lists, and that link labels need to be useful cues to the information they lead to.

INFORMATION SCENT

In the optimal rationality or the satisficing models of navigation, users must evaluate each link for the likelihood that it leads to the correct content. How do they know the likelihood? The information available is in the label of the link and any explanation that comes with it. If they visit a flower site and one link says "Flowers" and another says "Occasions," they have to select which one is most appropriate for finding Mother's Day flowers. People may judge this differently, but perhaps they'll decide that "Flowers" is too general and "Occasions" seems very likely to include Mother's Day. In either case, they would ignore the link that says "Our History" because it has no hint, or "scent," of the information they're looking for.

Information scent (also called *information residue*) is the shade of meaning in a label and its description that suggests the full meaning that people are seeking. In other words, people need meaningful local cues to help them locate distant content.

When people are "just surfing," not looking for anything in particular, then they are likely to be evaluating each link by how interesting it is (the scent of something interesting), as opposed to how well it matches a particular concept.

Figure 5-2.

Problems with Information Scent.

Where would you go on this site (*www.barebones.com*) to buy one of their products? Both "products" and "store" seem to suggest this task.

People may also navigate using *mental maps*. A mental map is an idea the user has of how the overall web site is structured. Using this concept of the site organization, users select the route that seems most efficient, even if the individual link they follow suggests nothing in particular about their goal. We help provide people with mental maps by the way we present the navigation bar or the way we organize the pages in a site map. People are more likely to navigate by thinking in terms of a mental map when the site provides a very strong model for its organization, such as well-known sequences (e.g., "page 2 of 10"), familiar physical spaces (e.g., maps), or well-known taxonomies (e.g., Animal—Mammal—Canine—Dog).

For sites that people use frequently, especially complex ones with no clear mental map, they may become experienced enough to navigate through *rote memorization*. That is, when they recognize a familiar path, they simply follow the same path they've successfully used before. You'll often see users follow the same inefficient path because they know the way. In such cases, they may rely on landmarks and orientation cues to confirm they're in the right place, and page *variation* can help people recognize their unique location (whereas most other design principles encourage consistency and uniformity).

Another view of user navigation behavior is known as *information foraging*. This approach suggests a comparison of people's information-seeking behavior to animals foraging for food. Think of people as consuming local information resources before they stray to other areas for more information. In other words, the cost of getting every last scrap from where you are is less than the cost and risk of seeking additional sources elsewhere, at least up to a point. Thus, we find people lingering on the first site they find rather than pursuing other sites that may be more useful, because if they abandon the site, they risk wasting their time when they fail to find more promising information elsewhere. The information foraging model also stresses that people modify their goals as they get additional information that might suggest they reframe their questions.

The most general approach that combines the previous models is the *information costs approach*. This approach says that users choose among strategies based on effort versus payoff; that is, the cost in mental effort and time leads to a tradeoff among planning, sense-making, scanning navigation options, and clicking. This approach suggests that if you want the user to get somewhere, you should lower the cost of all these activities. The information costs approach differs from the optimal rationality approach in that the latter ignores people's psychological limitations, whereas the former factors in psychological costs in choosing the best course of action. In the most general perspective of developing an optimal navigation structure, you should factor in the cost of *not* finding the information and the costs to you (as the designer) of organizing and maintaining the information. All of these navigation models are summarized in Table 5-1.

The Primary Cost Tradeoff: Scanning versus Page Traversal

Two major mental and time costs are involved in navigating: the cost of scanning and deciding among the range of link choices and the cost of clicking on a link and waiting for the next page to load. When people click through to a new page, they run a risk of not finding what they need and therefore backtracking. When pages load slowly, this cost is very high, and people will spend more time carefully reading through the links and choosing the most suitable option. On the other hand, when there are a large number of links (consider

CONCEPTUAL DESIGN

all the portals that show hundreds of options on a single page), then the cost of reading every link is high, and people will decide to try following a link rather than finish reading the remaining options.

This cost tradeoff affects how many links we display on a given page. If there are too many, people won't read all the options. If there are too few, people are more likely to make an error in their selection because the labels are less informative and specific. Because pages don't download instantaneously, people are generally more willing to read through lists of links than we expect, and so a larger number of links is appropriate.

This tradeoff also suggests that we need to minimize these costs, so keep the download time of pages short to minimize the page traversal time, and make link labels clear and legible to minimize scan time. A popular but ill-conceived technique is to use icons for links and to use rollovers to display the labels. This is called *mystery meat navigation* (you're not sure what meat you've got until you bite into it) or *minesweeping* (let's roll over everything and see if any surprises pop up; see Figure 5-3). The problem with such an approach is that you've dramatically added to the cost of scanning through the alternatives of where to go on the web site, thus significantly slowing down site navigation. As much as possible, try to make the navigation self-explanatory at a glance rather than forcing users through a problem-solving process.

Garden Paths

When people confidently follow a sequence of links that seems to lead to their goal only to find that what they're looking for isn't there, this is called a *garden path,* a pretty path that leads to nothing. At the end of a garden path, people have several options: abandon the search in exasperation (a not uncommon choice); backtrack using the Back button until they find a feasible alternate route; click on the Home button and start the search from scratch; follow the main navigation links to look in another area (saving one step versus going to the home page); or visit one of these pages that offer some help: Help, FAQ, Contact, Site Map, Site Index, Search. You'll see each of these strategies, so support each alternative.

Sense-Making

The process of piecing together a mental map of a site from the information provided is sometimes called *sense-making*. People may form a mental map from the moment they see the first page on your site, but they progressively refine this model as they visit each page. Since people may follow many different paths through your site, make sure that the sequence of pages they view will add up to a coherent story no matter what path the user takes.

Table 5-1.

Models of Human Navigation.

Navigation Model	Assumptions	Design Implications
Omniscience	Users have perfect knowledge. Users make no mistakes.	This is a best-case scenario that provides a useful point of comparison. Even when users are superhuman, they benefit from short, efficient paths to their goals.
Optimal rationality	Users only know what they've seen (they're information-limited). Users are psychologically perfect—they reason perfectly.	Also unrealistic, but a useful point of comparison. Make sure links provide adequate cues to the content they lead to.
Satisficing	Users avoid remembering and planning. Users make decisions based on information that is immediately perceptible.	Make sure pages function independently. Organize the page to make the most important content and links immediately visible.
Mental maps	Users actively use the cues available to try to infer the structure of a web site. Users will often take a path they understand that fits into this mental map rather than risk a shortcut that doesn't fit the mental map.	Organize the site simply so that users can easily conceptualize it. Design the appearance of the navigation bar and site maps to reinforce this mental map.

Navigation Model	Assumptions	Design Implications
Rote memorization	When users find a path that works, they tend to remember and repeat that path. Users avoid reasoning through alternatives if they already know a successful solution.	Since people will tend to repeat what worked the first time, make sure the most obvious solution is also reasonably efficient. Use distinctive landmarks and orientation cues to help people recognize where they've been before.
Information foraging	Users try to get as much as possible at one location before going elsewhere. Users refine their goals as they explore information.	Help users evaluate the scope of your web site and evaluate their progress through it. Enable spontaneous discovery by providing context, structure, and related topics.
Information costs	Users have limited knowledge and reasoning ability. Users can make tradeoffs to determine what mental resources to apply and therefore which strategy to utilize in navigating.	Minimize the mental costs of sense-making, decision-making, remembering, and planning. Different types of users, tasks, and mind-sets can lead to different navigation strategies, so support multiple strategies.

In forming this mental map of your site, users are also gauging the *scope* of your site, estimating how much information is available, how many pages are likely to be involved, how broadly you sample topics, and how specifically you address topics. They estimate the scope of the site based on what you explicitly say is the topic of the site, how comprehensive your links appear to be, and how detailed your page content is. For a large site, it can be very difficult to articulate for the user how much detail you provide, but communicating this may be essential to keeping the user engaged with your site. Knowledge of the scope helps users decide if certain information will be available on your site, decide when they've finished reading the relevant information (very important for information foraging), and decide whether they have the time to read the information now or need to return later.

Figure 5-3.

Minesweeping: Before and After Discovery.

Links like these (*www.microsoft.com*), which hide their labels until you roll over them, dramatically slow down navigation and increase the likelihood that the user will never discover the link that was most useful.

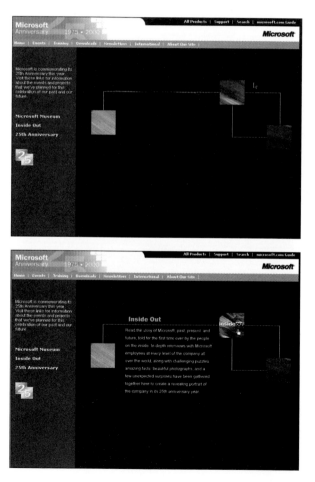

How the Browser Facilitates Navigation

A final piece in understanding how people navigate is to consider the tools the browser provides to users to enable them to navigate. Figure 5-4 is an illustration of such tools.

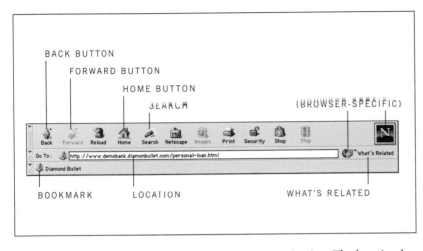

Figure 5-4.

Navigation Support in the Netscape Browser.

Here are examples of how browsers may support navigation. The location bar enables users to enter a domain name or extended URL to go directly to a site. People will use this to guess a likely domain name out of the blue ("I'm looking for flowers, so I'll try *flowers.com*"). Some beginners regularly confuse this with a search box and will enter their search terms here. Surprisingly, it works more often than you'd expect, contributing to the confusion. The Back button is used a lot, and sites should remove the button bar only after careful consideration, because this is users' most common resource when they've gone in the wrong direction. However, users will not always use the Back button, so you need to provide links on every page as well, even if they just go back a page. On the other hand, the Forward button is somewhat less commonly used than the Back button. Browser-specific buttons take people to specific sites, such as the Home button, Search button, Netscape's "What's Related" button, and standard menu items for browser-featured sites. Links are displayed by default as blue underlined text. Also, even when links are applied to graphics, the browser provides support for showing the URL of a link in the status bar when the user mouses over the link. ALT tags and link titles may also appear on mouseovers. Bookmarks/Favorites allow users to revisit favorite pages. The Go menu provides a history of visited sites, allowing users to backtrack to comfortable spots when they get lost.

THE PROCESS OF DEVELOPING AN ARCHITECTURE

An architecture for your web site comes from taking all of your materials and organizing them into a structure that helps the user navigate efficiently. You'll present this information in a site outline or diagram that is used to guide the development of the site. You may also create detailed specifications for the content, navigation, and maintenance of the web site. All of this design work will be based on analysis of the site requirements, the patterns and relationships inherent in the content, and user testing.

Developing an Architecture

A typical process for developing an architecture is as follows:

1. Review prior art

Review the results of your requirements and task analyses. Review earlier versions of the site you're developing and competitor sites. This develops a list of potential content pieces, candidate labels, and candidate organization schemes.

2. Evaluate your content

Identify content pieces for your site by reviewing what information you have available and what information your users need. Evaluate the quality and completeness of your content. Specify and design any content that is still needed. Create a content inventory, which specifies the complete list of content for the site and what pieces remain to be developed.

3. Create and evaluate your core structure

Brainstorm candidate content categories and site structures. Example structures are discussed in the next section on Organization Schemes. Create an organization of your content based on information structure, task structure, user types, and card sorting. Decide which content pieces belong together on a page. User test and refine the organization of the base architecture. This core structure should work well even before you've implemented helpful tools such as shortcuts and search engines.

4. Add shortcuts, redundant links, and supporting pages

Review your primary tasks and procedures and map them onto the site organization. Optimize the architecture to be efficient for the highest priority tasks. Review the primary user types and optimize for each of them. Add appropriate shortcuts and redundant links. Add necessary support tools, such as Help, Site Map, and Search. If possible, implement this architecture into a barebones web site for user testing.

5. Develop and evaluate the navbar and orientation cues

Refine the layout and presentation of the navbar and orienting information, such as headers and page titles. Establish final labels and graphics. Since the presentation of the navigation can have a strong effect on users' mental maps and their ability to scan the options, user-test this version of the design when possible.

6. Create final design specs

Get client sign-off on the organization and labels. Create a final site outline or diagram, final content specs, design rationale, and maintenance specs.

7. Implement the architecture and verify its implementation

Build the web site and update the specifications as needed. Test that the site conforms to the specifications.

8. Train site-maintenance staff

Web sites quickly stray from a coherent structure as pages are added and removed. Train those who maintain the site to correctly interpret and apply the maintenance specs, so they know the standards for updating the site and testing those updates.

Bottom-up versus Top-down Design

Two broad approaches to developing an initial architecture are bottom-up and top-down design. In bottom-up design, you gather all of the intended materials and categorize them, building up to higher levels of categories. In top-down design, you specify the top-level categories, and break each category down into smaller pieces until you've identified the lowest level of information. Top-down helps identify missing pieces that are needed to complete a category, and bottom-up identifies missing categories that are needed to include every piece of content.

As an example, consider constructing a web site about poetry. In the top-down approach, you consider what information to provide at the top level, perhaps Poets, Poems, and Forms. Then you break down each main topic. Forms might consist of Sonnets, Haiku, Free Verse, and so forth. Poets might be broken down by country or historical period. You keep breaking this down further until you have all the topics you feel you need.

In contrast, a bottom-up approach to a poetry web site might start with the question, "What materials do I have available or can I construct for this site?" You decide that you have a few hundred poems you're able to provide, and you then determine that each poem would go on a page of the site. Then you determine how those poems might be grouped. Perhaps one set represents

Love Poems, another set Nature Poems, and a third set French Surreal Poetry. Those form your low-level categories. If this is all you have, then you're done (and you avoid having to create all the material for Poets that the top-level breakdown suggested). If you also have other materials, you could group these under Poetry Genres and continue.

In practice, both top-down and bottom-up approaches are usually taken, going up and down the levels of organization and refining in each direction.

Representing the Architecture

In the course of developing a web site architecture, you'll need to diagram or otherwise represent the architecture to illustrate your ideas and communicate them with clients and your development team. The form of representation you choose will depend on your target audience, what it needs to do, and your ease of putting the diagram together and modifying it. Figure 5-5a–g presents a variety of ways to represent your architecture, including outlines, flowcharts, tree diagrams, sexy diagrams, wireframes, and page schematics.

Architecture representations are used by a number of people, and each type is best suited for a particular role. Table 5-2 presents the suggested representations for different roles.

Figure 5-5a.

Outlines.

Outlines are a traditional text representation suitable for simple lists or complex hierarchies. These are easy to construct and modify, but deeply nested hierarchies can sometimes be difficult to manage, and sequences and shortcuts are not represented easily.

I HOME

II ABOUT US
    A. Our Staff
    B. Our Culture
    C. Jobs
        i. Administration
        ii. Shipping
        iii. Customer Service

III FLOWERS
    A. Roses
    B. Violets
    C. Bouquets

IV SHOPPING CART → Enter Shipping Address → Enter Billing Info → Confirmation

V OUR DELIVERY GUARANTEE

VI CONTACT US

Whichever representation you choose, you'll need a way to represent several common concepts within the diagram. For instance, the home page needs to be easily identified and is usually obvious by its position at the top. Other pages may need to be marked according to their development status (e.g., "waiting for content for these pages," "these pages are planned for Phase 2," or "these target our international users"). Techniques for identifying these characteristics include annotating the diagram with comments, coloring nodes, grouping pages, using special borders (thick or dotted lines), and putting boxes around related nodes. Include a legend with your diagram if you end up using special markings.

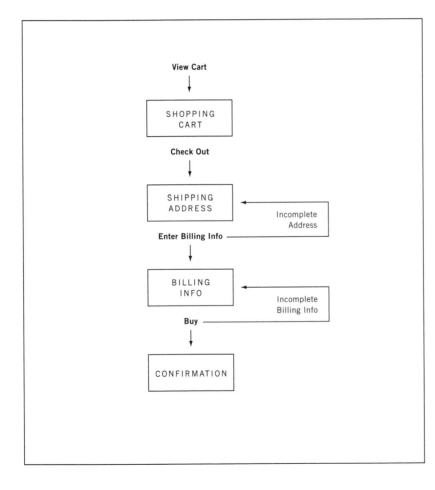

Figure 5-5b.

Flowcharts.

Flowcharts are particularly suited to sequential tasks with relatively limited branching. Good examples are lengthy question-answer sequences and lengthy registration and purchasing processes.

Figure 5-5c.

Horizontal Layout of a Tree Diagram.

Tree diagrams (5-5c and 5-5d) are quite common. They are generally more attractive and more readily understood than outlines but take more time to create and modify.

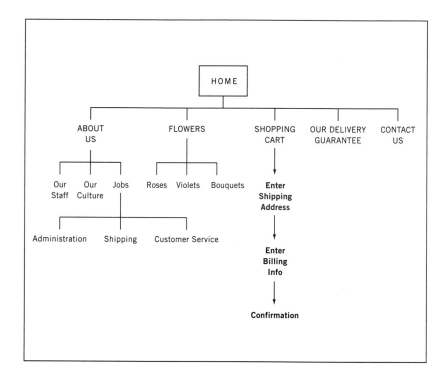

Figure 5-5d.

Vertical Layout of a Tree Diagram.

Horizontal layouts (5-5c) are quite common and appropriate for hierarchies without much branching, but because text is wider than it is tall, a vertical layout (5-5d) is usually more compact, allowing larger, more complex structures to be shown. Trees are limited in the size they can conveniently represent, but subtrees can be broken out into separate diagrams.

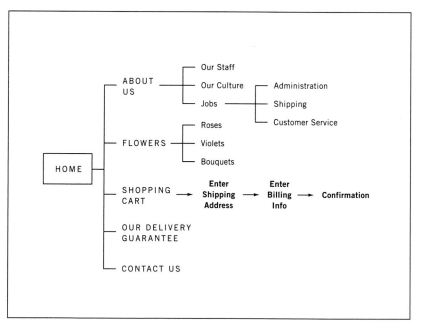

CONCEPTUAL DESIGN

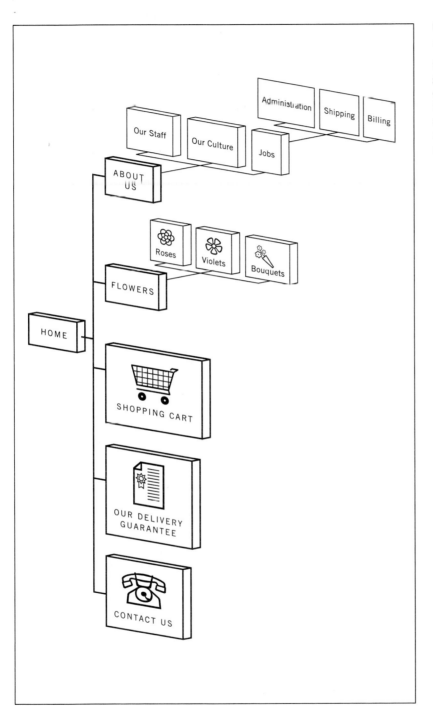

Figure 5-5e.

Sexy Diagram.

Sexy diagrams are simple tree diagrams that have been decorated and elaborated to impress the viewer. Such effort seldom adds real value, and these diagrams are particularly unwieldy in the design and development process.

Figure 5-5f.

Wireframe.

Wireframes (a working skeletal site) are simplified, working HTML prototypes of a site. Each page of the prototype is minimal, without final graphics, and often without content or with only a content specification. The wireframe is used to implement the site architecture and to check that, as you browse through the site, the navigation makes sense, the flow through the site is comfortable, and processes are efficient. Wireframes can be used for user testing of the architecture and as a form of specification for programmers and content developers.

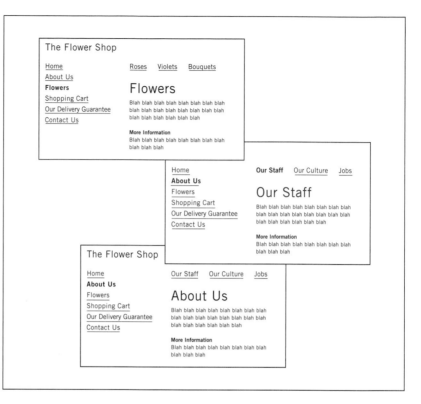

Figure 5-5g.

Page Schematic.

A page schematic is a single-page specification of the architecture showing roughly where each content piece is located on a page, indicating content requirements, such as navigation, page titles, and headers. A collection of page schematics can form a specification of the entire site architecture. Subnavigation can be shown on the navigation bar and used to indicate the entire architecture from a given page. A common early specification combines this page schematic with a list of content items needed for the final site (see Chapter 8, "Writing for the Web").

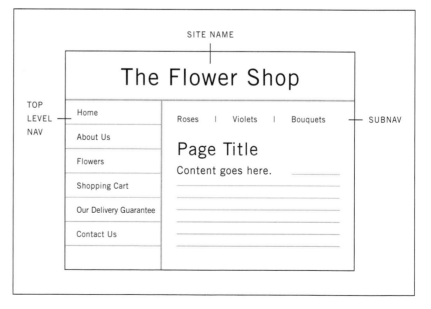

CONCEPTUAL DESIGN

Table 5.2.

Who Needs What?

Role	Architecture Representation Best Suited for Role
Production staff	An *outline* or *tree diagram,* with levels clearly indicated, a detailed list of pages, and navigation labels and content for every page.
Writing staff	A *page schematic* with navigation and content requirements for each page.
Quality assurance	A *comprehensive list of pages* with detail about each page. For ease of testing, this list of pages can be online, and each page listed can link to the corresponding page within a wireframe, so that the content of each page can also be verified.
Usability testers	An *outline* or *tree diagram* for annotating during testing, and a *wireframe* for actual testing.
Designers	An *outline* or *tree diagram,* indicating final labels, the number of options at each level of the hierarchy, and how much site navigation is displayed on each page.
Clients who act as decision-makers	A *"sexy" diagram* (presentation-quality), with detail corresponding to the business end of the site.
Clients who act as content providers	An *outline* or *tree diagram,* to decide on completeness, and a *page schematic* indicating navigation labels and content requirements for each page.

Six common diagramming conventions are shown in Figure 5-6. They include

• Using dotted outlines around pages to distinguish proposed pages from current pages.

• Drawing pages as a stack when they form a highly related series, such as a set of otherwise-identical product detail pages.

• Embedding boxes within a page box to indicate different content pieces within a page.

- Dotted lines to indicate shortcut cross-links that don't appear in the primary navigation.

- Arrows indicating links to or from external sites.

- Rounded boxes (or another shape) to indicate dynamically generated pages (such as search results).

Card Sorting

While we can determine the structure of a web site through analysis, when confronted with uncertainty, a good approach to take is to get our prospective users to suggest organizations for the site. The card sorting technique is a very useful approach to understanding what natural categories people have for the domain. It is especially appropriate when the designer is not a domain expert and needs the insight of the users or when several alternative organizations are possible. The card sorting technique has its roots in the psychological investigation of how people form concepts and categories.

How to Do an Open Card Sort

Several approaches to card sorting are available, but the most common is the *open card sort*. The steps for an open card sort follow.

1. Label the cards

Get a set of index cards and put the names of each low-level concept on a card. For instance, to organize animals, we'd put the terms "dog," "cat," "giraffe," "pufferfish," and so forth onto the cards. However, we wouldn't label any cards with categories like "mammal," "canine," or "plant-eaters"—we want the users to suggest such categories.

2. Brief the users

Bring in users and explain that the purpose is to generate an organization for the web site. Their instructions are "Organize these cards into groups. Remember, there is no one right answer, so choose the grouping that makes the most sense to you. After you've divided these cards into groups, label each group."

3. Let the users group the items and label the groups

Avoid interfering or answering questions about the categories—you want to see what makes sense to the users. If they don't understand a term you've provided, you might ask them to exclude it. After they're done, you can then explain the term, see if they would have called it something different, and ask them to fit it into their categorization scheme.

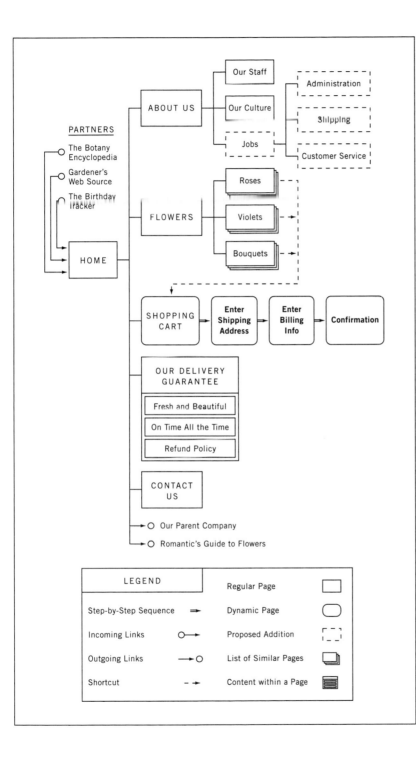

Figure 5-6.

Example Diagramming Conventions.

PARTNERS

The Botany Encyclopedia

Gardener's Web Source

The Birthday Tracker

HOME

ABOUT US

Our Staff

Our Culture

Jobs

Administration

Shipping

Customer Service

FLOWERS

Roses

Violets

Bouquets

SHOPPING CART

Enter Shipping Address

Enter Billing Info

Confirmation

OUR DELIVERY GUARANTEE

Fresh and Beautiful

On Time All the Time

Refund Policy

CONTACT US

Our Parent Company

Romantic's Guide to Flowers

LEGEND		
Step-by-Step Sequence ⇒	Regular Page	☐
Incoming Links ○→	Dynamic Page	◯
Outgoing Links →○	Proposed Addition	⌐ ⌐
Shortcut - →	List of Similar Pages	⬚
	Content within a Page	▤

4. Listen to other comments about the content

Allow users to suggest missing topics, topics that don't fit, and topics that they consider to overlap.

5. Group the groups, or subdivide the groups

For small sites, no further grouping may be needed. But for larger sites, you'll need to generate the next level of the hierarchy. Some users will have created a lot of groups, such as "canine," "feline," "rodent," and so forth. Ask these users to create larger categories that group together the groups they've already defined. Other users will have created only a few groups, such as "mammal," "fish," and "bird." Ask these users to look for subdivisions within any large group. Once again, ask for labels for the new groups they create.

6. Write down the hierarchy the users created, and repeat with more users

Usually, about five users are enough to have a sense of how people organize the domain, but when users have conflicting organizations, you may want to ask more. An example of a conflicting organization in this domain is having some users group "wolf" and "bobcat" as "wild animals" and "dog" and "cat" as "domestic animals," whereas others group "wolf" and "dog" together as "canines" and group "bobcat" and "cat" together as "felines."

7. Combine the results

Statistical methods exist to take these alternative hierarchies and find an organization that fits the data best (a technique called *cluster analysis*), but usually it's sufficient to eyeball the results and spot the dominant organizational schemes. A simple count of how many people grouped any two items together provides a useful metric of how confident you can be in grouping them. After you're done, you'll also need to do some cleanup, patching up incomplete categories and choosing among alternative group labels. You may even jot down which items were less certain; later information may help resolve the ambiguities.

Limitations

Card sorts are extremely sensitive to your original choice and phrasing of concepts on the initial set of cards. The organization is affected if your cards are misinterpreted or you fail to include every topic that will be on your site (or include topics that are beyond the scope of the final site). Thus, you may choose to include a brief description on each card. For example, rather than simply labeling a card "The NX47c Ultrathin," you may want to provide a description, such as "a low-cost and very small personal computer." In addition, you may ask users to suggest additional topics they feel are missing or suggest topics they feel should be thrown out.

CONCEPTUAL DESIGN

While user input on the grouping of items is extremely useful, their suggested category labels are not necessarily very good. They provide some helpful directions for the types of words users apply in their domain, but frequently labels suffer from problems of ambiguity, overspecificity, overgeneralization, double meanings, and inconsistency. User-suggested labels provide a good beginning for your development of optimal labels, but you will still need to analyze the labeling schemes.

Variations

A *closed card sort* constrains the users by providing the low-level concepts *and* the categories. The user must fit each concept into a predefined category. This approach is helpful after the categories have first been determined from an open card sort, and when content is being added to a pre-existing site.

Another approach is to do *similarity matching*. Using the same set of cards, you ask people to rate the similarity of every pair of cards (this is relatively fast if it's done on computer). Using the same statistical technique of cluster analysis, you can then determine how concepts are grouped, based on the items in the group being rated as similar. The main limitation is that you don't get the opportunity to ask the user what to call the groups, although you can get some idea by combining this with an open card sort. The main advantage of similarity matching is that you get more refined data from each user than with a card sort. For each user, a card sort tells you whether two cards belong in the same group or not, but similarity matching indicates the *degree* to which they belong in the same group, and also indicates how much a card may belong in other groups as well, allowing the data to reflect that concepts can be divided along several dimensions.

An alternative, reflecting the top-down approach described earlier, is to provide users with the top-level categories and ask them to generate lower-level concepts that they'd expect to find under each category. This can work well when users are experts in the domain. Regardless, you can't expect that users will be complete in the concepts they identify, but the exercise can suggest missing concepts and also suggest which concepts are most salient to users (the ones that are suggested first, and most often).

Testing the Architecture

After each design iteration for the architecture, some kind of evaluation is useful to make sure the architecture is effective. A critical paper-and-pencil test is to check whether the primary user tasks are obvious and efficient in the architecture. In Chapter 4, we discussed constructing task procedures. Follow through each procedure, making sure there is an obvious sequence of pages to follow within your site architecture to accomplish the procedure.

Whenever possible, you should also test the architecture with users to confirm that they are able to successfully navigate it. Until the site is actually constructed, a simple testing approach is to build a quick wireframe prototype of the site, with page titles and navigation buttons, but only minimal content (as much as is needed to perform the tasks). Ask users to perform their main tasks on the site, watching for labels they misconstrue or times they stray from the most efficient path, or times when they fail to complete the task. Fix any problems you find, and test again if the problems are serious. For more details about usability testing, see Chapter 12, "Usability Evaluation."

Architecture Review Checklist

The architecture review checklist (see Form 5-1; download from *http://www .mkp.com/uew*) summarizes many of the architecture design points that are presented throughout this chapter. While this list is good for design issues, it's especially intended to be used to critique an architecture. After developing a proposed architecture, step through this checklist to identify problems, or ask an outside reviewer to use this in critiquing your architecture from another viewpoint.

MAINTENANCE AND EXPANSION

Sites will grow and change. These changes may not even be under your control. Your site may require maintenance due to link rot (links to external sites that go offline or change their addresses), server upgrades, and new browsers that are introduced without total backward compatibility.

Change involves costs and risks. If pages are added or removed, this takes time and cost. It also may introduce errors and inconsistencies into your site. If these inconsistencies are left unchecked, your site will slowly degenerate, becoming less and less usable.

An architecture style guide can help to maintain a stable architecture throughout the changes. It specifies not only the standards used in the organization and labeling schemes, but also documents the policies, processes, and procedures for making changes and testing them. There are several typical procedures to document:

CONCEPTUAL DESIGN

1. Inserting a new low-level content piece. The style guide should document how to update the navigation, generate the new graphics, fix the navbars and titles, examine the need for shortcuts, and perform quality assurance.

2. Inserting a new category. Documentation should include determining what location is appropriate, deciding how many options are too many, and when the architecture needs to be reorganized.

3. Removing pages and/or categories, and saving data being removed in case it needs to be recovered. Documentation should include working with outdated links both internal and external, updating navbars, and performing quality assurance.

4. Archiving out-of-date information (but keeping it live). Old news stories and old product support information may need to remain online even if they're not actively relevant, necessitating their removal from the primary navigation and placement into an archival section of the site. Your documentation should include updating links and navbars and conforming to a systematic organization and file-naming scheme for archival data.

The cost of these procedures will be influenced by a number of design decisions, including the number, choice, and layout of links on each page, the number of external links, the decision to use text links versus graphics, the overall coherence of the architecture, and whether the site is statically coded or database-driven. Database-driven sites can automatically generate site maps, indexes, and navigation, which can dramatically reduce costs and ensure a higher level of quality through consistency. On the other hand, automatically generated site maps and indexes can suffer from some problems, such as including poorly labeled or redundant items, or missing important synonyms and rephrasings.

The style guide should include the rationale for the architecture and provide a labeling scheme for consistently naming new topics. Content policies for pages establish what can be said and how, as well as indicate what can link to where. For instance, there are frequent battles within companies over what gets linked from the home page, the most valuable real estate on the site. A policy for submitting link requests, and approving, prioritizing, and scheduling them can go a long way toward fairly and rationally resolving these conflicts.

Form 5-1.

Architecture Review Checklist.

Architecture Review Checklist

Process
- ☐ The site organization has been tested with users.
- ☐ Clients have reviewed the architecture for completeness and appropriateness.
- ☐ The site organization has been finalized and documented.
- ☐ A site maintenance plan is documented.
- ☐ All content has been acquired or planned for.
- ☐ Site logs and search logs have been reviewed for possible refinements.

Overall
- ☐ The architecture matches overall site requirements.
- ☐ The architecture makes sense at a glance.

Coverage
- ☐ No relevant content is missing.
- ☐ No unnecessary pages can be removed.
- ☐ The site has all necessary pieces, e.g.,
    - ☐ Home
    - ☐ About/Introduction/Overview
    - ☐ Contact/Feedback Forms
    - ☐ Site Map/Site Index/Table of Contents
    - ☐ Help/Frequently Asked Questions
    - ☐ Search
    - ☐ Error Pages
    - ☐ Privacy Policy/Copyright Policy

Task Analysis
- ☐ All important tasks and user types are supported.
- ☐ Common tasks flow along a natural and short sequence of pages.
- ☐ Important tasks are achievable in one section of the site, or appropriately cross-linked.

Organization
- ☐ The site is relatively broad and shallow, no deeper than 3 levels, no broader than about 16 options.
- ☐ Categories are placed at the right depth. Based on importance, no categories need to be promoted or demoted.
- ☐ Important options come first.
- ☐ Related options are grouped.
- ☐ The organization is flexible. Sections can be added and deleted without major reorganization.

Categorization

☐ Categories divide up the space sensibly.

☐ Each category has comprehensive coverage.

☐ All topics are in the correct category.

Orientation and Labeling

☐ Pages are clearly identified and explained, with clear page titles and good descriptions.

☐ Landmark pages are sufficiently distinct.

☐ Labels are clear, meaningful, and appropriate to their target content.

☐ Labels are consistent in specificity, tone, and usage.

☐ Link labels provide the scent of all subcategories.

☐ Scope notes are provided when useful.

☐ Users can gauge their progress through the information.

Links

☐ The link to the home page is explicitly indicated.

☐ External links are chosen with restraint, appropriate, and regularly maintained.

☐ Page links are minimal and clearly labeled.

☐ There are no dead-end pages—those without any outgoing links.

Navigation Bar

☐ The navbar indicates where the user is currently located.

☐ The user can see how the current page is positioned within the whole site.

☐ The hierarchy is clear. The user can determine which options are at the top level versus a sublevel.

☐ Text navigation is provided for users who are not viewing images.

☐ Navigation is at the top and the bottom of long pages.

☐ The user can quickly review all options without scrolling or rolling over the options.

Search

☐ Users can choose to either browse or search (though search may not be needed on small or very well structured sites).

☐ The scope of the search is clear.

☐ Search tips are provided, especially after too few or too many results are found.

☐ Search results indicate the number of matches and the total records or documents.

☐ Search results are comprehensive, precise, and relevant.

☐ Search results are ordered usefully.

☐ Search results provide the context and/or description of each match.

☐ Search results are categorized when there are a large number of matches.

☐ The search query is repeated in the results, and users can easily refine searches.

☐ Common queries produce good results.

☐ The search is robust with regard to misspellings, alternate spellings, synonyms, plurality, and prefixes and suffixes.

ORGANIZATION SCHEMES

In this section, we consider the various ways a site might be organized. The first step is to examine the nature of the information you're dealing with. Is it structured or unstructured? Is the information homogeneous (all pieces follow a similar pattern) or heterogeneous (no simple format works for everything)? Is the information specific and concrete or ambiguous? Do you have comprehensive coverage of information within a domain or just scattered pieces? Often, information can be massaged into a more coherent and complete form, so it's worth spending time getting to know your material.

Topology

An initial organizational question is what structure or *topology* to build. The topology is the primary way that pages are linked together. Figure 5-7 shows several options.

By far the most common topology is a *hierarchy* or *tree*. While hierarchies don't fit all types of information, they have several important advantages: navigation through a hierarchy involves relatively few steps, it's relatively easy to represent where the user is within a hierarchy, and hierarchies expand to fit more data relatively easily.

In a *linear topology*, pages are organized into an ordered sequence. Linear topologies work especially well when users must complete a process in a specific order, such as a purchasing process. Many other types of data, such as product lists, may seem naturally linear, but are still better organized into a hierarchy for efficiency of browsing. Avoid forcing users to view items in a specific order unless it is absolutely necessary to go in that order to complete a process or make sense of a storyline.

A *matrix or grid* can be appropriate when information varies along two dimensions or follows a two-dimensional map. While this is seldom adequate as the sole organization of the information, the information can be accessed as a hybrid between a hierarchy and a matrix. For instance, in a product database, the user should be able to view a list of products and click down to an individual product (a hierarchical organization), but from the individual product page, the user may click to view the next color or click to view the next product (a two-dimensional organization).

A *full mesh* is a set of pages that are fully interconnected—every page is linked to every other page. For a small web site or a small subsection of a site, this allows rapid navigation among related pages. For larger sites, however, a full mesh is not practical.

Figure 5-7.

Common Topologies for a Web Site.

Topology	Characteristics
HIERARCHY (OR TREE)	• Most common and well understood • Allows relatively fast navigation from one page to another • Expands easily to support more information
LINEAR TOPOLOGY (OR SEQUENCE)	• Good for processes, stories, and sometimes for moving through ordered lists of similar items • Can be time-consuming, so keep sequences short
MATRIX (OR GRID)	• Sometimes appropriate for two-dimensional data, such as maps • Should not replace other ways to access the information, such as search or an index, since it's tedious to get around
FULL MESH	• Connects everything to everything, allowing rapid navigation • Only feasible for small sites or small sections within a site
ARBITRARY NETWORK	• Sometimes appropriate when the structure is not well understood • Is often the de facto organization when no central authority can determine the organization • Can be aided by a secondary organization to help users find things
HYBRID	• The most common form in practice, as most sites are a combination of these various topologies to some degree • Needs to be made clear to users where the organization changes

Sometimes information doesn't lend itself to a formal structure, and an *arbitrary network* or *web* is appropriate. The World Wide Web itself appears to have this kind of structure, with sites linking back and forth with other sites with no dominant structure. This kind of linking may be appropriate in certain research scenarios where the best structure hasn't yet been discovered, and may be a necessary reality in any scenario without a central controlling authority. Even so, imposing a hierarchy above such a structure can make it easier to use the information within. For example, Yahoo! provides such an imposed hierarchy for the Web as a whole.

Most of the time, topologies should not be absolutely pure. It's fine to create shortcuts that cross from one subbranch of a hierarchy to another, and you'll often find that a subset of a hierarchy belongs under more than one main branch, requiring two branches to share a subsection. Hybrid designs often make more sense in a given domain than a pure approach. However, any such exception creates a potentially confusing situation for the user, so when you break out of the structure the user is expecting, provide strong cues about what you're doing.

Breadth versus Depth

Figure 5-8 shows two extremes in designing a hierarchical structure: broad, shallow trees with many branches from each node (meaning more links in the navbar) versus narrow, deep trees with few branches from each node (meaning fewer links in the navbar). As discussed earlier, the main tradeoff is between scanning time and page traversal time. In some cases, fewer links in the navbar means less mental complexity in making a choice, which would seem better. However, if the site is large, this initial decision will require that many more choices will need to follow, thus creating more opportunities for users to make a mistake.

In the end, up to a reasonable limit, having more links is better (that is, a broad structure), provided that the navigation is well organized. However, if the navbar doesn't fit on one screen, scrolling can make scanning the options significantly longer. Also, if the font size is small, scan time goes up. Thus, a practical upper limit to the number of links is roughly the number that will fit on a single screen at a reasonable font size.

We disagree with the common recommendation that a limit of seven links at each level is about optimal (usually argued for on the basis that people can remember about 7 ± 2 items). It's not clear to us why memory for a list of links should be a major factor in the task of navigation.

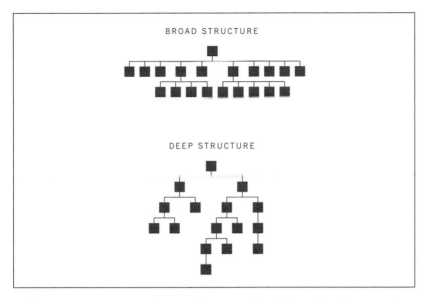

Figure 5-8.

Breadth versus Depth.

In fact, evidence suggests that people get confused about their location when in hierarchies that are deeper than three levels, and this suggests a limit to the depth, rather than the breadth, of a site. In one of the few studies directly addressing the issue of breadth (Larson and Czerwinski 1998), researchers found that two levels below the home page was in fact better than three levels (even if each level was fairly broad), and that 16 links in a navigation bar worked better than 8 or 32. That study had its own limitations, but we'd argue that, based on this study and the tradeoff of scan time and page traversal time, sites should generally be no deeper than three levels and no broader than about 16 options. Greater breadth is possible provided that the list is well organized (i.e., in a clear order and grouped well) and that the links are easy to understand without further explanation. This breadth and depth allows for over 4,000 pages, so should be adequate for many sites.

Semantics

Semantics refers to that aspect of the organization based on the meaning of the material. Some broad organizational alternatives are based on how you want to *conceptually* divide the top-level categories. Below are some alternative methods of organization.

Task-Based Organization

This approach organizes around the principal tasks that a user must accomplish on the site. The main navigation items are labeled according to these tasks, such as "Send flowers," "Choose a gift," and "Contact Us." Each choice goes to a page that either refines the task options or begins the first step of each task. Task-based organizations are usually the best choice, and where other organizations work well, it is usually because they fit the user's task well.

User Type

This approach organizes around the principal types of users who come to your site, so the main navigation includes options like "For our customers," "For our employees," "For shareholders," and "For vendors." Often, the second level of organization under these options is a task-based navigation, where the tasks are selected for each type of user.

Topical

The topical approach divides the domain into logical categories based on the information content rather than the users or their tasks. This works well when the user's goal is to find information related to a specific topic. An example is breaking up a "Products" section into logical product categories, such as "Cars," "Trucks," and "Vans" for an automotive site.

Organizational Structure

As a form of topical organization, sometimes a site will be organized around the internal structure of an organization, often because this is the easiest way to organize the collection of content for the site and to manage changes within each subsection. An example of such a site organization is "Our president," "Sales," "Customer service," and "Research and development." This is seldom the best way to organize information for your users except perhaps for an intranet.

Life Event

This organization is based on correlating with major events in a person's life. This is like taking a broad perspective on the task-based approach (each life event encapsulates one or more tasks) and may be appropriate in very general portals, with links like "Buying a car," "Buying a house," "Getting an education," and "Finding a job."

Implementation

This organization fits the way the site is implemented, such as dividing off secure areas from nonsecure areas or placing access to different databases into different sections. This may be necessary when connecting a new site to a legacy system (an old system that you're not able to significantly modify). This is seldom an optimal basis for architectural decisions, from a usability

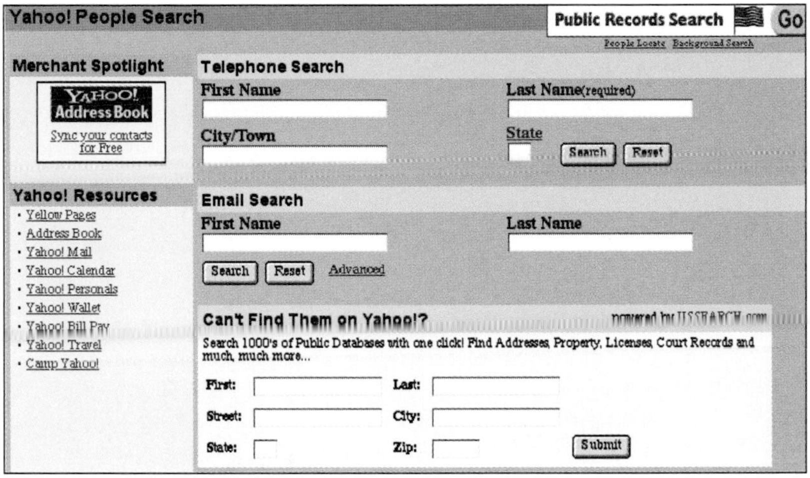

Figure 5-9.

Yahoo! People Search's Implementation-Based Design.

On this site, you can choose to search for a person's phone number or email address, but not both. There's no obvious advantage to this design over having a single search that returns both pieces of information, but presumably the site's implementation precludes it.

point of view. When necessary, the key is to make the transition between different organizations obvious to the user so you don't create a false expectation of consistency. Figure 5-9 shows an example of an implementation-based organization of the interface. It branches to separate pages, presumably based on which database is searched, rather than the more logical approach of going to a single page with combined results from both databases.

Systematic Organization When No Semantic Relationships Exist

When no meaningful organization of the information is apparent, it may be more appropriate to simply present the options as an alphabetical list. For instance, a list of people may not fit into logical categories.

How pure should you be in choosing an organization? Do sections always need to be mutually exclusive? Does the taxonomy have to represent exactly equivalent categories at each level? While some will argue for a pure classification system, you'll usually find that it imposes too serious a constraint on the organization, and you'll find that making reasonable exceptions will rarely confuse the user. In other words, if you were designing *pets.com,* your main navbar could contain Dogs, Cats, Fish, Reptiles, and Contact Us. Of course, you'd want to visually distinguish the Contact Us to make it perfectly clear, but this list is unlikely to confuse any users.

Terminology

Regardless of the way the organization is broken down, the perception of categories can be heavily influenced by the terminology used to label categories. Thus, "Buying a Car" and "Renting a Truck" focus more on providing information, while "Buy a Car" and "Rent a Truck" focus more on making the transaction. Some users will avoid clicking on "Car Buyers" because they're "just looking," but wouldn't have any trouble following a link labeled "Cars." Thus, select a label, and its specific phrasing, that sets up the right expectations:

Terminology	Example
Activity-Based	"Buying a Car"
Task-Based	"Buy a Car"
Role-Based	"Car Buyers"
Topic-Based	"Cars"
Org Chart–Based	"Sales Department"
Mixed	"Cars," "Trucks," "Vans," and "Customer Service Department"

Order

The order of options in a navigation bar guides the user's understanding of the overall organization and can have a major influence on the speed of navigation.

The order of topics affects a user's scan order and the memorability of items. When topics have no particular order, users will typically scan the items first to last, or sometimes last to first. In this case, the first few items will be spotted first and remembered best (a factor called *primacy*), and the last item or two will be similarly easy to spot and easy to remember (since they're the last items to be read, they'll be remembered best, a factor called *recency*). When topics fall into a predictable order, such as alphabetic or chronological lists, the user can scan more quickly to the item of interest.

When a logical or conventional order is available, it's often the best choice. For instance, products may be listed alphabetically or by price. However, especially at the top level of a site, frequently no logical order is possible. In such cases, the order should typically be by task priority—what is the most common or most important task or tasks? Place the most important options in the first few slots and possibly as the last item in the list.

Support Pages

While most of your site is probably organized around your core content, a variety of pages are provided to make it easier for your users to effectively use your content and complete their tasks. These include pages devoted to navigation (*router pages*), help pages, and error pages.

Router Pages

Router pages are designed to help people navigate to their destination. They include your home page, site maps, tables of contents, indexes, and intermediate pages where users choose among options to hone in on their target content. While these pages can be crucial aids to your user, avoid overusing pages with navigation but no content. Look for opportunities to provide users with applicable information at the first opportunity. That is, promote content to the highest-level page where you know the user would want it. Content pages can also provide routing functionality, by including standard navigation tools and by including relevant shortcuts. Avoid dead ends, where users get to a page with no outbound links. Whenever you have a good idea what information users may want next, include links at the bottom of the page to help guide them to the appropriate spot.

Help Pages

Some types of help pages may fall naturally into your site structure, such as Reference pages, Frequently Asked Questions, Customer Support, and Contact pages. However, context-sensitive help, where relevant information is provided from any point in the site, may involve hundreds of pages that don't fit into a natural site topology. For instance, you may want to provide help buttons in input forms, so that a user can pop open a window with examples of appropriate form responses. These types of pages can be diagrammed independently from your main site architecture, and you may indicate where they're used simply by marking pages from which help is available with an asterisk in your site diagram. An example of context-sensitive help is shown in Figure 5-10.

Error Pages

Similarly, error pages can occur from many different points in the site, and many different error pages may appear after form input. These usually need to be handled as a special case in the site architecture. Of course, you should design so that error pages are infrequently needed, but where they are needed, you should document what types of errors can occur after form input for each form. Typical types of user error include *missing data, invalid input values,* and *invalid passwords.* You should also list error pages that must be designed for the whole site, such as *file-not-found* pages. While most sites leave these as the default error pages provided by the server, careful design on these pages could help people correct their mistakes more effectively. For example, a file-not-found page should indicate what URL the user entered, suggest that the user check the spelling, provide links to pages the user was likely to be looking for, and offer recourse to contact someone for additional help or to report a bug. Figure 5-11 illustrates a user-friendly error page.

Figure 5-10.

Context-Sensitive Help.

Clicking on the help icon next to a form element brings up the help window below, which explains the purpose of the New User ID field (*www.rxprofit.com*). While the help icon could be used next to any field, it's used only next to those fields where users are most likely to have questions.

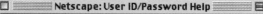

RxProfit Registration

To register with RxProfit, begin by completing the form below.

► indicates a required field

Login Information

New User ID: ► [   ] ❓

New Password: ► [   ] (must be at least 6 characters)

Re-type Password: ► [   ]

Contact Information

Name: ► [   ]

Title: ► [   ]

Company: ► [   ]

Address: ► [   ]

City: ► [   ] St: ► [⬍] Zip: ► [   ]

Phone: ► [   ] Fax: [   ]

E-mail: ► [   ]

Netscape: User ID/Password Help

You choose your own User ID and Password with which to login to the RxProfit system.

Your user name may be composed of an alphanumeric string, plus spaces and underscores. Other special characters are not allowed.

Passwords must be 6 characters or more in length, and are not case sensitive.

[Close]

Figure 5-11.

File-Not-Found Error Page.

When users enter an incorrect URL, this page doesn't just tell them it's wrong—it helps guide them to fix the problem with suggestions and alternative links on the site (*www.diamondbullet.com*).

diamondbullet.com

File Not Found

The page you requested is not located on the Diamond Bullet server.

○ If you got here by typing in the address line, check the spelling, punctuation, and capitalization and try again.

○ Diamond Bullet hosts many clients on our server. If you were trying to go to one of our client's webpages, see the clients page for a list.

○ Use the navigation on the bottom to browse the Diamond Bullet site.

○ If you followed a link to this page fill out the feedback form to inform our staff of the broken link.

Feel free to contact us if you have any further concerns.

who we are	usability	services	contact us
our profile	usability consulting	website design	contact info
our team	about usability	website hosting	our location
our clients		banking industry	feedback form
press releases		healthcare industry	
job openings			

Paths

A *path* or *trail* is a sequence of pages designed within an overall structure to provide a linear experience for the user, to provide a single coherent narrative within a larger collection of information. This may serve, for instance, as a guided tour through a web site.

A path can be built into a site so that the user will have only one single option at all points. Some designers use this approach to force users through a set of pages to ensure that the users see all the information the designers meant them to see. Thus, some have suggested the use of *entry* and *exit tunnels*, sequences of pages users must go through when entering or exiting a site before they have access to anything else, although this lengthens the amount of time spent getting to the desired destination, which decreases the probability they'll persevere to completion.

This narrow path approach is necessary for certain types of transactions, where each page depends on information gathered on previous pages. In "wizard"-style interfaces, a user goes through a sequence of pages, answering prompts on each page. This can be useful when it considerably simplifies the interface, provided that users can escape the process when they need to.

A site can also provide a "suggested" path without actually constraining the user to follow it. Including Previous and Next links on pages can allow users to easily traverse a path through your site, while the presence of a traditional navbar gives them the option of going directly to the information of most interest to them.

Paths can be built outside the structure of the site as well. For instance, other sites can build frame-based views on your content, allowing them to show the user a limited subset of interest. Similarly, a secondary window can be designed with Previous and Next buttons, which take users through a given subset of your information. These types of use make sense when someone is developing a tutorial or presentation and drawing information from a large collection of material.

WAYS TO PRESENT NAVIGATION TO THE USER

Navigation bars are so common that we simply can't avoid the shorthand of calling them navbars. The navbar provides the primary mechanism for users to browse your site, and the appearance of the navbar establishes a framework for users to understand how the site is organized.

The navbar doesn't have to be a comprehensive view of the underlying way the site is linked together. The navbar provides a useful *summary* of the overall organization. In fact, the site can have many convenient links that aren't represented in the navbar. Setting up shortcuts is critical to effective navigation.

Deciding Which Links to Show

Exactly which links should you show in a navbar? Too many links add clutter and confusion. Too few links make navigation paths longer and slow down navigation. In addition, too few links will miss the opportunity to indicate to users how the site is structured and where they are within that structure.

Typically people need to get to the following places from any particular page: the home page, any subpages underneath this page, and the page at the top of the current section. Depending on their task, people also need to access the next and previous pages in a sequence. When browsing quickly through sections of the site, accessing sibling pages, at the same level as the current page, helps users understand the scope of the site or to comprehensively search a site. To go up in the hierarchy to any level of generality, you need access to any page above the current page, in the sequence of ancestors. To have a visible reminder of the scope of the site, you need access to any of the top-level categories, and any of several types of helper pages, such as Contact, Site Map, or Shopping Cart, as well as any other page on the site.

Listed here are some of the most common navigation styles to satisfy these varied needs, but other navigation styles will undoubtedly evolve to satisfy the various tradeoffs.

Minimal Navigation

In its most minimal form, a site map or home page can link to all the pages of the site, and each page needs only one link, the link back Home:

> Home

(In this and the following examples, we present links in underlined gray that you would likely have visited in order to get to a page with this navigation, and present unvisited links in underlined black.)

In most cases, you can save a little time in browsing a hierarchical site by providing the list of links to subpages of your current page. Thus, when you get to the Products page, you'd want to see the subnav like this:

> Home
>
> **Products:** Furniture – Appliances – Electronics – Home Décor

When browsing through individual products, it's also useful to have Previous and Next links to quickly move through them, and an Up link (or "Back to Appliances") to get back up to the most recent category:

Home | Up | Previous | Next

This minimalist approach, especially without Next and Previous buttons, provides for a navigation scheme that is very low maintenance. To add a page or remove a page, you simply add or remove the single link to it from the category it's contained in. The navigation is short, succinct, and easy for the user to comprehend. On the down side, the navigation doesn't clearly indicate how the site is organized, and it's significantly more time-consuming to click through to your destination than other approaches.

Breadcrumbs

Breadcrumbs show the hierarchy of pages in the most direct path from the home page to the current page. This is a succinct representation of the site structure and your current location within the structure.

You are here: Home > Products > Appliances > Toasters > QuickCrisp Deluxe

or

Home → Products → Appliances → Toasters → QuickCrisp Deluxe (You are here)

Some users may confuse this list with a traditional navbar, where each of the options is at the same level. The use of the greater-than symbol (>) or arrow (→) is intended to help them understand that the breadcrumbs indicate an ordered relationship, and the "You are here" seems to help.

Breadcrumbs make it easy to browse to any level of the hierarchy quickly; and intuitively the set of links represents a good guess at where the user is most likely to want to go from here. That is, the user is much more likely, when looking at a toaster, to want to look at other toasters or other appliances than to want to skip over to the Furniture section of the site.

In an alternate implementation of breadcrumbs, it's possible with database-driven sites to list the *actual* path that a user took to the current location rather than the idealized hierarchy represented in traditional breadcrumbs. This may provide more relevant options to the user, but loses the ability to indicate the structure of the site.

Top-Level Categories

Providing a list of top-level categories helps define the scope of the site to the user and makes access to the primary information quick.

Home – About Us – **Products** – Locations – Contact Us

Toasters: QuickCrisp Classic – QuickCrisp Deluxe – NoBurn Safety Toaster

The subnav is shown for the current page, but intermediate categories are omitted, which keeps the navigation concise but makes navigation to those intermediate categories difficult. By providing breadcrumbs along with the top-level categories, you can largely address this problem. This works well for shallow sites of one or two levels of navigation, but for sites with greater depth, the absence of intermediate navigation can be confusing. (Note that while Home is technically above the other categories in the hierarchy, it's a common convention to list it at the same level as the other top-level categories.)

Expanding Outlines

One of the most common navigation styles is to show a list of options, and to expand each topic, like an outline, as each category is selected:

HOME

ABOUT US

PRODUCTS

    Furniture

    Appliances

        ovens

        microwaves

        toasters

           - QuickCrisp Classic

           - QuickCrisp Deluxe

           - NoBurn Safety Toaster

        blenders

    Electronics

    Home Décor

LOCATIONS

CONTACT US

This approach helps the user create a good mental map of the site organization. The vertical layout also lends itself well to vertical navbars on the left side of a page, and this enables items to be added and removed without having to redesign the layout of the page. The approach also works reasonably well in a horizontal approach, which you may see in text links at the bottom of a page:

Home – About Us – **Products** – Locations – Contact Us

Products: Furniture – **Appliances** – Electronics – Home Décor

Appliances: Ovens – Microwaves – **Toasters** – Blenders

Toasters: QuickCrisp Classic – QuickCrisp Deluxe – NoBurn Safety Toaster

The outline style is the closest alternative to simply showing all the links on the site and thus allows the fastest navigation of the options presented. This ability to get quickly to any piece of content rather than forcing users through tedious paths is called *direct access* or *random access.*

The main problem with the outline view is that the list becomes unwieldy as the number of options gets large. While it scales well to three levels of navigation, at four or more levels, it can become confusing and no longer space-efficient. In addition, while this organization is easy to provide in a database-driven site, it can be a monster to maintain if you are coding the site by hand, since changes in the structure require a lot of pages to be modified and tested.

Progress Bars

When pages fall into a natural linear sequence, a list of the pages with Previous and Next pages is a common convention:

1 2 3 **4** 5 6 **7** 8 9 | Previous Next

This is especially common for search engine results or for multipage articles and can work for multistep processes and any kind of ordered list (see Figure 5-12). Notice how the indication of visited links helps strengthen the paradigm by making it clear how far you've gone through the sequence and clearly indicating if you've skipped around.

Very Large Sites

None of the approaches described so far works terribly well for particularly large sites. On large sites, you need to carefully analyze the tradeoffs of all the information needs involved. A typical approach is as follows: include a breadcrumb trail, utility pages (Contact Us and Site Map), the primary nav (top-level categories), and a subnav listing subpages of the current page.

You are here: Home > Products > Appliances > Toasters [Contact Us] [Site Map]

Home – About Us – Products – Locations

Toasters: QuickCrisp Classic – QuickCrisp Deluxe – NoBurn Safety Toaster

As opposed to the outline approach, this avoids clutter, but it takes a little more time for the user to decipher, as each navigation bar must be interpreted.

Figure 5-12.

A Progress Bar.

Santa Monica Bank's Bus Sign Museum uses a graphical progress bar. The graphic links are quite attractive, but notice that they can't represent which pages have been visited.

Standalone Subsites

As sites become very large, one strategy is to create standalone subsites, where you include a link back to the main home (or a breadcrumb trail in the following example). The subsite is presented as if it were a site unto its own, with its own home page and dedicated navigation, thus reducing the apparent complexity for users. This works well if, as in this example, the user's main interest is really in Toasters.

You are here: <u>Home</u> > <u>Products</u> > <u>Appliances</u> > Toasters [<u>Contact Us</u>] [<u>Site Map</u>]

Toaster Home – <u>QuickCrisp Classic</u> – <u>QuickCrisp Deluxe</u> – <u>NoBurn Safety Toaster</u>

In this example we've removed the boldface from the "You are here" in order to place the visual focus on "Toaster Home," so that it really feels like its own site. Here you can also see why we distinguished utility pages from the top-level categories, as we did in the previous example. When the top-level categories go away, we still need access to some of the most common utility links, like Contact Us and Site Map.

Redundant Navbars

Providing a text navbar at the bottom of pages provides useful redundancy. If your main navigation is a set of graphic links, the graphics may not be accessible to users whose images are turned off or those using screen readers. Also, if a page is long, it's convenient to find navigation at the bottom of the page so that scrolling to the top of the page isn't necessary just to navigate.

However, if pages are short or of varying lengths, this redundant text nav can be unnecessary clutter and actually confusing to users, who assume that if they see two navbars on the same screen, there must be a meaningful difference between them. To minimize this problem, make sure there are no unnecessary inconsistencies between the two versions of the nav.

If the pages are always short and the main nav is presented as HTML text, then there is really no need for redundant nav.

Rescuing Lost Users

When the standard navbar isn't succeeding for users, it's nice to have alternative ways of finding things. We'll discuss giving users a Search option in more detail later. Other facilities for rescuing users who are lost include the following (these mostly correspond to utility pages, mentioned earlier).

Site Maps

Site maps (Figure 5-13a) aren't necessarily intended to show every link on the site, though if well-structured, they work well showing as much as possible. Site maps help reinforce a good mental map of the site and give the user an opportunity to evaluate the scope of the site.

Indexes

An index (Figure 5-13b) provides an alphabetical list of terms that users can look up to find their topic. Complete indexes need to anticipate the range of synonyms that may be used and should use *term rotation*, a standard technique in book indexes where multiword terms can be looked up by any meaningful word in the term. Thus, in addition to listing "usability evaluation" in an index, you need to list "evaluation, usability."

Tables of Contents

A table of contents (Figure 5-13c) provides a site outline, structured to show the intended order of topics and hierarchical relationships. Site maps are often just such tables of contents.

Help Systems

While help systems can provide a number of types of information, a simple introduction in the help system can explain complex navigation bars, suggest search strategies, and provide tips for finding common topics.

Contact Information

Many users who despair of finding what they're looking for will happily send a question to customer support or a site administrator. If you're prepared to handle these requests promptly and helpfully, this is a great way to help out those in serious difficulties. If you track these questions, you can also identify which aspects of the site require improvement.

Figure 5-13.

Navigational Utilities.

(a) Graphical site map, (b) index, and (c) table of contents.

(a)

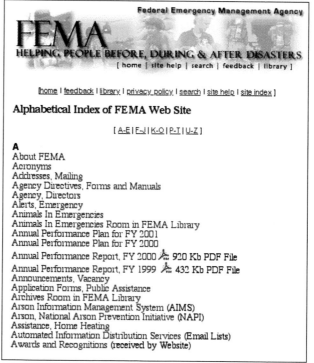

(b)

CONCEPTUAL DESIGN

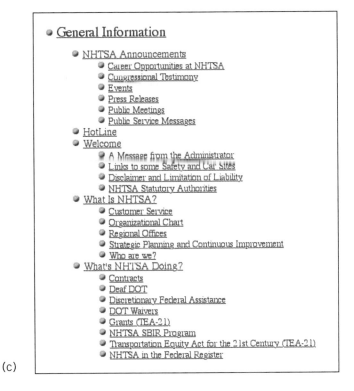

(c)

Live Customer Support

The technologies for live customer support are still somewhat in their infancy and may confuse the user further, but if you can organize it simply, this enables you to solve users' problems in realtime (of course, this means you have to have someone on staff to take these calls when they come in). Chat services enable text discussions with your users, and facilities to synch your browser with users help you understand the context of their questions. Live video connections can be even more compelling. "Callback" services allow the user to enter a phone number and get an immediate return call. This works best, of course, when the user isn't tying up the only phone line with an internet connection.

Just-in-Time Links

One of the most effective ways to help users find information is to anticipate where they'll want to link to from any spot and provide those most-likely links. For instance, if I'm registering for a conference, I'll also want information about travel and accommodations. If this information isn't in the same section, a cross-link is crucial. At the bottoms of pages, include links that cue the user exactly where to go when they get done reading.

LABELING AND ORIENTATION CUES

The actual terminology you use can significantly influence how well people can navigate. You must have links that clearly indicate where they lead (with effective information scent); and when people arrive at their destination, your site must provide appropriate orientation cues to indicate that the users have arrived where they expected to arrive.

Links and Labeling Systems

Work with a writer to design your link labels: getting this right is not as obvious as it may seem. Labels must communicate effectively, both in denotation and connotation, in meaning and feeling; they must be unambiguous, interesting, and appropriate to your overall corporate image. If you decide to use icons for your links, make sure you label them with words as well—icons alone are rarely clear, especially for newcomers to your site.

Labeling systems are standards used to ensure consistency in vocabulary, style, and spelling. Labeling systems, for instance, will specify a *controlled vocabulary*, which establishes the preferred terminology that will be used throughout the site. The controlled vocabulary helps ensure that you always choose the same word among two synonyms, for consistency. Thus, it might resolve whether your products are called "Products" or "Offerings" or whether you refer to your customers as "Clients" or "Customers." (When you design an index or a search engine, you have the opposite problem—that of enabling the synonyms, rather than restricting usage.)

The Home Button

Silly as it may seem, web page designers often seem to forget to include a link back to the home page. It's easy to overlook.

A common convention is to put the company logo at the top left of a site and link the logo back to the home page. While this convention is understood by many, we've seen lots of users who never think to click there, and if you don't have a link labeled "Home," they spend enormous amounts of time looking for it.

Always provide a clear, explicit Home button. We frequently put a "Home" label right below the company logo to help reinforce the convention. Even if you don't have a logo there, stick the Home button toward the top left, right where people expect it to be.

You Are Here

In a navigation bar, be sure to mark the current page being viewed, and don't link the current page. If the navigation bar shows several levels, mark the

ancestors of the current page as needed to make the hierarchical position obvious. "You are here" indicators include such simple techniques as marking the current location with a little arrow or triangle and coloring the name of the current page. For instance, in this example, the current page is for the product called QuickCrisp Deluxe, so it is unlinked. It falls into the Toasters category, so the Toasters link is in bold. Toasters is still linked so that the user can easily navigate up a level.

Appliances: <u>Ovens</u> – <u>Microwaves</u> – <u>Toasters</u> – <u>Blenders</u>

Toasters: <u>QuickCrisp Classic</u> – QuickCrisp Deluxe – <u>NoBurn Safety Toaster</u>

Page Links

Page links are links that, instead of taking you to another page, simply scroll you down to another location on the current page. When people see links, they typically assume that they'll lead to a new page, so to avoid confusion, it's a good idea to explicitly label such links, like this:

On This Page: <u>Lions</u> – <u>Tigers</u> – <u>Bears</u>

or

Scroll Down To: <u>A</u> <u>B</u> <u>C</u> <u>D</u> <u>E</u> <u>F</u> <u>G</u> <u>H</u> <u>I</u> <u>J</u>

These can be convenient shortcuts on long pages, but they can create some unusual navigation confusions. Imagine clicking on <u>Tigers</u> in the previous example: you view the tigers, browse around the page, scroll back to the top, and then decide this page doesn't have what you want. So then you click the Back button on your browser—and it leaves you in the same spot! You expected it to take you to the previous page, but it actually took you to the previous position on the same page when you last clicked a page link. For this reason, we recommend keeping page links to the absolute minimal usage. Label the page links clearly and avoid linking back and forth all over the page.

<u>Back to Top</u> links are also fairly popular. The theory is that they save scrolling time, and when used in conjunction with page links at the top of a page, a user can jump down to a particular item and easily jump back up to the navigation options. However, scrolling down to the exact spot is the hard part; scrolling back up to the top is fairly fast and easy, so this doesn't buy you much time. After using a series of page links and <u>Back to Top</u> links, a user will find that the behavior of the Back and Forward buttons is very confusing. Consider this tradeoff before using <u>Back to Top</u> links.

External Links

People have a variety of default assumptions about where a link leads, depending on how it's presented. In most cases, people assume a link will take them to another page *on the same site* unless something indicates otherwise. Thus, if you have a link that goes to an external site, make sure the link label is very clear to that effect or that the link visually indicates this, such as by being grouped with other obviously external links.

See-Also Links

People also generally assume that a link will take them somewhere within the same branch of the hierarchy that they're currently in, usually to a deeper level, unless something in the presentation clearly indicates otherwise. Thus, if you display an expanded outline, users won't be surprised if a link in the outline takes them to the appropriate other location in the hierarchy, but they'll be quite surprised if they click on one of the subnav options and find themselves in a completely different branch of the hierarchy. This problem presents itself when you have topics that naturally fall into more than one category. In this case, one of the simplest solutions is to pick a "primary" category for that topic, and in any other category, omit it as a normal navigation option, but present it as a "See also" link, which alerts the user that the link will go elsewhere.

Scope and Scope Notes

When people come to a site, they want to know what they will be able to find on the site. This is the *scope* of the site. What does the site cover? What is not included on the site? How much have I seen? What portion or how much remains to be viewed?

People can feel overwhelmed when they have no way to estimate how much information is available on a site. They have trouble determining when to stop looking when they can't gauge how much they've seen or how much more remains. They can't correctly evaluate whether to postpone the search until later if they believe they've already seen almost everything.

Provide a sense of the size and scope of your site. You can indicate this by presenting a clear explanation on your home page of what your site contains, by choosing clearly stated and comprehensive categories in your navbar, by ordering navigation options (so missing pieces are easily spotted), and by providing a site map or index.

One common technique used by databases to indicate scope is to show how many records are available in any given category. For instance, in the following example we indicate how many products are available in each product category, which helps not only determine the number of selections for any particular type of product, but also signals what type of product emphasis this store has.

Products: <u>Furniture</u> (12) – <u>**Appliances**</u> (17) – <u>Electronics</u> (55) – <u>Home Décor</u> (36)

Appliances: <u>Ovens</u> (2) – <u>Microwaves</u> (5) – <u>Toasters</u> (3) – <u>Blenders</u> (7)

Scope notes provide information that clarify the range of topics encompassed by a category (see Figure 5-14). Scope notes help provide the scent of information for what lies beneath by elaborating on the title of the link. Scope notes may be representative subtopics under each link or brief descriptions of each link, as shown in the following example.

Representative Subtopics	Brief Descriptions
<u>Furniture</u>	<u>Furniture</u>
<u>sofas</u>, <u>chairs</u>, <u>lamps</u>, …	A variety of comfortable home furnishings.
<u>Appliances</u>	<u>Appliances</u>
<u>microwaves</u>, <u>blenders</u>, …	Kitchen appliances for the amateur chef.
<u>Electronics</u>	<u>Electronics</u>
<u>stereos</u>, <u>TVs</u>, <u>VCRs</u>, …	Consumer electronics for your home media experience.
<u>Home Décor</u>	<u>Home Décor</u>
<u>baskets</u>, <u>florals</u>, <u>candles</u>, …	Decorative knickknacks with an arts & crafts feel.

Orientation Cues

Pages need to be clearly identified so that users know where they are at all times. People can pop into any page from a search engine, so they need to be able to identify what site they're on, what page they're on, and how it relates to their information needs. Use clear site titles, page titles, and tag lines.

Page Titles

Use page titles that are as close as possible to the link titles that users followed to get to the page. For instance, if a link says "Appliances," be careful about naming the linked page "Kitchen Appliances" or, worse yet, "Kitchen Gear." While this may provide useful additional information, it is usually better for the link to be consistent with the page title. Otherwise users may think they clicked the wrong link, especially if they were looking for nonkitchen appliances. On the other hand, some minor differences will rarely confuse people, such as a link called "Toasters" that goes to a page called "Our Toasters."

Pages should be labeled both in the `<title>` tag in HTML, and with a large, obvious title in the body of the page. While the `<title>` tag may seem sufficient, most users never seem to notice the title in the title bar of the window.

Figure 5-14.

Scope Notes.

Examples of scope notes provided as representative subtopics and brief explanation.

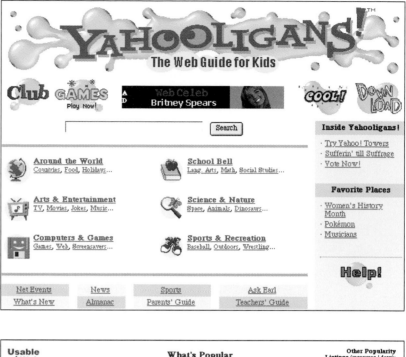

The title you provide in the `<title>` tag should be meaningful without any additional context, such as when it gets reported in a search engine. A common convention is to have the site name followed by the page name, as in "XYZ Corporation—Toasters." Some people like to pad titles with keywords to improve their performance on search engines, but this usually undermines readability. Of course, the portion of the title that names the page should exactly match the page title you show in the body of the page, whenever possible.

Landmarks

Some degree of variety in page design helps the user to have a strong sense of the location within a web site. Consistency remains important, and certain features, like the site name, page title, and navbar, should be kept as regular as possible. However, some simple changes can help users understand where they are in a site. Using colors or large symbols to identify major sections of a site helps users recognize when they've skipped from one section to another.

In addition, significant pages can be made unique by modifying the layout (as a regular variation on the layout themes of the site) or by using a particularly strong page element, such as a large table, image, or typographical element (such as a bulleted list). Common and clearly identifiable pages can act as landmarks that help users ground themselves within a site, and help users avoid getting lost in a morass of same-old, same-old template pages.

SEARCH TECHNIQUES AND SEARCH ENGINE DESIGN

Does every site need a search function? Certainly not very small sites. However, on larger sites, users often choose to search rather than browse, or at least they express a desire for the ability to search when it's not available (more than half of users seem to prefer searching; see Nielsen 2000, 224–25). However, just because people want search capabilities doesn't mean we should provide them. For instance, if users try searching but can't find what they're looking for, then it might have been better not to have provided that function in the first place. In fact, there are two very good reasons searching may fail: users may have very poor search strategies, and your site may have a very poor search engine.

How People Search

Most people are relatively poor at searching. They use terms that are too broad or too narrow. They overconstrain the search. They don't consider synonyms. They don't know how to filter out documents that are irrelevant. As a result, we need to help out as much as we can.

Traditional information retrieval makes use of Boolean queries. Boolean searches rely on logical expressions of what constitutes a good result, where search terms are combined with AND, OR, and NOT. Boolean searches can sometimes be an effective query format for trained experts, but most people are highly unsuccessful with Boolean searches. One key problem is that natural language usage doesn't match logical expressions exactly. In English, when I say I want information about "cats and dogs," I usually mean that I want information about "cats," "dogs," or "cats and dogs." However, in a Boolean query for "cats and dogs," I wouldn't find any information about "cats" alone.

This is an instance of a general problem: people generally assume that if they provide more information, they'll get more and better results; however, most search engines are designed such that the more information that is provided, the further constrained the search and the fewer the results. In practice, if someone starts describing a man they've met as "tall and dark-haired, with a scar on his cheek," they usually assume you'll also think of the not-so-tall person who is dark-haired with a scar. They also assume that if they give you more information (e.g., that the person has a talking parrot and smells like sea salt), you'll be more likely to correctly identify the person, even if they got one of the details wrong. However, traditional database searches are usually written such that a single incorrect search term will mean that you get no match.

Most traditional database searches suffer from being too rigid in their results. They include all matches and only exact matches. People are much more successful if they can also see near-matches, ordered by the closeness of the match.

Another example of this problem is with *parametric searches* (see Figure 5-15). This type of search provides a form with multiple options and is typical for database searches with multiple fields. While this type of advanced search enables a more powerful search capability for skilled searches, many people will either assume they must fill out all form options (and thus overconstrain the search) or that filling out an additional field will provide more opportunity for matches. Because of these assumptions, an implementation that ranks the degree of match will be more effective.

Figure 5-15.

Parametric Search.

While it works well to ask most travelers to specify their origin and destination, many travelers will have flexible dates and times, and so these should be treated as preferences on which to rank the results rather than as a basis for forcing strict matches (*www.nwa.com*).

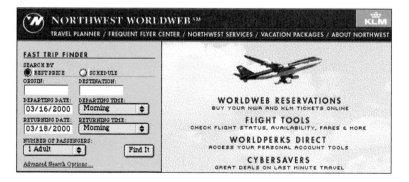

CONCEPTUAL DESIGN

An advanced search option is a nice feature for experts, but most users will be most successful with a single text box in which to enter their keywords. Typical syntax for web searches is to support a plus sign (+) before required keywords, a minus sign or hyphen (-) before keywords that must not appear, and quotes around multiword phrases that must appear in the order presented, and to require that capitalization match if users enter uppercase or mixed-case search terms (lowercase terms should match *any* capitalization).

Search Engine Design

Search engine development is much harder than most people realize. If you want a search engine for your site that works as well as Google or AltaVista, your best bet is probably to buy it, and expect to pay quite a bit. On the other hand, if you can't afford to build or buy a good search engine, you may be better off without one. A search engine that gives poor results will not do your users any favors.

Some search engines can be obtained for free, and some search engine software is available in the public domain. While these tools can be quite effective, be sure that they provide the search features that are needed for your application.

Traditional database searches work by comparing search strings to each record in the database, and they return a match if the keyword exactly matches the record (or is a substring of the item in the record).

Full-text retrieval systems try to address several problems with this approach. They speed things up by *indexing* the information, and they use several rules of thumb to estimate the degree of *relevance* of each match, based primarily on how many times the keyword appears in the matching document. Indexing creates a list of all terms in the whole set of documents, with references back to the documents. Thus, at the time of the search, the search term is looked up in the index and the matching documents are immediately found. When more than one search term is used, the set of documents is combined from the list provided in the index for each term.

Desirable Search Engine Capabilities

Following are some advanced search engine capabilities that you'll want to try to support.

Fuzzy matches are matches that don't fit the search query exactly but would probably be interesting to the user to a certain extent. For instance, if I look for "pet food" and there are no matches at all, there's a high probability I'll be interested in documents about "dog food" or "cat food" or "feeding your furry companions."

Spell-correction allows you to find matches even if the searcher spelled something wrong or the document spelled something wrong. If I search for "wierd events" [*sic*], I want the search engine to find documents with the phrase "weird events."

Alternate spellings refers to the ability to find permissible alternate spellings of terms, such as some very common British and American alternate spellings: "colour" and "color," "grey" and "gray," "organisation" and "organization." When people search for one, they are usually interested in the other as well.

Synonyms are alternate terms with the same meaning. When someone searches for "dogs," they would usually be interested in "canines" and "puppies," although perhaps to a lesser extent. A smart search engine expands the scope of its search to recognize synonyms and related terms.

Stem words are root words, that is, versions of words without any prefixes or suffixes. When people search for "anarchist," often they will also want to find "anarchy" or "anarchism," so the search engine needs to understand how to handle different word forms, how to strip prefixes and suffixes, and, more than anything, how to handle singular and plural forms of words. This can be extremely difficult in general because someone searching for "democrat" is not necessarily the least bit interested in documents about "democracy."

Stop words are terms that are deliberately *not* indexed in the search engine. These typically include function words (determiners, conjunctions, prepositions) such as "the," "and," and "of," and include terms that are so common as to be of limited use. For instance, the terms "web" or "home" don't tend to contribute to a search of web pages because they are so common.

What Makes for Good Search Results

The quality of search results is usually characterized by three factors: precision, recall, and relevance.

Precise search results contain the fewest possible incorrect matches. If you search for "gravy," you shouldn't be getting documents about "gravity."

Recall refers to the completeness of the search results. Complete search results include as many appropriate matches as possible, without missing anything that might be related. If you search for "dog," you shouldn't just find out about pets, you also want to find "Dog Star," "Three Dog Night,"

"Reservoir Dogs," and references to someone's chili tasting like dog food. Complete results should show every match, no matter how obscure.

Relevant search results put the best possible matches at the top of the search results. Relevance means that the result gives you information that is actually useful to your purpose as a searcher. In general, this is at best an educated guess. If you're looking for "dog," then a page called "Everything You Ever Wanted to Know About Dogs" is much more likely to be relevant than a page about bad chili.

When you've got your search engine working, you'll want to test it and make sure it gives the kinds of results you would hope for. Test the search engine results, especially for the most common queries, and verify that the results returned make sense. If not, fix the search engine. When you test the search results, check that the results are precise, comprehensive, and relevant. Check that the presentation of results is comprehensible.

Keep a log of search queries that users enter, especially those that return no matches. Often this will indicate information that is missing from your system, or synonyms or keywords you need to add to your search engine.

Displaying Search Results

The following provide a set of suggestions for effective presentation of search results.

Use Domain-Specific Terminology

Use terminology relevant to your domain. Avoid terms like "record," "field," or "database." For instance, instead of saying "55 records found in the database," specifically say "55 matching products found in the store."

Repeat the Query

Your presentation should repeat the search query so people don't have to remember exactly what they searched for as they evaluate the results (e.g., "Searching for: 'cats and dogs'"). When possible, repeat the search query in another search box. This makes it easier for the user to refine and repeat the query.

Specify the Number of Results

Specify the number of matching results found. Sometimes it's also useful to specify the total number of documents or database entries (e.g., "36 matches out of 10,000").

Provide the Title and Description of Each Result

List the title and description of each match. For instance, when listing matching web pages, provide the title, URL, and description:

> "The World's Best Cat Nip, www.catnipfromheaven.com, 'organic farm-grown catnip that will make your cat beg for more.'"

Help Users Find Similar Documents

As people refine their ideas about what they're looking for, one common need is to find similar documents. Each result could contain a link such as "More like this . . ." Thus, when users find a match they're happy with, they can easily find similar items without having to construct a good query to do so.

No Results

When no matches are found, give search tips for specifying queries more effectively. Depending on the features of your search engine, you may want to suggest that users try synonyms, alternate spellings, or shorter queries. You might suggest actual search terms that you know will work, and give tips on proper query syntax. Finally, this is an appropriate place to list topics so that the user can browse rather than search.

Too Many Results

When too many matches are found, consider providing search tips to help refine the query, such as using more specific search terms. Categorize the results to help users narrow down their queries, as shown in the following example:

> **Searching for: "pets"** returns **500 matches** (out of 10,000 documents).
>
> Choose a category of interest:
>
>> Pet food (220)
>>
>> Pet supplies (150)
>>
>> Training and housebreaking pets (50)
>>
>> Veterinarians (43)
>>
>> Celebrity pets (37)

Multipage Results

When more results are available than can be listed on a single page, be sure to specify what set of results, within the entire list, is currently being shown (e.g., "items 11–20 of 55").

Sorting Results Listings

Sort the results from most relevant to least relevant. If you can't gauge relevance well, use a logical order, such as alphabetical order.

EMBEDDING YOUR SITE WITHIN THE FRAMEWORK OF THE REST OF THE WEB

Your site must be effective within the framework of the entire Internet. This means people need to be able to find your site when they're looking for it and be able to identify both that your site exists and that it contains pertinent content. Your site will link to other sites and be linked from other sites, and you'll want these links to be meaningful and reliable. In addition, your site should work well with automated tools, such as search engine spiders.

It's a good practice to mark up your pages with information that helps automated tools understand your content. Pages can be designed to work effectively with other tools by following HTML standards as closely as possible. Using style sheets or XML is helpful in separating content from formatting as much as possible. Use the `<title>` tag to label pages clearly and unambiguously, and use metatags to specify keywords, descriptions, and related information. See the sidebar "The Dublin Core Element Set" for more information on metatags.

Your site may have one or more *gateway pages*. These are pages intended to be entry points into your site. The home page is an obvious gateway page. Other gateway pages may include pages that are targeted to specific user populations, interest areas, or pages that are simply expected to be extremely popular because of their valuable content. Gateway pages may accidentally evolve (because of their popularity), or they may be designed as such, presenting themselves as a main page and often having their own domain name. These pages are convenient pages to advertise, so that specific target audiences can go directly to a view of the site intended for them.

Your site benefits from strong orientation cues, such as an obvious site logo, a large page title, and a distinctive page layout, which help new arrivals at your site by informing them where they are. Very effective orientation cues also help people understand the relationship between your site and other external sites. For instance, if you are creating a site for a local city government, you might add to it a set of links to related governments, such as US Government > Michigan > Washtenaw County > Ann Arbor. For those unfamiliar

THE DUBLIN CORE ELEMENT SET

Metatags appear in the <head> portion of an HTML document in the following format:

```
<meta name="Title" content="Put your title here.">
```

The Dublin core element set provides standards for metatags. The following metatags are suggested:

Title: *A name for the document*

Creator: *The name of the person who wrote the document*

Subject: *Keywords describing what the document is about*

Description: *A text description, such as an abstract*

Publisher: *The name of the person or organization that is making the document available*

Contributor: *The name of others who contributed to the document*

Date: *Authorship or publication date, recommended in formats like YYYY or YYYY-MM-DD*

Type: *Type of document, such as home page, novel, poem, or technical report*

Format: *The data format, size, and duration (when appropriate), and software required*

Identifier: *A unique identifier such as a URL or ISBN (for books)*

Source: *The original source or sources of the document, when appropriate*

Language: *The language in which the document is written*

Relation: *Related resources and their relationship*

Coverage: *The scope of the site, especially any time frame or location covered by the document*

Rights: *Intellectual property rights, such as copyright or trademarks (which can be a link to a more complete statement)*

If you decide to apply these metatags strictly, you'll want to look up the formal specification. The details are beyond the scope of this book.

The Dublin set is a useful starting point, but doesn't cover every type of metatag that could be useful. Noticeably absent are tags for privacy policies and security specifications, and for self-labeling of content to mark information containing, for instance, sex, violence, profanity, or other adult content. If you have other types of needs, you can create your own metatags, or check out specific standards that are evolving in different domains.

with your city, this type of breadcrumb trail gives them helpful context, and for those with an acute interest, it gives them easy access to related sites. In addition, if you can convince related sites to adopt the same convention, you can create a community of easy-to-navigate sites.

Similarly, you may want to add links to related external sites in other types of structures, such as linking to a web-ring about your topic area, providing links to general indexes related to your company or topic area, or providing quick links to search engines that automatically search for your topic.

CONCEPTUAL DESIGN

Conceptual design uses the site requirements to first establish the tasks of the site and then develop the information architecture. The architecture defines the structure of the site as a whole with minimal concern for the detailed visual layout. However, as we refine the navigation, we need to start addressing visual design issues, which Chapter 6 elaborates on.

06

MOCKUPS AND PROTOTYPES

PAGE LAYOUT

Because first impressions are critical in establishing a user base, a well-structured, highly usable web page gives you an edge. Page layout is concerned with the immediately available "look and feel" of your site. This is the user experience—and it may be the most critical aspect of a successful and usable web site.

This chapter discusses page layout and the constraints unique to web site design that can cause usability problems. We review design principles useful for maintaining and reinforcing the usability of your final product.

THE GOALS OF YOUR LAYOUT

The primary objective of graphic design is effective visual communication. A properly designed page structure should enforce a consistent hierarchy of design elements where the relevant elements are emphasized and the content is displayed in a logical and orderly manner. This doesn't mean pages need to be humdrum and uninspiring. Aesthetics is an element of usability, and the overall design fails if the other objectives of visual communication are poorly served. Good design may be aesthetically pleasing, but *great design* takes note of aesthetics in a usable context. The following goals will keep you on track to achieving usability at the individual page level: simplicity, consistency, and focus.

Keeping watch over these goals will allow you to creatively explore the design space while maintaining a highly usable page design. In a vast information space such as the Web, the user can be gone in the blink of an eye. Ease of use and relevance of information are critical to emerging a winner.

Simplicity

Keeping the page structure simple allows the page to support the content. A simple page ensures that page titles are recognized as page titles, that navigational elements are clearly for navigation, and that the information contained within the page is salient to the user. Additionally, a simple structure gives the designer control of the information presentation.

A truly elegant design reduces the page to its required elements. This allows each element to be intimately tied to its message and increases the page structure perceived by the user. An elegant design also enhances the flexibility and adaptability of your site (i.e., it facilitates future additions and changes). In addition to supporting the structure of your page, this approach conserves screen space and bandwidth.

MOCKUPS AND PROTOTYPES

Consistency

A consistent layout aids user navigation and synthesizes the elements within your page. It also establishes unity across several pages. It should be immediately obvious to users that they are at the same site whether they are on the "About Our Company" page or the "Job Listings" page. Consistency increases ease of use, reinforces a sense of structure, and decreases learning time associated with navigating your site.

Consistency applies to the overall site, the distinct page structures, and the individual graphical elements. Having consistent elements within your page strengthens the structural relations among elements while reducing clutter and visual noise. Predictability and consistency allow a user to easily scan the display to find the relevant elements and information details.

Consistency should manifest itself throughout your page: aligning elements along common axes, using consistent sizes and line strokes, repeating font styles for headings and navigation. A consistent page layout establishes a framework for the user, and conscious manipulation of elements within this framework can have a strong impact on the user.

Focus

Once you've planned for a consistent and simplified layout, the third goal comes easily: place emphasis on the key elements of a page.

Focus is the process of ensuring that key elements are the center of attention. The element of emphasis—whether it be a label, title, or icon—should immediately communicate the information contained on that page. While the page structure will provide *visual* emphasis and support, remember that your labeling scheme is essential for establishing *meaning*. Thus, the page structure can only support and reinforce whatever meaning is created through your initial choice of icon or label.

Focus enables you to control the users' gaze, as well as establish key areas within the framework of the page. By establishing a focal point, you can be sure to get the important information to the user right away. Increasing the size of specific elements, highlighting elements with color, increasing the stroke or size of a font—all these things can be used to make an element of the page stand out.

Why Do All of This?

By keeping the pages consistent, focused, and minimal (as in Figure 6-1), you retain control over the content of the page and facilitate user navigation and comprehension of the site structure. At a more practical level, you minimize development time and assist error detection prior to rolling out the product. In other words, having a consistent layout makes it much easier for your quality assurance team to find inconsistencies and errors in the layouts.

PAGE COMPONENTS AND BASIC PAGE LAYOUT

You can begin to think about page layout by making a list of the various page components you'll need to incorporate into the design. This list should be a result of your requirements and task analyses. Features such as navigation tools, body text, headers, and footers can all be included. Also, if there are specific pages you will be prototyping, be sure to include any unique data or information on the list. Common page components include headers and page titles, body text, footers, logos, navigation and subnavigation, bulleted lists, images and diagrams, and interactive elements.

Once you've determined the basic elements to include on the page, you can begin developing the page structure. Understanding all the common elements will help when it comes time to begin prototyping.

Figure 6-1.

Simplicity, Consistency, and Focus.

This page allows users to immediately identify the site (by allowing the logo to stand out) and where they are within the site architecture (reinforced with the title and navbar highlight). In addition, the format of the body allows users to skim and quickly acquire the main point of the page (to present the primary team members associated with this research group). The overall simplicity of the page, and the use of consistent elements, establishes a focus that allows users to quickly grasp the page's content.

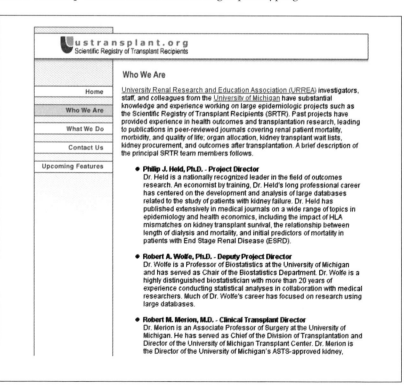

MOCKUPS AND PROTOTYPES

Begin by examining each component individually and ask why it is needed. If you can't answer the question, throw it out! Then ask how this component relates to other components. Find the related components and be sure to reflect that relationship in the visual design and layout of the components. Reduce the page to its minimal components. If you are unsure of a component, discard it. If discarding it ruins the layout or prohibits effective use of the page, then you will need to find a way to add it back in.

Remember, less is better! Having less on your page now will facilitate future growth and expansion of your site. If it's stuffed to the gills right away, you'll have no room for future expansion.

SOME COMMON PAGE STRUCTURES

Once you've identified the basic page requirements, you can begin to brainstorm various layouts. You should always take a look at other page layouts before developing your own. Look at other sites on the Web, determine if their layout might be useful, print out the ones that are, and focus on the strengths and weaknesses of each style.

Review your list of elements required for your pages and see how they might fit into different layouts. Reviewing different layouts will keep you from getting stuck in a rut and may reveal several layouts that you would not normally have considered. The examples in Figure 6-2 demonstrate several common page layout styles often found on the Web.

Figure 6-2.

Common Page Structures.

While not exhaustive, this figure illustrates the flexibility attainable in page layout. Can you think of other designs not shown here? Which are your favorites and why? What are the drawbacks to each of these designs (e.g., too little room for text)?

PAGE LAYOUT TECHNIQUES

Just where do you put all these elements? When you've decided on what to include in your page, and you have the required elements, how do you decide where to put things? This section investigates the development of a page layout. It begins with a quick look at page templates.

Creation of Page Templates

Development of a novel set of page templates can be used to guide the design and provide a flexible framework for future growth. The advantage to this method is that it achieves consistency and long-term time savings. The disadvantage is the difficulty in achieving appropriately flexible templates for future additions and changes while retaining a unique and aesthetically interesting page.

What Do We Mean by Page Templates?

Using templates doesn't mean using a preformatted "boilerplate" solution proposed by your favorite WYSIWYG package, but rather establishing a grid or page architecture unique to the site you're designing. Nor does this mean that you need to adhere strictly to the established framework. There are times when it makes sense to establish a unique page (e.g., a page illustrating a site map may require a slightly different use of screen space than the rest of the site pages).

Why, Then, Would One Want a Template?

A template is useful for maintaining consistency throughout the site. If the navigation is in the same place on the vast majority of pages, the user will expect it there. Consistency across the pages will facilitate integration of the site structure into the users' conception (or mental model) of the site. An accurate mental model reduces the cognitive effort required to search and find things within the display. If each page is unique, the user will need to search for elements within the page, and the cognitive and perceptual strain will be much greater.

The use of a page template allows you to establish a consistent and simple page structure throughout the web site. By reducing clutter and eliminating excessive attention-grabbing elements, you can ensure the user is focused on the critical content areas. The consistency afforded by a template is useful for both the designer and the programmer. Once a common page structure has been established, it is easier to implement new pages, and mistakes and inconsistencies are more easily detected. The sidebar "Attention to Detail" describes another benefit of consistency within a web site.

While page templates have been discussed here, their actual creation often occurs after the mockup stage is completed. For this reason, a detailed discussion of their creation is reserved for Chapter 7. However, you'll want to keep in mind that it is a goal to develop a page that will have consistency and a common layout throughout.

Simplification and Reduction

A major way to improve the usability of your site is to increase the user's comprehension of the elements and structures contained within the page. This is achieved through simplification of the page structure, and reduction of the elements contained within the site.

Reducing the number of visual vertical lines within your page is one way to simplify the display. Figure 6-3 demonstrates the vertical structure of a page and how inconsistencies and excessive arrangements can be simplified. Limiting your page to four or fewer vertical alignments is a good way to maintain control over the structure, although this is by no means a rule. Remember: If your page seems cluttered and you can't quite pin down the reason, it is often due to an excessive number of vertical alignments within the page structure.

Any element that breaks the perceptual boundaries of a page has a strong influence on attention. Reduction of the number of attention-grabbing elements will help to simplify the page for the user while strengthening the focus on the important page elements (see Figure 6-4a). This can be both good and bad. For example, if a fairly static page has new information added to it, you may want to make that information stand out. However, too much of this can contribute to a cluttered page that is difficult to parse (see Figure 6-4b). You should strive to develop a page that has a hierarchy of focused elements throughout the page.

ATTENTION TO DETAIL

People often wonder why their site doesn't look quite as professional as others. Consistency can have a major impact on the users' perception of the quality and professionalism of a web site. Small errors in spelling, inconsistencies in layout, and minor design errors—while often not consciously detectable to the novice user—may lead to a subtle impression that a site lacks professionalism.

Figure 6-3.

Blocking Out a Layout.

This figure illustrates how minimizing the number of vertical alignments (indicated by the blue bars) contributes to page structure. The page on the left has four primary vertical alignments, while the page on the right has nine.

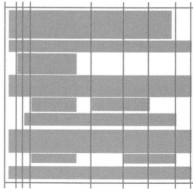

MOCKUPS AND PROTOTYPES

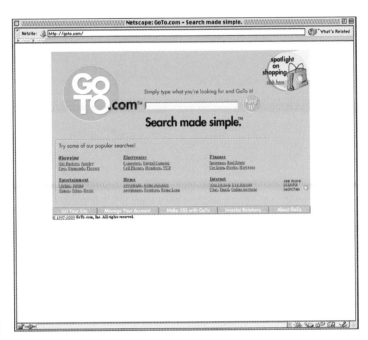

(a)

Figure 6-4.

Grabbing Attention.

Breaking the perceptual boundaries of a page can be a useful technique for drawing attention to an element. (a) When done with a single element, it can be quite effective, as in *Goto.com*'s spotlight in the upper right corner. However, too many items (b) can lead to a loss of effect, as seen on the Discovery Channel's overhanging elements in the upper-left and upper-right portions of the display.

(b)

Contrast

Contrast is critical to overall balance and structure, differentiating elements within a display, and controlling the users' gaze. Contrast allows structure to emerge from the page. A full page of text will be viewed as a solid mass with no clues as to how the user should proceed, while an overly graphic page containing too many highly contrasted elements will disrupt the ability of the user to find the relevant content.

Contrast can exist across several visual dimensions: shape, color, size, or position (to name but a few). It's important to develop a feel for how these differences can affect the user's perception of the page. Highly contrasted elements grab the users' attention, whereas more subdued contrasts require conscious effort to be noticed. While the use of contrast will be discussed further in the design elements section, it's important to keep in mind that too many highly contrasting elements will lead to an unbalanced and confusing display. Too little contrast leads to a dull page with no hints as to the underlying structure and may look accidental rather than intentional. Contrast is only effective when the intent is obvious.

Use contrast to draw attention to particular elements of the display. Contrast also helps to develop a hierarchy of focal elements to rhythmically move the user's eye across the page.

Contrast and consistency go hand in hand. Make similar things look similar. Make different things look different. Leave nothing to chance.

Balance

Balance is used to establish a feeling of consistency and a harmonious layout. A page is balanced when the elements of the display come to a physical equilibrium and the page is equally weighted around a particular axis. In other words, the "physical weights" of the design elements should equal out across the page. Balance is a particularly tricky issue when dealing with the dynamic nature of web pages. Therefore, it is even more critical to establish a well-balanced framework for your page if you are to stand any chance of succeeding when dimensions start changing!

Symmetrical or asymmetrical layouts can be used to achieve a balanced page (see Figure 6-5 and Table 6-1). While symmetrical pages lend themselves naturally to a sense of balance, asymmetrical pages can be unique while still achieving a sense of balance. A well-balanced display will greatly enhance your ability to establish focus and guide the movement of the user's eye across the page.

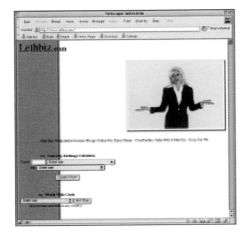

Figure 6-5.

Balance in Page Layouts.

From top to bottom: symmetrically balanced, asymmetrically balanced, and poorly balanced layouts.

Table 6-1.

*Symmetrical versus
Asymmetrical Layouts.*

Symmetrical	Asymmetrical
Highly organized, well-balanced structure	Often more aesthetically pleasing and unique
Easier to implement	Placement specific (i.e., not as good for content that changes often)
Highly flexible and adaptive (i.e., easier to revise or change)	

To develop a well-balanced page, begin by identifying a central axis along which the page will be balanced (this is often a vertical axis in web site design because the horizontal structure is more constrained than the vertical structure). Arrange the information and data about the axis so there are equal weights on both sides of the axis. View the page from a distance or blur the image by squinting slightly to ensure that the visual weight is indeed even.

Repetition

Repetition means to have some element or aspect of the design repeated throughout the design space. It is all about consistency. In fact, it is consistent repetition that brings about a unified design space. Having consistently repeated elements throughout the design space reinforces the structure and identifies your site as a cohesive whole. It is a continuous effort that brings about the unity of the design.

Repetition is often found throughout a great design. Some of the important elements of repetition include headlines and titles that use the same typeface, weight, and size; shapes that are consistently used and vary on one dimension (e.g., size); and bullets that use a consistent design element (e.g., a circle) and are used in a consistent fashion throughout the site.

Repetition can enhance perceptual grouping and reduce visual search time for the user. At a more practical level, it directly contributes to usability by minimizing download times through caching.

Repetition reduces clutter by reducing the number of unique items in the display and lending a low-level graphical structure to the page, while at the same time presenting a visually stimulating layout. Figure 6-6 illustrates how repetition helps to establish an overall page structure that is less cluttered and more cohesive.

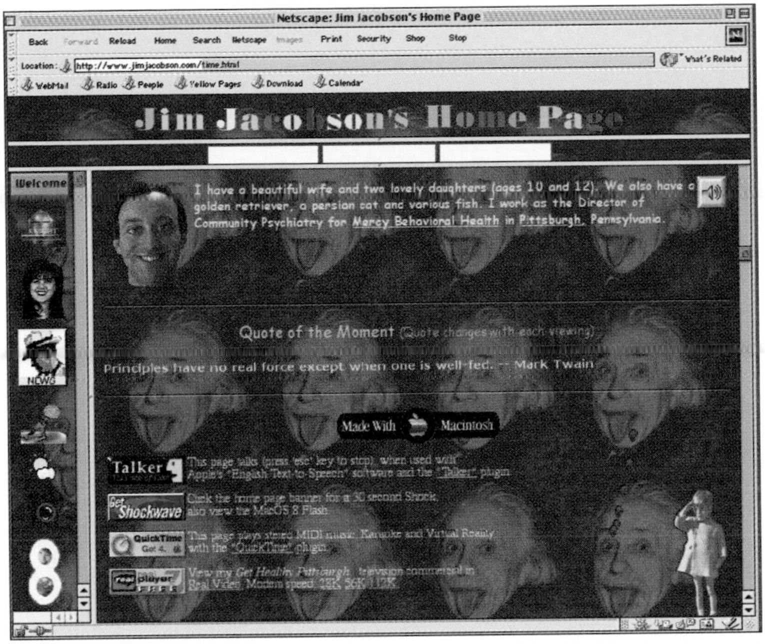

(a)

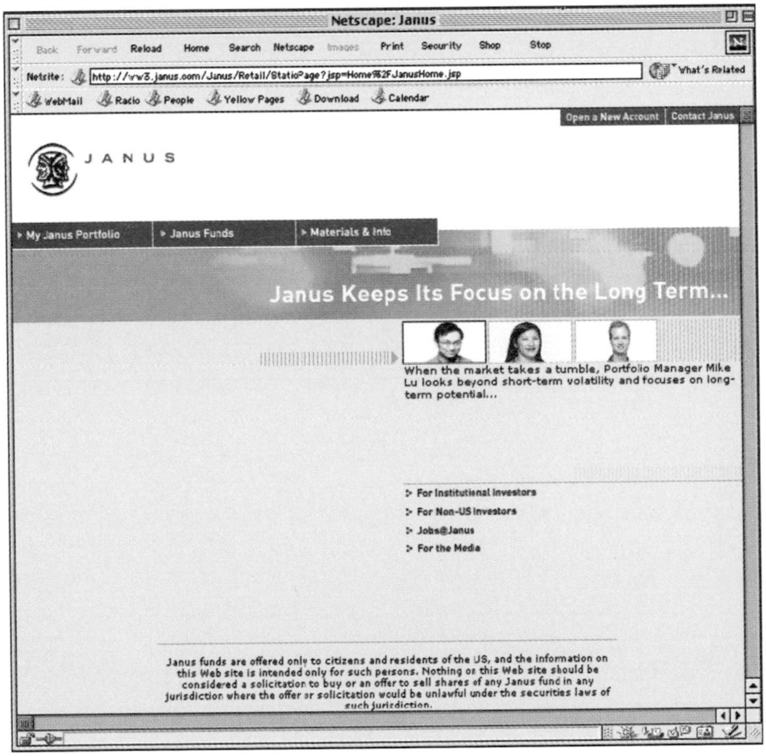

(b)

Figure 6-6.

Disjointed versus Unified Elements.

It's hard to believe, but these two pages have close to the same number of design elements (images, buttons) and the same amount of text. The figure in (a) fails to unify the design space in part because of the lack of repeated design elements (each element is unique in color, stroke, and style). By contrast, the figure in (b) demonstrates a visual hierarchy and repetition of design elements (repeated colors, similar font size and stroke) that reduce the visual noise and structure the elements within the page, creating a unified design space.

Repetition of elements also has a very practical application. By using the same graphic in various positions on your page, you may reduce the download time by limiting the number of unique graphics on the page. Often, when an element is used in several places on one page or on several pages, the image becomes cached on the user's local machine. This means that the next time the user needs to get that image, it is retrieved from memory on the user's local machine rather than having to be downloaded across the network.

Finally, repetition can be used to establish branding of your site. For example, repeated logos can help to establish a brand identity while at the same time reinforcing to users that they are at the proper site.

In summary, you'll want to use repeated elements on your page for the following: to develop a hierarchical structure according to the location, size, and hue of the repeated elements; to reduce download time for unique graphics by having repeated elements that may be cached locally; and to facilitate branding.

Gestalt Principles

A successful page layout uses the techniques just discussed to provide a framework for a strong design. The details of your presentation can add overall coherence to the structure of your site and can be achieved by following established perceptual principles.

The Gestalt psychologists of the 1920s described several general principles of perceptual organization: proximity, similarity, and good continuation, among others. When used properly, these perceptual guidelines can be the glue that holds together a finely crafted web site. By perceptually grouping objects, higher-level comprehension of the display can emerge. For example, a display that has 15 graphical elements may be perceptually presented as three groupings, thus reducing visual search time and simplifying the display while at the same time providing visual groupings that hint at the context of the page.

Proximity

The principle of proximity states that objects (e.g., shapes, text, buttons) that are close together tend to visually organize themselves into groups or units (see Figure 6-7).

Similarity

The similarity principle says that objects that look alike tend to organize themselves into groups or units. This is apparent in Figure 6-8. Note how the squares that previously grouped as columns now group as rows. This is due to the similarity of the objects. With effort, one can see it the other way around (i.e., as columns), but the key here is to learn to create a design that doesn't require mental effort on the part of the user.

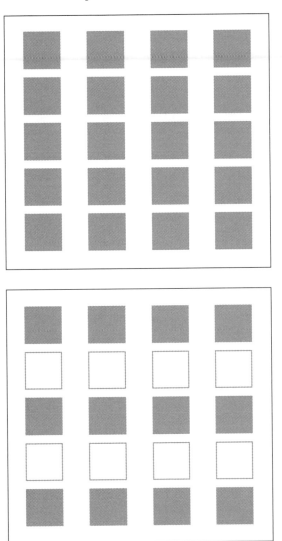

Figure 6-7.

Proximity.

These objects stand out as four columns because they group according to their vertical proximity.

Figure 6-8.

Similarity.

These objects stand out as five rows because they group according to similarity of shape and color.

Good Continuation

The principle of good continuation suggests that you will see the drawing in Figure 6-9a as two lines (A-D and B-C), as in Figure 6-9b. This is because of the common movement, or good continuation, of a curve or delicately changing line. It is just as likely that this figure illustrates lines A-B and C-D, as in Figure 6-9c. However, good continuation dictates that a human will perceive the image as the former combination of line segments.

Figure 6-9.

Good Continuation.

From left to right: Good continuation suggests that it is much more likely an individual would see the first illustration (a) as being composed of line segments A-D and B-C as in (b), rather than as line segments A-B and C-D, as in (c).

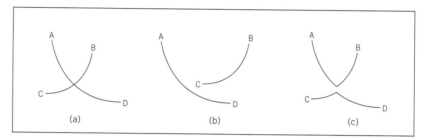

Applying the Gestalt Principles

As with most guiding principles, it is important to know when they should be applied, ignored, and most important, when they should be broken.

For example, your site should take advantage of good continuation by consistently aligning objects along a common curve within a page (see Figure 6-10a). The example in Figure 6-10b, while admittedly somewhat contrived, demonstrates how your page may look cluttered if good continuation is not present in your design style.

Breaking the Rules

Well, here comes the exciting part: breaking the rules! While it is important to know how the Gestalt principles can be used to group and cluster elements, it is just as important to understand the features that will make elements or items stand out. For example, grouping by similarity helps elements hang together, but as Figure 6-11 illustrates, it is also a great way to make items pop out.

One thing you'll want to remember is that this pop-out effect is a scarce resource. If too many elements pop out, then the effectiveness of this trick decreases. So when do you use these effects? By understanding your users and their wants and needs, you'll get a better idea of what elements should stand out for them. Use the pop-out effect to attract attention to frequently changing items or content areas (e.g., special offers, changing news items, or meeting times), to highlight current navigation or locations, and to display critical information.

MOCKUPS AND PROTOTYPES

(a)

(b)

Figure 6-10.

Gestalt Principles.

The Gestalt principles can be used to organize a visual display. In the first illustration (a), proximity is used to group the icons, links, and text as separate elements. Similarity is used in the scale, shape, and backgrounds of the icons. Good continuation can be found in the visual arc upon which the icons are arranged. Failure to use these principles often results in a cluttered and disorganized design, as seen in (b).

Figure 6-11.

The Pop-Out Effect.

Search results displayed from two
common search engines. The site in
(a) merely lists the matches, while
the results in (b) are displayed with
the search terms in bold. Note how
the bolded words pop out. Less effort
is needed in finding the terms.

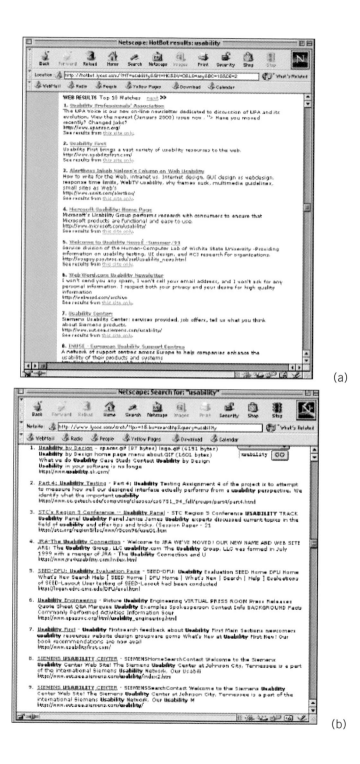

(a)

(b)

MOCKUPS AND PROTOTYPES

Human vision is an amazing system. With very little effort, we detect spiders creeping around in the periphery of our vision, recognize incoming objects in plenty of time to dodge, and easily spot patterns and disruptions of patterns. The application of the Gestalt principles allows users to focus their cognitive efforts on other aspects of their task. For example, a pop-out helps move the recognition of a target element from a time-consuming visual search to what is called *pre-attentive processing*. This lets our visual system do the work without having to waste precious (and limited) mental resources on the task. The example in Figure 6-11b demonstrates offloading of a search task from the cognitive to the visual system. By offloading the cognitive effort required in a search for particular elements, you can greatly reduce the mental load required of your user and free up processing for more difficult tasks that a visual display cannot solve.

PAGE LAYOUT CONSTRAINTS, COMMON PITFALLS, AND SOLUTIONS

The design space of a web page is significantly different from that in traditional print media. Page dimensions are dynamic mobile entities that refuse to remain constant, colors possess a startling knack for cross-platform saturation vacillation, and inner-page dimensions are as obscure and unpredictable as the weather. Design in this environment must be flexible, and your page layout is the key to maintaining a highly usable site across a wide range of systems. Understanding the potential pitfalls and constraints unique to web site design is essential.

Page Layout in Web Site Design . . . It's Just How It Is

Times they are a changin'. Books have had thousands of years to develop, and in that time elaborate aids for finding information have developed. A table of contents provides an overview of a document and enables the reader to immediately grasp the scope of a book. An index allows readers to find all instances of a particular concept. Such tools and aids are being developed for the Web, but the aids so useful for traditional documents are not always good solutions for web-based documents. The structures of the documents are quite different, and this poses several critical problems that must be understood and resolved. Table 6-2 summarizes several major differences between traditional and web-based documents.

Web documents live within a highly flexible and dynamic design space. This means that the page dimensions are always changing. In traditional print media, you know the exact dimensions of the final product. Thus, you can rely

Table 6-2.

Differences between Traditional Paper Documents and Web-Based Documents.

Traditional Paper-Based Documents	Web-Based Documents
Static, stable structure	Dynamic, often uncontrollable dimensions and structure
Often stand alone, or are complete within their surrounding environment	Can be seen as individual elements, within a larger context, or grouped with other elements and materials not originally conceived of by the author (e.g., another web site creating a collection of links that its designers believe are related)
Often dense, large, and well-defined beginning and ends	Often smaller and less well-defined beginnings and ends

on the structure of the design space and can reliably place elements within the page. On the Web this is not so. For the most part, web pages lack a reliable structure—the following are a few consistencies on which you can rely.

Users See the Top of the Page First

Users are required to scroll down the page to see any content that is below the fold. Although it may seem like common sense, an important guiding principle results from this: present the most useful information at the top of the page. If a user needs to wait for a 60-kilobyte graphic at the top of every page, and then has to scroll down the page to get to the relevant information (or worse yet, has to scroll down only to find out this is the wrong page), that user won't be staying there for long!

The Top Left Edge Is Stationary—Everything Else Can Change

The only placement you can truly rely on is that the upper-left corner of the display will be the same on most browsers. This is much less interesting than the fact that the right and bottom edges will be *consistently inconsistent* across your user base! Thus, the "sweet spot" of the page is the upper-left corner. If you have information you must get to the user, make sure it is in this general area. The farther it is to the right, or the farther down the page it is, the less likely it is that *every* user will see the information (see the sidebar "Do Users Scroll?").

Here are the basic requirements of web-based pages that you need to keep in mind. Pages load top down. The top-left edge is stationary and the right and bottom edges will vary (in other words, you can't be sure of where these edges will be on any given user's machine). Some browsers won't display the contents of a table until everything within the table has been downloaded (therefore, don't enclose your whole page within a table unless you want the user to sit idle until the page is completely downloaded). Some browsers will repaint the screen every time the window is resized. Thus, complex graphical designs and backgrounds may add an additional wait time for users.

DO USERS SCROLL?

In our experience, some novice users do not use the scroll bars to see content below the fold. While it may seem unreasonable to attempt to address this problem, there are things you can do to help. By including the necessary navigation within the minimum viewing area (see Table 6-4), you can be assured that you're doing your best to enable novice users access to your information. For a more detailed discussion of this topic, be sure to see both Nielsen's and Spool's accounts (Nielsen 2000; Spool 1997).

Resolution and Page-Width Restrictions

The two major concerns for determining the proper page width are screen resolution and the printing requirements of your users. You need to ask, Who are the major users of this site? What kinds of systems are they using? How important is printing for this population? The answer to these questions will help to determine the requirements of your design. Without careful consideration of page-width constraints, you may unknowingly limit access to your web site (see Figure 6-12).

Solving the Page-Width Problem

Currently, we recommend that sites be designed to work well on a 640×480 screen. The rationale behind this is based on an extensive investigation of the tradeoffs involved. Rather than give you a directive—"If you don't design pages of x width you're wrong!"—we have laid out a detailed account of the tradeoffs involved in choosing the appropriate page width for your web site. Understanding the tradeoffs involved and how they will affect the end user is the key to making a sound decision.

There are several approaches to solving the restrictions of resolution and page width. Three of the most common page layout solutions are variable width, fixed width, or a combination of the two (see Table 6-3).

Table 6-3.

Common Page-Layout Approaches and Tradeoffs.

	Advantages
Variable Width	Maximizes use of screen real estate and provides the most information possible for a wide variety of monitors, browsers, and font settings (see Figure 6-13). Allows users to adjust the display to fit their personal desires (e.g., larger text). Printers can effectively repaginate the information to fit within their constraints.
Fixed Width	You can develop layouts that work very well for a vast majority of users. Consistency throughout your site reinforces the site structure and allows users to easily recognize the structure without having to deal with different layouts on different machines. Layout is highly predictable (little variation among most browsers). Considerably simplifies coding.
Variable and Fixed Combination	Can develop a page that adapts to both wide and narrow screens. Can control the minimum column widths to maintain text readability (doesn't allow the layout to be too narrow).

	Disadvantages
Variable Width	Legibility suffers with extremely high resolution and wide monitors (due to the inability to follow from the end of one line to the beginning of the next).
	Legibility suffers with low-resolution and small monitors (e.g., imagine having to read several paragraphs at two words per line).
	Loss of control of items within the page and in relation to one another (due to dynamic rescaling of the page).
Fixed Width	Users with high-resolution monitors complain about the excess space surrounding the page (see Figure 6-15).
	Not the most efficient use of space for all resolutions (i.e., space is wasted on high-resolution monitors).
	At very small widths (e.g., 300 pixels wide), elements of the page can be cut off (however, developing for a low-end system ensures that only a very small portion of users will be cut out of the picture).
	If set to a fixed width wider than a printer's resolution, some printers may yield cut-off pages.
Variable and Fixed Combination	Consistency is not guaranteed.
	Control is less than with fixed width, but greater than with variable width.
	Difficult to implement.
	Changes can be difficult.
	Loss of control of items within the page and in relation to one another (due to dynamic rescaling of the page).

Figure 6-12.

Page-Width Problems.

Sapient's home page
(*www.sapient.com*) limits access to a
section on client case studies. In
image (a), the blue icons on the far
right take you to the case study
pages. However, image (b) demonstrates what happens when the window size or screen resolution is not
adequate.

(a)

(b)

MOCKUPS AND PROTOTYPES

Figure 6-13.

Variable-Width Designs.

Variable-width designs adjust to the
browser window size.

Variable Width

Variable-width solutions take advantage of the flexibility and adaptability of
screen size, browser size, font size, and cross-platform differences. A purely
variable-width solution would have the page structure completely dependent on
percentages and relative sizes of the elements within the page (see Figure 6-13).

In general, variable width is a tough solution to choose. There are several
ways in which it can go wrong. A major problem occurs when the browser
width is set too narrowly, and the user ends up seeing one or two words per
line. On the flip side, really wide monitors can have lines of text equally long.
This can prohibit the user from easily finding the beginning of the next line.
Additionally, you have very little control over the layout of page elements within the page. If your design calls for having graphical elements aligned to more
than just the body (i.e., there are strict relationships between graphical items),
this will be a hard pill to swallow. On the positive side, this layout method
makes the best use of the users' browser dimensions and can maximize the
use of space to display the most information possible.

There are a few things you want to watch for when designing variable-width
solutions. At a small width, text areas may suffer. When pages resize, they
tend to maintain the width of your images, and the bulk of the resizing will

occur in your text region. Be sure to check this to ensure that your text is still legible. Develop flexible foreground graphics that don't rely on positioning against the background or to one another (this is a design problem that is unique to the Web and is a fun challenge for any web designer). Remember to thoroughly test your pages by adjusting the font sizes and browser height and width (a detailed approach to this is covered in Chapter 11, "Pre-Launch and Post-Launch"; however, you should be implementing some of these tests early on).

Fixed Width

Fixed-width solutions require a thorough examination of your users and their possible systems. There are several options and each requires a tradeoff: designing for the lowest common denominator, designing for the majority of users, designing for high-level machines and users, or designing for a known user base (e.g., an intranet).

Designing for the lowest common denominator is the one way to be sure that roughly 99 percent of all users can use your site. This requires developing a screen layout that will print effectively without clipping and without requiring users to adjust their print settings (thus no more than 520 pixels wide); will work on low-resolution monitors (e.g., 640 × 480 pixels) with low color depth (e.g., 8 bit); and supports text-only browsing. If this is your target audience, then there are several constraints you'll want to follow (it's not as simple as developing screens that fit within a 640 × 480 design space). Table 6-4 shows the minimum adjusted requirements that need to be made when using a fixed-width solution geared toward machines at specified resolutions.

Table 6-4.

Common Page Width, Height, and Resolution for Fixed-Width Solutions.

This table presents the recommended dimensions in which your design should fit given specific target platforms and display resolutions.

Target Platform	Screen Space Used by the Browser (in Pixels)	TARGET RESOLUTION SAFE AREAS (Width x Height)		
		Screen Resolutions		
		640 × 480	800 × 600	1,024 × 768
PC				
Internet Explorer 5.0	43 × 160	597 × 320	757 × 440	981 × 608
Netscape 4.5	46 × 125	594 × 355	754 × 475	978 × 643
MacOS				
Internet Explorer 5.0	53 × 152	587 × 328	747 × 448	971 × 616
Netscape 4.7	44 × 130	596 × 350	756 × 470	980 × 638

MOCKUPS AND PROTOTYPES

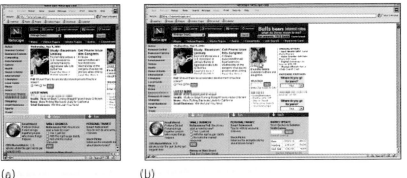

(a)   (b)

Figure 6-14.

Problems with Fixed-Width Designs.

Fixed-width designs offer the most control over the layout. However, common complaints of fixed-width solutions are (a) pages are often cut off at small window sizes, and (b) excessive white space occurs in the margins of high-resolution displays.

You'll note that the recommended sizes are significantly smaller than the actual screen size. This is due to the browser requiring a certain amount of the page width within which the actual web site is displayed. This percentage varies from browser to browser and across platforms. This means that when choosing 640×480 resolution as your target width, you'll need to make sure your page is sufficiently smaller than 640×480 pixels. Thus, 520×295 pixels is a requirement that we often use (the following paragraph elaborates on the rationale between these numbers). While 640×480 screens are most likely a small percentage of new monitor sales, a considerable number of people still use them. Additionally, some people with high-resolution monitors set them to lower-resolution settings to ease reading and legibility in their day-to-day work.

Making Fixed Width Work

A common complaint when developing fixed-width layouts for the lowest common denominator comes from users with high-end machines who look at the page and complain that there is too much additional space surrounding the page (see Figure 6-14b). Below are a few tips useful for satisfying both the low-end and high-end users of your web site. First, center the site. This won't work if you need to depend on alignment of foreground and background images. However, it guarantees that the page will be presented in the center of the browser window and tends to resolve the complaint of only using a small amount of screen space on the left-hand side of the screen. Second, use a background image as a decorative solution on the right. This may present bandwidth problems, so if you use a large background image to do this, you'll want to be sure that it has a minimal palette and is graphically simple. One way to do this is to use low-resolution graphical elements in the right-hand margin.

Figure 6-15.

The Browser Also Uses Screen Real Estate.

The release of Internet Explorer 5 for the MacOS introduced a tabbed pane on the left that resulted in even further restrictions on available screen width.

There are some things to remember when using a fixed-width solution. The lowest common denominator fixed-width size to use is 520 pixels wide. This will work for printing and on 640 × 480 monitors. Some combinations of printers, printer settings, browsers, and operating systems will not work with pages beyond 520 pixels in width. Anything above this may be cut off (see Figure 6-14a). Thus, if it is important that your pages are printable for all your customers, you may want to consider 520 pixels as a maximum width or provide an alternate means for them to get printed information from your web site. If printing isn't a concern, then the next width you need to worry about is that required by users who are running machines with a resolution of 640 × 480 pixels. To leave plenty of horizontal space for margins, windows, scroll bars, and window borders, we use a maximum width of 595 pixels. New browsers seem to be using more and more of the available horizontal space. You never can tell when a new browser will use those 10 pixels you are relying on (see Figure 6-15). If you plan on having your web site available for a long period of time and want to do minimum maintenance, you may want to plan a little extra buffer zone for future browser modifications.

If you know your user base very well (e.g., as you would on an intranet), or are willing to dismiss a certain percentage of users (e.g., an interactive art exhibition may choose to reduce potential viewers to gain additional screen real estate), the same logic as above can be applied. You may be able to rely on a wider design, but you should still determine the exact width that will work for

MOCKUPS AND PROTOTYPES

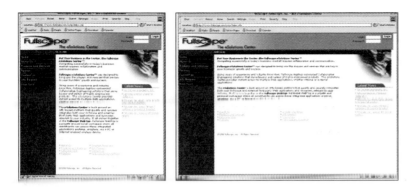

Figure 6-16.

A Combination of Variable- and Fixed-Width Layouts.

Using a combination of techniques allows you a flexible design that maintains legibility by limiting the width of text in wider displays, yet maintaining the ability to rescale for smaller displays.

your target platforms. Discover your user base, understand the limitations of their systems, and thoroughly test any implementation on a variety of browsers and operating systems.

Another solution is to use both fixed-width and variable-width page layouts (see Figure 6-16). By using a combination of the two, you can set a minimum width for particular areas of the page (e.g., the major text body) and allow the page to increase in size as the user sees fit. This allows a minimum width for a text area (e.g., 200 pixels) while making use of the flexibility available by the use of a variable-width setting

Page Layout in Web Site Design...Here's What You Can Do

So how do you get around all of these constraints? Once you are aware of the constraints, you can do several things to address them.

Place Critical Information at the Top of the Page

Pages load top-down. There is no way around it, short of developing your own bottom-up browser. So be sure to include the most relevant information at the top of the pages. Let users know right away whether or not they are on the right page. Using this space to display a large graphic is usually not going to facilitate information-finding. Similarly, an enormous, intricate title does little more than reinforce to the user what the general topic of the page is. Give the user some information. An opening paragraph that is highly descriptive of the page contents or a quick bulleted list of the major topics is much more useful than a company logo. Users should be able to determine whether or not the information they are looking for is on this page. The quicker this is resolved, the more usable your site will be (not to mention the happier users will be, and the higher your user retention rates will be).

In web site design, the top of the page is the most critical area. This "sweet spot" is the most dominant area of the page. It loads first, is accessible to the highest proportion of users, and is virtually guaranteed to be seen. Use this space wisely. Put the most critical information here. Introduce the contents of the page, provide the user with the novel and unique information of the page, and be sure it is quickly accessible. In other words, use this space sensibly and efficiently. It is the area of the page that packs the most punch, so spend the extra time to make sure it is well structured and designed.

Mind the Gap

In addition to the basic structural constraints of web pages, there are subtle differences between browsers you need to understand before building your web page. These differences are manifest in the sizes of gaps and gutters, fluctuating alignment of background and foreground images, and color changes for standard links, to name but a few!

Different browsers have a variable number of pixels at the left and right edges of the browser window (often between 5 and 10 pixels; see Table 6-5). This variation can become particularly tricky when trying to deal with issues of alignment and exact registration of items on the screen. A common occurrence of this is in the layout of navigation at the left edge of the screen. Often people develop graphics or layouts that rely on single-pixel accuracy. This can lead to surprising results.

While there are several ways to get around the problem of differing gap sizes (including the following suggestion), it is important to understand that such differences occur across platforms and browsers. The message to remember is that pages should be designed flexibly enough to tolerate small shifts in exact alignment.

Table 6-5.

Gutter-Width Size Differences for Some Common Systems and Browsers.

	Netscape 4.7 (MacOS) / 4.5 (PC)	IE 4.5 (MacOS) / IE 4 (PC)	IE 5
MacOS 9.0	8 pixels	8 pixels	10 pixels
Win98	8 pixels	10 pixels	10 pixels

In any event, these problems can often be controlled with cascading style sheets. However, style sheets can pose additional problems you need to be aware of (see Chapter 10, "Usability in Software Development"). The following code fragment can be used in the body tag to control the minimum border on newer browsers. Beware, though, older browsers will ignore these tags!

```
<BODY leftmargin=8 topmargin=8 marginwidth=8 margin
  height=8>
```

The **leftmargin** and **topmargin** tags are for Explorer, while **marginwidth** and **marginheight** work for Netscape.

The best way to deal with layout problems that occur due to slight shifts in layout across platforms is to design graphics that don't rely on single-pixel accuracy. While this is the best solution, it also takes some time to learn. However, with enough practice this becomes second nature.

Common Page Layout Problems

Following are design flaws and constraints frequently encountered in page layout:

- Misaligment of foreground and background images

- Changing gutter sizes at the left edge of the browser

- Overlapping foreground images not allowed (although there are several tricks to get around this, such as using an image as a table cell background, using style sheets, or drawing them as a single image)

- Font size differences from system to system, machine to machine, and browser to browser

- Dynamic restructuring of pages not thoroughly tested

Dynamic Font Sizes and Line Spacing

Keep in mind that in the development of a web page, the fonts displayed on the screen are dynamic: they have the ability to increase and decrease in size. This can affect your layout, the spacing in between items, and line-spacing on the page. What looks nice on Netscape and the MacOS may look completely different on Internet Explorer and Microsoft Windows.

What about White Space?

Is white space useful or not? There are a few key ideas to keep in mind when thinking about whether or not to use white space within your page. While white space can be wasted space, it can also effectively support and organize the structure of the elements within the page. For example, setting a "New" section apart from the rest of the page makes use of white space to support the user. However, you'll want to keep in mind that if you use line-spacing within your text, you run the risk of font changes multiplying the white space. While vertical white space can be useful for differentiation between content sections, horizontal space is at a premium—gratuitous use of horizontal white space is a no-no.

HOW DOES PAGE LAYOUT AFFECT USABILITY?

Quite simply, when graphics and layouts become cluttered or misaligned, they unintentionally create complexity and additional visual features within the display. Instead of providing structural support for the information and facilitating the users' creation of a mental model of the site, these problems become attention grabbing, competing with intentionally designed elements in unpredictable ways. From an efficiency standpoint, these additional features increase the time it takes a user to parse the screen. In addition, they increase the probability that users will not be able to find the information they are seeking or will become confused. At the very least, they will make the display look excessively cluttered and unprofessional.

07

MOCKUPS AND PROTOTYPES

ENVISIONING DESIGN

Developing a highly usable web site requires a thorough understanding of the design space. This can only come from a persistent exploration of alternative designs and from early involvement of users in the design process. Refining the design across several stages will lead to a solution that is highly usable, cost-effective, and carefully matched to the project requirements.

Successfully envisioning the design space can be achieved using an iterative process of mockups and prototypes. Mockups provide visual representations of *page structure* often focused on creating effective visuals. Prototypes explore both visual and interactive representations of *page structure* and *site structure* and focus more on content, architecture, and interactions. Using a combination of mockups and prototypes allows you to get the design right the first time around when the cost of change is reasonable and an exploration of wide-ranging alternatives is possible, rather than repairing a design after the site has been fully implemented.

THE GOALS OF ENVISIONING DESIGN

The web designer's goal is to create a site that seamlessly integrates strong and effective visuals, clear and intuitive navigation, and exciting and useful content. All of this can be achieved through a set of well-integrated mockup and prototyping processes.

A successful approach to mockups and prototypes can yield great benefits including getting everyone involved, exploring and defining the design space, and providing for early user testing, as well as cutting costs, reducing errors, and improving quality.

Get Everyone Involved

Designs and abstract ideas are difficult to talk about without tangible artifacts to represent the ideas. Concrete examples are useful for getting everyone involved and on the same page. Examples in the form of mockups or prototypes open communication channels and guide conversation toward explicit and useful comments and ideas.

In addition to providing the design team with a common artifact for discussion, mockups and prototypes also provide a more tangible product for clients to examine. This makes the product "real" to clients and can be an effective way to win their involvement and support early in the process. (Early client involvement has some risks, however; see sidebar "Potential Pitfalls of Early Client Involvement.")

Mockup and prototyping techniques help to increase involvement by providing common artifacts for examination, facilitating communication among the design team (users, clients, and designers), and fostering early client buy-in to the project.

POTENTIAL PITFALLS OF EARLY CLIENT INVOLVEMENT

If your client is not accustomed to being involved early on in project development, you may experience some backlash in response to the "unprofessional" look and feel of early examples. This can be easily diffused by describing (ahead of time) the procedures used and reassuring the client that these are tools to facilitate development.

Also, because mockups and prototypes are deliberately incomplete, clients can sometimes be distracted by the fact that they don't fully implement every project requirement, guessing perhaps that you've forgotten important elements. Early on, stress to them that the purpose is to help them communicate and clarify their goals, and throughout the process, be sure to specify which aspects you're prototyping and which aspects are being neglected. For instance, an early mockup may be used to capture a visual style but not be intended to represent the final navigation labels or content.

Some clients like to ask that a mockup be correct in every detail. For some purposes, this may be useful, but in most cases, it is better to explain to them the cost tradeoffs involved and the logic of quickly iterating low-cost alternatives before building high-cost representations of the site.

Explore and Define the Design Space

Mockups and prototypes also provide an artifact that can help to define the limits of the design space within which you are working. Mockups and prototypes help by providing tests of feasibility and proof of concept, exploring various visual and structural arrangements, eliminating guesswork early on, and detecting errors at the earliest stage possible.

Provide for Early User Testing

Early and rough representations of content and functionality allow you to bring users into the design process in ways that traditional spec sheets and abstract definitions don't. Providing a concrete example—even when not complete—is more useful for examining how a user might react to a design. Mockups and prototypes provide a tool for early user testing, which in the long run will allow the site to be developed more quickly and cost-effectively.

Mockups and prototypes provide a mechanism for gathering user data at the beginning of the design process, the means for gathering user feedback early in the design process, and a framework that allows user testing at the beginning of the design process.

Increase Quality, Cut Costs, and Reduce Errors

Design prototypes can provide you with early buy-in from your clients, a valuable user testing platform, a low-cost method for determining the feasibility of specific design ideas, and a method for catching errors early in the design cycle. The end result of all of this is quite simple: you'll be designing user-centered, cost-effective, high-quality, successful designs.

THE FIDELITY OF MOCKUPS AND PROTOTYPES

Prototypes and mockups can vary from very coarse-grained, fuzzy layouts of the general page requirements done on paper (low-fidelity), to fine-grained, highly elaborate, and polished digital versions of the web site (high-fidelity). This range provides the designer with levels of refinement useful for testing and exploring varying details of a given design. For instance, early paper mockups may be used to gather feedback on the basic functionality or visual layout in a quick and efficient way. In contrast, fine-grained prototyping methods may be used to gather detailed information on the *processes* involved in traversing several pages, or a subset of tasks.

The general rule, then, is that low-fidelity mockups are useful for discovering larger problems and are more suited for the early stages of design, whereas high-fidelity mockups are more useful for refining the details of the design and are thus more effective in the later stages. It's usually good to invest in several low-fidelity mockups early on, and use a high-fidelity mockup or prototype in the latter stages. However, don't be afraid to mix both types at different times, as they reveal different types of problems.

MOCKUPS

Mockups are primarily single-page, static representations of the design space. They are used to refine the visual design and facilitate communication among the design team (i.e., designers, users, and clients). Mockups focus on the look and feel of the design while attempting to tackle the more complex page layout problems that might be encountered in a web page. In addition, mockups can be used for user testing. Simple user testing can reveal whether users understand the basic page structure or whether they find icons or button labels straightforward and intuitive. Several mockup methods are discussed in this chapter: thumbnail sketches, paper mockups, and digital mockups.

Thumbnail Sketches

Thumbnail sketches are small, rapidly rendered sketches used to develop a broad spectrum of design ideas (Figure 7-1). Thumbnail sketches are typically used at the earliest stage of design, often before the requirements have been finalized.

Figure 7-1.

Thumbnail Sketch.

Thumbnails are small, unrefined, rapidly rendered explorations of the design space.

The key to developing thumbnail sketches is quickness. Each sketch should only take 15 to 20 seconds. This way, you can generate a lot of thumbnails in a very short time. You might wonder, What is the use of developing a bunch of quickly rendered sketches of designs that may never be used? Quite simply: idea generation.

Imagine the following. If you produce one sketch per minute for 30 minutes, you will have a nice selection of ideas to work from. It is likely that 15 of these sketches will be too similar and that 10 of them just won't work. So half an hour's work leaves you with 5 *diverse* sketches. But it buys you more than that. It also gives you 10 or so ideas that you know *won't* work, and you'll know not to go down that road. Perhaps more important, it has enabled you to begin to envision the possibilities of the design space.

Thumbnail sketches allow quick explorations of the major design components and design space. They also allow you to develop a broad array of design ideas, and to focus on the ideas, not the details of the display.

Paper Mockups

Once you've developed a good set of thumbnails that interest you, you're ready to take the next step. Paper mockups are slightly higher-quality (although still fairly rough in comparison to the end product), rapidly rendered representations of your major design decisions (Figure 7-2). They allow you to explore page layout and arrangement as well as more aesthetically driven issues such as color palettes. They are much larger than thumbnails (usually at least 8×10 inches and often larger) and are drawn in dimensions closer to the final design. This gives you a more realistic understanding of the limits of the page size and allows you more room to perform semidetailed investigations of the design space.

Figure 7-2.

Paper Mockup.

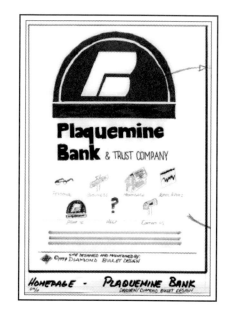

Paper mockups effectively envision the design space, identify potential difficulties early in the design process, and provide a device with which to begin user testing. Among designers, clients, and users, paper mockups quickly produce presentable ideas and facilitate communication.

Digital Mockups

Digital mockups are higher-quality, rapidly rendered representations of major design decisions (Figure 7-3). They allow you to explore page layout and arrangement as well as more thorough investigations of color and palette choice. For web design, digital mockups are the only accurate way to explore the color and contrast issues that might arise in an online environment. They

Figure 7-3.

Digital Mockup.

Digital mockups often appear more refined and provide an accurate representation of color and type.

are often created in paint programs (e.g., Adobe Photoshop) or illustration programs (e.g., Adobe Illustrator or Macromedia Freehand).

Typically, digital mockups present a level of refinement beyond that of the paper mockup. However, there are tradeoffs involved in the use of digital mockups. Users, designers, and clients perceive digital mockups differently than they do paper mockups, so you should be careful about how early in the design process you choose to implement digital mockups (see the following section for more details). For this reason, we tend to view digital mockups as useful in the later stages of design refinement.

Differences between Paper and Digital Mockups

There are some interesting differences among the perceptions conveyed via paper and digital mockups. It's better to use paper mockups early in the design cycle for one major reason: clients tend to view paper mockups as a *conceptual* rather than a finished product. The strength of this cannot be overlooked. One of the biggest problems we've encountered with digital mockups is that clients tend to view them as final, unchangeable products.

Paper mockups are perceived as less polished and more conceptual. As such, they tend to provoke more comments and often lead to more engaging discussion. Clients and users become more open in their suggestions for change and are more vocal in describing the perceived inadequacies of the design. In this way, paper mockups generate more useful feedback on broader design issues.

By contrast, clients viewing digital mockups tend to focus on the details of the layout and on issues such as font choice, exact spacing, label names, or colors. While it is good to get this level of feedback, it is often a bit premature to receive this advice in the first round of mockups. Thus, we tend to reserve digital mockups for later in the mockup process when we are nearing a final page design. See Table 7-1 for a summary of the strengths and weaknesses of both types of mockup.

THE MOCKUP CREATION PROCESS

Far too often designers spend time refining the details of a page without first exploring the overall structure and layout. If designers learn to spend more time in the initial investigation of content and structure rather than diving right in to the details of a page, their end product will be vastly superior. Wait until the page requirements have been explored and rearranged before deciding to work on the visual details of the page. This will allow you to support the individual page structure with visual design rather than having the design determine the structure of the page.

Selecting Pages to Mock Up

Choosing which pages to mock up can vary depending on the stage of the mockups—that is, whether you are in the early stages of mockup creation or in the later refinement stages. The goal of your mockups is also important. You may choose a slightly different subset depending on whether the mockups are primarily being used for internal development and user testing, or whether their main goal is to be used for client review and sign-off on the look and feel.

Choosing Pages for the Early Stages
In the early stages of mockup creation you'll want to focus on pages that explore the most detailed and difficult design problems. These are often pages that include vast amounts of data, are dynamically generated, or deviate significantly from the rest of the pages (e.g., order forms). The goal here is to learn as much about the design space as possible, so you really want to push hard to explore and tackle some of the most difficult problems.

Choosing Pages for the Later Stages
Later in the refinement and review process you may be primarily using the mockups to get client approval on the look and feel. If this is the case, you should try to choose a subset of pages that demonstrates the diversity of the design as well as pages that will be the most visible to visitors. This often includes the home page, a detailed subpage (perhaps a favorite product of the company), and other pages that are more diverse in structure.

Table 7-1.

The Strengths and Weaknesses of Paper and Digital Mockups.

	Paper Mockups	Digital Mockups
Strengths	Quick to produce.	Easy to refine.
	Easy to redraw.	Easy to change colors and move elements around within the screen.
	Present a "sketchy" feel.	
	Focus remains on the content of the page and not necessarily the details of the graphics.	Allow quick changes to color palettes.
		Easy to quickly produce a wide variety of choices based on a particular style (e.g., pages with different palettes, slight font changes, etc.).
	Can be presented anywhere they can physically go.	
		Readily available for display on the Web.
		Multiple alternatives of one style easily accomplished.
		Maintain a polished, finished look and feel.
Weaknesses	Multiple alternatives of one style can be difficult and more time-consuming to produce (e.g., making many color alternatives can be difficult).	Maintain a polished, finished look and feel.

Choosing Pages for Internal Use

Pages selected for internal use should focus on those that provide the highest payoff—that is, the pages that will be visited most often by users or pages that are critical for achieving crucial processes such as product purchasing. In addition, it is often useful from a design standpoint to tackle the most difficult (often the most content-rich) pages. This will provide you with the knowledge that your design is flexible and scalable enough to handle pages deep in the hierarchy, or those with excessive amounts of content.

When choosing pages, you'll want to ask yourself, Is this the most important page in the design? Is this where I want to focus my efforts? If the answer is no, then you may want to look for a page that contributes more to the overall design.

Choosing Pages for Client Review

The goals change somewhat when you are choosing pages for client review. While you still want to choose pages that allow you to learn about the design space and also enable user testing, you may need to be prepared to make some sacrifices in the name of salesmanship. You should still keep as your goal choosing pages that are critical to the design; however, if your clients are at all interested in image and branding, they are going to want to see the home page. Thus, when developing mockups for client review, choose a home page and some combination of subpages that includes those critical to learning about the design as well as some that represent the most highly trafficked areas. See Table 7-2 for a summary of issues involving the choosing of mockup pages.

Techniques

There are several techniques that can be used for developing mockups. The following presents a selection of shortcut techniques for representing common elements of web pages. These techniques are quick, effective ways of simulating design elements and interactive areas of the display. However, the key to developing good solid technique is practice, practice, practice.

Greeking

Greeking refers to a way of displaying an approximation of the text that will appear on your page (Figure 7-4). It is a simple way of showing how much text will appear on any given page and its approximate layout and format. This allows the designer to effectively envision the space occupied by text without worrying about the actual body text that will be inserted in the final site.

MOCKUPS AND PROTOTYPES

Table 7-2.

Choosing Pages to Mock Up.

Mockup Stage	Internal Audience	External Audience
Early	Choose the most critical pages based on users and user goals.	Choose pages with highest visibility.
	Focus on content-rich pages to ensure solutions for the pages with heaviest content.	Choose a variety of pages that demonstrates the breadth of the design (e.g., home page, low-level subpage, pages with dynamically driven content).
	Choose pages that require multiple sources of data (e.g., dynamically generated pages that require data from a database and dynamic content creation).	Choose the most frequently visited pages (based on user testing and knowledge of user base and site goals).
	Choose pages that involve several members of the design team.	
Late	Choose the most critical pages (e.g., entry page to online sales area, personal portal area, home page, etc.).	Choose pages that demonstrate the diversity of the design.
	Choose the most difficult pages (e.g., deepest in hierarchy, pages with the most content).	Choose pages that will be frequently visited.
	Choose the most highly visited pages (e.g., home page, various entry points).	Choose pages that are important to the client (e.g., famous products, areas of expertise, etc.).

Figure 7-4.

Greeking.

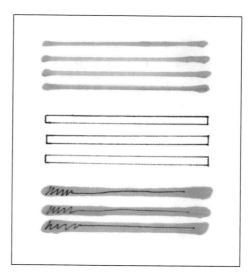

Shadows

Drop shadows can be useful to suggest elements that are interactive or "click-able" (Figure 7-5). A simple shadow on the lower right edge provides the viewer with the perception of a raised element, which can be used as a device for illustrating interactive objects in the mockup, even if they are not used in the final design.

Highlighting

Highlighting can be used to represent a selected item, identify the current page in navigation, or announce an item currently in focus (i.e., in the range of the mouse pointer; Figure 7-6). Highlighting a particular object provides visual feedback to the user about the current state of the page or an event. This is often a useful technique for demonstrating the current location within the larger site structure, or simply showing activation of a current setting or feature.

Outlining

Outlining provides a simple way to present an image in a low-resolution fash-ion (Figure 7-7). Instead of taking time to painstakingly get every detail right, outlining provides sufficient information for mockups, prototyping, and user testing. This is often a useful technique for presenting icons or images within your prototypes (read more on icon design in Chapter 9, "Design Elements").

Sketching

It is rarely worth the effort to make an illustration or photo final in an early prototype or mockup. Sketching images into the mockups provides

Figure 7-5.

Shadows.

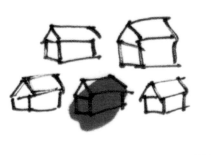

Figure 7-6.

Highlighting.

Figure 7-7.

Outlining.

a placeholder for the image, preserving the scale and demonstrating the content (Figure 7-8). It also provides a sufficient image for user testing. The key to sketching is practice. Round out the forms. Don't worry about exact details; basic proportions and placement are more important than highly refined details.

Photo Placement

Photo placement can simply be indicated using a square with lines extending across opposite angles (Figure 7-9). This is generally simpler than sketching or outlining and performs the useful task of indicating that a picture is supposed to be in a given area, along with presenting the basic dimensions of the image. This is often quite useful for developing mockups of pages where there are several dynamically driven content pages with images embedded.

These techniques are but the tip of the iceberg. They are techniques we have found useful and employ most often. However, keep in mind that there are several other fantastic techniques waiting for your adoption and integration! The key to developing good mockups and prototypes is to develop solid techniques and creative solutions through practice.

Figure 7-8.

Sketching.

Figure 7-9.

Photo Placement.

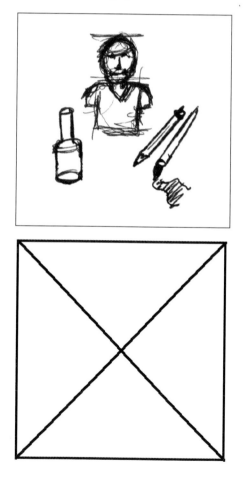

 MOCKUPS AND PROTOTYPES

Step-by-Step Mockup Example

There are nine basic steps for creating a static paper mockup. These steps will take you to the final design.

1. Begin with Thumbnails

Start by developing thumbnail sketches based on the basic requirements of the page (Figure 7-10). Don't worry about the constraints—just draw! After you've developed several sketches, go back and examine which ideas might be feasible and spend a few minutes redrawing those that seem promising.

Figure 7-10.

Develop a Set of Thumbnail Sketches.

2. Create a More Refined Sketch of the Chosen Thumbnail

Once you've selected the most promising thumbnails, choose one for mocking up in more detail. However, before starting on the mockup, you should sketch a slightly larger, more refined drawing with the elements you want in the display (Figure 7-11). This will be used as a reference drawing for the mockup.

Figure 7-11.

Start with a Sketch.

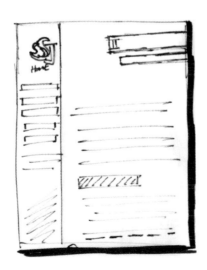

3. Draw Page Boundaries

Begin by drawing the page boundaries in dimensions close to those you expect the final screen dimensions will be (Figure 7-12).

Figure 7-12.

Draw the Page Boundaries.

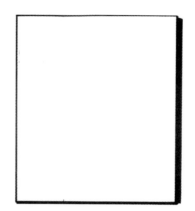

4. Rough the Basic Page Elements and Structure

Start by partitioning off the major elements of the screen: navigation areas, headers, footers, content area, and any others you may have (Figure 7-13).

Figure 7-13.

Establish Areas for Basic Page Elements.

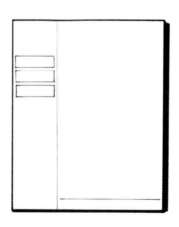

5. Put in Key Graphics, Logos, Main Labels, and Titles

Once you've established the basic page boundaries, sketch in the major elements of the page (Figure 7-14). This should include the navigation elements, the page titles, and major labels. You should attempt to sketch in the type at a size that closely approximates the final design specs. For example, make the page title slightly larger than the body text and make the font appear bold. Don't overdo the sketches, but take the time to get clean outlines that accurately reflect the final proportions. For large text, such as titles, take the time to portray the actual font. This small amount of time will vastly improve the final look of the mockup and allow you to realistically understand how the design works.

Figure 7-14.

Add Key Graphics, Logos, and Page Elements.

6. Greek Body Text and Photo Placement

Once the basic page structure is there, you can approximate the page content with text greeking and image placement (Figure 7-15).

Figure 7-15.

Add Text Greeking.

7. Refine with Details

Now that you have structured all the basic elements of the page, you can refine with details such as adding shadows and highlights, and touching up

areas of the display (Figure 7-16). This stage may require more or less time depending on the goal of the mockup. If it is an early mockup primarily for internal use, you may want to skip the step entirely. However, if you are presenting this mockup to clients or a review committee, then you'll want to spend some additional time here.

8. Check the Mockup for Missing Requirements

Once you've completed the mockup, make sure that all of the page elements are included by checking the guidelines in the Mockup Checklist (Form 7-1; download from *http://www.mkp.com/uew*). Note that this checklist includes criteria for both paper and digital mockups.

This checklist can be used to ensure that your mockup is a suitable representation of the final product. It's good to have a checklist such as this to serve as a reminder of layout issues and to prevent proposing a mockup that is ultimately unusable. Many of the principles included in the checklist come from Chapter 6, "Page Layout," and Chapter 9, "Design Elements."

You may want to customize this example checklist to your own design standards. Individual guidelines may vary from project to project, but changes should be thoughtfully considered and explicitly documented.

9. Prepare for Client Presentation and Review

If you plan to present the mockup to clients, mat the mockup on a suitable mounting board. This will make it easier to distribute, and you won't have to worry about the page getting sullied. Paper mockups can also be digitally scanned for presentation online, which is especially useful when the mockups will be reviewed by remote clients.

Mockup Checklist

Layout
☐ Simplicity, consistency, and focus.
☐ Contrast, balance, and repetition.
☐ Proximity, similarity, and good continuation.
☐ Critical elements stand out.
☐ Critical information appears toward top left of the page.
☐ Works for printing and at a variety of window sizes (e.g., 520 pixel maximum width of your design).
☐ Provides appropriate focal point, emphasis, and hierarchy of information.

Background Image
☐ Can be compressed to a reasonable size.
☐ Aligns with the foreground images.
☐ Will tile appropriately.

Navigation
☐ Navigation is scalable.
☐ The most complex page can be developed using this framework.
☐ Proper page titles and link labels have been used.

Text/Fonts
☐ The typeface matches the page style.
☐ The number of typefaces is limited.
☐ The use of typefaces, weights, and emphasis is limited.
☐ HTML text is aliased (jaggy) and presented in the expected font.
☐ Font size is flexible.
☐ Text links are underlined.
☐ Text links are different colors for visited and unvisited links.
☐ Body text, titles, and labels are legible.

Images
☐ A consistent light source is used.
☐ The compression of the mockup does not lose too much visual quality.
☐ The images are used to support the content of the page.

Color
☐ Color is used appropriately (e.g., for grouping, pop-out effects, and so forth).
☐ Color is appropriate for dark, light, and grayscale monitor settings.
☐ Contrast is appropriate for dark, light, and grayscale monitor settings.

Client Requirements
☐ Required logos, fonts, and colors are included in the mockup.
☐ Page titles, button labels, and link names are accurate.
☐ Appropriate identifying images and marks are included.
☐ The client address is correct.

THE MOCKUP REVIEW PROCESS

When developing mockups for review, be sure to have comprehensive procedures in place to facilitate the process. The following presents a set of procedures to promote communication, serve as a valuable reminder of areas for review, and promote the integration of feedback into the next stage of design. Having a smooth-running method of review will enhance communication, reduce delays, and provide for a more thorough integration of both client and user comments.

Mockups can be created for either external review or review by the users and clients (whether they are external or within another or even the same division). Regardless of the target audience, mockups are designed to promote communication and understanding of implementation ideas. The following materials are developed primarily for working with external audiences; however, with minor tweaking they can easily be adapted for use within the design team.

Developing a System of Multiple Drafts

Mockups are most useful when they are used in an iterative fashion to refine design ideas based on user testing and feedback. Developing a system of multiple drafts that progressively refine the design lays the groundwork for such use. Form 7-2 presents a sample schedule for mockup development across several drafts. (Download from *http://www.mkp.com/uew.*)

The initial draft consists of three mockups that are fairly diverse in style and display a wide variety of solutions. It is good practice at this stage to provide a combination of navigation and page layout alternatives as well as a wide variety of stylistic choices (e.g., various colors and fonts). However, be sure to explain that any combination of colors can be used with any of the structural designs. In other words, you want to avoid the instance of a client or user really preferring the structure and layout of one option, but choosing another because of a color preference.

There are a few things that should be noted regarding the mockup development schedule. The number of mockups produced at each draft stage decreases as you get further into the process. As you reduce the number of mockups, you should begin to refine the subset you are working with. The further along in the process you are, the more focused and refined your mockups should become. Figure 7-17 illustrates a model of the draft system.

Form 7-2.

Sample Mockup Development Schedule.

Sample Mockup Development Schedule

Week 1: Idea Generation
20 Thumbnails

Week 1: Draft 1
3 Paper mockups (home page)

3 Paper mockups (subpage)

Week 1: Review Stage
Select design or combination of designs, gather
feedback, and prepare next iteration

Week 2: Draft 2
2 Digital mockups (home page)

2 Digital mockups (subpage)

Week 2: Review Stage
Select design and get detailed feedback for
final mockup

Week 3: Final Draft (Draft 3)
1 Digital mockup (home page)

1 Digital mockup (subpage)

Week 3: Final Review Stage
Make explicit any changes that need to occur
when beginning production on the site

When working with clients, be sure to establish a draft system beforehand. Describe the system to the clients, and be sure they understand the consequences of making changes, requesting additional drafts, and so forth. This helps to prevent the seemingly infinite mockup cycles that are all too common when working with clients. It also helps to solidify the design and allows the clients an opportunity to feel involved in the development and design of the web site.

Figure 7-17.

Draft System Model.

Mockup development should follow an inverted pyramid model where the number of drafts and the diversity of styles are reduced as a solution is approached.

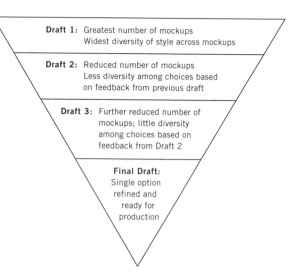

Draft 1: Greatest number of mockups
Widest diversity of style across mockups

Draft 2: Reduced number of mockups
Less diversity among choices based on feedback from previous draft

Draft 3: Further reduced number of mockups; little diversity among choices based on feedback from Draft 2

Final Draft: Single option refined and ready for production

Mockup Review, Approval, and Sign-Off

It can often be very difficult to achieve closure with your client. Once iterations begin, the client can continue requesting alterations for what seems like an eternity. One of the ways to circumvent this (and also help keep the developer on track) is to have a predetermined system of mockups and approval. This doesn't need to be set in stone; it only needs to *appear* to be set in stone! Have a preset number of drafts established up front. Make a preset agreement and stick to it as best as possible.

The mockup approval form shown in Form 7-3 can be used after each draft stage. (Download from *http://www.mkp.com/uew/*.) The upper right corner indicates which draft this represents out of the total number agreed upon and planned for (e.g., "Mockup Style Review Form, Draft 2 of 3). This serves as a gentle reminder that the iteration process cannot go on forever. As long as this has been explained up front, there should be no problems.

Making Use of the Mockup Style Review Form

By breaking down several of the categories in the review form, it helps to focus clients on what it is they may or may not like about a given design. This also serves as a reminder to the reviewer to examine things like color, scale, and layout, as well as naming conventions. In addition, the form provides an area for the reviewer to write comments.

While the form itself is a useful tool for recording comments, it is perhaps even more useful in that it gets the reviewer to think about the design at a deeper level. After the client has filled out this form, you should follow up with a phone conversation or meeting. The form then serves as a device to clarify issues and concerns, and will give the designer a grasp of the most critical areas to remedy in the next draft stage.

Tips for a Successful Mockup and Approval Process

Managing the mockup and approval process can be a difficult task. However, there are several things you can do to make this a more fluid process. Presenting high-quality and accurate representations while keeping communication channels open will help to eliminate the majority of problems.

Make Mockups of Realistic Quality

To prepare for review, make sure that your mockup conforms to appropriate technical constraints and is realistic in its form. Ensure that the mockup's overall quality does not exceed the potential quality of the final result. You want to avoid producing a mockup that will have a higher resolution than the final web site, exceeds screen width limitations, or has text at a higher resolution than can be realistically achieved (e.g., don't display anti-aliased body text when it will be aliased on the final web site).

Leave Out Bad Alternatives

People inevitably choose your least favorite design alternative. If you aren't comfortable with a particular design you've generated, then throw it out. Design selections should only be made from among alternatives that solve the design problem well.

Keep Communication Channels Open

Let people know as soon as possible when snags are encountered. Some snags are expected, and if stakeholders are notified early on, they usually don't cause large problems. It is usually the last-minute updates or unexpected problems that get you into trouble.

Be Explicit

Let everyone know up front what to expect. State the number of drafts, the number of mockups for each draft, and the general area of focus that the mockups will be examining (e.g., the home page and a product page).

Discuss Costs for Additional Work

Let those involved know up front that changes are costly. Not only do additional mockups cost more money, they may offset the original target dates (if you've built in some slack time to your processes, you should be able to give a little here).

Form 7-3.

Mockup Style Review Form.

Mockup Style Review Form

Date sent _____   Draft ____ of ____

Project _____

Project contact _____

Signing this form signifies the completion of the mockup style review process unless additional drafts have been previously arranged.

Please return this completed form when you have finished reviewing the mockups to

Company name:

Address:

Phone/fax numbers:

☐ Mockups are available for viewing online at
　　[*http://www.yourcompanyhere.com/clientname/mockups*]
☐ Attached as a printout are the following: ☐ Home page ☐ Subpage

Mockup style to proceed with:

1   2   (3)   (4)   (5)   (Other When Available):

Please review the following categories, and feel free to mix comments regarding multiple styles.

Color scheme
Do you want any color changes?   ☐ No   ☐ Yes   If Yes, please explain:

_____

Size
Do you have size constraints, limits, or specifications?   ☐ No   ☐ Yes
If Yes, please explain:

_____

Navigation
Do you have navigation or button title changes (refers to wording on the buttons or links)?   ☐ No   ☐ Yes   If Yes, please explain:

_____

Is the navigation and button look acceptable?   ☐ No   ☐ Yes
If No, please explain:

_____

Are the general positioning and layout of navigation acceptable?
☐ No ☐ Yes If No, please explain:

_____

Graphics

Are there any specific photographs or images you would prefer to see on the final web site? ☐ No ☐ Yes If Yes, please explain:

_____

Are company logos and other identifications included and correct?
☐ No ☐ Yes If No, please explain:

_____

General layout/look and feel

Does the overall layout support your needs?
☐ No ☐ Yes If No, please explain:

_____

Does the look and feel match the image desired by your company?
☐ No ☐ Yes If No, please explain:

_____

Briefly describe the reason for preferring the mockup style you have chosen:

_____

_____

_____

_____

☐ **Additional comments are included with this form**

I have reviewed the final mockup style for this project and have determined that it is
☐ Ready to proceed to the final draft
☐ Ready to proceed to the next previously ordered draft
☐ Not ready; I would like to purchase additional drafts

Approved by:

_____

Date of approval:

_____

Get a Signature

Be sure to get a signature from the responsible contact on the client side *before* proceeding with the next stage of work. While nobody likes to point fingers, it will help to protect you in case clients suddenly change their minds.

PROTOTYPES

While mockups are primarily single-page, static representations of the design space, prototypes provide a more useful framework for investigating interaction and overall site structure. They are often more useful for user testing and examining the tasks and processes involved in the *use* of the web site (prototypes may consist of several paper mockups strung together to represent a particular process or task of interest). There are several types of prototypes, including storyboards, wireframes, and high-end prototypes.

Prototypes allow you to examine a small portion of the web site in detail. For example, you may choose to prototype the transactional portion of a banking web site. This can be done by creating a prototype that deals primarily with the pages involved in the transaction process. Prototypes allow detailed investigations of particular aspects of a web site and can support user testing without having to wait for the entire site to be available. Alternatively, prototypes may be used to examine the entire architecture of the web site while reducing the content or level of visual refinement.

Prototypes allow early user testing and shorten overall development time by identifying problems early in the design cycle. They differ from the final site in many significant ways. The details of final development are often omitted. They provide less thorough but adequate samples of the pages (i.e., they may not be completely debugged, or have complete functionality or elegant algorithms running behind the scenes). They often use static data that is preprocessed (which eliminates the need to spend time developing things that may not be used).

Storyboards

Storyboards are sequences or snapshots of screens that focus on the possible actions and movements a user may take through the site (Figure 7-18). Developing storyboards generally takes a little more work up front than paper or digital mockups because of the number of screens that need to be created. However, they provide a means for gathering more detailed user testing data. Storyboards needn't capture *every* detail of the web site. Rather, they only need to capture the site's major functionality (or a subset of functionality) and present the user with the illusion of interaction in the given area of interest.

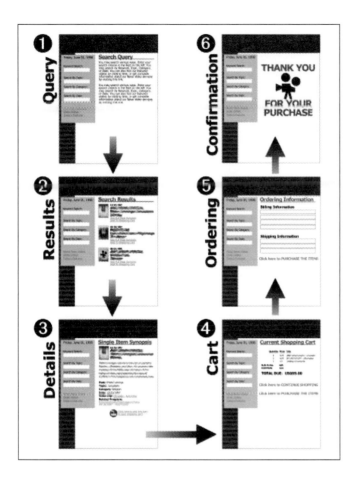

Figure 7-18.

Storyboard Example.

Storyboards often focus on detailed processes or tasks.

Storyboards typically present a subset of the overall functionality of the site. Thus, they may focus on a particular process such as a transactional interface, or a particular area of the web site such as the Products section.

There are several ways to create storyboards, but two of the simplest are to use a series of paper mockups or use a presentation software package (such as Microsoft Powerpoint). Alternatively, quick and bare bones HTML pages are commonly used.

Storyboards are often developed as sequences of paper mockups or sketches that describe the basic functionality of a process or present a broad architectural overview without the detail of a final site. They can be structured in a fashion that permits user testing of the process or area under investigation. Alternatively, they can be presented to a group (see Figure 7-19) and used to aid conversation or site structure design decisions.

Figure 7-19.

Paper Storyboard.

Paper storyboards can be used for group discussion, user testing, or to establish design requirements.

Figure 7-20.

Digital Storyboard.

Digital storyboards can be created using familiar presentation software packages.

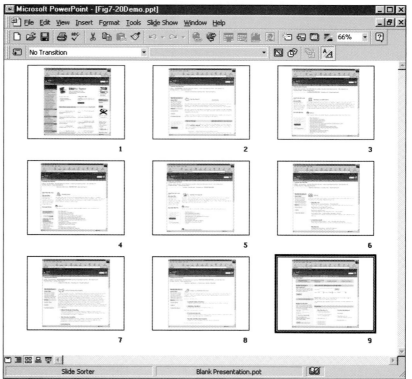

Presentation software such as Microsoft PowerPoint can be used to create sequences of images similar to the paper storyboards (Figure 7-20). With a little tweaking, this can result in a presentable site structure that can be used to gather user and client feedback. In addition, these slide shows can be made into interactive user testing devices. This can be done by providing links to alternate slide numbers. The tradeoffs between paper and digital storyboards are presented in Table 7-3.

Prototyping Tip for Redesigns

Since much of the work of the web designer comes in the form of redesigning previously unsuccessful sites, paper-based storyboarding can yield excellent results early on. Start by printing pages from sections of the old site that you find problematic. Use your favorite mockup techniques to retool the printouts—for example, taping new pieces of paper over the top of the existing ones, whiting out and redrawing, and so forth. Photocopy the new versions to minimize the perceived effects of the changes (this helps to keep the new changes from standing out to the user). Begin testing the new pages.

Wireframes and High-End Prototypes

Wireframes and high-end prototypes provide tools for examining user behavior throughout a task. They can also be used to collect more elaborate and detailed information about how users approach your site. In general, they focus on the structure, scope, and detailed processes of your web site (e.g., an ordering process; Figure 7-21).

Wireframes are often simple HTML pages (or other simulated pages) with a minimum of information and links that can be produced quickly with a site design program such as NetObjects Fusion or a WYSIWYG editor such as Macromedia Dreamweaver. While wireframes traditionally focus on navigation and architecture, they can also be used to test naming, labeling and categorization schemes, aesthetic and branding issues, basic user interface capabilities, use patterns, and functionality (e.g., ordering processes).

In addition, several benefits can be derived from wireframe prototypes. They can resolve uncertainties in the design (operation sequence, functionality, look and feel) and help spot implementation problems early on. You can explore an interactive look and feel and use wireframes to explore design interactions in user testing. Finally they can aid in refining the design.

High-end prototyping is often done in software development but may not be applicable to all web site design projects (it depends on your budget and the time you have to develop the site). However, if you have the time and the

Paper Storyboards

Strengths
- Create quick mockups of the pages (or series of pages) of interest.
- Can be arranged in a structured fashion that can be used for site structure demonstrations or user testing.
- Can be taped or pinned to a wall for analytical use and group discussion.
- Flexible enough for informal and formal user testing.
- Changes to the design can easily be made *during* user testing.
- Changes can easily be made by photocopying the current screens and adding or deleting elements.

Weaknesses
- Limited in scope, low level of interactivity and content.
- Time-consuming to make large changes compared with digital prototypes.

Digital Storyboards

Strengths
- Easy to rearrange components and slides (or pages).
- Useful for presentations to clients.
- Maintain a more engaging and realistic environment for users during testing.
- Often higher quality than paper storyboards, and dramatically easier to maintain a consistent look across many pages.

Weaknesses
- Limited in scope, low level of interactivity.
- Harder than paper to make spontaneous changes while testing users.
- More rigidly linear than other prototypes.

Wireframes and High-End Prototypes

Strengths
- Can explore overall structure.
- Provide a more intuitive and presentable demonstration of site structure (in comparison to traditional system specs and diagrams).
- Great for user testing.
- Explore naming conventions and architectural issues.
- Code can be used for text-only version of site (see sidebar "Double Dipping: Putting Wireframes to Use").
- Useful for proof-of-concept technical demonstrations and for early testing of difficult software systems.

Weaknesses
- Time-consuming to develop.
- Only partial implementation of system.

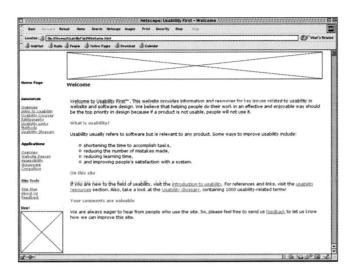

Figure 7-21.

Wireframe.

Wireframes typically focus on the architecture and navigation.

budget, it is more than worth the effort. Gigantic or highly complex web sites require high-end prototypes. They experience the same sort of payoffs from high-end prototypes that large-scale software development projects do.

High-end prototypes have similar benefits to wireframes and in many cases are simply more refined and content-rich versions of wireframes. In addition, high-end prototypes are often used to test algorithms, user preferences, and highly detailed specifics of the design. See Table 7-3 for a comparison of the strengths and weaknesses of various prototyping methods.

You should continue elaborating mockups and prototypes until you're satisfied you have a final design specification. When you are satisfied that it works well, looks good, and that details have been worked out, it's time to prepare the final design and content of the site. The following three chapters on production cover creating the final specifications, elaborating all the details, and, finally, creating the finished material for the web site: text, graphics, and code.

DOUBLE DIPPING: PUTTING WIREFRAMES TO USE

While wireframes can be created at different levels of granularity, more complete versions can actually be used as highly accessible text-only versions of the web site. For example, a well-refined wireframe fleshed out with all the content can make the perfect solution for a text-only browser, PDA, or screen-reading software.

08

PRODUCTION

WRITING FOR THE WEB

WRITING TO COMMUNICATE

Text conveys the content of a web site and helps to reinforce the brand through its tone and style. Given the importance of text in carrying the message of the site, how can text be written to communicate effectively? What makes words *usable?*

The text of a web site should be constructed around three primary goals: draw the reader in, help the reader orient, and convey information. To do this, you need to make your content interesting, enticing, and easy to read. Offer the reader a pleasant reading experience. Help readers decide where they are and where to go next. Help them determine if what they're seeing is relevant, and lead them to places that are relevant to them. Don't waste words. Give readers useful information at the earliest opportunity.

Tasks and Goals

Text needs to be written to support the user's tasks and goals and to suit the intended audience. For the writer, the audience and goals are known from the results of a requirements analysis, and the tasks are defined from a task analysis. The text can then be written around these tasks and goals. For instance, write headlines that match possible goals. If a person may be looking for the price of a product, then write a headline that says, "How much does this cost?"

Write to help people navigate the web site. Help guide the user's actions. Give the user information that aids in decision making. Put things in the order that people need them. Make the steps clear. Directly state what options are available. Of course, the Internet is full of sites that fail to communicate well (see Figure 8-1). The advice in this chapter will help you avoid common problems.

Figure 8-1.

A Page That Doesn't Communicate.

This company home page (*www.bearcreek.com*) has no orienting or descriptive text. A home page should answer some basic questions: What does this company do? Who is this site intended for? Why should it matter to me?

PRODUCTION

Readability and Legibility

For text to communicate effectively it must be comprehensible. *Readability* refers to how much sense the words and sentences make to readers, how clear the vocabulary and grammar are. *Legibility* refers to the visual quality of the text, whether readers can see it well and make out the letters and words.

To make highly readable text, substitute simple words for difficult or obscure words. Replace long sentences with short ones. Replace passive sentences with active sentences.

Some word processors have built-in indexes of readability that you can use to evaluate your prose. These usually indicate a grade level for which the text is appropriate. For the adult mass market, most writing should be targeted at the sixth- to eighth-grade level. However, use these automatic evaluators critically: most of them are designed for evaluating essays and reports and don't necessarily assess headlines, bullet points, and links appropriately, and thus may yield misleading scores. The best way to handle this is to omit sentence fragments from your evaluation and assess only prose passages.

To present highly legible text, use large, easy-to-read fonts and high contrast. Visual limitations such as nearsightedness are extremely common, and illegible text can cause eyestrain as well as make a site completely inaccessible to a large segment of the population.

Types of Writing

While we often think of writers as being responsible for long passages of prose, words are actually used in a diverse set of circumstances (see the different genres of writing in Figure 8-2a–e). To communicate effectively, writers need to thoughtfully compose even the most mundane uses of text, such as page titles, button labels, instructions for form completion, and spec sheets. The Web also enables new types of writing, such as links, animated text, and dynamically generated text. For example, in the dynamic text of Figure 8-2e, users can click on text in a visual thesaurus, and words move and fade as they follow the chain of synonyms.

The Writing Process

The process of writing needs to be organized around several important objectives: to deliver complete and accurate information, to present the information in a useful format for the reader, to achieve a consistent and natural style without typos or other writing errors, and to coordinate among multiple writers drawing from a variety of information sources.

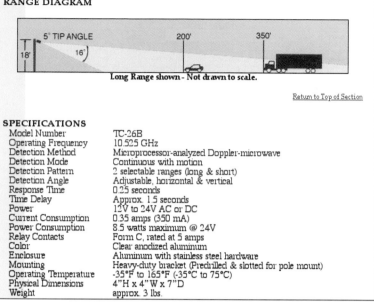

RANGE DIAGRAM

5° TIP ANGLE   200'   350'

18'   16°

Long Range shown - Not drawn to scale.

Return to Top of Section

SPECIFICATIONS

Model Number	TC-26B
Operating Frequency	10.525 GHz
Detection Method	Microprocessor-analyzed Doppler-microwave
Detection Mode	Continuous with motion
Detection Pattern	2 selectable ranges (long & short)
Detection Angle	Adjustable, horizontal & vertical
Response Time	0.25 seconds
Time Delay	Approx. 1.5 seconds
Power	12V to 24V AC or DC
Current Consumption	0.35 amps (350 mA)
Power Consumption	8.5 watts maximum @ 24V
Relay Contacts	Form C, rated at 5 amps
Color	Clear anodized aluminum
Enclosure	Aluminum with stainless steel hardware
Mounting	Heavy-duty bracket (Predrilled & slotted for pole mount)
Operating Temperature	-35°F to 165°F (-35°C to 75°C)
Physical Dimensions	4"H x 4"W x 7"D
Weight	approx. 3 lbs.

News & Events

University of California, Berkeley

[Home] [Campus Map] [Search]

| Highlights | About UC Berkeley | News & Events | Departments | For Students | For Faculty & Staff |

Online Calendar

The Campus Calendar of Events

Care & Use of Animals at UC Berkeley
Fact sheet about the campus' animal care program

Tidal Wave II
Enrollment challenges facing UC Berkeley

Ethnic Studies Update
Get the latest information about what's happening with Ethnic Studies.

Redefining Health Science Research
UC Berkeley scientists are excited about a major new research and education initiative designed to tackle health problems of the 21st century.

Top Stories

Professor finds talking with hundreds of students no laughing matter
Associate Professor Michael Ranney's jokes were falling a bit flat, his humor sometimes failing among the 200 students in his UC Berkeley lecture course. So Ranney decided to take an innovative approach to engaging his students -- he met with each of them individually in his office for five minutes. The experiment, which took him 17 hours to complete and nearly cost him his voice, definitely got the students' attention.
(press release, 17 Feb)

New imaging technique could aid in design of better superconductors
An exciting advance by physicists at UC Berkeley could help unlock the secrets of high-temperature superconductors.
(web feature, 16 Feb)

Law professor John P. Dwyer appointed new dean of Boalt Hall
John P. Dwyer, the John H. Boalt Professor of Law at the UC Berkeley School of Law (Boalt Hall), has been named to succeed Herma Hill Kay as dean of the law school. The appointment requires approval by the UC Board of Regents. It is expected that Dwyer, one of the most prominent environmental law scholars in the country, will assume the deanship on July 1, 2000.
(press release, 15 Feb)

Revised model of protein-drug interactions could make job of drug designers a little easier
While most people may have difficulty distinguishing a person from his or her mirror image, proteins in cells have no such problem. They are exquisitely selective, able to latch on tightly to one molecule but reject its mirror image.

More News

- UC Berkeley Press Releases
- Berkeleyan: campus newspaper
- Web Features
- Berkeley Magazine: Cal's magazine for alumni & friends
- Letter Home: a newsletter for parents of Cal students
- Calendar of Events
- Cal Sports News
- UC Newswire: news for the UC system
- Daily Cal: independent student newspaper

Entertainment

- Cal Performances
- SUPERB productions: student-run entertainment events.

Mmmmm! Tastes So Good!

By Stephanie Jorgl

Miss Charlotte Kruk was born with a sweet tooth, smack dab in the heart of Silicon Valley. One day, while working on a sculpture project at San Jose State University, she came up with a tasty idea: recreating 1950's fashion by designing cute, tart little dresses — but out of a recycled materials.

"I needed something sensational for my show at school," says Kruk. So she decided to use candy wrappers as the theme for her designs, and to create a whole exhibit to communicate the importance of appreciating the package, beyond just consuming the contents.

"I hated the stuffy sort of gallery scene about the art department — I mean, everybody who is anybody knows that the people just come for the food. So, I decided to really exaggerate that concept by naming the exhibit 'And I Earned Every Calorie,'" says Kruk. "Naturally, the crowd ate it right up!"

You Are What You Eat

First came the Bit O Honey bikini and the Tootsie Roll gown. Then, Kruk's roommate spotted an ad for the

Kruktart on Display

The pieces have been shown and sold in art galleries and museums, including the San Jose Museum of Art and the San Jose Institute for Contemporary Art and featured in newspapers, magazines and on television.

Not only has she recently been featured on the Roseanne Show and the Home and Family Show at Universal Studios, but her dresses have been written up by Jane Magazine, West Magazine and the fashion syndicate Mary Gottschalk.

An Expensive Sweet Tooth

Now, it might all sound a bit sugar-coated, but Kruk's dresses sell for a pretty chunk of change. The Junior Mint dress was snatched up by a bank president's wife for $1,600, and a jeweled copper headdress — with candy wrappers mounted beneath the glass inlays — sold for $2,300.

And with the wild flavors that Kruk is used to putting into her fashion art, it's no surprise that she uses a tangerine iMac to design, maintain and serve her dandy candy website. Go Live, Photoshop and Illustrator are all she uses beyond her trusty circa 1970 Elna "Happy Homemaker" sewing machine — and the candy, of course.

Figure 8-2c.

Essays and prose fiction (www.apple.com/hotnews /articles/2003/03/kruk).

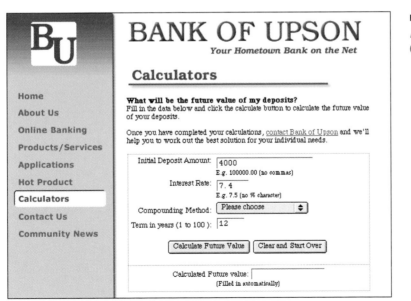

Figure 8-2d.

Forms (www.bankofupson.com).

(Continued)

Figure 8-2e.

*Dynamic text
(www.visualthesaurus.com).*

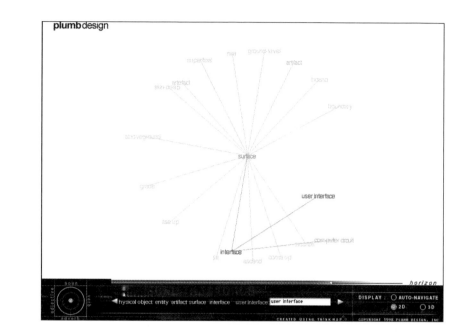

The following process achieves these objectives but needs to be applied flexibly to respond to the demands of the project. See the sidebar "The Writing Process" for a concise summary.

1. Plan the Project

The planning meeting for developing web site content is usually combined with an initial planning meeting for the entire web site project or comes soon after the requirements analysis is completed. The planning meeting must answer the questions that follow.

What Content Will Be Required for the Site?

This generally is drawn from an initial outline of the site and a good understanding of the main tasks and goals being supported.

Where Will the Text Come From?

Will the text be written by the client organization, a marketing firm, a freelance writer, or the web site designers? Or will the text be repurposed from existing marketing materials? This is a good time to ask whether the client minds if client-supplied text is edited to optimize it for the Web (reformatting, breaking the text into smaller chunks, adding headlines, and rephrasing to fit the specific online context). In our experience, most clients are happy to allow their text to be modified within reasonable limits.

What Project Deadlines Need to Be Set?

When will source materials need to be provided? When can interviews take place? When will final text be delivered?

2. Define a Style Guide

All but the smallest of web site projects will involve multiple authors, and a style guide is a crucial element in achieving consistency, quality control, and consideration of usability principles in the writing. A style guide (see sidebar "Example Content Style Guide") establishes writing standards in terms of tone, voice, structure, and layout, and it states common usability guidelines. It explains preferred file formats (e.g., which word processor to use). Finally, a style guide specifies corporate standards, such as trademark and logo usage and preferred slogans and terminology.

Usually the *writing* style guide will be developed alongside a style guide for the graphic elements of a page, specifying common fonts, colors, and layouts. The style guide is used not only by the writers but also by the HTML programmers and testers, who use it to verify that they are interpreting and formatting text correctly. When possible, it's good to include a writing sample with the style guide for other writers to imitate in preparing materials. In some cases, it may be enough to simply ask that the writers imitate the style of a favorite web site.

It's okay if your style guide gets modified as you go. It's rare that you'll know all the important considerations until you've started writing. Just make sure that all of your writers are kept up to date on any changes, and watch out for the hidden costs of rewriting if you make a change that forces major restructuring of what's already written.

3. Collect Information

The content of the site may come from any number of sources, depending on the nature of the site. In many cases, library research, newspapers, and other web sites may provide critical information. In particular, competitive web sites may help to identify important pieces of information that need to be conveyed and may even suggest how to structure the information for maximum impact.

Brochureware

For corporate sites, much of the information may come from company literature, marketing materials, brochures, technical reports, user manuals, and so forth. In many cases, the simplest approach to getting this information online is to reuse the text from those sources. Web sites based entirely on previously existing collateral are often derisively called *brochureware* because the text can seem flat, dense, and irrelevant. Text developed for print often relies on the fact that readers can skim easily and skip pages quickly as they flip through a lengthy brochure. Reusing this print material can be an important time-saving approach, but it requires that writers reorganize the material and break it up for more effective reading online.

EXAMPLE CONTENT STYLE GUIDE

This style guide provides your client organization with standards for developing and presenting text. Such standards minimize the complexity of editing content for consistency. Specific standards will almost certainly vary for each organization. A style guide should rarely allow poor usage (such as using blue text for headers), but may often disallow perfectly good usage in order to maintain a coherent style (for instance, this guide strictly prohibits text in all caps, which might otherwise be acceptable in some limited contexts).

This document establishes some standards for writing in order to achieve a consistent voice and content that is both readable and effective for web site users. These guidelines will also be used by the web site developers to proofread web pages.

Writing Style

- Use the active voice.
- Refer to our company in the first person (when pronouns are used at all), such as, "We put our customers first." (That is, never refer to our company as "it" or "they" or "the company.")
- Refer to the reader in the second person, as in "Our customers are important to us. Your needs drive all of our efforts."
- Use direct, simple sentences.
- Divide the text into small, easy-to-read chunks.
- Provide factual and content-rich information. Avoid anything that would be perceived as advertising copy or fluff.
- Put the main themes at the top of every page. Put the main themes in the first sentence of each paragraph.
- Present lists as bulleted items, not as prose.
- Use clear section titles, and liberally include headings where they help users to quickly find information.
- Avoid ambiguity. Avoid trying to draw people in with incomplete teasers. Give them the information they need as soon as possible and as succinctly as possible.

Formatting

- Align all text to the left, including headers and paragraphs.
- Separate paragraphs with two line breaks. Put one blank line before headers and no blank lines after headers.
- Don't use smart quotes (curly quotes). Use only straight quotes and apostrophes.

(Continued)

- Avoid special characters that may not be available in HTML. If you have the opportunity, you can save the developers a lot of time by providing a printed copy of any pages that use unusual characters, with those characters highlighted. Examples of special characters that may require extra work to reproduce include em dash (—), copyright (©), trademark (™), registered trademark (®), cedilla (ç), umlauts (ü), micro (µ), yen (¥), pounds (£), degrees (°), and Euro (€).
- Use bold to highlight words and phrases. Do not use italics (which can be difficult to read on the screen). Do not use all caps.
- Do not rely on variations of font and font size. These are not reliable across platforms on web browsers or with different user preference settings.

Spelling and Trademarks

- Make sure all trademarks, service marks, and registered trademarks are labeled according to the standard corporate reference.
- "Web site" is two words.
- Use American English spellings throughout.

Writing for Search Engines

- Make sure your text includes common terms that may be used to search for your information.
- For each page, provide a one-sentence (25 words or less) description of the page that will be used in a hidden description field (this is the description many search engines will provide in their listing of search results).
- For each page, provide a short set of keywords that will be used in a hidden keywords field.
- With your keywords, include common misspellings and alternate spellings (e.g., "web site" and "website").

Content Delivery Format

- The web site development team can convert between several text formats, including Word, PowerPoint, Excel, plain text, RTF, Quark, and PageMaker. However, new content will be easiest to work with if it is created in Word or in plain text. Please do not convert your text to HTML. It is also helpful to provide the development team with a paper version to verify the format of the text and for proofreading.
- Graphics content can be delivered in almost any standard graphics format, including EPS, Photoshop, TIFF, GIF, JPEG, Freehand, Illustrator, BMP, and PICT. To maintain the highest quality, avoid using a compressed format, such as GIF or JPEG, and provide the highest-resolution version you have. If electronic versions are not available, we can scan camera-ready print versions.

Interviews

When text needs to be written from scratch, the most common approach is to interview subject matter experts, usually people within your client organization who have expertise in the area you're writing about. For technical specifications, interview the engineers. To determine the marketing message and emphasis, interview the marketing organization. Interviews need to be scheduled with ample time because of the frequent need to reschedule. Tell the interviewees ahead of time how long the interview is expected to last, what topics will be covered, and what materials they can bring to help out. In many ways these interviews will be similar to the user interviews discussed in Chapter 3, "User Needs Analysis," especially when designing intranet sites. During the interviews, be efficient, focusing on the information you need.

Purchasing Content

A final way to acquire content is to purchase it from external sources. For instance, you may wish to buy an article from a freelance writer or buy a tip list that you found on another web site. In many, if not most, cases you won't be permitted to modify the text or redistribute it in any form other than that for which it was purchased. Be sure to clarify who owns the copyright, and if you don't own it, identify what you are allowed to do with the text.

4. Write

The process of composing online text is the same as writing for other media. First, collect all of the information together and make notes. From the notes you should be able to form an outline and rearrange the information into a clear flow and group related items. After that is done, divide the material into appropriate pages and sections and write the text. Finally, review the written text and keep rewriting.

Writing material from scratch is a time-consuming process, so it's helpful to get feedback on your writing approach as soon as possible. Review the detailed outline with others, and draft a representative web page to review with clients and users before completing the text for the entire site. You can often coordinate this with the initial design mockups by asking the client to review and approve the mockups and the text together. As with design mockups, early review helps avoid the problem of needing to redo a substantial amount of the writing work.

5. Review, Test, and Rewrite

At this point, the writing needs to be evaluated and revised. Review the text in the following ways to uncover potential improvements: proofread, test users, have it reviewed by a trained editor for voice, tone, grammar, and so forth, have it reviewed by all the stakeholders (clients, fellow designers, users, and subject matter experts), and review all web writing guidelines and your own style guide to make sure the writing conforms.

Then swallow your pride and make the changes that are necessary. Be sure to allocate time in your project planning for rewriting. It will be very tempting at this stage to skip it when deadlines are pressing.

Form 8-1, the Writing Guidelines Checklist, is a useful tool for evaluating whether your writing will be effective. (Download from *http://www.mkp.com/uew/*.) Many of the individual guidelines are taken from this chapter, although the list doesn't attempt to follow the exact order of presentation as the chapter.

HOW PEOPLE READ

Most key principles of writing are derived from an understanding of how people read. This ensures that readers are able to see the text, understand it, remember it, and apply it to their own situation.

What's the Task?

People read differently depending on what they're trying to accomplish. Think of reading as goal-directed. When sports fans get their latest copy of *Sports Illustrated* in the mail, they may read it cover to cover. However, when someone goes to the library to find out who won the 1927 World Series, they search and scan to get to the information as quickly as possible, and they're very unlikely to stop and read an advertisement or a special-interest story.

Scanning the Page

In studies by Morkes and Nielsen (1998), 79 percent of test users always scanned the page rather than reading every word (though 16% *did* read word for word, so things aren't perfectly clear-cut).

Users were more successful at remembering the content of a web site when the text was more concise, more objective, and more scannable (with bulleted lists, headings, and highlighted keywords). Online readers typically scan the text for the most salient features, trying to complete their tasks with minimum distraction and without reading any more than they have to (Figure 8-3).

Writing Guidelines Checklist

Content
- ☐ The content of the web site provides value to the user.
- ☐ The writing supports the reader's task.
- ☐ The user is not required to read or navigate through irrelevant material to reach relevant material.
- ☐ The text includes a call to action.
- ☐ The reader interacts with the text as much as possible.
- ☐ The information is accurate, authoritative, and up to date.
- ☐ The information will be easy to maintain.
- ☐ Items that need to be regularly updated have been documented.

Readability
- ☐ The text is comprehensible and targeted at the right reading level.
- ☐ Sentences are short, direct, concrete, and active.
- ☐ New information is grounded in known information.
- ☐ Text is in lay language, avoiding jargon, insider references, and obscure humor.

Legibility
- ☐ The typeface is legible and the font size is sufficient.
- ☐ Italics are avoided except at large sizes.
- ☐ Boldface and all caps are only used for short pieces of text. (Boldface is preferred over all caps.)
- ☐ Text has sufficient contrast with the background color and is not placed over a conflicting pattern.

Scannability
- ☐ Emphasis is provided with appropriate headings, lead-ins, and pull quotes.
- ☐ Opening sentences and paragraphs summarize the content.
- ☐ Text is short, simple, and concise.
- ☐ Text is specific and objective.
- ☐ Text is broken into useful chunks and bulleted lists.

Orientation
- ☐ Page titles provide useful orienting clues.
- ☐ Headings match the reader's goals.
- ☐ Readers know where they are and what each page is about.

(Continued)

Pagination

☐ The text is divided between pages based on user tasks (i.e., pages are divided so users can skip portions irrelevant to them).

☐ If scrolling is required, the user has appropriate cues within the text that more material is present, and horizontal rules are avoided.

☐ Pages are self-explanatory: each page stands on its own.

Technique

☐ Fundamentals are sound: grammar, spelling, capitalization, and punctuation.

☐ Tone is natural and accessible.

☐ Style is consistent.

☐ Terminology is unambiguous.

☐ Active sentences are used.

Links

☐ Static text is *never* blue or underlined.

☐ Text links are left in the default color.

☐ Different types of links are distinguished graphically (e.g., audio clips vs. video clips).

☐ Link text is descriptive and specific.

☐ Email links explicitly show the email address.

☐ Links don't cross punctuation or line breaks.

Forms

☐ The order of steps through the form is clear.

☐ Submit buttons are clearly labeled with descriptive text.

☐ Reset buttons are avoided.

☐ Required fields are clearly labeled.

Metatext

☐ Metatag description and keywords are provided for each page.

☐ Non-body text is specific and consistent: titles, ALT text, captions, headings, and buttons.

Writing for Screen Readers

☐ Text is concise.

☐ The top of the page contains meaningful, page-specific information.

☐ Link names are self-explanatory.

Format

☐ The layout does not depend on a specific typeface or font size.

☐ The specified typeface works well on all platforms.

☐ The default font size of the browser is used.

☐ Semantic tags, rather than format tags, are used wherever possible.

☐ Text aligns with graphics on the page and with other text blocks.

☐ All centered text on the page is centered around one axis of symmetry.

☐ Related text doesn't appear in multiple columns.

☐ Headings are closer to their body text than to other text on the screen.

Intellectual Property

☐ The copyright notice is present and in the correct format.

☐ Trademarks and service marks follow corporate standards.

☐ Company branding is strictly adhered to.

☐ No information is confidential or sensitive.

Standards

For each of the following, specify the standards this site will follow:

- Person: ☐ 1st and 2nd person (recommended), or ☐ 3rd person

- Commas before the last item in a list: ☐ "A, B, and C" (preferred), or ☐ "A, B and C"

- Punctuation within quotes: ☐ traditional punctuation ("text,"), or ☐ logical punctuation ("text",) (preferred)

- Header alignment: ☐ left, ☐ center, or ☐ right

- Paragraph format: ☐ double-space between paragraphs, or ☐ indented opening of paragraphs

- Common spelling, hyphenation, and capitalization conventions, e.g., ☐ Internet or ☐ internet, ☐ web site or ☐ website, ☐ email or ☐ e-mail

- Preferred file format for text files (e.g., plain text, RTF, Word, HTML)
  _____

- Preferred file format for figures (e.g., EPS, Photoshop, TIFF, PICT, BMP, gif, jpeg) _____

Figure 8-3.

Scanning the Page.

People take in what they can at a glance, so the focal point of the page is very important (*www.pets.com*). (a) The original web site. (b) What web users typically see when they look at a page. (c) What their dog sees.

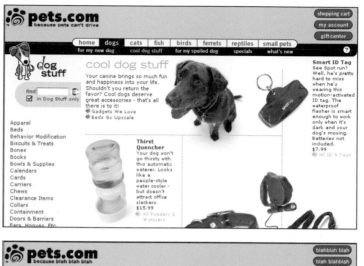

(a)

(b)

(c)

Of course, this doesn't mean there won't sometimes be articles that people might want to read from head to toe, such as research articles, news stories, or fictional narratives.

Morkes and Nielsen also found that their users hated "marketese," marketing fluff with exaggerated and empty claims, and that credibility was important. Credibility was influenced by "high-quality graphics, good writing, and use of outbound hypertext links."

Literacy

Consider the literacy level of your target audience. Are you targeting an international audience? Many of your readers may be nonnative speakers who will appreciate direct, concrete statements and common terminology.

Will children be browsing your web site? If so, keep the vocabulary and complexity appropriate to their grade level. Keep in mind that, while reading is fairly automatic for literate adults, this skill develops over several years. If you have a large header saying "Click here to buy," adults will read it without effort and without even specifically intending to. But readers in their first few years of learning generally must explicitly make an effort to read, even when the text is at the appropriate reading level.

The problem of designing text for young readers is that you must overcome what is essentially just an extreme case of the adult tendency to skim the page. Readers of all ages are looking for a least-effort approach to getting to their goals. Young readers are even more inclined to infer their required next step from the layout of the page and the most salient elements—the big fonts and bright colors. They almost solely read text that's isolated and brief and text that occurs along their critical path.

The Given-New Approach

A common problem for any writer stems from knowing too much about the topic and unconsciously relying on implicit assumptions. The reader then fails to understand references in the text. To achieve a writing style that flows from one item to the next, each element should first present a "given" piece of information and then follow up with new information in relation to the given information.

In direct, active sentences, the given-new approach is typical. This is also called the *topic-comment* approach. For instance, in the sentence "My car broke down," the topic is "my car" and the comment, or new information about the topic, is "broke down." The approach applies at all levels—sentence, paragraph, and page. Ground your comments in terms of what is already known, and establish new information from which you can branch out. Because the writer already knows all the information, this can be difficult to put into practice, but an editor can spot the problem right away, so rely on a second pair of eyes.

Levels of Processing

Readers' memory for what they've read is increased through more active engagement with the text. Glancing over the surface structure of a page will leave the least memory trace. Actively reading for meaning will increase retention of a passage. Actively visualizing as you read and thinking through implications and relationships with other things you know will further improve memory for the passage. A writer may encourage these activities with a phrase as simple as "Visualize this . . ." or "Imagine what you could do with this. . . ." Integrating the material through multiple modalities, combining text with illustrations or diagrams, will produce greater memory for the content.

A way to even further engage the reader and increase memory for your message is to bring the reader into the passage by personalizing it. If you have profiles of your users, then use their names, refer to their interests, appeal to their concerns. If the users can be encouraged to interact with the content, then they will be even more likely to retain what they read. Get them to choose preferences, choose options, and determine the outcome of a passage.

Reading on a Screen

For a variety of reasons, text is less legible on a screen than at the same size on paper (Figure 8-4). Text on a screen usually has less contrast than on paper, and the angle of viewing is less flexible, meaning that readers have more difficulty adjusting reading conditions to their specific needs, and thus may have greater eyestrain and neck strain in reading. Another contributing factor to poor legibility is screen resolution. In particular, words in italics can be particularly hard to read on the screen at small sizes because of inadequate screen resolution. As a result, increasing the font size may be necessary to improve reading conditions, and text should be displayed at a maximum contrast between foreground and background.

Type that appears within graphics can be tweaked for improved legibility, but small sizes should be avoided. In addition, avoid putting any text over a patterned or textured background—this creates visual noise that makes the text harder to interpret (Figure 8-5).

Figure 8-4.

Text Legibility Is Critical.

Text is less legible when it has strong shadows, is too small, or is in italics, as in this example (*www.secure -banking.com/home*).

Figure 8-5.

Legibility over a Background.

This chart on *www.fidelity.com* exemplifies a typical problem. While the background stripes are attractive, they shouldn't ever go behind content, especially text at such a small size. It may still be possible to decipher these numbers correctly, but the stripes slow down the interpretation. The number "6" (in red) can be mistaken for an "8," and because of the stripes, the central horizontal bar might be missed and it could be confused with a "0." A careful choice of fonts, or hand-tweaking of the letterforms, could avoid the top loop of the "6" forming a full circle as it does.

WHAT TO WRITE ABOUT

What's the first thing a visitor to your web site needs to do? What's the second thing? What must the readers absolutely do before leaving the page: Contact you? Make a purchase? Bookmark the site? In writing, focus on the reader's tasks first. More than anything else, include a *call to action,* an opportunity for the user to take the most important step relating to your business goals.

Provide Value

Give the reader a reason to come to your site. Your site *specializes* in something. That means you're a *specialist* at something. Share your knowledge. Don't just throw the reader a bone; make sure it has some meat on it. If you can't pay your readers money, then give them information, tutorials, spec sheets, tips, links to other web resources, anything it takes to convince them to tell their friends that you have something on your site that they can't get elsewhere.

Marketing

When you're talking about your products and services, be factual. Provide information, not hyperbole. It's okay for your information to have character, style, and a point of view, but make your products relevant to the reader— state the benefits and uses. Make the site vital.

Quality of the Information

Users prefer information with legitimacy, information that is honest, accurate, up to date, and based on reliable, expert sources. Information should not only live up to these standards but needs to convey a sense of authority as well. Whenever possible, provide precise, detailed information and provide sources and dates. This is particularly appropriate in subject areas such as health and politics, where conflicting and misleading information is very common.

Keeping Current

One of the most common problems is keeping the web site up to date. When calendars are not updated regularly, links pages have broken links, or pages have "Under Construction" signs for indefinite periods, the reader's trust is undermined. After seeing so many web sites that have stayed online without ever having been updated, visitors are quick to conclude that an out-of-date site is one that will never be updated, and so they'll seek other sites that are more current.

Writers need to plan for the effort required to maintain information that goes online. Some maintenance problems can be avoided by leaving out links that may be unreliable and omitting dates and events that won't be removed in a

Figure 8-6.

"Coming Soon," but When?

Clicking the "Coming Soon" link at *www.thebettyfordclinic.com* doesn't give additional information. (Is this actually even *the* Betty Ford Clinic? The design style certainly doesn't suggest that this is the official site.)

timely fashion. Never label a site "Under Construction"—all web sites evolve over time. If it's important to let the reader know that more will be coming (see Figure 8-6), let them know what it will be and when it will arrive, as in "Coming Soon! Our product spec sheets will be online in June." Then be accountable to the date you've promised. This lets readers know specifically when they can return to find the information they need. If you can't guarantee the deadline, then don't announce anything.

Types of Pages

Different types of pages have different content needs, depending on the purposes they serve. The following provides suggestions for several of the most common kinds of pages.

The Splash Page

A splash page is a visually rich and exciting page that visitors see when they first enter a web site (Figure 8-7). In theory, visitors see the splash page, get totally thrilled by the site, and then click through to the actual home page. Splash pages are usually intended to show off what a company can do to excite their customers with flashy animations. Instead, what can happen is that visitors wait a long time for the splash page to download, can't figure out what the company is about, have difficulty figuring out what to do next, and abandon the site before entering it. A splash page adds one more step for users to get to the content they need, and thus one more opportunity for them to give up before completing their task. Don't do it!

The Home Page

While some sites abandon the idea of a home page, it's a convenient metaphor that users understand (Figure 8-8). They can always return to the

Figure 8-7.

Splash Page
(*www.cocacola.com*).

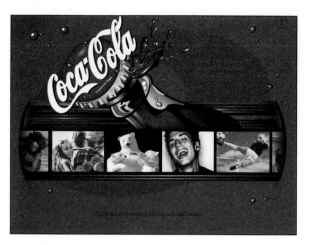

Figure 8-8.

Home Page
(*www.franceweb.fr /poesie*).

home page to reorient themselves. When a visitor first enters a web site, the home page has a lot of responsibilities to fulfill. It needs to download quickly, communicate the nature of the site (e.g., what the company does), establish the corporate image, communicate what information and services are available on the site, keep the users interested so they will explore further, and help route the users to their appropriate subpages.

About Us

While information about a company—its history, mission, and values—is easy for a company to put together, About Us pages tend to get very few hits. Still, an About Us page or section can provide useful information (Figure 8-9). Readers know what information to expect there, and the few who

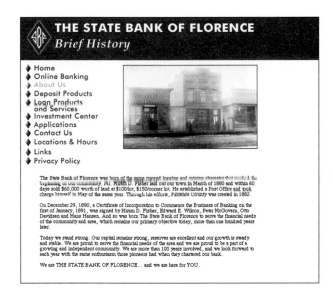

Figure 8-9.

About Us Page
(*www.florencestatebank.com*).

have an interest will visit. Others will just ignore it. A problem with many About Us pages is that they say nothing meaningful. Marketing messages such as "we have the best customer service at a competitive price" don't mean anything without concrete details or examples. What aspects of your customer service make it so good?

Products and Services

The Products and Services page is often the most important piece of information for marketing and e-commerce sites, so focus on making it easy to access, extremely clear, and detailed (Figure 8-10). Often, when you have relatively few offerings or they fit into well-defined categories, you'll want to avoid having a Products or Services page, and instead simply include direct links to each product, product category, or target market from every page of the site. For instance, a pet food store would be better off having top-level links to Cat, Dog, and Fish Products than having a Products page that links off to these categories. This saves a step for the user and helps communicate the types of products you offer right from the navigation bar.

Contact Us

Avoid having a Contact link simply pop up an email program with the email address. This can be confusing (especially when users are sharing a computer, so the email isn't configured right for all users), but also misses the opportunity for other types of contact. In many cases, when contact needs to be

Figure 8-10.

Products and Services Page
(*www.medstat.com*).

encouraged, full contact information (address, phone, email) should appear on every page. If that's not done or there are too many possible contact addresses to list on every page, a dedicated page is useful and appropriate (Figure 8-11). Put the most important contact information at the very top of the Contact page, and if other email addresses or phone numbers are listed, be clear which one should be contacted for what type of question. Rather than relying on email, feedback forms are often more convenient. They don't depend on users having their email configured correctly, and feedback forms can include specific questions to help more clearly identify the user's needs. Prepare a plan for responding to any email you get. If you're not ready to provide timely responses to questions, don't encourage people to contact you.

Privacy Policy

While privacy policies are not needed for many sites, they are important whenever information is being collected about the user. While most users won't read the policy, the presence of one can increase trust and may protect you from customer complaints. Think carefully about how you need to use the user information, and make sure you actually conform to the policy you specify. Don't simply promise users that you "won't spam them." That's subjective. Instead, tell them exactly how you will and won't use their information. The HON Code of Conduct (see Figure 8-12) goes even further than the typical privacy policy with detailed usage guidelines.

◄Home

Company Profile
& Contacts

Qualitative
Research Services

Quantitative
Research Services

Marketing
Planning Services

Client & Project
Descriptions

Ann Arbor
Area Resources

Contact
PTM Research

Company
PROFILE & CONTACTS

PTM, founded in 1983, has an excellent reputation for quality marketing research and consulting services. Our team of experienced professionals uses a comprehensive range of strategies to help you achieve your objectives. We use standard and innovative approaches that are individualized to meet the diverse needs of our clients.

Key Team Members

Deborah Babcock, President and CEO

A marketing analyst and researcher for almost 25 years, Deb is experienced in all facets of marketing research, both qualitative and quantitative, as well as marketing planning and communications. She has spearheaded projects ranging from product marketing plans to nationwide marketing surveys and community public opinion polls. Deb holds a summa cum laude BBA from Saginaw Valley State University and has completed quantitative and qualitative research course work through the Burke Institute and Anderson Niebuhr & Associates. She is a member of the American Marketing Association and serves on the board of directors of numerous community, trade and nonprofit organizations.

Figure 8-11.

Contact Us Page
(*www.ptmresearch.com*).

Health On the Net Foundation

**HON Code of Conduct (HONcode)
for medical and health Web sites**

Principles

HONcode

▶ Introduction
▶ How it started
▶ Self-regulation
▶ Users
▶ Principles
  ▶ Chinese
  ▶ Danish
  ▶ **English** 📄
  ▶ Finnish
  ▶ French
  ▶ German
  ▶ Italian
  ▶ Japanese
  ▶ Polish
  ▶ Portuguese
  ▶ Russian
  ▶ Spanish
  ▶ Swedish

Authority
1. Any medical or health advice provided and hosted on this site will only be given by medically trained and qualified professionals unless a clear statement is made that a piece of advice offered is from a non-medically qualified individual or organisation.

Complementarity
2. The information provided on this site is designed to support, not replace, the relationship that exists between a patient/site visitor and his/her existing physician.

Confidentiality
3. Confidentiality of data relating to individual patients and visitors to a medical/health Web site, including their identity, is respected by this Web site. The Web site owners undertake to honour or exceed the legal requirements of medical/health information privacy that apply in the country and state where the Web site and mirror sites are located.

Attribution
4. Where appropriate, information contained on this site will be supported by clear references to source data and, where possible, have specific HTML links to that data. The date when a clinical page was last modified will be clearly displayed (e.g. at the bottom of the page).

Justifiability
5. Any claims relating to the benefits/performance of a specific treatment, commercial product or service will be supported by appropriate, balanced evidence in the manner outlined above in Principle 4..

Figure 8-12.

Policies Page
(*www.hon.ch/HONcode/Conduct.html*).

Copyright Policy

Copyright law applied to online content is still in its formative stage. As such, if you have considerable concerns, you should definitely consult with legal counsel for specific ways to protect your information. In most cases, identifying each web page with a copyright notice (e.g., "© 2001 Acme Products, Inc.") should suffice. However, those who want to show caution in specifying how their content should and should not be used may find the need for a more detailed page of copyright information.

Help

In user testing, we've found that users will frequently try out a Help or Frequently Asked Questions page when they have trouble finding information. So, while your ideal site will be extraordinarily easy to use, a more realistic approach is to use a Help page to help introduce people to the site, answer frequent questions, and guide people to the relevant sections of the site (Figure 8-13). Write the help text from a task-based point of view: each section of help should specifically address a particular task and goal of the user and give step-by-step instructions, rather than simply describing the pieces of the web site. Provide your contact information for a final level of customer support, so users can ask questions directly by phone or email.

Site Map

For very small sites, a site map shouldn't be necessary. At around 20 pages or less, the navigation of the site can be made sufficiently clear to avoid a site map entirely. When a site map is needed, avoid unusually large graphics. People don't usually go to the site map to see nice pictures. They're there in order to get somewhere else. Make the structure very clear and focus on revealing the hard-to-find sections that may not be apparent from the primary navigation (Figure 8-14). Large sites won't be able to list *every* page, so they'll need to decide which pages can be omitted in favor of listing the section. Give descriptive text explaining each section, so users don't have to depend on section titles alone.

Error Pages

Easy to overlook, well-designed error pages are essential to helping users resolve their most difficult problems (Figure 8-15). An extremely common error is an incorrect URL, producing a "404 Not Found" message.

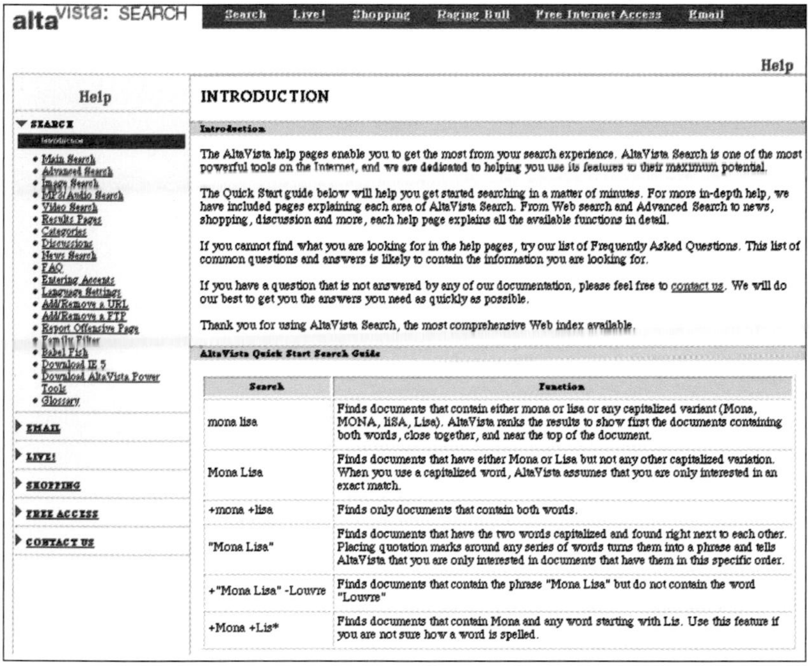

alta^{vista}: SEARCH Search Live! Shopping Raging Bull Free Internet Access Email

Help

Figure 8-13.

Help Page
(www.altavista.com).

Help
▼ **SEARCH**
Introduction
• Main Search
• Advanced Search
• Image Search
• MP3/Audio Search
• Video Search
• Results Pages
• Categories
• Discussion
• News Search
• FAQ
• Entering Accents
• Language Settings
• Add/Remove a URL
• Add/Remove a FTP
• Report Offensive Page
• Family Filter
• Babel Fish
• Download IE 5
• Download AltaVista Power Tools
• Glossary
▶ **EMAIL**
▶ **LIVE!**
▶ **SHOPPING**
▶ **FREE ACCESS**
▶ **CONTACT US**

INTRODUCTION

Introduction

The AltaVista help pages enable you to get the most from your search experience. AltaVista Search is one of the most powerful tools on the Internet, and we are dedicated to helping you use its features to their maximum potential.

The Quick Start guide below will help you get started searching in a matter of minutes. For more in-depth help, we have included pages explaining each area of AltaVista Search. From Web search and Advanced Search to news, shopping, discussion and more, each help page explains all the available functions in detail.

If you cannot find what you are looking for in the help pages, try our list of Frequently Asked Questions. This list of common questions and answers is likely to contain the information you are looking for.

If you have a question that is not answered by any of our documentation, please feel free to contact us. We will do our best to get you the answers you need as quickly as possible.

Thank you for using AltaVista Search, the most comprehensive Web index available.

AltaVista Quick Start Search Guide

Search	Function
mona lisa	Finds documents that contain either mona or lisa or any capitalized variant (Mona, MONA, liSA, Lisa). AltaVista ranks the results to show first the documents containing both words, close together, and near the top of the document.
Mona Lisa	Finds documents that have either Mona or Lisa but not any other capitalized variation. When you use a capitalized word, AltaVista assumes that you are only interested in an exact match.
+mona +lisa	Finds only documents that contain both words.
"Mona Lisa"	Finds documents that have the two words capitalized and found right next to each other. Placing quotation marks around any series of words turns them into a phrase and tells AltaVista that you are only interested in documents that have them in this specific order.
+"Mona Lisa" -Louvre	Finds documents that contain the phrase "Mona Lisa" but do not contain the word "Louvre".
+Mona +Lis*	Finds documents that contain Mona and any word starting with Lis. Use this feature if you are not sure how a word is spelled.

Figure 8-14.

Site Map
(www.pages.ebay.com).

eBay™

home | my eBay | site map | sign in

Browse | Sell | Services | Search | Help | Community

▶ Tell eBay how you want to be contacted.
▶ Cars on eBay? Buy or sell YOURS now!
▶ Preview Smart Search — simple way to refine search.

Search | tips
☐ Search titles **and** descriptions

Browse
· **Categories**
  Antiques & Art
  Books, Movies, Music
  Coins & Stamps
  Collectibles
  Computers
  Dolls, Doll Houses
  Great Collections
  Jewelry, Gemstones
  Photo & Electronics
  Pottery & Glass
  Sports
  Toys, Bean Bag Plush
  Everything Else
· **Featured** don't miss!
· **Hot**
· **Grab Bag**
· **Great Gifts**
· **Big Ticket**
· **Gallery**
· **Category Overview**
· **New Today**
· **Ending Today**
· **Completed Auctions**
· **Going, going, gone**
· **eBay Official Time**

Services
· **Services Overview**
· **Registration**
  Register now
  Confirm registration
  I forgot my password
· **Buying and Selling**
  Manage My Items for Sale
  Revise my item
  Add to my item description
  Change my item's category
  Feature my item
  Fix my gallery image
  Promote your listings with link buttons
  Cancel bids on my item
  End my auction early
  Relist my item
  Mister Lister bulk upload
  PowerSellers
  Services
  Seller Accounts
  Check my seller account status
  Make payments toward my account
  Place or update my credit card on file with eBay
  Request final value fee credit
  Cash out your credit balance
  Buyer Tools
  Billpoint Online Payments
  Retract my bid

Community
· **Community Overview**
· **News**
  Announcements
  Cool happenings
  Latest buzz on new features
  Calendar
  Letters to the founder
· **Chat**
  Chat Rooms
  The eBay Cafe
  The AOL Cafe
  Discuss eBay's Newest Features
  Wanted Board
  Holiday Board
  Emergency Contact
  eBay International
  Category-Specific Chat
  Advertising Collectibles
  Antiques
  Barbie Bulletin Board
  Beanie Babies
  Books
  Car Chat
  Coins
  Comics
  Computers
  Diecast
  Dolls

Figure 8-15.

Error Page
(*www.diamondbullet.com*).

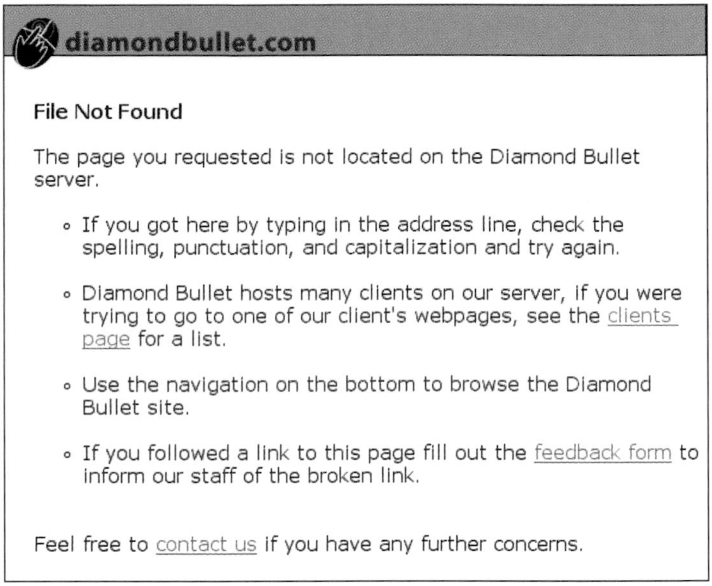

Such a message isn't terribly helpful to the user. A good error page needs to have the following:

• A clear identification of the problem (don't use obscure error codes).

• A clear set of options for resolving the problem. That is, if the error represents a missing page, provide tips on finding the correct page and access to a site map or search engine.

• A page style consistent with the rest of the web site, providing branding, and helping the user understand the source of the error.

Be sure to test that your error pages display correctly on all browsers.

Elements of a Page

For most sites, the elements of a page are relatively straightforward, but for complex interactions it's helpful to create a page schematic. A page schematic is an abstract page layout that specifies each content element on the page, such as titles, headers, navigation buttons, body text, footers, sidebars, metatags, and advertisements. Used in conjunction with a site outline, the page schematic unambiguously identifies every piece of content that will be needed for a site. This works especially well when multiple writers must coordinate their efforts. Without it, pieces can be left unspecified and the HTML coders end up patching in their best guesses for these pieces or scrambling to coordinate with the writers at the last minute.

Navigation

The navigation area need not be simply an arbitrary list of links. Rather, you should order and group the links, and provide appropriate emphasis. On some pages, such as the home page, a brief description may be associated with each link. The navigation area may also be used for bylines or announcements, but keep in mind that users won't be expecting other information within the navigation.

Page Titles

Users need to understand where they are in a web site. In fact, given that they may end up on a subpage directly from a search engine or outside link, the page needs to identify the web site itself as well as the particular page within that site. A web site name and logo are common forms of site identification. The page title should be specified within the `<title>` tag and will appear in the window's title bar. This title is especially useful for outside sites such as search engines to identify the page. However, users rarely read the title within the title bar and redundancy is extremely helpful. Most pages will benefit by having an obvious page title at the top within the displayed page.

Body Text

In your main body text, plan the sequence of ideas carefully. Break up the text into meaningful chunks. Lead the readers' eyes with headers, bullet points, and appropriate emphasis. Use topic sentences, and proceed from most to least important. Your goal is not to captivate every reader, but to draw in readers who need your information, and let readers know that they can leave if you aren't going to provide the information they need. Avoid sensationalism. "Shark kills hundreds!" will work as a teaser for a movie preview, but it will annoy readers of a journal article if you are referring to hundreds of fish.

Quotes and Sidebars

Pull quotes and sidebars help break up the monotony of long pieces of text. Pull quotes are phrases from the body of the text that represent an important and interesting statement (Figure 8-16). A pull quote usually appears in a distinctive font in the margin or as a floating element within the text. Readers may browse the page by reading pull quotes, so the highlighted statement should not be misleading, and can be useful to draw a reader in to a long passage.

Sidebars provide information that doesn't fit into the main flow of the text, such as anecdotes, summaries, or alternative perspectives. Keep sidebars short so that readers do not lose their place while scrolling up and down to read them.

Figure 8-16.

A Pull Quote.

A pull quote highlights an important phrase and helps readers scanning the passage to preview the content.

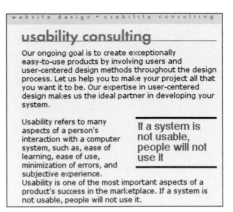

The Footer

A footer typically contains text links, copyright information, privacy policy and usage policy links, and credits. Text links help provide redundancy when the primary navigation uses graphic links, and they are especially useful at the end of long pages to help guide the reader to the next page. Text links are not always appropriate in a footer when the primary navigation uses text links and the page is so short that additional text links provide more clutter than assistance. Including the URL of the page in the footer can help users locate the page again after they've printed it.

Last Updated Date

Some people recommend placing a last-updated date in the footer, such as "This page last updated on July 9, 1995." This information may be valuable to some users who can learn whether the information is current. An older date may indicate that the site is not maintained regularly. Similarly, a recent date suggests regular attention to the site. With so many pages being created and many of them not maintained at all, this can be a significant data point. On the other hand, a common problem is that people maintaining the site forget to update the date.

Maintaining the date becomes a maintenance problem in itself, and an incorrect date is far worse than no date at all. Some automated tools will update this date every time the page is modified—an excellent solution for those who have these tools available. However, most corporate sites prefer that users assume that *all* pages are up to date and should only put information online that can be maintained regularly. In this case, pages of static content should not identify their last-updated date, and dates should only be indicated where

appropriate for time-sensitive material (e.g., conference announcements, coupon expiration dates, and news items). Information that is two years old may be perfectly accurate, but it gives the impression of not being so if the date is identified.

Corporate Identity

Before beginning a writing project, obtain the corporate guidelines for trade-mark use. Trademarks and service marks protect the use of names, symbols, and phrases. As with all intellectual property, the degree to which a trademark can be enforced depends on a variety of factors such as whether the trademark has been registered, the degree to which it is used consistently, and the degree to which the company is diligent in protecting its trademarks. Be sure to determine which product names and slogans are trademarked and how they should be written and used. Capitalization and spelling must be exact, and some guidelines may require that trademarks only be used as adjectives or that they occur with the term "brand" whenever used (e.g., "XYZ brand pota-to chips," not "XYZ chips"). Incorrect usage may weaken the enforceability of the trademark or be misleading to the consumer.

Advertising for Somebody Else—Links, Credits, and Awards

Should you make references to other web sites by providing link pages, by putting up an award that someone granted your site, or by listing credits for vendors or partners? As with all decisions, it boils down to whether these help your users accomplish their goals and are consistent with your business goals. A links page can be useful but should provide focused, relevant infor-mation. Check all links to make sure they are stable and credible. Ask your-self, Does linking to an outside site, or putting its medallion on your page, contribute to your bottom line (see Figure 8-17)? Does it lend authority to what you have to say, or does it lower your credibility? If it's irrelevant, omit it.

WRITING STYLE

For maintaining consistency in your writing, writing style should be established in your style guide, including the choice of voice, person, tone, and formality.

Voice

The active voice is generally better than the passive voice. Active sentences are more direct and easier to understand. Passive sentences are only appropriate for formal, conventionalized speech, or in the rare occasion when no active agent can be determined.

Preferred: Active voice—"We offer the following services."

Undesirable: Passive voice—"The following services are offered."

Person

First-person sentences are generally best. (First person includes *I* and *we;* second person includes *you* and *you all;* third person includes *he, she, it,* and *they.*) Most corporate or organizational web sites prefer the first-person plural, *we.* Most individual sites should be written in the first-person singular, *I.* The "royal" *we* (using *we* to refer to yourself as an individual) should be avoided. Refer to the reader as *you.*

Preferred: First and second person—"We want to provide you with the best service possible."

Undesirable: Third person—"XYZ Corp. provides customers with the best service possible."

Tone

Fit the tone to your organization and the image it wants to project, but for online text, don't be afraid to be informal, casual, chatty, direct, and hip. Avoid educated words. It's possible to go too far and be too casual for some sites, but overly formal writing is the more common error. Cyberspeak should push the edge toward a more personal tone. Readers are accustomed to this online. Their attention spans are shorter, and their tolerance for the bland is lower. Slang and idiom are fine, even preferable to help communicate clearly, but pull the reins in if you intend to be understood across cultures and across language communities. Most of all, be sure the tone is appropriate to your audience.

Use humor cautiously. Your audience can be rather broad, and you can't be sure of the context in which they're reading your jokes. Avoid using hip terms if they obscure your meaning. Natural, conversational language should help clarify, not complicate, the meaning. While you may use slang (and even technical jargon for a technical audience), avoid using insider language that is used within your organization but which your users may not know.

Grammar, Spelling, Capitalization, and Punctuation

Make your teachers proud by getting the basics of grammar, spelling, capitalization, and punctuation right.

Standards

Decide what standards guide to use, whether it's the *Chicago Manual of Style* (1993), Strunk and White's *Elements of Style* (Strunk 1979), or *Wired Style* (Hale 1996). The *Columbia Guide to Online Style* is useful for getting online references right.

Determine standard spellings and capitalization. Will you use American or British English spelling? Will "Internet" be capitalized? Is "web site" or "home page" one or two words? As words come into common use, they tend to lose their capitalization, and two-word combinations become hyphenated and then close up into single words. Therefore, cutting-edge usage usually drops the hyphen on common word pairs.

Consistency

Be consistent in what you write. For instance, when you have a list of three or more items, should you place a comma before the final conjunction (i.e., should it be "A, B, and C" or "A, B and C")? We suggest the first because it is completely unambiguous—the second version might be interpreted as the item A and the combination of B and C. However, for such relatively minor differences, self-consistency is more important than exactly which standard you follow.

Punctuation

Decide if you'll use "traditional punctuation," where commas and periods occur inside the quotes (a standard that helped make the presses more reliable in the ancient days of movable type), or if you'll use "logical punctuation", where punctuation comes outside the quote unless it's intended to be part of the quoted text. Pick a convention and stick with it.

Sentence Fragments

What could possibly be more important than having perfect grammar? Simplicity. Clarity. And having fun along the way.

Your English teacher may not approve of using sentence fragments, but as long as your reader is happy about what's going on, you're doing well. While you want to avoid obviously awkward and incorrect grammar, feel free to break the rules responsibly when it improves the readability of the text. Don't feel that you have to follow strict grammar rules as long as your sentences are clear and your grammatical variations are inconspicuous. Often, sentence fragments can communicate more quickly and with less clutter.

Writing Guidelines

The following are detailed usage guidelines that address some of the most common problems with online text.

Watch for Ambiguity

Does an "Order Now" button order an item immediately, or does it take you to a page where you can specify your order? This type of confusion makes users nervous and steers them away from buttons that might have undesirable effects. A link that says "Enter Order Information" is less ambiguous. Watch out for other types of confusions such as these:

- "Correct Order": Does it mean that the order is correct or that you want to fix the order? Avoid noun/verb/adjective ambiguities like this one (see Figure 8-18).

- "Correspondent": We needed a link for this on a TV news web site. However, in user testing several users chose this link when they wanted to contact the business, confusing it with the term "Correspond."

- "Confirmation" and "Verification": What's the difference between confirming an order and verifying an order? Nobody's sure. Avoid subtle distinctions like these.

Provide Emphasis

Provide a hierarchy of information. Go from most to least important, from overview to detail. Keep key information at the top, and show the structure by choosing appropriate headers and subheaders. The most important information should be the most obvious and should require the least amount of effort to read.

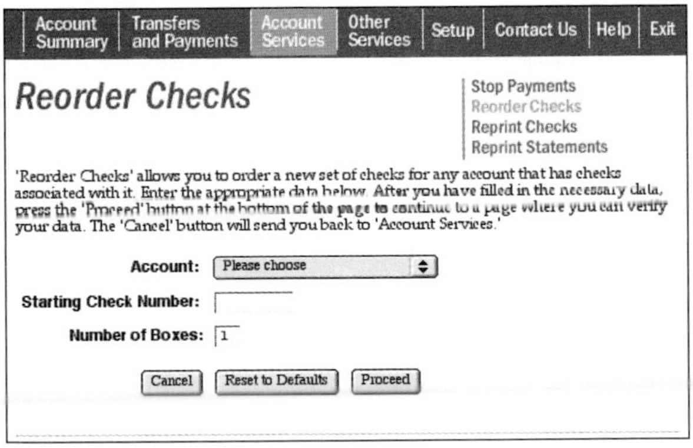

Figure 8-18.

Ambiguous Titles.

"Check Orders" was the originally proposed but highly ambiguous title for this page. This is from a web banking application that allows users to order a new set of blank checks when their checks run out. "Order Checks" is ambiguous too. In the end, we chose to call it "Reorder Checks," making it clear that "Reorder" is being used as a verb.

Highlight text in useful ways. Consider highlighting lead-ins in bold or with a font that stands out. A lead-in is a phrase that starts a paragraph and draws the reader in, like a topic sentence. Use pull quotes to break up long passages of text and help the reader skim the text for interesting entry points. Finally, relate text to the associated graphics. A good design works to integrate the text and graphics into a coherent message and style.

Be Direct and Concise

Keep your language simple and avoid wordiness. Answer readers' questions as soon as possible, using appropriate topic sentences. Imitate the style of journalism: start articles with answers to the questions of who, what, where, when, why, and how. Avoid using teasers that open questions in the reader's mind without answering them until much later. Especially avoid teasers that create a desire for more information that isn't satisfied until another page.

Be Specific and Objective

Instead of saying "We're the best," say why: "Our prices are the lowest," "We rated number one in surveys of customer satisfaction," "We have the lowest return rate in the industry," or "If our moms can love us, so can you." This is not only more useful to the reader, but it lends authority by being factually based. Avoid labeling things generically. Instead of saying "Our Services," it's usually better to say what those services are: "Legal Services," "Shipping Capabilities," "Consulting," or "Auto Repair Services."

Break Up the Text

Use short paragraphs that divide information into useful chunks. Sometimes only one or two sentences are needed in any given chunk.

Use Bulleted Lists

Bulleted lists are helpful to highlight the parallelism in multiple items. However, a common mistake is to use unusual, custom-designed bullets. Avoid bullets that look like buttons and resist using shadows and three-dimensional shading. Bullets should help the user identify the structure of the text but shouldn't draw attention to themselves. Even the default bullets (•) will sometimes be mistaken for buttons by novice users. If you take the time to select custom-designed bullets, we've found that open circles (○) or small dots (·) work best.

Use Frequent Headings

Headings help the user skim to the relevant portion of the text. They should fit the user's goals and match the question the user has in mind:

How do I contact XYZ Corporation?
Call us toll-free at 1-800-XYZ-CORP.
24 hours a day, 7 days a week.

Or the heading can be presented as a phrase:

Contacting XYZ Corporation
Call us toll-free at 1-800-XYZ-CORP.
24 hours a day, 7 days a week.

Or better yet, if you can keep it short, use a heading that both matches the user's question and answers the question:

Call us at 1-800-XYZ-CORP
Toll-free. 24 hours a day. 7 days a week.

What makes a bad heading? One that doesn't match the user's goals even while it gives information. One that gives the least important information first:

BAD: **Toll-free service 24 hours a day**
          You can call us at 1-800-XYZ-CORP.

Another troublesome approach is a heading that tries to be a teaser, to sound fun and interesting, but fails to explain what information the section will contain:

BAD: **And a friendly voice answered, "Hello, can I help you?"**
          You can call our friendly salespeople at our toll-free help line
          at 1-800-XYZ-CORP.

HOW WRITING FOR THE WEB DIFFERS FROM WRITING FOR PRINT

There are some basic aspects of the web experience that affect the way text is written. For instance pages are easy to fix and change and are therefore more transient than paper. The user population generally has some knowledge of computing and the Internet. The context of the Web is usually more informal than paper. Technology constrains the display and navigation of the text. And text can contain links and other interactive elements.

Non-Body Text

When writing, don't forget the non-body text such as titles, ALT text, captions, headings, metatags, and buttons. In many cases, these "labels" may be more useful to the user than the body text. These labels need to be written with appropriate language for successful search engine matches.

Every page needs to have a clear title to help orient people within the page content. Most users don't read the page title that appears in a window's title bar, so it's not safe to rely solely on the `<title>` tag to communicate a page title. However, the `<title>` tag is still necessary both to meet user expectations and to support automated tools evaluating a page (such as search engines). Make sure that page titles match the link labels that go to them; otherwise, users who click the Contact Us link may be confused when they reach a page titled "Feedback Form."

ALT text is text that appears in place of an image before the image loads or when the user has images turned off (Figure 8-19). Be aware that ALT text may be clipped when the text appears within a graphic that is too small to display the text.

Figure 8-19.

ALT Text.

ALT text provides helpful clues about an image that may be displayed when a user mouses over the image. ALT tags are also critical, as shown here, to help users who are browsing with their images turned off (usually to speed up download). Remember, though, not to rely on the text being visible if the graphics are too small to display the ALT text without chopping it off.

Text-Only Browsing

Even in these modern days, users will sometimes browse without downloading images, relying on the text content of pages. People have different reasons for doing this, but a common reason is that images take dramatically longer to download. This is likely to become less common over time, but is likely to remain an issue in the short term.

In addition to voluntarily choosing to turn images off, some users may not be loading images because they are constrained by technology, usage environment, or visual impairments. For instance, many users of PDAs (Palm Pilots and related devices) are limited to viewing only the text portions of a web document. Users may also prefer voice interfaces for hands-free web navigation, such as in-car interfaces or certain industrial environments, and voice interfaces will require good text design.

Supporting Screen Readers

Screen readers are devices used to speak the text of a web page. These are primarily intended for people with visual impairments. Text can be optimized for screen readers to minimize the aggravation of waiting for long passages of text and to help people using voice navigation to move around quickly. A good way to test pages for their accessibility by screen readers is to view them in a text browser with a keyboard interface, such as *lynx* (see Figure 8-20).

With screen readers, users may have facilities to jump easily to the next heading or next link, but otherwise scanning the page can be quite difficult. As users jump to each link, they'll hear the link being read aloud, so link text needs to be especially self-explanatory, avoiding labels like "click here." To optimize the speech synthesis, avoid acronyms, unusual spellings, and unusual characters. The speech synthesizer is likely to spell out odd characters and words that it can't pronounce. Write tersely, and get to the point quickly. Make sure the pages start with meaningful, useful text, rather than, for instance, advertising copy or lengthy lists of links. Generic header text at the top of every page may be difficult to skip in a voice interface.

Scrolling

How long should a page be? Unlike with paper documents, people can't easily gauge how long a web page is. Text "below the fold" (using the newspaper analogy, text beyond the first screenful of text that the user sees) may not seem to exist at all unless there are clues that the page continues onward. Furthermore, horizontal rules can create "false bottoms" (see Figure 8-21). As soon as readers see horizontal rules, they often assume they've reached the

PRODUCTION

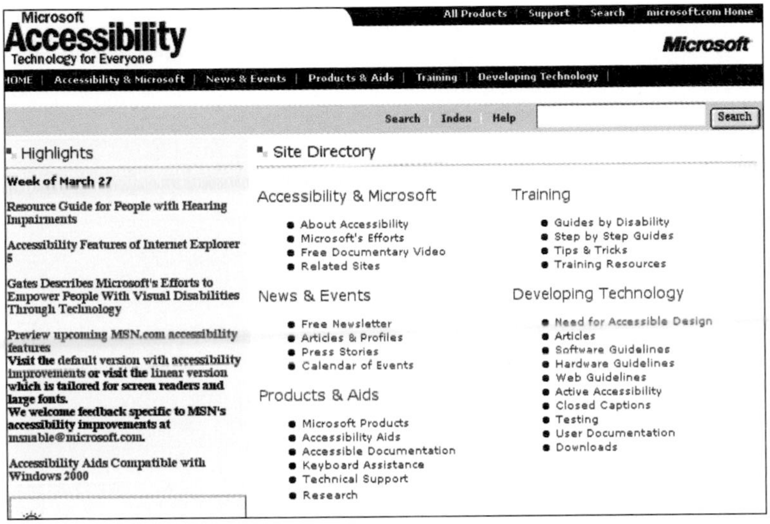

Figure 8-20.

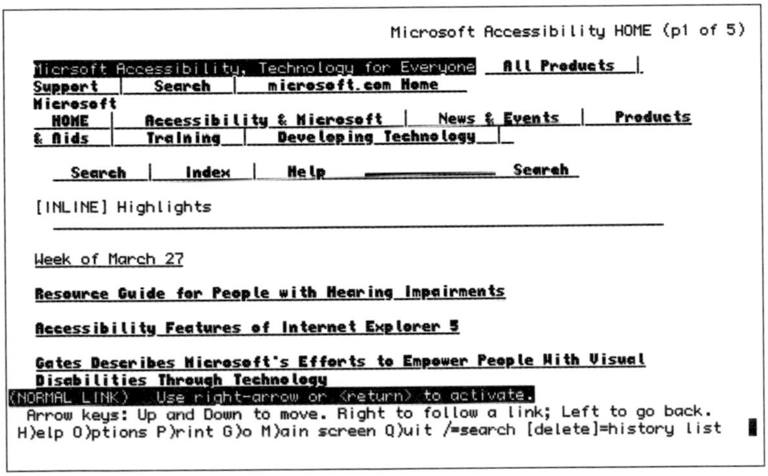

Accessibility for the Visually Impaired.

(a) Typical browsers display this graphical view of Microsoft's accessibility page (*www.microsoft.com /enable*).

(b) The corresponding view in *lynx*, a text browser, gives an approximation of the text that would be spoken by screen-reading software.

end of the text (thus, horizontal rules should be avoided in most contexts). For a suggestive study of readability, especially addressing "the fold" and horizontal rules, see *Web Site Usability: A Designer's Guide* (Spool et al. 1997).

You often need to direct readers' eyes and direct their scrolling to move them past the end of the screen. How? Text and images that are cut off in the middle will imply that more is below, encouraging users to keep scrolling. Vertical lines can also be used to imply that the page continues on.

Figure 8-21.

False Bottoms.

A page with a "false bottom" (a) seems to end even though more information is available; but when it's seen with a split image at the bottom (b), this implies that more is available.

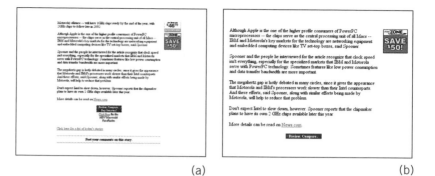

(a)   (b)

Breaking Text into Multiple Pages

At a certain point, text needs to be broken up into multiple pages to improve navigation and download time. When this is done, some pages may be needed as *router pages,* such as home pages and site maps, whose primary function is to display the structure of the web site and help people find relevant content. In most cases, every page should have useful content and only specifically designated router pages (e.g., site maps) should contain navigation alone. A common mistake is to have a main page for a section that contains only links to subpages and doesn't actually provide useful summary information.

Pages should be divided up to support the task. Ask yourself, Does the content belong together because of a unified theme? Will it be easier to scroll to the content or to follow a link? Most often it makes sense to divide the content into more pages up until the point where additional pages disrupt the flow of work or make navigation significantly more difficult (see Figure 8-22).

Figure 8-22.

Page Broken Up That Should Be Unified.

In this example, a news article is arbitrarily broken into multiple pages. You need to do this in a printed newspaper, but there's no especially good reason to do so on a web site.

Internet standards-based ISP/ASP arena. The Sun-Netscape Alliance appears to have a clear advantage with its iPlanet messaging server products already widely deployed. Assuming the IMCS vendors can get scalability and reliability right, two questions remain. First, are their rich feature sets attractive enough to open some space in the seemingly closed society of the ISP/ASP? Second, will companies, large and small, agree to outsource this business-critical function to ASPs? The next year should bring some answers. We remain skeptical that the commercial IMCS vendors can move into this arena with any big numbers.

The shipping versions of the IMCS products from Lotus, Microsoft and Novell have been available for many months: Microsoft Exchange 5.5 since the fourth quarter of 1997, Novell GroupWise 5.5 since the fourth quarter of 1998 and Lotus Notes/Domino R5 since the first quarter of 1999. Until now, the vendors have been providing service packs (to fix known bugs) and supplying small enhancements. Lotus and Novell won't ship new versions of their IMCS products until mid-2000 or later. Microsoft released Beta 3 of Exchange 2000 in October and is shooting for a new version to be released in the second quarter of 2000.

PAGE: 1 | 2 | 3 | 4 | 5 | 6 | NEXT PAGE

When using multiple pages, make sure that each page stands on its own. Don't assume that users have had to navigate from the home page to get there except when you force them to go through a page such as a login screen. Often users will arrive at a subpage through a search engine or a cross-link on another web site. Pages should indicate what web site they belong to as well as help the user identify where they are within that web site.

Forcing a Message in Front of the User

As users browse, it's often possible to force them through a specific screen or path, usually for marketing reasons. For example, when users enter a web site, they may see a splash page that they need to click through before gaining access to the remainder of the site. A set of screens that one must click through is called an *entry tunnel*. One screen leads to the next and on to the next before a user ever has the option of navigating to the relevant subsection of a site. This approach to advertising, known as *interstitial advertising,* places ads on the path between useful links. For advertisers this can be a powerful technique, since users must interact with the ads in order to continue— unlike television commercials from which the audience can escape by walking to the kitchen for some avocado dip.

Other methods of forcing a message on the user include bringing up dialogue boxes and opening up new browser windows with additional information (Figure 8-23). Marketing people may love these techniques, but they add window management work for users. Interstitial advertising adds steps to users' tasks, thus slowing them down, distracting them from their primary task, and increasing the likelihood that they will abandon their current goals and possibly leave the site altogether.

Links

Web technology grew out of hypertext research in the 1980s and early 1990s. Hypertext research studies the creation of nonlinear documents, where links connect documents in associative webs. This allows users to guide their own reading rather than having authors do it for them. However, the result is often a fragmented and confusing traversal of links. Thus, a web author can still assist the user by structuring the way links are organized.

Blue and Underlined = Click Me

Writing for an interactive medium requires a special sensitivity to the user's thinking process and requires that you make distinctions unnecessary in print. First of all, we must distinguish which text is a link and which text is static text. Blue and underlined text is readily recognized by

even inexperienced users as links. Various studies have shown that using another color for a link dramatically reduces the number of click-throughs for that link, and using graphics for the link reduces the number of click-throughs even further. The most straightforward explanation of this observation is that users are simply less certain that other colors might represent links and are therefore unlikely to notice those links or are more reluctant to try them out.

Thus, for maximum click-throughs, we recommend that you avoid changing the default color of text links. If you decide to override the default, make sure that links are extremely obvious (see Figure 8-24).

Users can set preferences in their browsers to change the default link colors and the default underlining of links. In some cases, you may need to shift link colors to a different shade of blue for legibility (for instance, when a black background is used), but this may still confuse users who have altered their default link color or turned underlining off, so alternate background colors need to be considered carefully. Since different browsers can sometimes have different default colors for visited links (e.g., purple and green), it's a bad idea to shift the color of a visited link.

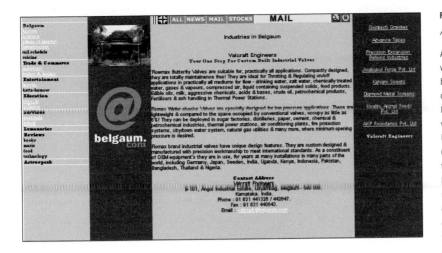

Figure 8-24.

Appropriate Link Color.

A common design problem crops up when using a dark-colored navigation bar. Default blue links aren't legible on dark backgrounds, so it's tempting to change the link color to something visible on a dark background. Unfortunately, as on this web site (*www.belgaum.com*), the lighter links then won't show up well on a light background. Style sheets can be used to produce different link colors on different parts of the page, or you can avoid designs where links would fall on dark backgrounds, so the default blue links can be used.

Some designers like to use black links because black creates a more relaxed color scheme, but this is extraordinarily likely to confuse users, especially those who have link underlining turned off.

Other designers like to use red links because red is an especially salient color, but the logic of doing so is somewhat flawed. Yes, red is very salient, and this means the users' eyes will be attracted to red words, and users may be more likely to click those words, but we're not trying to get users to follow links just because they are perceptually salient. If that's all we wanted, we could use the `<blink>` tag on all links. We want users to click on links that are relevant to their tasks. Instead of using red for links, use red to draw the user's attention to important content.

Never display *static* text in blue or use underlining for anything other than a link (see Figure 8-25). Alternative shades of blue may be acceptable in certain limited contexts, such as when the typeface and font size are changed to make headlines, but these should be user tested to confirm that users don't confuse them with links.

In addition to the high recognition value of blue underlined links, text links have a distinct advantage over graphic links because browsers support differentiating between visited and unvisited links, which is not possible when graphics are used. Users quickly learn to take advantage of this information when browsing; without it, they often find themselves needlessly revisiting pages on a site that they don't remember having visited earlier.

Figure 8-25.

Link or Not a Link?

"Chapter 3" (in the table of contents) is actually not a link, but static text presented in blue and underlined, presumably to make the links look more uniform. But the result is that users are uncertain why the links aren't working when they click there (*www.cox.smu.edu/faculty/sconger /pdews/ch3.htm*).

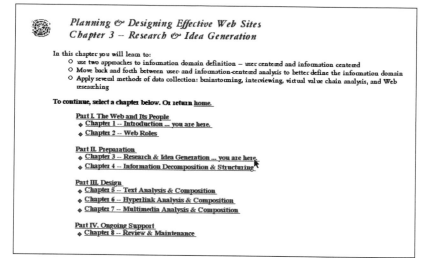

Link Color, Underlining, and Consistency

Use blue underlined links whenever possible, but no matter what, make sure your link style is consistent. In all fairness, ensuring consistency can be extremely difficult for very large sites, such as Microsoft's, as can be seen in Figures 8-26 through 8-31 (*msdn.microsoft.com*), which demonstrate a variety of common problems in displaying links.

Types of Links

Not only do you need to distinguish which text is interactive, but you want to indicate what type of interactivity is implied by a button or link. A linked word may lead to the definition of that word, to reference material, to more detail on the topic, to another section of the web site, to an outside site, or to another location on the same page. Some hypertext systems use menus or multiple colors of links to indicate different types of references, but web technology doesn't facilitate making these distinctions. When graphics are associated with links, the graphics can indicate the kind of link by their style.

Another useful way to indicate the type of link is to use a link title. A TITLE parameter is available for links in some browsers; these show a specified message when the user positions the mouse pointer over a link, as seen in the following example.

```
<a href="http://www.usabilityfirst.com/" title="a
reference web site for usability">Usability First</a>
```

The TITLE parameter helps disambiguate the type of a link without an extraordinarily detailed explanation within the body of your text.

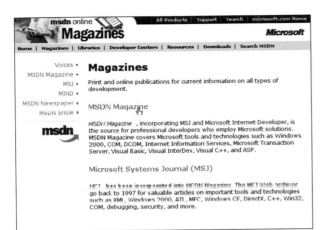

Figure 8-26.

Links: Blue and Not Underlined.

Although Microsoft Internet Explorer shows links as underlined by default, on their web site they turn off underlining through style sheets.

Figure 8-27.

Links: Inconsistent and Not Underlined.

This page shows at least five different link styles, and the relationship between them isn't very clear.

Figure 8-28.

Links: Inconsistent Underlining within Same Page.

Although Microsoft doesn't use underlining for links, on this page they turned underlining back on for *some* of the links. As a result, users have no way of knowing which items of text represent links and which don't—they have to explore every single text item to find out.

Figure 8-29.

Links: Inconsistent Color between Pages.

Microsoft's usability page uses a different link style. The rest of the site uses blue nonunderlined links, but this section uses black underlined links.

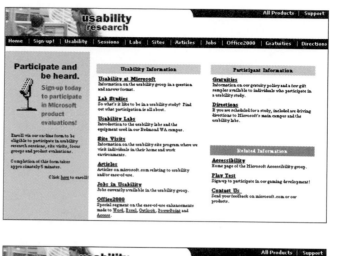

Figure 8-30.

Links: Black Links Are Hard to Spot.

Black links are a bad idea because the user might have underlining turned off, as shown here, and wouldn't see any links at all.

Figure 8-31.

Links: Visited Link Color.

If black is the default color for unvisited links, what color should visited links have? No matter what, don't use blue for the visited links, as was done here. The user is likely to have the opposite interpretation.

Writing the Text of a Link

A link name should answer the questions, Where will I end up? What will this do? Be descriptive, not obscure. Longer link names can be better if they provide more useful information, but not if words are redundant or implicit. Thus, "About Us" is better than "About the Company" because it is shorter and because "the Company" doesn't usually provide any useful information to the user. In an unambiguous context, simply "About" is even better. Still, "About" is relatively vague, and if you have a specific story to tell, it's better to be interesting and informative in the link. If your About section is really a corporate history, in some cases the link should say something like "Our Growth: from a garage in 1977 to a multinational empire today . . . " (see sidebar "User Testing Link Names.")

Do not let a link cover punctuation or run across multiple lines. This tends to make one link look like two or more. You can often prevent undesired word-wraps within a link title by using nonbreaking spaces (in HTML).

Also, make sure the meaningful words in a sentence are linked, not just the "click here" text, as shown in the following example.

BAD: <u>Click here</u> for information about our products. <u>Click here</u> to read about our service guarantee. <u>Click here</u> for testimonials from our customers.

The problem with linking to "click here" text is that users can't scan the page to assess where to click—all they see is a sea of links to "click here."

BETTER: Click here for information about <u>our products</u>. Click here to read about <u>our service guarantee</u>. Click here for <u>testimonials from our customers</u>.

Of course, the "click here" text is clichéd and vacuous. While it's okay to say it now and then, and sometimes even more clear to do so, in most cases you can edit out the "click here" and use more meaningful wording.

EVEN BETTER: <u>Our products</u> are effective and affordable. <u>Our service guarantee</u> ensures your 100% satisfaction. Still have doubts? Read our <u>customer testimonials</u>.

At this point, a remaining problem is that the text is too generic and too subjective. What are "our products"? Who would consider them affordable? The following example still gets the marketing message across, but in no uncertain terms. This last version provides dramatically more useful information than the original version with only a few extra words.

BEST: Our tennis shoes cost less than name brands. Our service guarantee promises no waiting in line EVER! Our customers will tell you that they prefer XYZ Shoe Stores.

Don't hide an email address within a link. If you want an email link on every page, instead of linking Contact Us with a *mailto* link, link the actual email address (e.g., dbd@diamondbullet.com). Everyone recognizes an email address, and by displaying it, users can select and copy the address, print it out, or write it down. A common problem, especially when computers are shared, is that email preferences are not correctly configured in the web browser, so this enables users to see the address and type it directly into their own mail software.

USER TESTING LINK NAMES

You can grab users to generate and test link names fairly quickly and easily, much as we describe testing icons in Chapter 9, "Design Elements."

Generating Link Names

Write down a list of descriptions of each web page, and ask users to brainstorm labels that would be appropriate for each page (in most cases, you'll want the link names and the page titles to match). Combine ideas from several users, or select the most common suggestions for link names.

Testing a Link

If a link may stand alone on a page without any description, the best test is to provide users with a link name and ask them to explain what type of page the link would go to. If the description of the target page is inaccurate, you'll often understand from the testing what types of changes are likely to be helpful.

If links are likely to occur in groups, as in most navigation bars, test the set of links as a group. Users are likely to make better predictions about a link if they can rule out possibilities or gain contextual clues from adjacent links.

When to Use PDFs

The proprietary Portable Document Format (PDF) from Adobe has become a common standard for delivering documents over the Web because its formatting can be practically guaranteed on all supported platforms (Figure 8-32). The PDF format is especially appropriate for document printing because of its organization around the size of a printed page. The PDF format is also useful for archival documents that you do not intend to modify because updating a PDF document essentially means regenerating it, and users can be prevented from modifying the document. PDFs are also commonly used when large numbers of documents are already formatted for print and the cost of converting them to HTML (and maintaining both print and HTML versions) would be prohibitive.

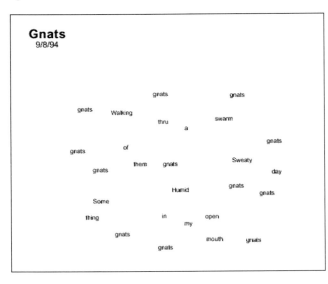

Figure 8-32.

An Example Use of PDF.

A PDF can be used for documents whose formatting would be difficult in HTML, such as this visual poem.

Not all users will have the PDF plug-in for their browser, and PDFs may be entirely inaccessible to some users (such as those whose screen readers can't handle the format). As with other plug-ins, there are a variety of reasons users may not want to download the software (security, memory available on their platform, compatibility, not wanting to spend the time or interrupt their task, uncertainty of the benefits), so PDFs shouldn't be used when you need to guarantee that the information is accessible to all of your users. However, when the user population is known (as on an intranet), you may be able to guarantee that all users have the plug-in.

TEXT FORMATTING

How can text be formatted and organized on a page to facilitate reading? HTML introduces a number of formatting complexities that aren't an issue for print documents. The user may change font sizes, default colors, and layout properties. The sizes of the screen and of the browser window are variable.

The Unpredictability of Typefaces and Font Sizes

The exact appearance of text in HTML is not entirely predictable, thanks to platform differences and the ability of users to modify font preferences. We therefore discuss some common solutions to achieving desirable typefaces and font sizes.

Typeface

While it's possible to specify a particular typeface within HTML, typefaces are not sufficiently consistent across systems to confidently ensure the user will see a specific typeface. In most cases, we can only consistently distinguish among serif, sans serif, and typewriter typefaces. For some purposes, we may be able to specify a more interesting typeface that will improve the appearance for a small class of users, but it's rarely worth the effort. In the cases where it's absolutely critical to get the right typeface, the text can be created as a graphic, but this should rarely be needed.

At the time of this writing, the common serif typefaces are Times, Times Roman, and Times New Roman. The common sans serif typefaces are Arial and Helvetica. The common typewriter typefaces are Courier and Courier New. These options work in a wide variety of circumstances. Unfortunately, other popular typefaces, such as Futura and Optima, are not reliable in HTML text. Futura, for instance, is available from dozens of type manufacturers with widely variable spacing and quality, and so, even if the user actually has Futura, you can rarely be sure what name it goes by or what it will really look like.

Among the common typefaces noted above, there is still a big problem. Most of these typefaces were designed deliberately for print, not for the screen. As a result, while Times may be moderately legible on the screen, it's not the best option, and Helvetica appears cramped and cluttered on the screen. Most platforms have typefaces called *screen fonts* specially designed for easy reading on the screen. On the Mac platform, Geneva is a particularly legible sans serif screen font and is an excellent choice for small text (but isn't very attractive at a large font size). Verdana is a sans serif screen font from Microsoft available for both Mac and PC platforms that works quite well in most contexts (although Geneva is still probably preferable for very small text); however,

Verdana does not come standard with all systems, so you can't really depend on it. We suggest that you include Verdana and Geneva as the first options in specifications for sans serif typefaces (but exclude Geneva for larger text), with more standard sans serif typefaces as backups when those are not available, as shown in the following example.

```
<font face="Geneva, Verdana, Arial, Helvetica">
```

Font Size

In conventional HTML, a web page doesn't specify a particular font size, but merely sizes that are relatively smaller or larger than the default. This allows each web browser to determine the best default font size to work with, and each user can raise or lower the font size easily to optimize the legibility or compactness of the text. Pages can then be displayed in very large sizes for presentations or for the sake of users who are visually impaired.

The problem is that the layout at different font sizes may not be optimal. At small sizes, the page can seem cramped, and the graphics may dominate the text without connecting effectively with their associated text. At large sizes, the text can have unacceptable line breaks and may actually not be able to fit into the screen space allocated for it.

As a result, extra space needs to be left in any layout to allow for variable sizes of text. This is particularly a problem when text is laid out in tables, as individual columns may not be able to accommodate wide words.

Text-entry form elements use the default fixed-width font size (which the user may change independent of the variable-width font used for most of the body text). When text-entry fields have a large font, they grow quite large; for this reason, it's usually a good idea to keep no more than one large text-entry field per line in a form. See Figure 8-33 for an example of how font size can affect the layout of an online form.

The Optimal Font Size Is What the User Wants It to Be

What font size should you specify? It's usually best to keep the majority of text in the default font size (`<font size=3>`, which is usually around a 12-point font), and for small amounts of text, to bump it up or down a size as appropriate (`<font size=2>` or `<font size=4>`). Some designers like to make most text large (`<font size=4>`, which is usually around 14 points)—a good idea to improve the legibility of the text for most readers. Others like to use smaller text (`<font size=2>`, which is usually around 10 points), which allows for more text on the screen and improves the visual texture of the screen, aesthetically speaking.

Figure 8-33.

Font Size and Page Layout.

(a) When the fixed-width font is at a typical size of 12 point, the form works fine.

(b) However, if the user selects a larger fixed-width font of 18 point, the layout of the form breaks, which in this case is merely slightly unattractive (the form expands outside the regular margins), but in the worst case leads to form elements that fall outside the viewable area.

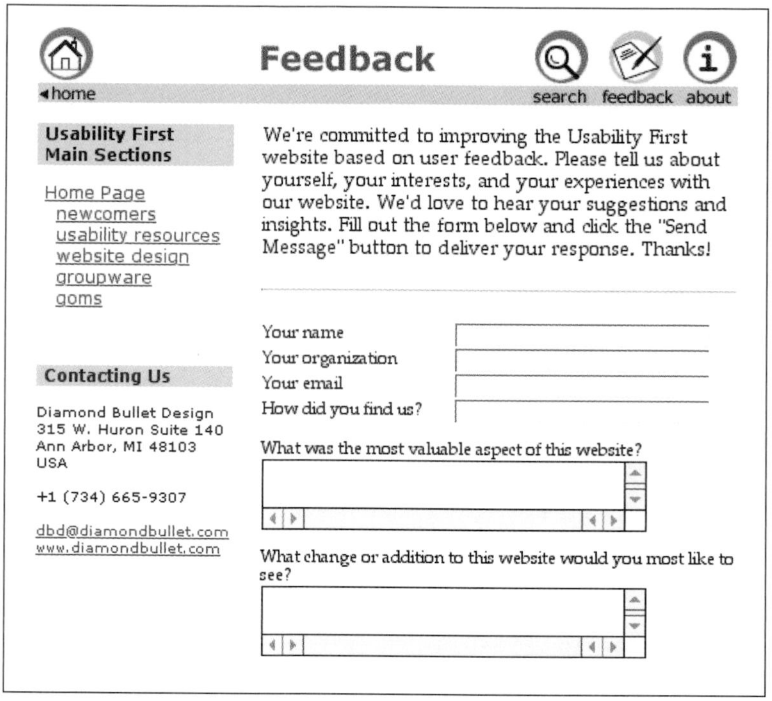

(a)

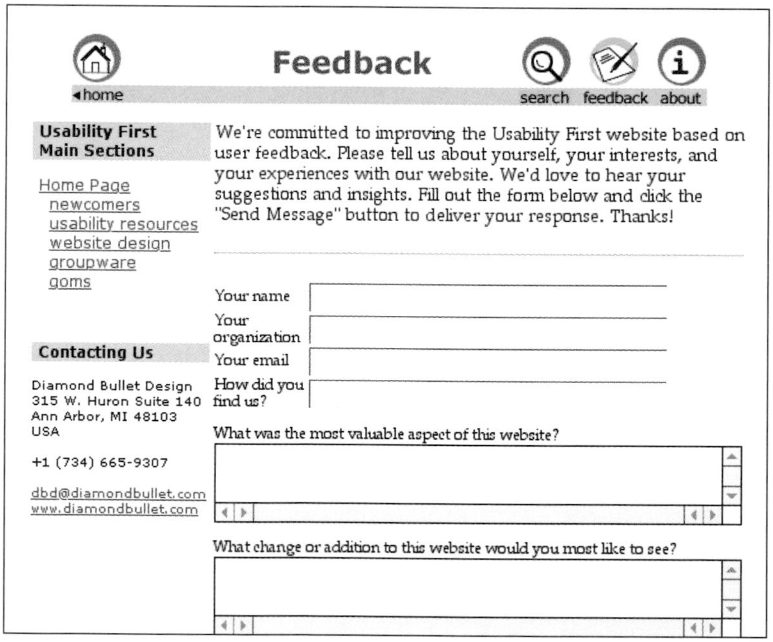

(b)

In our experience, when we've built a site around a nondefault font size, we regularly receive complaints from users about unusual font sizes, whether they're too small or too large, and we've *never* heard this complaint about the default font size. What happens is that some platforms exaggerate the sizes of fonts, making large fonts look very large. In addition, those users who do adjust their font sizes have adjusted them for their own optimal legibility, and any modification from their preferences will frustrate them. Those with limited vision will make their fonts larger, and if you've set the size as large, they'll get sizes that are too large. Those who like to see as much text as possible will adjust their fonts to be smaller, and if you've set the size as small, they'll get text that is too small to read.

Style Sheets

Style sheets can be a great way to control some basic font formatting, including typeface, font size, color, and style. This control enables the designer to create a finely crafted layout by setting the font to a specific point size, which the user won't be able to modify without overriding the style sheet. Unfortunately, current browsers make it difficult for novice users to override the style sheet, so setting absolute font sizes can be a bad idea if some users need to modify those sizes. However, when designed well, style sheets can help a lot in creating and maintaining a style for the text consistently used throughout the web site.

Type Effects

Text styles can be varied to provide emphasis and add visual interest to the page (see Figure 8-34). Font colors can be varied and large fonts can be used. Decorative fonts may add appeal when you know the user's system will include the font. If you're targeting multiple platforms, the appearance of these type effects will probably not be very consistent, so don't rely heavily on spacing and alignment of the text, and leave plenty of space for display variations.

Avoid using boldface or all caps for long pieces of text. These styles slow down reading for a user, so they should only be used to provide emphasis. Never use underlining except for links. Avoid the `<blink>` tag, or you will be cursed for all time by users whose brains exploded after seeing your page. Avoid italics except for large font sizes. In body text, use black text on a white background whenever possible for optimal legibility.

Semantic versus Format Tags

HTML can specify the formatting of tags either in terms of their semantic content (what the *meaning* of the text is) or in terms of their format (how they will appear on the page). The semantic tag `<strong>` indicates that the words need to be emphasized, somehow or another, and typical browsers will display such words in boldface. The format tag `<b>` indicates that the words need to be in boldface, regardless of whether that indicates emphasis in a specific context.

There is a tradeoff between using semantic versus format tags. The advantages of using semantic tags are as follows:

- Users with very different browsers can still get the proper interpretation of the text, regardless of how it is displayed. For instance, users with screen readers can hear `<strong>` words emphasized in the speech synthesis, whereas the speech synthesizer may have no good way to distinguish words in bold or italics.

- Various automated tools can interpret pages constructed with semantic tags. Thus, when an automated tool sees an `<h1>` tag, it knows that it is seeing a primary header, and that the following text represents a new section. However, if it sees headers displayed as `<font size=4 color="red">`, it has no idea what role the text plays within the document and can't infer anything about the document structure.

- In combination with style sheets, semantic tags can usually achieve the appearance the designer desires.

The advantages of using format tags, by contrast, are as follows:

- The designer can control the appearance of the text and can therefore choose a meaningful, usable format. This gets around the problem of browser defaults and user customizations that format semantic tags in unusable and unattractive ways.

- Using format tags improves the predictability of how the page will appear on different systems.

For most situations, the weight of this tradeoff falls on the side of using semantic tags.

While it's rare to encounter a situation where the difference between semantic and format tags is obvious, an old example is the `<blockquote>` tag. Semantically, `<blockquote>` is supposed to indicate that a block of text is being "quoted" within the document. This shouldn't indicate any specific format. However, almost all browsers show block-quoted text as indented from the primary text, and therefore HTML programmers use the `<blockquote>` tag to indent. In fact, many web page layout tools clearly imply that the role of the `<blockquote>` tag is to indent text, which is counter to the spirit of using it as a semantic tag. The problem with relying on it as a format tag is that some browsers may actually choose not to indent block quotes. For instance, early versions of Explorer displayed block quoted text in italics rather than indenting it.

Alignment

Text blocks need to follow the same principles of good alignment as graphics. Text should align appropriately with the graphics on the page. Left-aligned text is the default and usually the most attractive alignment. Centered text should be restricted to only small text blocks, such as titles and footers, and shouldn't be used for body text. Large amounts of centered text slow down reading considerably.

A common mistake is to alternate too much between centered and left-aligned text. This clutters the page and looks inconsistent. In most cases, making everything left aligned is a good solution to this problem.

Another common mistake is to have multiple axes of symmetry for centered text, such as when moving from a single column to two columns. In almost every case, a page will look cluttered unless all centered text on the page is centered along the same axis.

Multiple Columns

Multiple columns of text can make a more attractive layout and create lines of text that are shorter and easier to read. This is why narrow columns are standard in magazines and newspapers. Online, the primary problem with multiple columns is not being able to follow the flow. When the user is interested in the material in both columns, or when one column has text flowing into the next (as when you use the `<multicol>` tag), the user is forced into scrolling up and down several times to follow the flow of the text or is forced to read both columns simultaneously before scrolling and remembering the content of each while scrolling (see Figure 8-35).

Therefore, you should either stick to one column, so the user can scroll linearly and follow one train of thought, or use multiple columns *only* when your columns contain unrelated information—that is, when a user would clearly ignore one column while reading the other. Using a column for navigation, advertising, cross-links, or very short sidebars is an effective strategy.

Figure 8-35.

Multiple Columns.

Apple's web site (*www.apple.com*) makes frequent use of multiple columns. Fortunately, they tend to write very short passages into the side columns, which minimizes the need to scroll, but this succeeds only if the font size selected by the user is relatively small.

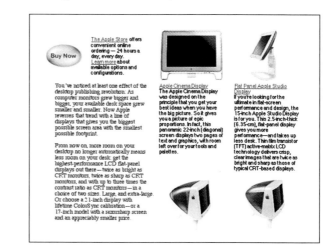

Grouping Text Chunks

Because of the nonlinearity of the online reading experience, it is important to follow some text grouping principles. Keep blocks of text together that are related. Use line breaks to separate paragraphs. Group headings with the text that they label. Make sure the heading is closer to the paragraph it identifies than it is to other paragraphs. Don't put a horizontal rule underneath a heading to make it stand out because the horizontal rule makes it look like it doesn't belong with the text below. If one blank line between sections doesn't clearly delineate the sections, use two blank lines.

GETTING YOUR MESSAGE ACROSS

In too many web sites, writing is an afterthought, if it's considered at all. This leads to beautifully designed frameworks that say nothing. The opposite problem is to write several pages of dense paragraphs. But readers aren't mindless sponges—they won't sit passively and absorb everything you throw at them. They'll skip it. Text needs to be relevant and easy to read. If it doesn't solve people's problems, they won't bother with it.

The bottom line: Tell people what they want to know. Tell them what they need to know. Get down to business and tell them something meaningful and concrete. Be clear and concise. Get every detail right.

09

PRODUCTION

DESIGN ELEMENTS

The goal of this chapter is to consider ways in which basic visual design elements can be made usable within the context of web design. Rather than reviewing all of graphic design, this chapter merely provides a window into aspects of design that may be particularly tricky or influential in the way they affect the usability of a web site. As such, this chapter will not teach you how to be creative, but rather, serves as a reminder of things to watch for when creating visual designs for highly usable sites.

Previous chapters took a high-level approach to page layout and design. This one explores the details, imagery, and elements contained within each page. It covers the following goals of graphic design for the Web: establishing design parameters, including visual elements, style, and scope of the site; color and typography as design techniques; designing page elements, such as icons, forms, and navigation; and animation and multimedia.

GOALS OF GRAPHIC DESIGN FOR THE WEB

Graphic design for the Web requires an understanding of the goals and trade-offs involved in the development of a relevant graphical display. It should support the user and facilitate communication of the intended message. Be sure to keep in mind the following ideas when designing your pages.

Practical Tradeoffs

Graphic design for the Web is not just about aesthetics. Rather, it is a tradeoff that must be resolved by taking into account the site's goals, the schedule and technological constraints, and the aesthetics of the web site.

Use-Based Presentation

Graphic design provides a visual way to manage how people interact with information. Through a combination of understanding user needs and effectively presenting available content, graphic design can be used to support and structure the display to enable communication. A designer should determine the layout based on the goals of the users.

Supporting Meaningful Content

The effective communication of information lies at the heart of successful web design. Part of this communication is portraying and supporting ideas through graphic design. In and of itself, graphic design cannot solve all of your problems. If the proper content isn't there, a well-designed graphical page will do little to support the user. However, graphic design *can* provide very strong support for a well-constructed message.

ESTABLISHING THE DESIGN PARAMETERS

Several factors influence your major design decisions. As early on as possible, you need to determine what visual materials are available to use within the site, the style of the site, and the scope of the site.

Gathering Relevant Materials

Start by gathering as much information as you can about the given organization. It is your goal to uncover what is needed to make a successful site. While this varies according to your relation with the client, the Web Site Materials Request Form (Form 9-1; download from *http://www.mkp.com/uew/*) can serve as a useful way to gather information from your client.

Be sure to gather *all materials* that your client currently uses in marketing, promotion, and public relations. Even pieces they no longer use can be useful in giving you a feel for the company as well as for understanding styles they no longer consider suitable or pleasing. Be sure to mark up materials they like and want to emulate, as well as materials they dislike and don't ever want to see again! Often you can learn as much from materials they dislike as from materials they like.

The Web Site Materials Request Form, or a similar form, can be used to remind clients of everything that might be of use to the designer in the early stages of design. Send this form to your clients when the project begins. This will help facilitate the gathering of information needed before designing the first mockups. Even if you are meeting with the clients for an initial design meeting, such a form can be useful for preparing them to have everything ready for the meeting and will facilitate a quick start. Early reminders for such items as accreditation seals and membership logos are often valuable to a web design project because such details can easily be forgotten until the late stages or even until after the launch.

Defining Your Web Site Style

You need to establish the targeted style, voice, and point of view of your web site. This is particularly crucial when you are working for a client whose organization is not thoroughly familiar to you. The overall style of the site is determined by analyzing information collected from an array of sources. Marketing departments often have a good deal of investment in the public image a site should present, but you may have additional insight based on your early user needs analysis, where you've heard from interviewees or focus group participants what style the users prefer.

Web Site Materials Request Form

Project _____

Project Contact _____

Date _____

**Please mail the following materials as soon as possible.
(Please include this form with requested materials.)**

Check off included materials

☐ Corporate style guide for printed or electronic materials

☐ Names of typefaces

☐ Pantone, CMYK, or RGB preferred colors

☐ Logo in digital format (vector format or high-resolution raster)

☐ Photographs of desired or suggested material (scanned digital images preferred)
(e.g., key personnel, products, locations, events, community service projects)

☐ Samples of all print materials
(e.g., flyers, brochures, ads)

☐ Audio and video clips
(e.g., advertisements or promotional materials)

☐ Digital or multimedia materials
(e.g., promotional CDs)

☐ Samples of newspaper or magazine articles or advertisements

☐ Accreditation seals and membership logos

☐ Maps to locations

☐ Written permission to use copyrighted materials

Acceptable submission formats

File formats:

    Text: Plain text format, RTF, Microsoft Word
    Graphics: EPS, GIF, JPEG, TIFF, Photoshop
    Other: .aiff, .wav

Mediums:

    Digital: Zip disks, Mac or PC formatted floppy disks, CD-ROMs
    Other: Photographs, printed materials, analog audiotapes, VHS videotapes

Send to:

Company Name
c/o _____
123 Any Street
OurTown, CA 91221
USA

Phone
(123) 555–1313

Fax
(123) 555–1414

Additional comments:

_____

_____

_____

_____

Materials sent by:

_____

Date:

_____

Defining your web site style requires understanding your clients and their position within their domain and business environment. Should they portray a corporate image, a playful image, or a contemporary image? You won't know this unless you have close ties to your clients, or you do a lot of probing and investigating. The Client Interview/Web Site Information Worksheet (Form 3-1 in Chapter 3, "User Needs Analysis") provides a worksheet that can be used to establish the way clients view themselves within their local and competing business environments.

Get your clients to provide you with a list of competing companies. If they have web sites, be sure to have your clients take a few minutes to go over the sites with you. Identify ways in which they are successful and ways in which they don't succeed.

The second half of the Client Interview/Web Site Information Worksheet provides a place for recording information about the content that needs to be included in the design and provides a means for gathering any information on preestablished style guidelines that a given company may already have (e.g., specific fonts used, logo requirements, etc.).

Once the style is established, your design elements will need to be created to fit this style. Thus, the style may affect the font chosen (e.g., corporate vs. playful), the icon style (e.g., bulky vs. elegant), the color (e.g., striking contrasts and bright colors vs. subtle and subdued), or any element on the page. The style you establish provides the voice for the web site, implying a frame of mind and providing a point of view.

Determining the Scope and Scalability of the Site

Before you get started with the development of your site, determine the approximate scope of the site: How many pages will it have? How many options will there be at each level? How deep will the site go? This will help determine the style of navigation needed.

In addition, you should consider how much the site will change and grow. While you always want designs that are scalable (i.e., easy to add new pages and navigation), some sites will likely require more dynamic growth than others. This can be determined in part by asking clients to describe their future plans for growth. However, you should beware of relying too heavily on a client's assessment. Most estimates on growth can be wildly off and very misleading. It is best to approach this question with common sense and a conservative perspective. Assume that the site will need to grow massively, unless you have good reason to believe otherwise. Set scalability as your goal and design accordingly. This may make your initial design more difficult to achieve, but in the long run it will pay off, particularly if there is a need for major growth.

COLOR

Color can be effective and powerful but has certain limitations. Technological constraints include the fact that color calibration between monitors is relatively poor, and that colors appear differently on different hardware platforms. In addition, users may be using devices with either black-and-white screens or reduced-color screens. Human constraints include differences in color preferences, in cultural meanings, and in color perception. In addition, color blindness is relatively common (about 4% of all people) so it is usually unsafe to depend on people's ability to accurately distinguish colors.

Make It Work in Grayscale

As a result of these limitations, make sure your designs work in black and white. While you can still design in color, if you want to distinguish between two colored areas, make sure they contrast in brightness as well as in color, and that this difference in brightness is sufficient. To test whether a design works without color (Figure 9-1), convert the design to grayscale and make sure it's still possible to use.

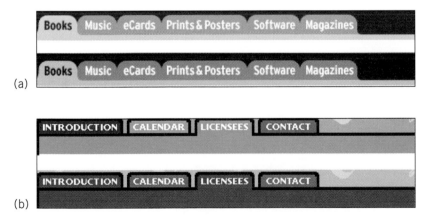

(a)

(b)

Figure 9-1.

Testing in Grayscale.

Testing color choices in grayscale can reveal when the brightness differences are good (a) and when they are not (b). The selected tab should stand out in both the color and grayscale versions. Notice how the "Books" tab stands out in both versions (a), while the "Licensees" tab stands out in color but not in grayscale (b).

Color Perception

Watch how colors work together. Certain pairs of colors do not work side by side, because the edge between them will appear to vibrate; these include red/green, blue/violet, and red/blue. If you need to put these pairs of color next to each other, you can reduce the vibration effect by separating them with a solid black line. You can also reduce the effect by increasing the difference in brightness between the two colors. Keep in mind that it's not good enough to make subtle changes that improve it "just enough." Because of differences in the color calibration of monitors, you can't be sure that they won't fall back into an unacceptable range on certain monitors.

People also have difficulty focusing on thin blue lines (the blue receptors in the eye are the least acute). For this reason, avoid highly saturated blue for sharp lines or detailed work.

Effective Use of Color

While we've discussed several concerns with the use of color, color is also extremely effective at accomplishing certain perceptual effects. Some good uses of color include making things pop out (one bright color among dull colors is easy to spot), emphasizing important information, grouping related items and reinforcing layouts (by providing redundant color cues to highlight which items are meant to be more prominent than others), and increasing comprehension and memorability.

TYPOGRAPHY AS A DESIGN TECHNIQUE

Great typographical layout can make the dullest of designs look clean and professional. This section focuses on the use of lettering and typography as design elements. This means using type for accents and titles and in graphics, rather than as basic body text (for tradeoffs between graphics-based text and HTML text, see Table 9-1).

Good typography relies on the ability of the type to create a visual contrast between fonts as well as across the page as a whole (e.g., body text or headlines). There are a few simple ideas that can help you to make the presentation of type communicate effectively.

Match the Typeface to the Content

Match the style of typeface you choose to the style of site you want to produce (Figure 9-2). For example, if your client is looking for a highly professional but somewhat modern look, you'll want to use a typeface that supports that feel. Thus, you wouldn't use old gothic type, but rather something more elegant and formal, such as Optima.

Get to Know Your Typeface

It's difficult to know the quirks of a given typeface until you've seen it in action. Select a typeface and use it for *everything* you do for a few weeks. Use it on letterhead, memos, in word-processing documents. Make it large, make it small, make it wide, and make it tall. After a few weeks of this, you'll know how the typeface works best. Is it a good font for large titles? Is it better and more suitable for long text passages at smaller font sizes?

Don't Go Overboard

A mistake that beginners often make when discovering the world of typography is to go overboard in their use of different typefaces. Very subtle changes in font size or weight can contribute to large perceptual cues, particularly if

Using Graphics for Text	Using HTML Text
The designer has total control over typeface and font size and can therefore guarantee the visual quality.	Text downloads faster than graphics.
Layout can be controlled because the graphic will not vary in size.	Fonts can be controlled and modified with style sheets.
The edges and contrast of the letterforms can be controlled by the designer for clarity.	Users can modify the font size to suit their visual acuity.
Leading and kerning can be controlled.	Many users browse with images off.
Visual effects are enabled, such as .gif animation and JavaScript rollovers.	PDA and mobile phone interfaces are often text browsers.
Branding can be maintained.	Text enables voice-only interfaces (e.g., for the blind).
Text can be layered and integrated with graphic elements.	Text restructures itself more easily to suit different browsers and window sizes.
	Modifications can be made more easily.

Table 9-1.

Tradeoffs of Using Graphics for Text versus Using HTML Text.

Figure 9-2.

Match the Typeface to the Content.

Each of these typefaces has a particular feel and speaks with a particular
voice, expressing the style and brand
identity of your site.

the vast majority of your page is similar in scale, weight, and structure (see
Figure 9-3). On the other hand, make sure that if you intend for something to
be distinguished, it has sufficient contrast to eliminate any ambiguity.

Using Variations on a Single Typeface

When creating subdued, formal, and highly structured text, it is often useful to stick with the same typeface throughout the design space (see Figure
9-4). For instance, a form design can often benefit from using the same
typeface throughout. This allows you to easily draw attention where you
need to and also to direct the flow of a user's eye across the page with deliberate control (there are methods for defining areas of emphasis; see sidebar
"The Squint Test").

> ### THE SQUINT TEST
>
> A good way to determine if the emphasis is in the correct areas is to squint
> or blur your vision when looking at a page. By blurring the details, the more
> obvious areas stand out. Sit back from the monitor, squint your eyes until
> the page becomes blurry, and look for areas that stand out more promi-
> nently than you intended or areas that are clumped together when they
> should stand out.

Welcome

Welcome to Usability First™.
This website provides
information and resources for
key issues related to *usability*
in website and software design.
We **believe** that helping people
do their work in an effective
and *enjoyable* way should be
the top priority in design
because **if a product is not**
usable, people will not use it.

What is usability?
Usability usually refers to
software but is relevant to any
product. Some ways to **improve**
usability include:
- shortening the time to
accomplish tasks,
- reducing the number of
mistakes made,
- reducing learning time,
- and improving people's
satisfaction with a system.

Welcome

Welcome to Usability First™.
This website provides
information and resources for
key issues related to usability
in website and software design.
We believe that helping people
do their work in an effective
and enjoyable way should be
the top priority in design
because if a product is not
usable, people will not use it.

What is usability?
Usability usually refers to
software but is relevant to any
product. Some ways to **improve**
usability include:
- shortening the time to
accomplish tasks,
- reducing the number of
mistakes made,
- reducing learning time,
- and improving people's
satisfaction with a system.

Figure 9-3.

Making Text Stand Out.

This example demonstrates how bold
type stands out much more when the
rest of the page is consistent (as on
the right), as opposed to the mixture
of styles used on the left, which
obscures the bolded font. Look
for the bolded phrase "improve
usability" in each of the columns
and note how it is much easier to
see in the more subdued example.

Variations

of a single typeface allow you to

CONTROL THE PAGE

AND WHERE ONE

looks

helps to create subdued, formal designs

useful for controlling rhythm and
STRUCTURE WITHIN A DESIGN

Figure 9-4.

Variations on a Single Typeface.

Variations on a single typeface can
provide an interesting look and feel
and can be used to effectively move
the user's eye across the page. They
give you control of the user's gaze
and thus allow you to clearly present
the structure of the page and communicate the critical information.

Figure 9-5.

Contrasting Typefaces.

Contrasting typefaces can create
exciting tensions and a dramatic
feel. However, too many typefaces
can result in a cluttered and
confusing display.

Contrasting typefaces

distinctive dramatic EXCITING

Using Contrasting Typefaces

Contrasting typefaces can create a very strong visual impact. (See Figure 9-5 for examples.) However, too many contrasting typefaces produces a cluttered page. A confusing hodgepodge of graphical intensity can lead users to despair rather than to your information!

Changing the Typeface on a Single Dimension to Emphasize Structure

By varying one dimension of a typeface, you can effectively structure the visual space, reinforcing the uniformity of most elements on your page and giving clarity to the single distinction that you want to make. For example, increasing a single typeface in point size can effectively create a focal point in the page and help relate key elements in the display. Changing the weight of the stroke has a similar effect. Type can be varied on any of a number of dimensions, but it's easiest to retain control over the structure of the page by varying only one dimension. Type can be varied along these dimensions: width of the stroke, size of the font, and color of the font.

ICON DESIGN

While icons are not necessary for links, when carefully designed, they can often make the links they identify more prominent, more attractive, more comprehensible, and more memorable. However, when not carefully designed, they can do more harm than good. There are few things more frustrating, for example, than clicking an icon expecting one thing to happen only to find a completely different action taking place. Icons, like the rest of your design, should support the user's task. Thus, icons should be used only when they effectively aid comprehension or communication. If they are being used solely to make your page look good, you need to be sure that they in no way detract from the communication and usability of the page.

Characteristics of good icons are as follows: they should be identifiable outside the context of the page, unambiguous, distinct and memorable, familiar, consistent (both across icons and across pages), and attractive.

Icons can be used as compact graphical representations to facilitate navigation. They are most effective when used to complement a link where the text alone doesn't provide a clear definition of the link. Use icons to clarify the meaning of your link labels.

It's useful to provide a text link along with your icon. A text link can be read by screen readers for the visually impaired. If you choose not to include text links, be sure to include adequate ALT tags to provide for screen-reading software.

Icon Development

Icon development follows much the same pattern as the processes mentioned throughout this book: mockup, test, and iterate. When developing mockups for your icons, it's often good to tap your domain experts. It is reasonable to do the first couple of iterations with simple paper-based representations. Later on, as the icons become more refined, you can move to digital representations and begin testing on the screen. In this section we describe how you can be lazy and let the best icons design themselves.

1. Shirk Responsibility: Brainstorm Icons

Start off by giving as many people as possible a list of concepts. Then ask them to draw, sketch, or simply describe the images they would use to support such concepts. It's always easier to let others do your work for you, and it provides you with some data regarding the most common themes. Starting this way is similar to the development of thumbnail sketches for page layout. You quickly get a large selection of ideas from which to base your further development. In addition, you learn which ideas might be common across the selection of people you've gathered for the brainstorming. For this reason, it is often beneficial to involve as diverse a population as possible. Better yet, let the developers of your initial icon concepts be as close as possible to your target population of users.

To brainstorm possible ways of representing a concept in an icon, a simple worksheet can be used to elicit ideas from people, and it only takes a few minutes (see Form 9-2; download from *http://www.mkp.com/uew/*). List the names of the icons you want down the left column. Give descriptions if needed. In the second column, ask them to give synonyms, related terms, and describe objects that they associate with each concept. Many people won't feel comfortable drawing potential icons, but they can still suggest visual ideas that

Form for Brainstorming Icons

Instructions: We're designing a web site for a business that wants to disseminate materials and research findings to the public sector. As someone who currently works in this area, we'd like your feedback on how we can illustrate the following concepts on the web site using icons.

Icon Name	Write any words or phrases you associate with this concept, especially any objects or visual concepts you think of.	Draw any ideas you have for an icon to represent this concept. Even a very rough drawing is helpful.
Case Studies/ White Papers		
Late-Breaking Results		
Our Services		

will help you to come up with an icon. In the last column, ask them to draw some candidate icons. These sketches will usually be pretty rough, but they help you to identify prototypical visual concepts.

2. Limit Your Options

On the first pass, you may want to choose a subset of icon designs to continue refining. You should pay particular attention to those icons that people suggested most often. However, you'll want to be sure that you haven't mislabeled the concept or that the icons aren't just a simple, but inaccurate, metaphor for the concept you are attempting to visualize.

3. Refine with Details and Begin Testing

At this point you should have several alternatives for each concept that you want. Here you might want to begin to develop higher-resolution or slightly more detailed versions. You'll also want to begin an iterative testing process using a mixture of tests described in the following section.

You should also begin testing your icons in black and white. An icon should be able to convey everything it needs to in grayscale form. If you require color for the meaning to be clear, in most (although not all) instances this means your icon is not properly communicating to the users.

4. Go against Your Intuitions and Choose the Best

Once you have tested and refined the icons several times, it should be obvious which are the best choices. Often this may go against your original inclinations—but who are you to resist! At this point, you have combined the minds of several individuals along with testing data to determine the best solution. Be humble. Do what's right. Of course, it will be up to the graphic designer to make these icons as visually appealing as possible, but a lot can be gained from utilizing the power of numbers.

In summary, there are several tips to follow when developing icons: take advantage of others in the initial development of ideas; start with simple sketches; refine initially in black and white or grayscale; and develop an iterative system of testing and redesign.

Icon Testing: A Questionnaire Approach

Questionnaires can be a useful alternative or supplement to task-driven user testing (described in Chapter 12, "Usability Evaluation"). The following sections describe some alternatives for identifying successful icons to use in your design. A similar set of approaches can be used to test link labels.

Interpret This Icon

Once you have candidate icon designs, you need to know whether your design makes any sense. A simple approach is to show the icons to users and ask them to write down what they think each icon means. You can use a simple worksheet (see Form 9-3 for an example; download from *http://www.mkp.com /uew/*), or if you have a mockup of the site ready, show them the mockup and simply ask what they think each icon means in context. Don't expect people to guess the icons correctly all the time, but identify your worst icons and keep working on them.

Match the Icon to Its Concept

While optimally icons will be recognizable in any context, many times it's fair to assume that your users will understand the context and won't be guessing the meaning of an icon in a vacuum. For instance, if your users are domain experts, they'll know what types of features to expect on your site, so they'll have a head start in figuring out what an icon might do. Thus, in some cases, all you need to do is make sure that your set of icons can unambiguously be mapped to the correct concept. Form 9-4 demonstrates a simple way to test this. (Download from *http://www.mkp.com/uew/*.)

DESIGNING ONLINE FORMS

Online forms are frequently designed in a fashion that makes them both frustrating and downright unusable. Forms should help improve the interaction and level of engagement for users. However, too often forms adopt improper controls (such as drop-down menus and radio buttons), provide the user with inadequate feedback, or simply don't work.

Great progress can be made by simply applying the consistency principle to all of your forms. Use common conventions, make form layout similar across forms, and take advantage of what users already know about or are comfortable with. When using forms to submit data, you must be consistent!

A great way to achieve consistency is to establish a style guideline for all your online forms. This is simply a guide that developers and designers can consult that makes the layout, interactions, formatting, and labeling of forms explicit. A style guide serves as a reference and is particularly valuable when designing sites with several forms or working on a site that continually adds new forms and data over time.

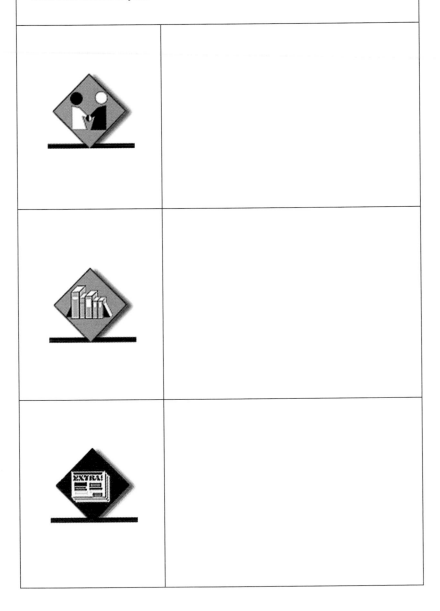

Form for Testing Whether an Icon Is Recognizable

Instructions: We've designed the following possible icons for a web site representing a business that wants to disseminate materials and research findings to the public sector. In the right-hand column, please write what each icon means to you.

Form 9-4.

Form for Testing Whether a Set of Icons Maps Uniquely to a Set of Concepts.

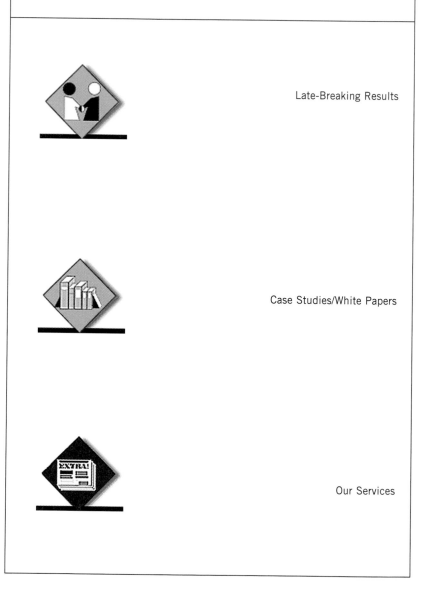

Form for Testing Whether a Set of Icons Maps Uniquely to a Set of Concepts

Instructions: We've designed the following possible icons for a web site representing a business that wants to disseminate materials and research findings to the public sector. Please draw a line connecting each icon to the concept that it best represents.

Late-Breaking Results

Case Studies/White Papers

Our Services

The style guide should address form layout, standard widget use and guidelines, labeling conventions, interaction guidelines for multiple-page forms, and techniques for presenting feedback to the user. In addition, a style guide should provide a graphic demonstration of each recommendation.

Overall Form Design

Online forms should present a clear step-by-step procedure for the user. Often, it's good to label the steps numerically within a page (1, 2, 3) so that the user can quickly see the sequence. In the absence of numbers, make sure the next step is always clear. A common problem is to have a submission button that is not obvious and that the user never presses. If the steps occur across multiple pages, it's helpful to note the total number of steps by labeling them as "1 of 4," "2 of 4," and so on.

Keep Forms Short

As in surveys, most people don't like to fill in much information. Minimize the number of form fields. You can make the respondents' job easier by allowing them to use checkboxes and radio buttons rather than fill in free-form text fields.

Identify Required Fields in the Form

Boldface text or asterisks next to the required fields are common conventions. We've found that small arrows or triangles work well too. Required fields can prevent you from getting information that's useless—for example, it doesn't do any good for respondents to ask for more information if they don't provide you with contact information. However, never require any more information than the bare minimum you need. If users get blocked in submitting the form, there's a greater likelihood of their becoming frustrated and giving up.

Form Elements

There are several common elements that appear in forms (see Figure 9-6). They should be used in consistent ways and should never go against the standards.

Introductory Statement

Every form should have a few sentences at the top of the page detailing what the form is and describing any constraints of the form.

Labels

Labels are the descriptive text used to communicate what information is being requested.

Controls

Controls allow users to make selections and input data. There are several different types of controls. These are defined as follows.

Text fields: *These allow users to type in responses using their keyboard.*

Drop-down menus: *These allow the user to select a single value from a list of choices. Drop-down menus should always be populated with a default value. The label used for the default value should be a description of the contents beginning with an action word—for example, "Select a State," where the rest of the choices are state abbreviations (e.g., CA).*

Scrolling lists: *These provide a list of preset values from which the user can select any subset.*

Radio buttons: *These serve a similar function to drop-down menus. They are used to present a list of choices from which the user can make a single selection. Radio buttons are more direct and easier to use than drop-down menus. However, they do not scale well when there are a large number of choices.*

Figure 9-6.

Basic Form Elements.

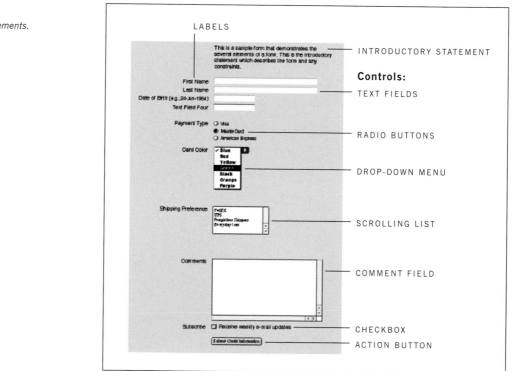

Checkboxes: These are similar to scrolling lists in that they provide a list of elements from which the user can select any number of choices. Checkboxes are more direct and easier to use than scrolling lists. However, they do not scale well when there are a large number of choices.

Action Buttons

Action buttons are used to trigger an action. A Submit button could trigger the sending of data, and a Reset button could clear the contents of a form.

There should only be one Submit button per form, and this button should be clearly labeled. Instead of "Submit," label it "Send This Message" or "Submit This Order" or whatever specific text is relevant to the form.

If you have a Reset button, this too should be labeled clearly, with text like "Clear All Values" or "Restore Default Values." However, we actually recommend you *don't* use the Reset functionality on a form because it generally causes more harm than good. It is not necessary for short forms, and for long forms it poses the risk of wiping out monumental efforts on the part of the user—with no opportunity to undo its effects! Still, Reset buttons can be useful when there are default values contained within the form that are difficult to reconstruct. When using them for such cases, remember to label the button "Reset to Default Values" or something appropriately descriptive.

Form Layout

A key to developing highly usable forms is to develop a consistent layout that is used on all forms throughout a site. Here we address some layout issues that are exclusive to forms, but you'll want to keep in mind the general layout practices discussed in Chapter 6, "Page Layout," such as screen size and dynamic resizing effects.

Introductory Statement

As mentioned earlier, the introductory statement should be placed at the top of every form. In addition, if this form is part of a multistaged process, you'll want to be sure to indicate where the user is in the process (e.g., "Stage 1 of 3" or "Background Information → **Detailed Bug Report** → Response and Feedback").

Labels

In general, labels should be placed to the left of the designated control. This creates a visually consistent layout and helps to clarify the layout when a form includes grouped controls such as radio buttons. If you put the labels above the controls, the relationship between label and control is less clear (see Figure 9-7). Placing labels on the left of the control allows users to visually group the items based on proximity.

Figure 9-7.

Putting Labels Above or Below the Controls Can Lead to Confusion.

In long forms, users can be confused about whether the label refers to the control above or below. The problem is compounded if the controls are all the same size.

First Name

Last Name

Title

Company Name

Mailing Address

City

State/Province

Zip/Postal Code

Country

Phone

Fax

Email Address

Labels should be right aligned so that the end of the label is flush against the corresponding control (see Figure 9-6). On the Web, where font size is not set in stone and pages can be dynamically resized, left-aligned labels can end up far from the controls they are intended to label (see Figure 9-8).

Controls

Controls include areas where the user enters data, selects a choice, or chooses a subset of choices. These typically include text fields, drop-down menus, and scrolling lists. The size of text fields should reflect the expected size of the input. For example, if the user is expected to enter a middle initial, the text box should be small. Controls should be left aligned so that the left edges are flush against the labels (see Figure 9-6).

Figure 9-8.

Poor Alignment of Labels and Controls.

Poorly aligned labels and controls make data entry difficult.

Contact Us
Before you complete this form, you may want to consult our frequently asked questions (FAQ's). Our FAQ's can answer most customer questions faster than contacting us through this form.

Please note that this is not secure email. Therefore, do not send any sensitive account information. To learn more about security, click here. If you wish to send us a secure email, you can do so once you are enrolled and logged in to the main Cardmember Services site. Click here if you'd like to enroll.

All fields are required:
Full Name:

Contact Phone #:

Home Zip Code:

E-Mail Address:
Please make sure that you've entered your e-mail address correctly; if your e-mail address is incorrect, we won't be able to respond. Thank you.

Last Two Digits of Account:
(required for First USA account inquires only)

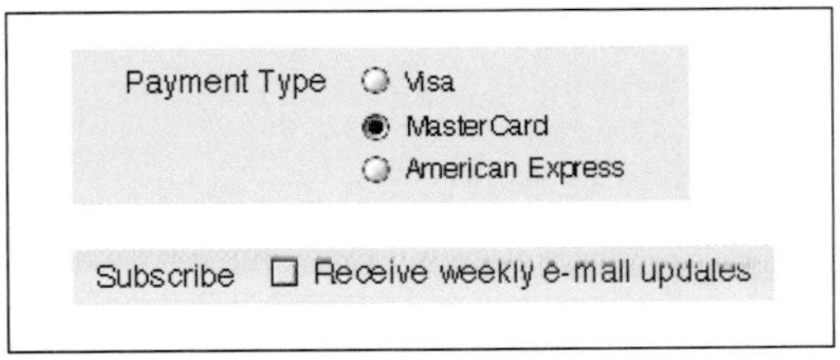

Figure 9-9.

Layout of Checkboxes and Radio Buttons.

Checkboxes and Radio Buttons

Checkboxes and radio buttons often require additional levels of layout. They typically have a high-level description of the group (e.g., "Payment Type") and then require labels for each of the subchoices within that group (e.g., "Visa"). The high-level group label should be placed to the left of the control and right aligned. Subchoice labels should be placed to the right of the control and should be left aligned (see Figure 9-9).

Action Buttons

Action buttons should be placed at the bottom of the form. Studies have found that users go directly to the bottom of a form to look for a Submit button (Spool et al. 1997), and placing them elsewhere on the page leads to users overlooking them. Action buttons should be left aligned underneath the controls (see bottom of Figure 9-6).

NAVIGATION

Once you've worked out how to display individual links (e.g., as icons), you need to determine how the navigation as a whole will be displayed. The structure of a site is intimately tied to its presentation. In fact, the perceived structure, established by the way navigation is displayed, can be significantly more important to the usability of the site than the actual underlying structure.

Presentation

Visual metaphors help organize the information and make the options more memorable. While most navigation will be presented as lists of text labels or icons, links may also be organized in maps, diagrams, or other pictures. For example, an approach that seems to pop up periodically is a room metaphor, where links are associated with objects in a three-dimensional scene, such as a room with a "help desk." However, unless your domain is architecture or furniture, a 3D room is most likely to be a stretch that confuses the users rather than helping them. Visual metaphors should be used when they *clarify* the content but avoided when they conflict with or confuse the interpretation of the content (see Figure 9-10).

Figure 9-10.

Visual Metaphors.

This site (*www.packardchildrens hospital.org*) is organized around a city block metaphor, where each section is represented by a building. Does the metaphor support navigation or confuse it? For instance, where does the "post office" go? Who are "our friends"? What is the building labeled "health professionals"? Is that designed *for* health professionals or *about* health professionals?

If you use them at all, find metaphors that are strongly related to your subject domain (Figure 9-11). When no obvious metaphor is available, avoid them altogether and use a simple list of links.

Navbar Layout

While other layout issues were covered in Chapter 6, "Page Layout," some of the basics of navigation layout are presented here. The main issues are coping with limited screen real estate (i.e., the amount of space available on a given display) and clearly indicating the relationships between multiple navigation bars.

Screen Real Estate

Dominating the problem of fitting information into limited space on the screen is the fact that English words are longer horizontally than vertically. Actually, English is a fairly dense language, and other European languages typically require even more horizontal space. (Some languages such as Japanese and Chinese require less horizontal space, on average, and more vertical space. They also allow convenient vertical layout of words when needed.)

The primary impact of this is that while horizontal navbars require very little vertical space, they can't hold a lot of items (see Figure 9-12). Multiline horizontal navbars are possible, and even common, but they can be confusing because the second line may be interpreted as a separate list or a subnav. Because horizontal navbars can fit very few items, they will necessarily vary in shape (i.e., vertical space) on different pages, creating design inconsistencies. In addition, if you need to add more options at a later time, you'll have to introduce a new layout when the list gets too long.

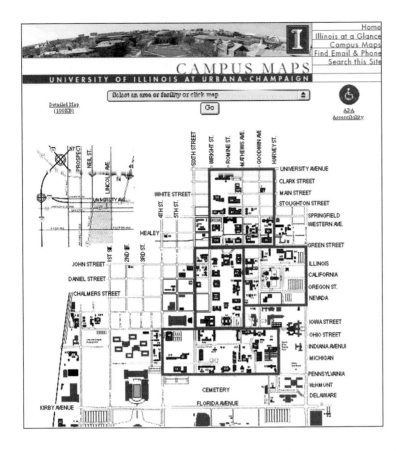

Figure 9-11.

Links within a Map.

Clicking on an outlined region of the map takes you to a detailed map. This visual organization of the navigation works effectively because it is directly connected to the information content as opposed to being imposed on the content (*www.uiuc.com*).

A vertical navbar (see Figure 9-13) doesn't suffer from this maintenance problem as much, but instead limits the length of individual link labels (thus putting pressure on you to create less meaningful labels). Vertical navbars also steal horizontal space that would otherwise be available to the body text.

One solution is to use drop-down menus to present navigation options (Figure 9-14). This saves screen space but is somewhat more difficult for users. We recommend it only for lists of shortcuts, not as a substitute for the primary navigation.

The limits of screen real estate have driven many sites to implement cascading menus in DHTML (see Figure 9-15). Compatibility issues are a factor here, but if carefully tested, it's possible to design this to work with the most common platforms. Because so many interaction styles are possible, it's important to test that users are comfortable with your implementation. If you decide to go this route, keep the menus simple and straightforward, imitating the behavior of standard desktop menus. Avoid multilevel menus (where one submenu leads to another level of submenus), which are more cognitively complex and more difficult for people to select with a mouse. People vary greatly in their motor ability to accurately point at links, and complex cascading menus can be among the most difficult to accurately manipulate.

There are still other ways to present navigation elements. See Figures 9-16 through 9-19 for some examples.

Figure 9-12.

Horizontal Navigation.

Horizontal navbars leave plenty of room for the main content but can't accommodate many options (*www.nationalgeographic.com*).

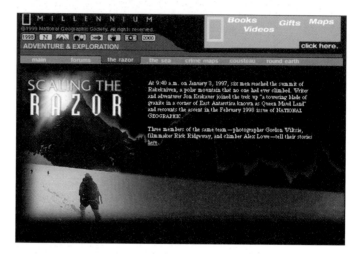

Figure 9-13.

Vertical Navigation.

Vertical navbars can extend to display many items well, but they take a lot of horizontal space away from the content (*www.clearidea.com*).

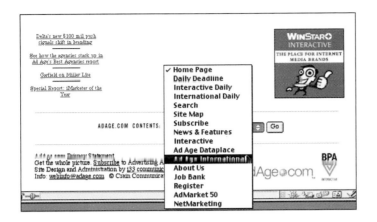

Figure 9-14.

Drop-Down Menus.

Drop-down menus are good for shortcuts and take little space. Standard HTML drop-downs use the standardized menus of the user's operating system, so they're consistent and easy for users to learn (*www.adage.com*).

Figure 9-15.

Cascading Menus.

Cascading menus in DHTML can give your site a coherent appearance, but their inconsistency with standard menus makes them harder to use (*www.westbankcorponline.com*).

Figure 9-16.

Sideways Text.

Turning the text sideways allows a vertical layout without taking space away from the content. However, this decreases legibility and suffers from the same lack of flexibility as a horizontal navbar—only a few options can be displayed well (*www.sapient.com*).

Figure 9-17.

Scrolling List.

A scrolling list is an alternative to a drop-down that works better for very long lists and makes some of the options visible at all times. Its drawback is that its navigational function is not obvious to users (*www.shop.com*).

Figure 9-18.

Navigation Using Tabs.

Tabs are a popular metaphor for horizontal navigation that give a strong sense of which section you're currently in (*www.seuss.com*).

Figure 9-19.

Combined Approaches to Navigation.

Combining horizontal navbars, vertical navbars, drop-downs, embedded links, and other methods allows you to squeeze in a lot of options for a complex site (*www.garden.com*).

Subnav Design

Several different navigation bars may be on a screen simultaneously, including top-level categories, multiple levels of subnav, breadcrumbs, and utilities. Users must determine which is which, and your responsibility is to make this obvious. If users see two lists of links, how are they to know what each represents? There may be two lists of links at the same level, a main nav and a subnav, a main nav and a subnav many levels deeper, a main nav and a breadcrumb trail, or one of several other alternatives.

You can indicate the relationship between a navbar and its subnav in several ways. You can put the subnav below and to the right of the main navbar, make the subnav smaller, or draw a line from the category in the main navbar that the subnav represents. It's also possible to enclose the subnav within a frame encompassed by the main navbar, or to use typography to indicate the primacy of the main navbar over the subnav—that is, to indicate the relationship by changes in font size, capitalization, indentation, color, or contrast. For instance, the main navbar can be in all caps, the first level down in title case, and the second level down in lowercase. Figures 9-20 through 9-24 illustrate several different ways to design subnavigation.

Figure 9-20.

Outline Format.

Navigation appears in outline format, and the subnav on the left is subordinated by graphic style and capitalization (*www.adams.com*).

Figure 9-21.

Section-Oriented Subnav.

Subnav appears below section title and is subordinated by graphic style and capitalization (*www.cbbonline.com*).

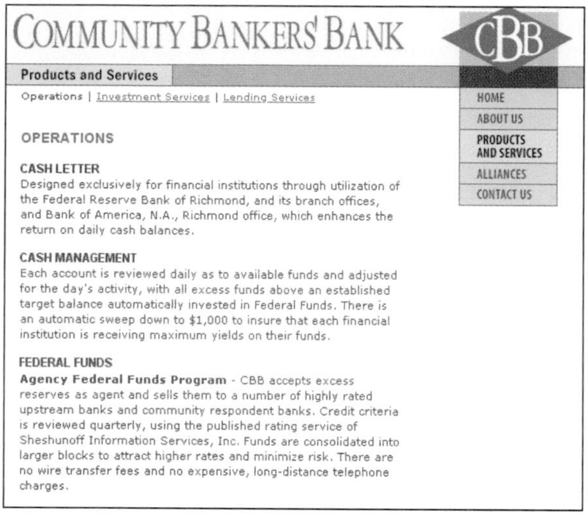

Figure 9-22.

Tethered Subnav.

Subnav is connected to main navbar by a line and is differentiated by capitalization (*www.languatutor.com*).

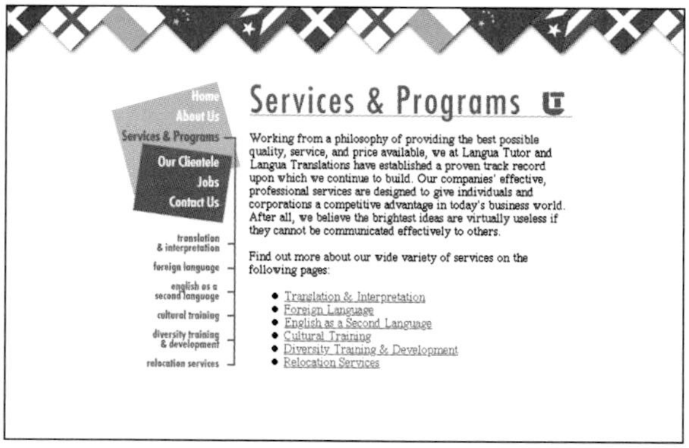

Figure 9-23.

Embedded Subnav.

The main navbar heads the page and the subnav appears within the body of the page (*www.heritagecommerce corp.com*).

Grouping Navigation Items

When your site is organized in a shallow structure (i.e., few levels of depth), you may have lots of links at the same level, which can be more easily scanned if they are grouped into related items. These groups help make a more sensible page, but they need to be carefully presented to avoid two problems: (1) a group may be mistaken for a subnav if it's not presented as being at the same level, and (2) people quickly become accustomed to using only one group and may be blind-sighted to the presence of the other group. See Figure 9-25 for an example of a complex site with multiple navigation groups.

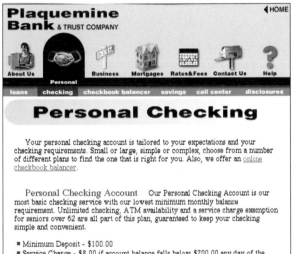

Figure 9-24.

Tiered Subnav.

The subnav is below the main navbar, below a shadow indicating that it is dominated by the main nav, and set in lowercase (*www.plaqbank.com*).

Figure 9-25.

Multiple Navigation Areas.

There are at least six groups of navigation on the first screenful of this page (*www.cnet.com*). This grouping helps to identify which links are related and which aren't. However, it can be difficult to grasp how these groups relate to one another, and people often overlook less salient groups, such as the horizontal text links at top right.

Isolating the Navbar

The navigation bar can also be isolated from the content of pages by putting it in a separate window or frame. On the plus side, an isolated navbar can make site maintenance easier, may slightly improve the speed of the site, and can improve the apparent stability of the navbar. On the down side, separate windows can create difficulties in window management, especially on small screens. They also make it more difficult (though not impossible) for the programmer to customize breadcrumbs and provide indicators of the current page.

INTERACTIVITY AND MULTIMEDIA

Choosing to integrate multimedia into your designs can come with a huge cost: restricting user access to your site, distracting users to the point of departure, or simply crashing their browser. At the same time, interactivity and multimedia elements can be very powerful for conveying information beyond that of text, diagrammatic representations, or static images. This is a tradeoff! If you choose to integrate such twinkles, you must be sure to understand their limitations and make a conscious effort to provide the most highly usable context possible.

There are times when interactivity and multimedia can be used to increase comprehension or facilitate understanding and information retrieval. In addition, they can be used to enhance the user experience. However, these advantages must be competently weighed against the restrictions and distractions such techniques often incur. The goal of this section is to make you aware of the potential usability issues involved in employing interactivity and multimedia and to allow you to make a conscious choice of the tradeoffs involved in adopting such techniques.

Animation

Animation can be a very powerful means of conveying information. It is also a very effective way to mislead, distract, and aggravate users. Animation has repeatedly been shown to distract users. Users would escape from animations by covering the screen with their hands or scrolling animated objects off the display (Spool, Scanlon, Schroeder, and Snyder, 1997). Animation triggers our attention through our low-level visual processes, and as such it is difficult to avoid. However, users do adapt and may ignore your animation entirely.

Thus, animation can cause problems, particularly if you are developing a site where users are searching for information or skimming the page contents. However, there are some advantages to animation. It can be used to help people find information more easily or to describe processes that are difficult to explain simply with text or static diagrammatic representations (see Figure 9-26). Animation can also make information significantly more engaging for the viewer.

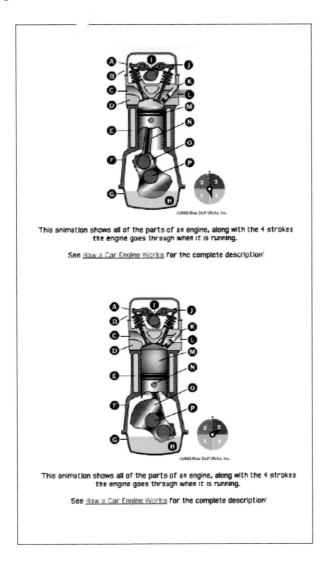

Figure 9-26.

Animations Help Clarify Explanations at howstuffworks.com.

If you plan to use animation on your site, be sure to keep some of these guidelines in mind. Animation should support the user's goals and tasks. You can use animation to elaborate or clarify processes that are not possible to describe in text. That is, animation can be used to convey content, not merely to decorate. Try to keep the animation from looping infinitely (if the user has stayed on a page long enough, it is likely he or she is looking for information on that page and an animation will only serve to distract). Use only a single animation per page, and use it to bring the viewer to the focal point of the page. Animation seriously distracts the eye, so multiple animations can cause a conflict as to where to look on the page.

Macromedia Flash

Flash movies enable highly interactive, animated, multimedia experiences. The use of Flash involves some significant tradeoffs. At the time of this writing, a major concern is what percentage of users actually have the plug-in installed (and the latest version of the plug-in). While Flash can be used quite effectively to provide higher levels of interactivity and more interesting online animation, each use must be carefully considered to make sure that it provides value to the end user without causing problems. The following are some tips for applying Flash with minimal disruption for users.

Always Provide Alternate Methods to Get the Information

Not everyone will want to experience your Flash site, regardless of how great and cool it is. Always provide an alternate and easy way for users to get to your content. If users don't have the plug-in, make sure they see something meaningful.

Make Sure Users Have Control

Give users buttons to skip introductions, animations, and so forth (e.g., "Skip Intro . . ."). The navigation *must be* available and accessible to the user. It is *not* fun to search for navigation, particularly when you are searching for information. Embed a link within the HTML of the page that allows users to skip through animations. Ensure that this is *always* visible to the users. Allow users to turn sound on and off and to control volume levels. Give users access to the Macromedia Flash contextual menu (this enables zooming, sound control, rewinding, and adjusting quality to fit local processing power). Provide navigation that allows users to tab through the choices for accessibility.

Give Users Feedback on the State of the File

Be sure to include a status bar to indicate how far along the movie is in its loading process. Keep the user informed of processes. Provide feedback about status (e.g., loading, clicks received, etc.) and total file size. When you tackle highly interactive interfaces that don't follow a web paradigm, read up on traditional user interface design for applications. Most of the problems have been solved before and are very applicable to Flash development.

Put Movies on Separate Pages

Link to portions of different movies using URLs. This allows users to bookmark specific sections of the site.

User-Test Your Flash Sites

Be sure to perform proper user testing of your web site. Perhaps you'll decide those straight HTML pages are better after all!

EFFECTIVELY INTEGRATING VISUAL DESIGN ELEMENTS

Whether you are integrating conceptual ideas into your pages (e.g., color or typographical principles) or specific elements (e.g., icons, buttons, forms), the development and integration should follow the pervasive usability procedure described throughout this book. This requires understanding the utility of specific elements in relation to user tasks and needs, a method for developing quick and easy drafts of the ideas, a means for testing the true utility of specific elements, and a refinement and review process for the chosen elements. Following this approach will lead to a design that serves to effectively communicate the information and ideas intended.

10

PRODUCTION

USABILITY IN SOFTWARE DEVELOPMENT

The software development phase of the web site development cycle is the last chance to prevent usability problems prior to final testing. It is also a time when unforeseen issues can arise, often where they are not expected. Many potential pitfalls are technology specific and may change over time. In this chapter, we focus on production issues that are likely to continue to cause problems irrespective of the current version of HTML standards. You will find some overlap with the usability issues covered in earlier chapters, but here we discuss techniques for preventing those problems in development. This chapter covers usability issues in the production process, web site engineering techniques, engineering web site components, and usability of web technologies.

USABILITY PROBLEMS

Many of the usability problems that are created during the software development process relate to the extra time it takes users to accomplish their tasks. Download time and system performance time continue to be among the top user complaints. Other issues are caused by server-side problems, inconsistent development practices within a site, changes to a site over time (beyond the Version 1.0 release), and poor use of other non-HTML technologies. There is not necessarily a one-to-one relationship between usability problems and solutions. In some cases, a single technique will address multiple problems. In other cases, multiple techniques are needed to address a single issue. This section discusses such problems. The next section discusses solutions.

Poor Response Time

Speed, speed, speed! Users can't get enough of it. It seems that as soon as hardware and communication technologies speed up enough for acceptable performance, software developers create products that are bigger and slower. A rule of thumb from the early days of client/server systems was that system response times longer than a tenth of a second were noticeable to users and could adversely affect usability. Even fast web pages today take several seconds to display and sometimes much longer. Overuse and misuse of graphics is a primary contributor to slow download time, as are poorly coded pages. Until technology allows us to achieve display speeds closer to a tenth of a second, users will continue to complain about speed.

Response time, however, is not just download time. It is a combination of data transfer time, server processing time, and browser-side display time. Often the real time-delay culprit isn't just the transfer of page contents, but

PRODUCTION

the processing time on the server side. Serving a static web page is a relatively simple task for a web server, but for more complex, dynamic pages, the web server may have to perform database queries, process credit card transactions, or request other services from legacy systems. Each server task contributes to the overall time. Overloaded servers, slow database integration systems, and inefficiently coded server transactions all contribute to slow response time.

A third contributor to poor response time is the time it takes the web browser software to display a web page's screen image. Overly complex or nested HTML table code can add considerably to display time. Unused size attributes for image tags can make progressively downloaded data unusable because the browser constantly shifts screen objects as new objects are loaded. This often makes it practically impossible for users to read any text that may have been displayed earlier.

Web Page Code Inconsistency

Another problem that can surface in production is that different pages written by different coders can be implemented in completely different ways. These differences can change the appearance slightly or dramatically, and can also affect how the page appears while downloading. For example, the decision to code using a single table, multiple tables, or no tables can have a noticeable effect on the final page and how it is presented to the user.

In addition, the use of different coding styles, over time, can become a nightmare for maintenance. The web site *will* change. That is a given. How much the changes will cost, however, is completely up to you. For example, what if your client wanted to make a global change to the size of the buttons on the navigation bar? What would normally be a simple change completed in a matter of seconds from a consistent code base (e.g., one built from templates) could take hours for code written inconsistently by multiple people. Usability is also important for programmer productivity.

Platform Incompatibilities

Many usability problems stem from the ways different browsers, or even the same company's browser implemented on a different computing platform, can interpret the same HTML or JavaScript code differently. For example, JavaScript code that makes use of time and date functions requires separate functions for older versions of Netscape and Internet Explorer because the JavaScript routines were implemented with incompatible outputs. In addition, proprietary and nonstandard extensions of HTML and JavaScript are sometimes incompatible with various browsers and platforms.

Poor Use of Technology

Companies are always trying to find some technological edge to set themselves apart from the competition. The Web has provided such companies an endless supply of bleeding-edge technology with which to wreak usability havoc on hapless users. Early on we saw a proliferation of huge, beautiful graphics that served no other purpose than eye candy. Then came animated GIFs, movies, Java applications, Flash, and so on. While each of these is very useful for some purposes, they are often used more for their name than for any useful purpose. For example, many companies are creating splashy Flash presentations in place of their home page because that's the hot technology of the moment. This type of design often requires users to download and install the latest plug-ins and requires that the user wait for an extra data file to download, sometimes without any way to bypass it (other than pressing the Back button).

Related to poorly used technology is proper technology that is poorly implemented. In addition to being compatible across platforms, an implementation must be sufficiently robust to handle common user behaviors and errors. For example, what happens if the user clicks on a link before the web page is finished loading? If JavaScript or other hidden code has not been loaded, any calls to nonloaded JavaScript functions will fail, leaving the web browser and the user hanging.

Poor Product Documentation

Documentation is another often overlooked part of web site production. Whether the project will be maintained in-house or by the client, documentation is very important for using, maintaining, and extending a web site. How will the system be used? How will it be updated and maintained? Throughout this book, we've provided techniques and examples for documenting various parts of the web site design process. A site that does not explain how users can most efficiently use it is a usability problem for the users. A site that is delivered without adequate documentation on how it can be best managed, maintained, and updated is a usability problem for the client. Poor documentation of your own web site will, of course, become a usability problem for you and will likely cost much more in lost productivity than the cost of creating proper documentation.

WEB SITE ENGINEERING TECHNIQUES

When building small web sites, coding and production details can usually be kept in the head of a single developer. Any development effort larger than a handful of pages, however, will benefit from some basic software engineering techniques. This section focuses on simple, practical techniques that you can easily apply to web projects. For a more rigorous, comprehensive treatment of software engineering theory and techniques, see one of the standard software engineering texts, such as Pressman's *Software Engineering* (1997). A classic treatment of organizational and practical software development issues can be found in Fred Brooks's *Mythical Man-Month* (1975).

Following proper software engineering techniques (or modifying them for web development) can have a substantial impact on overall system usability primarily because it enables developers to achieve higher quality. This allows developers to systematically meet usability goals on time and within budget. It also allows for better client communications and improves usability for the system's development team.

Software engineering processes are similar in spirit to the overall web development process covered throughout this book, and they follow similar principles of iterative design and pervasive evaluation. However, software development has its own, unique contributions to usability (see the sidebar "Why Software Engineers Are Critical for Usability"), and they are reflected in the following engineering techniques.

Software Requirements and Specifications

Software requirements should be driven by usability requirements and task analysis. Establishing requirements and specifications has a long history in software engineering and is a basic component of most standard engineering methods, such as the Waterfall (Royce 1970) and Spiral methods (Boehm 1988). What those methods do not include are clear linkages from usability requirements. They typically specify what will be built and how it will function, but not why it is needed or how it will be used. Consequently, many systems are built that function according to specification, but are useless.

From task analysis, we've established the pages needed for each task and the system functions required for each page. This is a blueprint for the overall system requirements. That is, we can say, "This is the behavior required by the system." The next step is to take each system function and completely specify its design. This includes a detailed description of what it does, a description for how it will be implemented, a range of acceptable inputs and outputs, and a list of things that can go wrong and what will be done in each event. This allows the interfaces between system functions and components to be verified to ensure that the outputs from one component are those expected as input to the next component. For example, when a user enters an account and password to log in, client-side validation can be written in Javascript to make sure the account name contains only valid letters and numbers before passing the data to the server for back-end processing. However, we cannot rely completely on validation done on the client side. For a more robust system, the back-end software at the server should also specify what will happen if bad data does come in from the browser (perhaps as part of a communications failure or a security breach), and what to do if a password or user name is incorrect. This level of specification is driven by, but not replaced by, usability requirements.

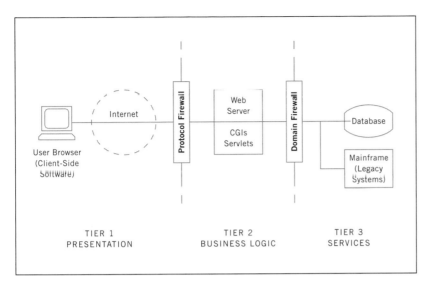

Figure 10-1.

A Sample 3-Tiered Architecture.

The implementation of a web site is divided into three layers, or tiers. Tier 1 is the Presentation tier, which includes all of the user-interface components. Tier 3 is the Services tier, which provides database and legacy system services. Tier 2 is the Business Logic tier, which connects Tiers 1 and 3.

3-Tiered Architectures

A systematic divide-and-conquer approach can be applied to the software development portion of the web site production process by dividing the problem into discrete parts and addressing their respective development issues separately. One paradigm for doing this is to decompose the system architecture into three tiers, or layers (Figure 10-1). This approach, referred to as a *3-tiered* (or, more generally, n-*tiered*) *architecture* (see White et al. 1998; Sadtler et al. 2000), divides the architecture into the following tiers:

Tier 1. Presentation Tier: Includes the user interface, typically a web browser

Tier 2. Business Logic Tier: Includes the web server and any server-side programs that run under it, such as CGIs or Java Servlets

Tier 3. Services Tier: Includes legacy systems, databases, and other back-end services

The Presentation tier refers to the user platform. Typically, this is a web browser running on a personal computer, but it can also refer to a Java applet running in a browser, a Java application running by itself, or any other client software capable of accessing the web server. The Business Logic tier includes the web server, CGIs, and other web server technologies that run within the web server (such as server-side includes), or in support of it (such as server plug-ins). For many web projects, only Presentation and Business Logic layers are used. For more complex sites, such as those serving dynamic content or web applications, a third tier, the Services tier, is also used. The Services tier includes databases and other legacy systems that provide information and back-end services (such as transactions) for the web server.

There are many advantages to using a 3-tiered architecture, including easier development and maintenance and improved scalability and security. By separating the services, business logic, and presentation, system components can be more focused and cohesive, and less coupled, or dependent, on how other system components are implemented. In addition, by logically (and physically) separating the tiers, components of any tier can be upgraded or maintained relatively independently of the other tiers.

Finally, 3-tiered architectures are often used to map out security measures for the system. Typically, this is done by placing firewalls between each of the tiers. In a standard deployment, the firewall between the Presentation and Business Logic tiers is called the *protocol firewall,* and it limits which services can be provided by the Business Logic tier to the Presentation tier. For example, the protocol firewall may allow HTTP requests through to the web server, but not Telnet requests that would allow outside users to control the web server. Between the Business Logic tier and the Services tier, a *domain firewall* is placed that only allows services to be provided to machines within a trusted domain, that is, those in the Business Logic tier.

This type of security structure provides a multilayered defense against potential security threats from outside the system. The main goal for many companies is to protect the legacy systems inside the Services tier, as that tier may contain the most sensitive and mission-critical data. The Business Logic tier serves as a buffer zone, often called the *demilitarized zone* (DMZ), which protects the security of the legacy systems in the event that any single machine is compromised.

Of course, good security contributes to system usability because an exploited system may not be able to provide the information or services to the users when they need it. Perhaps more important, users expect that companies collecting personal information over the Web (e.g., credit card numbers) will safeguard that information. A system that is not secure will not be trusted and will not be used.

Mapping Control and Data Flow

Once the necessary pages and the system functions that will support them are specified (but not necessarily built), data and control flow can also be designed and specified. There are several visual representations, which build on the 3-tiered architecture approach, that can assist developers in ensuring complete functional coverage and facilitate communications among the design team and in communicating designs to customers. The visual aids that will be discussed here are the static design, the dynamic trace, and system latency diagrams. (See White et al. 1998 for other system design techniques.)

Static design diagrams illustrate the logical organization of web applications. They are meant to convey an overview of the system that is especially useful for client communications. Figure 10-2 shows a simplified static view for a business-to-business e-commerce site. In the Presentation tier, the high-level user tasks are represented by thumbnail screens consisting of "login," "get account information," and "purchase products." The web server is represented in the middle tier, and database and transaction services are shown in the Services tier. Firewalls separate the tiers. This logical view may or may not represent the actual number of machines needed. For example, database and transaction servers could coexist on the same machine (although not recommended), and the web server could be distributed to multiple machines for better performance. Likewise, more user screens are required than are shown in this type of view.

A *dynamic request trace* specifies the data flow for accomplishing specific user tasks and the order in which the information exchanges occur. This view goes a layer deeper than static design diagrams, showing the sequence of events that the system will perform as the users perform their tasks. Figure 10-3 shows a simplified dynamic trace for a purchase task. Here, the user presses the Order button after selecting the items for purchase. The request

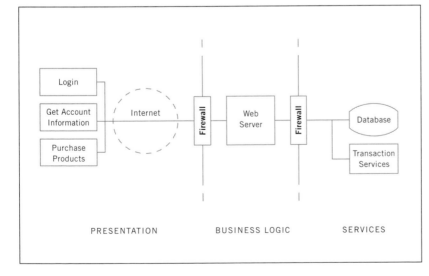

Figure 10-2.

Static Design Diagram.

The system is presented in terms of its high-level, logical components. The boxes on the left represent high-level user tasks that will be implemented. The simplicity of the static design diagram makes it especially useful for communicating with the client.

Figure 10-3.

Dynamic Request Trace.

This diagram traces the flow of data through the components of the system. This particular example shows how a purchase request is processed and a confirmation page is generated.

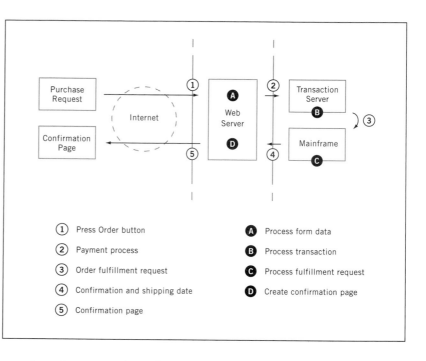

goes from the user to the web server, then to the transaction server for payment processing, then to shipping for order fulfillment, back to the web server with confirmation data, which formats the confirmation into HTML and sends a confirmation page back to the user.

System latency diagrams are useful for showing how much each system function contributes to overall task time. This is especially useful for optimizing system performance and reducing the effects of bottlenecks. Figure 10-4 shows a latency diagram for the purchasing task just described. Here, we see that the major contributors to response time are the transaction and database services. Increasing web server performance at this point would be ineffectual for reducing system response time. Instead, the focus should be on the subsystems providing the transaction and database services. Software, platform, and network issues are all potential culprits, as are any back-end services that go outside the enterprise, such as bank or credit card transactions.

Version Control

Version control is another technique for making the programmer's job easier. It provides a means for maintaining stable versions of your web site or system during and after the production process. Version control provides a layer of abstraction for programmers that allows them to focus on the

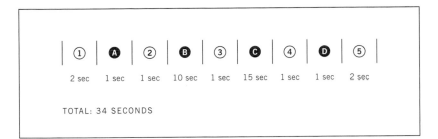

TOTAL: 34 SECONDS

Figure 10-4.

Latency Diagram.

This diagram shows the time taken
for each step of the process in Figure
10-3. This format makes it easy to
identify steps that are time consuming (such as B and C), so that efforts
to speed up the process can focus on
these problem areas.

changes or enhancements to the system without worrying so much about file level questions like, Is this the current version of the file? It is also used to ensure that one developer doesn't overwrite another's changes and allows programmers to work on one copy of the code while other programmers can still use the previous stable version of the code. Code files are then "checked in" after all necessary changes have been made. Of course, this is especially important when more than one person is coding.

Several commercial and open-source version control systems exist (e.g., CVS and Voodoo), each with its own capabilities. Most version control systems provide a means for tracking changes to documents or files, including who is making the change, what they did, why they did it, and when it was done. Some version control systems lock files so that only one person at a time can make modifications.

For simple projects, version control can be accomplished without support software by maintaining a central repository of code and making clear who works on which files. In such cases, it is especially important to make periodic backups of the code when it reaches a stable, working state. This allows developers to dial back to a previous working version if something dramatically wrong happens during development.

Asset Management

Asset management is the systematic practice of tracking various system resources, such as images, content files, Java applets, and HTML files. Some form of asset management is necessary for almost any size project. Asset management exists in some integrated development environments, but it can also be done with just a spreadsheet.

A practical technique for tracking production is to create a spreadsheet with one line for each web page and one column for each element that needs to be tracked (see Figure 10-5). For example, columns might exist for HTML, text, graphics, navigation, JavaScript, and so on. The status of each element can be

Figure 10-5.

Page-Tracking Spreadsheet Used for Asset Management.

A spreadsheet like this one can be useful for tracking the progress of content, which can be difficult to manage when the development is distributed among several people.

	HTML	Text	Graphics	Navigation	JavaScript
HOME PAGE	Tested	Done		*In testing*	Due 12/1
ORDER PAGE	Need to fix	Waiting for client	Done		
CATALOG PAGE	Tested	In progress			

tracked in the individual cells. Creating a database for tracking bugs is also a useful technique both during and after production.

Development, Staging, and Production Servers

Another development practice that can improve usability is the use of staging servers. A staging server is a duplication of the actual server platform (the production server) that can be used to test software, hardware, and other system compatibilities. This is separate from the development systems that the software developers will be using to create the system. Because there are so many possible interactions among server technologies, databases, system software, security, and other legacy components of the system, staging servers give the development team a safe place to holistically test the system. This keeps other live systems safe from development code, which may contain errors. If no other systems are live on the production server, a separate staging area can be set up on the actual production machine. However, this should be avoided, because any testing on the production server increases the risk of crashing the server.

Choosing Web Site Development Tools

With a plethora of web site development tools available, how do you choose ones that will support usability in the development process? Because of the rapidly changing landscape of development systems, no single tool will meet every organization's needs. We can, however, list some of the more useful features to consider when evaluating tools for your own development needs. Just as it's critical to understand the users when developing a web site, it is perhaps even more critical to understand your own developers when choosing a development environment. Simply using freely available tools is not always the most cost-effective path. When evaluating tools, consider at least four broad areas for the usability of the tools: project management, site and asset management, coding support, and technology support.

Project Management

What support does the tool provide for project management functions? In particular, support for the following areas would be helpful:

- Collaboration and version control—support for development teams working on a single code base, which limits version confusion and prevents mistakenly overwriting more recent code.

- Design notes—the ability to add notes or tasks to individual pages regarding status or tasks.

- Project management facilities—support for maintaining project task status, assigning tasks to team members, and producing status reports.

Site and Asset Management

How usable is the functionality for building the architecture of the site and managing the digital assets?

- Site maps—can the site be designed visually in either a tree structure or in outline form?

- Site importing and exporting—can existing sites be imported or exported?

- Asset views—can all assets of a particular type be organized in a coherent manner?

- Template creation—can page templates be created easily?

- File transfer—can modified pages be automatically transferred to staging and production servers?

Coding Support

How well does the tool support the coding of individual web pages? The following features are particularly useful:

- Text coloring—use color to automatically differentiate between HTML, scripts, and content.

- Syntax checking—check code syntax for valid constructs.

- Link checking—check links for invalid or dead links.

- Accessibility checking—make sure that ALT tags and other code elements are used to ensure equal accessibility to the content.

- Code indenting—help the developer organize the code in a readable form.

- WYSIWYG and code views—switch easily between code and page layout views.

- Script editing and debugging—provide tools for editing and debugging the scripting language of choice.

- Table creation—provide graphic tools for laying out tables and form views for specifying exact parameters.

- Form creation—provide drag-and-drop or other tools for rapidly creating HTML forms.

- No code mangling—automated tools should never change code you've written by hand.

Technology Support

Every organization and development team has certain technologies in which it specializes. How well does the tool support the use of those technologies?

- Dependence on nonstandard server technologies—does the development environment depend on server technologies that will limit how you deploy the site?

- Style sheets—is there support for creating, maintaining, and using style sheets?

- XML—does the environment support XML?

- Database integration—how easily can you create database-driven sites?

- Plug-in support—does the environment support third-party plug-ins for technologies it does not directly support?

- Project-specific technologies—can you easily develop sites using technologies with which your development team is proficient?

New development environments and new versions of existing tools are continually becoming available. For productivity and, ultimately, for the usability of the web sites you are developing, your team should have usable development tools that fit the way they work and that support your organization's development processes.

ENGINEERING WEB SITE COMPONENTS

To improve project management of web site projects, it is useful to separate the technical components that go into a web site's development. The categorizations made in this section are not necessarily distinct, but are made based on the roles you might assign to various programmers, the skills required, and the usability issues that might come up.

Web site development can be decomposed into two broad development efforts: client side and server side. Client-side development consists of three general areas: HTML page construction, client side scripting, and client side programming. HTML page construction refers to formatting the content and layout of individual pages with HTML, as well as integrating other technologies into HTML pages, such as Java or Flash applets. Client-side scripting includes JavaScript or Visual Basic scripting that is sometimes included as part of a web page and interacts with the visual components on the page itself. Client-side programming includes Java or Flash programs that run primarily on the user's browser platform.

Server-side development can also be categorized into at least three possible components: CGI programming, database and enterprise integration, and database development. CGI (common gateway interface) programming refers to general-purpose server-side programming, such as form parsing, date calculations, and other numeric processing that is difficult or impossible to do on the client side. CGI programs are typically developed using PERL, C++, or a scripting language. Serving the same purpose as CGI programming (but technically different from it) is Java Servlet programming. Database integration is how database technologies are tied to the dynamic web pages. Although CGI programming is often used to access databases, the issues involved with database integration are specific to accessing databases. Database integration is sufficiently different from other forms of web development that it deserves separate consideration. It includes Java Server Pages (JSPs), PHP, and Active Server Pages (ASPs). Database development includes the design of databases that feed dynamic web pages or that service transactions. Server-side development encompasses CGI and other server-side technologies such as PERL, C++, or Java programs.

The following sections describe techniques for preventing the types of usability problems discussed at the beginning of this chapter. Some techniques address a single problem only, but others alleviate multiple usability problems. Each technique will be explained, and the usability problems it solves will be pointed out.

HTML Page Construction Techniques

In any large project, it just isn't possible to hand-code each page individually. For any large web site project, it's necessary to begin by creating, testing, and debugging templates. Even after mockup pages or other prototypes have been user tested, it's still necessary to build solid templates to make sure they can actually work for the data they will contain or the function they will serve. To start, identify how many different types of templates will be necessary, even if it is just as a sanity check for early design phases. For instance, mock-ups may have been created for a home page and subpages, but what about product pages? If any set of pages will contain a vastly different type or set of data, a new template should be created and tested. Also test the boundary conditions with regard to page content. That is, if you test how a template works for the pages with the most and least content, you can be reasonably sure it will work for everything in between. Finally, make sure to get approval for any new templates that the client did not review during the mockup stage.

HTML Coding Guidelines

These are some general principles to follow in the process of coding HTML.

Code for Speed

Test download times for the slowest reasonable connection that users will have. For the general public, assume no faster than a 28.8-baud modem connection. (For users connecting through a cellular phone, 14.4 baud is often the maximum achievable rate.) Is the response time still reasonable at that speed? Maximum download time can be estimated by summing the file sizes for all components of your pages. Anything more than about 100K per page may create unreasonable delays for users with slower internet connections.

Code for Rendering

Reduce the number and complexity of any tables that are used, so that pages will display faster. Large, nested tables are more difficult to parse and take longer for browsers to render. Generally, the fewer the tables, the faster that users will be able to use screen data. In addition, ensure that all size attributes are used for image and applet tags. Otherwise, browsers may adjust the rendered layout on the fly, making changes as new information is downloaded. This creates an unstable and potentially confusing user experience, as screen elements jump around while the page is progressively updated.

Code for Accuracy

Use HTML syntax checkers to test the validity of your HTML code. Improperly formed syntax will display unpredictably in different browsers and with different user preferences selected. Also check for common mistakes that simple syntax checkers may not find, such as table data that is outside of <TD> tags.

Code for Maintenance

Document page code liberally with comments so that sections are easily found later. It is especially important to mark header, footer, navigation, and content sections. To the extent possible, also separate content and HTML tags onto different lines. While this sometimes cannot be done because it will change the layout, it is easier to select an entire line or block of lines if the entire block is content. This minimizes the need to select text from within a line of HTML tags, reducing the possibility of introducing syntax errors while updating content.

Code for Search Engines

Add necessary metatags and text so users can find your pages. Search engines work on the basis of relevance: they find pages with keywords and descriptions similar to the terms you're searching for. Those pages with the most words or word meanings matching a query will be returned first. It is therefore important to include keyword and description metatags with every page. They should include some general terms that describe your entire web site and some that refer to the specific page. For example, the Giraffe page described in Chapter 4, "Task Analysis," might include some keywords describing the company and children's toys, as well as keywords describing the specific stuffed giraffe product shown on the page. It is also prudent to include any common misspellings or variations in your keywords, as users don't always know or take the time to figure out the correct spelling for what they want. It is not, however, ethical or legal to include competitor's trademarked or service-marked terms in your keywords. Some search engines also index the content of your pages (especially the first 200 characters of the page), so include as many relevant keywords in the text as is reasonably possible (without detracting from the message, of course).

Keep in Mind Evolving HTML Standards

In addition to following current HTML standards as closely as possible, pay attention to new standards, so that your code is likely to be compatible with future browser releases for as long as possible, and so porting the code to new versions will be a minimal strain. See the sidebar "Why XML Is Good for Usability" for details on one of the most important standards that is likely to influence future web development.

WHY XML IS GOOD FOR USABILITY

XML (Extensible Markup Language) is a markup language for organizing structured information. Like HTML, XML consists of tags used to mark parts of the document. However, while HTML contains tags for specifying both the semantics of the content and how it should be displayed, XML makes a clear distinction between the two.

For example, the HTML <H1> tag (a semantic tag) indicates that the author intends the content to be a high-level heading. It specifies the semantics of content, and the text it marks is typically displayed by browsers in a large bold typeface. The same result could be achieved by using the <BOLD> and <FONT> tags (display tags), but they give no indication as to the purpose of the content. XML forces the author to use semantic tags only for marking document content, and to use separate style documents (either XSL or CSS files) to indicate how the semantic tags should be displayed. It is also extensible, so that document authors (or standards committees) can define appropriate semantic tags specific to the content of the document. For example, an online parts catalog might have tags such as <PartName>, <PartNumber>, <PartDescription>, <PartImage>, and <PartPrice> to describe each part. A separate style sheet might then specify that <PartName> should be displayed as 14-point, bold Helvetica type, <PartNumber> should be displayed in a 12-point monospaced font, and so on.

Content Reuse

The power and structure of XML have several important implications. The forced separation of semantics and display makes reusing content straightforward. For example, by changing only the style sheets, the information used for the online parts catalog can be used to create a print version of the catalog (say, with three products per page) or it can be formatted into a tabular form (say, with 30 items per page). This ease of reuse has the potential to improve usability, because it makes it more likely that information will be displayed in a format that better supports the user's needs.

Platform Optimizations

Similarly, the separation of semantics and display supports customized data formatting for individual platforms. This means richer designs can be created, because design elements do not need to be reduced to the lowest common denominator supported by all browsers. For example, the same structured content can be used to serve both desktop users connected with a T1 line and handheld users with a cellular connection without compromising the quality of the user experience.

PRODUCTION

Domain-Specific Searches

A third benefit of XML is that semantically tagged documents can be more efficiently searched than standard HTML. This is especially true when the meaning of the semantic tags is known to the user conducting the search. For example, if the user knew that a specific search term was included in the part name of a desired product, the search engine could limit its search to content marked with the <PartName> tag of each document. Not only is this technique faster than searching through the entire product page, but the results are more relevant as well. This feature of XML can greatly enhance the usability of search tasks.

Improved Data Sharing

Finally, XML has the ability to improve the usability of data communications. Prior to XML, companies and organizations defined *special-purpose* communication protocols and data structures. Every time a new relationship was formed, a significant effort was taken to integrate the new protocol within the existing infrastructure. That included, for example, high-level translation, so that the data Company 1 called "PartName" got mapped into what Company 2 called "ItemName." It may also have included the order in which the fields were sent and even the order in which the data bits were transmitted.

For example, EDI (Electronic Data Interchange) is an existing standard protocol, frequently used for conducting electronic transactions among banks and other companies. Although EDI has been in use for decades, there is still confusion about how best to implement it. Now, banks and other companies, such as those in the automotive industry, are using XML to improve on translation by defining standard semantic tag sets for particular domains. Thus they have document definitions for everything from automotive parts to mathematical equations, and more are being defined all the time. Having a standard definition for data elements that need to be shared or communicated, as is the case with XML, means that the only translators that need to be built are those between the standard definition and the internal definition. This greatly facilitates the flow of information and increases the likelihood that users will have the right information at the right time.

Client-Side Scripting Techniques

Client-side scripting languages, such as JavaScript and JScript, can be programmed to provide user interface elements that are not possible in traditional HTML. In general, client-side scripting makes dynamic behavior possible without accessing the web server. For instance, events such as mouse-overs (when the cursor is moved over an object) can be detected and used to create useful feedback for users. Mouse-over events can be used to trigger a visual cue to the user by changing a graphic to indicate that an object is clickable. This effect is called a *rollover*. Rollovers can also be used to provide contextual help by presenting messages that explain what will happen if the user clicks on the object.

Another good use for scripts is validating user-supplied data in forms prior to sending the data to the server. This allows common user errors to be detected and responded to without the latency associated with a server request. Scripts can be used to program other sophisticated behaviors such as interactive forms that update calculations when information is changed. Despite these positive aspects, scripting also tends to be overused, complicating the interface and slowing user interaction with bloated script code and gratuitous graphics. Rollovers, for example, when used to hide the full description of a link whose title is insufficiently descriptive, force the user to engage in minesweeping (moving the mouse to discover hidden information) in order to do a task.

To implement successful client-side scripts, code defensively. Be thorough and cautiously rule out possible errors in order to produce robust code. Put all script subroutines in the head portion of the HTML page. This prevents the user from calling routines that have not been defined. Wrap these routines in comment tags so that older browsers will ignore them. Specify which script and version you're using if you are using routines that are not backward-compatible with older browsers. Know which routines are not cross-platform-compatible and find other solutions.

In addition, follow good software engineering practices. Scripting languages are very similar to general-purpose programming languages and can be just as difficult to debug. Factor the scripts into small, cohesive subroutines that perform one function only. Such routines are easier to write, test, and debug. For complex scripts, consider creating flowcharts or structure charts to prevent logic errors. Declare all variables and document their purposes and types. Document each subroutine similarly. Keep page-specific variables and constants at the top of the code so you don't have to wade through all the code to customize it for every page.

Client-Side Programming

You may include Java, Flash, or other plug-in programming on the client side if it contributes to usability. The usability issues with client-side programming are similar to those of scripting, only multiplied. The user interaction techniques for Java applets are very rich, providing limitless

PRODUCTION

interface possibilities. Unfortunately, that power comes with a price. Java applets must be downloaded each time the user visits a page; applets typically run slower than normal programs; and they take a significant amount of time to download. In addition, the Java Runtime Environment takes extra startup time the first time any applet is run during a browser session. Client-side programming shares the general guidelines of scripting—that is, code defensively and use good programming practices.

There is one additional client-side programming rule of thumb: Put users in control. Let them have a choice about whether to use Java or plug-in technology, provide alternatives, and make the choices clear. Do not require them to download your code without knowing why they are doing it and how long it will take, or without providing an alternative.

CGI Programming

CGI programming allows for outside programming languages to be used on a web server to extend the capabilities of HTML. CGI programs are typically written in PERL, C, C++, or a server-platform-specific scripting language. At one level, every CGI program behaves the same: it takes user input from the browser, does some processing, and sends a response page back to the browser. Despite this seemingly simple approach, most end-user applications currently in use on the Web (e.g., bulletin boards, calendars, web-based email) have probably been implemented, at some time, as a CGI program.

CGI performance can be limited because CGI programs tend to require a separate process to run in. This requires additional system overhead and can cause scalability problems. CGI programming also lacks good debugging tools, so CGI programs must be tested on a real web server, even while in development. The CGI protocol is thus very powerful, but it also has some inherent performance limitations that may not allow it to scale well without additional hardware and software server support.

Depending on the application, CGI programs may have access to sensitive information on the web server (e.g., database records or transaction files). Since they are often compiled, CGI programs are also less likely than HTML to change over time. Therefore, prior to deployment, extra care should be taken to understand the security and long-term implications of CGI.

As with other aspects of software development, you should code defensively. Don't depend on client-side validation for your inputs. Communication or security problems could alter the assumption of valid data. Also, write your code for easy maintenance. Separate the response code from the logic code, either in a segregated section of the code or, preferably, in a separate file. Response pages are most likely to change, so separating the response page from the CGI code enables an HTML programmer to make the changes and you won't need to put a software engineer on the job.

Database and Enterprise Integration

Database and enterprise integration is a very powerful technique for creating a wide variety of data-driven and transaction-driven web applications. Although this web development component is similar and shares many of the characteristics of CGI programming, this specific application of CGI-like programming has a unique set of constraints and issues associated with it. Many database queries follow a common sequence of interaction steps: generate a search string and submit the search; view the list of returned records (hits) and locate the correct record; and view details of the desired record.

Database Interaction Guidelines

Database and enterprise integration is about providing web access to what are often huge repositories of information. Care should be taken to provide sufficient capabilities in the interface for the users to achieve their goals without being overwhelmed. Some suggested ways to structure a user's interaction with databases include the following:

Provide Users with Just Enough Search Capability
Databases often contain much more information than we can usefully search. Unless the user really needs advanced search capabilities, Boolean arguments on every data field make the search task overly complicated.

Limit the Number of Returned Records
Don't just dump out all 500 records in response to a query. Give the user a choice about how many records to return, if possible. Chances are, if the return list is too large, the user will want to refine the search anyway.

Provide Sufficient Information in the Return List
Display search results in a logical order and with enough detail so that the user can distinguish one from another without viewing their details.

Database Development

As discussed, databases are an extremely powerful tool for web development. For lightweight applications (those with relatively few records or infrequent use), a lightweight database engine such as Microsoft Access or Filemaker Pro is just fine. Databases can be rapidly created in those environments and web applications rapidly prototyped. For heavyweight applications like an e-commerce site serving thousands of requests per second, an industrial-strength database management system is required. High-performance database management systems such as DB2 or Oracle, however, have significant development overhead and typically require highly trained professionals to set up and maintain.

USABILITY OF WEB TECHNOLOGIES

With the proliferation of web technologies, how do you decide which to use? When considering whether to use a particular technology, you need to ask the following questions to keep from failing your users by getting caught up in the most recent fad.

- Does this technology provide real value to the user?

- Is it cross-platform?

- Is it standard (do people need to download a plug-in)?

- How much of the user's time will be saved?

- How will users use it?

- How much learning will it require?

- What are the overall benefits to the user and provider?

- What are the development and maintenance costs?

- Will the extra complexity add significant risk to the project?

Example: Usability of Frames

Frames are sometimes used in web pages to enable convenient navigation. However, they also introduce a variety of problems, many of which have to do with how the browser supports frames. As an example of weighing the trade-offs in applying a certain technology, here is a list of pros and cons for frames. While our experience is that frames are most often a problem for users, consider which of these issues applies to your situation and choose accordingly.

Advantages of Using Frames

Frames can provide a technical solution that facilitates a successful user interaction. Frames can improve quality by making software development easier, primarily by facilitating the separation of content and navigation. Following are a few of the most common advantages.

Nonscrolling page components: Certain items, such as ads and navigation, can remain on the screen at all times.

Uncluttered printing: Printing is more content-specific, since usually only a single frame is printed. This can be useful, for instance, if users want to print pages from an online manual for inclusion in a preexisting document and they want the printed format to match that of the current document. The surplus navigation will not be printed.

Mandatory home page traversal: Because bookmarks only capture the URL of the frameset, you can make sure that all bookmarks will lead to your home page. This can be useful for very dynamic sites where the content changes often (no "Document Not Found" errors). It's also useful if you want to force the user to come in through the front page (so they see current events, new postings, etc.).

Easy maintenance: Frames make it easier to change navigation, if it's only in one frame (but if pages are dynamically generated this shouldn't be a big deal). Other maintenance may be easier because page components can be separated.

Easier development: Frames can decrease development time because content can easily be developed independently of navigation. Checking for consistency across pages is also simplified (although frames themselves can sometimes be tricky to implement correctly).

Embedded external sites: Frames can be used to keep people from leaving your site when they click external links, by displaying external pages within a frame.

Increased speed: Pages load faster, although there isn't a big difference as long as graphics are reused between pages of the nonframe version. The main speed advantage of frames is the reduction of screen refresh time, generally not download time.

Disadvantages of Using Frames

Despite these desirable advantages, frames create a more complicated and confusing user interface, and they introduce new design problems. The frequency with which we observe these usability problems generally leads us to avoid the use of frames.

Confused printing: The print command usually prints the most recently selected frame. In many cases this is a navigation frame, not the desired content frame, which can be extremely confusing to users.

PRODUCTION

Inefficient use of screen real estate: Frame layout is extremely difficult for small window sizes (anyone with a smaller monitor). For smaller windows, a logo, a navigation bar, and ads can use up half the window or more.

Inability to bookmark subpages: Bookmarks don't work as users expect, so it's not possible to bookmark a subpage within a frame. Only the home page can be bookmarked.

Confusing Back button and History behavior: The Back button in the browser does not always behave as users expect (should you return to the previous frame or the previous frameset?), and the History does not show subpages within a frame, so browsing back to previous pages is extremely confusing.

Impracticality of navbar changes: Changing the appearance of the current page in the navbar is not practical with frames. This can be done by reloading the whole frameset, but this means you have less of the speed and maintenance advantage of frames.

Incompatibility with redundant text links: We generally recommend including a text version of links so that people with graphics turned off can still navigate. If you use frames, you will need to do one of the following: only use text links for navigation (less interesting, less customizable); only use graphics links (in which case users can't easily navigate with images turned off); include text and graphics in your navigation frame (confusing and ugly); or include text navigation at the bottom of your content frame (and thus you don't get the ease-of-development advantage of frames).

Unpredictable search engine behavior: Sites built with frames don't interact well with search engines, since an individual frame can be indexed as a page, so that when a user visits the page, they're missing the other frames in the frameset (such as the navigation).

Complicated keyboard controls: Users can normally scroll through a page with the scroll buttons on the keyboard (arrows, page up/down, home/end). With frames, this only works when the user explicitly chooses the frame first. In most cases, this is only an inconvenience. For users with motor disabilities, this can make the page significantly less accessible.

Potential problems when scrolling is turned off: If you turn off scrolling in a frame, make sure all the content correctly displays on small monitors and small window sizes.

Problems on small screens: While frames can work on desktop machines, they don't translate well onto small screens, such as mobile phones and PDAs.

In many cases, the benefits of frames can be duplicated in HTML without frames. This example illustrates how we go about evaluating the use of a new technology—we systematically weigh the tradeoffs to determine whether use of the technology is justified in each situation.

PRINCIPLED SOFTWARE DEVELOPMENT

The software development portion of web site production is typically not considered a prime source of usability problems. This chapter, however, points out many places where usability issues creep in. These potential usability problems can be detected and eliminated by following some simple guidelines and a systematic, well-documented software development process. Good software development practices lead to improved usability, and a thoughtful software developer makes countless daily design decisions that can dramatically affect the user experience.

LAUNCH

PRE-LAUNCH
AND POST-LAUNCH

The steps involved in launching your site are as critical and relevant to success as requirements analysis, writing, or page layout. Just prior to launch, extensive final quality assurance is required, and at launch, several critical items must be tested. After launch, you'll need to promote and maintain your site and to continue testing and evaluating its performance.

Quality assurance is central to a pervasive usability approach. After all, a site that doesn't work correctly certainly isn't usable. Making a seamless transition to a live site requires an extraordinary amount of planning. And having an error free and easily maintainable design contributes to the overall usability of your web site.

The launch of your site is not an isolated event achieved the instant the site is ready to go live. It requires weeks (if not months) of preparation. This chapter reviews the procedures that should accompany your approach to the launch as well as ways to track and target changes once the web site is up and running.

Keep in mind that this chapter is structured chronologically for expository purposes. Several of the subjects here should be part of a pervasive framework and integrated much earlier in your design process. For example, code testing is not a one-shot review at the end of the design process, but rather an integrated process that is undertaken throughout the design process.

IN THE MONTHS BEFORE THE LAUNCH

If you spend any time chatting in web design circles, you probably already know that you are more likely to find the Holy Grail than you are to find a web site that has launched on time. However, there are ways around the constant truancy of web sites.

Developing a Pre-Launch Schedule

A pre-launch schedule can keep you on track and remind you of the smaller issues that often lead to delays. A postproduction checklist will allow you to review items quickly and efficiently. The following section reviews many areas that often turn up as last-minute problems. By scheduling time for the following processes, you can ensure that you'll have the extra time at the end of a project to deal with truly unexpected events that will undoubtedly transpire.

Pre-Launch Planning

Testing aside, some preparation is necessary for the final launch date. Technical planning ensures that your server will be available, your domain name and security certificates are working (and payments are up to date), your server has been tested with all the software services that will be required at launch, and capacity and security plans are in place. You also need to coordinate with the business end of your site, making sure that marketing doesn't announce the site before it's ready (they're very eager) and that they do announce it when it is ready, that business partners and customers are ready to conduct business through the site, and that internal support staff and support processes are ready to go.

Registering Your Domain Name

One of the crucial planning steps is to make sure you've selected and registered your domain name before launch. This is something it's wise to do very early in your project, and it must be done before going live.

Choose a domain name that is easy for your users to guess, to remember well, to type quickly, and to type without spelling problems. Whenever possible, most businesses will want to get a *.com* address, because browsers will default to *.com* when the user omits the extension.

In addition to your primary domain name, consider getting alternatives that users might enter when they guess alternative spellings or abbreviations, when they choose to hyphenate or not hyphenate multiword names, and when they misspell your name (see Figure 11-1). You can find out what these alternatives might be by asking your prospective users what they think the domain name for your business is, and asking them to type it in so you can see what misspellings they make (or ask them to type it over and over again as quickly as they can, and you can count how commonly each misspelling occurs). Also consider whether you need to register *.net* and *.org* alternatives for your name and abusive misspellings of your name (to prevent other companies who use a domain name similar to yours from creating a parody of your site or competing with you).

THE CHALLENGE OF QUALITY ASSURANCE TESTING

Quality assurance (QA) processes should occur throughout the production process. QA needs to start at the beginning of a project and never end. While QA is continuous, it reaches its pinnacle in the final stages of the production process before the web site is launched.

Figure 11-1.

Consider What the User Will Type to Visit Your Site.

The window in (a) is what we got by typing *amnesty.org*, which doesn't work. When we entered *www.amnesty.org*, we got the site for Amnesty International, as shown in (b). Be sure to activate your domain name to work both with and without the *www.*, since people will often type the shorter version.

(a)

(b)

Why Bother with Quality Assurance?

QA may seem painful at times; however, its benefits greatly outweigh the growing pains involved in establishing quality assurance processes. QA serves several purposes:

- Providing design guidance early in the design process

- Eliminating errors as early as possible

- Achieving an overall cost savings by catching errors early

- Providing guidelines for changes, additions, versioning, and so forth

- Verifying that the original site requirements are still meaningful

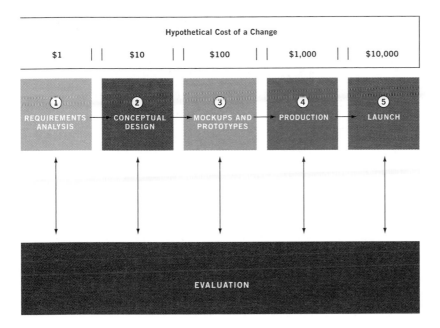

Figure 11-2.
Catch Problems Early.

Quality assurance needs to start early in the development process because the cost of fixing a given problem increases dramatically as the project progresses.

A major benefit of developing pervasive QA measures is the cost savings from instituting error-saving devices early on in the design process. In software development, the earlier you catch an error, the less expensive it is to fix (see Figure 11-2).

In addition to catching errors at the earliest stage possible, properly recorded QA measures provide a reference manual for the design. This can help to eliminate repeated errors, minimize the chances of breaking something when performing a fix (a much more common occurrence than any of us would like to admit), and provide a rationale for the course of the design.

Integrating Quality Assurance Measures

There's no limit to the level at which you can integrate quality assurance measures into your process—you can always keep improving your site. However, 100 percent quality requires infinite cost. You'll never develop a product that is perfect. Even if you test the product thoroughly, your test or tester might be wrong, in which case you will need to test the test. This leads to infinite regress. Thus, you need to designate a level of quality that can be targeted in a cost-effective way.

The level of quality often depends on the cost of failure. For example, an interface that is used to ensure that people receive life-saving medicine in time will require much more testing and a higher level of error-free operation than an interface for a game that has no life-threatening costs to the users. Thus, determine a critical level of error-free workmanship and set this as your goal. Do this up front and by weighing the costs of any mistakes that may make it into the product. This can then be used as a guide for your quality assurance measures.

Regression Testing

Regression testing is retesting after you've made a fix. Regression testing verifies two things: that the fix you made actually fixed the problem that had been identified, and that the fix you made didn't break anything else in the process.

A vast majority of problems are caused by designers and coders trying to fix things. Too often this happens because, when making minor changes or "obvious" fixes, no thought is given to testing the site after the changes have been made.

The introduction of new problems can be minimized by documenting the changes made and the tests performed and making sure retesting is part of the process. This documentation allows you to understand the implications of changes and any important dependencies that may exist, thus facilitating later changes as well.

Quality Assurance Feedback Methods

Your quality assurance processes need to test not only that things are working properly, but also whether or not the original requirements were sufficient. Thus, something may work fine and according to the requirements, but if the requirements were ill founded, then all you've gained is the knowledge that a bad design has been properly implemented.

You need to develop a method for informing earlier stages of design based on testing experiences. This feedback loop allows you to reevaluate and correct earlier assumptions when they may have catastrophic implications. You want to minimize the probability of having to correct earlier assumptions, and having a well-planned design process will help, but you also need a way to inform people of problems at the development and requirements levels. This means establishing processes for informing your design team about how they need to change things and what the critical differences need to be.

QUALITY ASSURANCE TESTING BEFORE THE SITE IS LAUNCHED

Several things need to happen before you can even begin to think about launching your web site. Functional specifications must be created, formalized testing procedures need to be in place, test completion criteria should be met, and methods for reporting and making changes must be in place.

Task-Based Testing

Examining the processes that users will most likely be interested in and ensuring that they occur flawlessly is the goal of this type of testing. This is not a completely comprehensive approach to testing, but rather a matter of placing emphasis on exploring the most common paths of the web site.

You should focus on testing the possible paths a user might take through the web site for the most common or critical tasks. Develop some specific questions that the user might have and then evaluate whether or not users could achieve these goals. For example, a library site may expect the users to find directions to the site, find the database of documents and successfully search and find an item, and perhaps find contact information in order to call the library.

Draft a formal listing of the process tasks and results tasks that users should be able to achieve. You can then test that each of the processes can be achieved in a reasonable way, note those that are problematic, and use your formalized feedback mechanisms to alert the whole design team of problems. As an example, Table 11-1 presents typical results from a QA test performed by a quality assurance specialist. A similar task-based approach to user testing is covered in Chapter 12, "Usability Evaluation."

This method is not guaranteed to catch every problem with your web site. However, it will help to identify the larger issues and will let you know if your major tasks can be achieved. It will not test every possible behavioral path through the site. Task-based testing often catches the most glaring problems—that is, those related to the subset of tasks you've chosen to investigate—and is more useful in the early stages of design. The best testing will occur with a suite of tests that includes both task-based testing and a more comprehensive testing process.

Task or Process	Completed Task?	Comments
Can get from home page to contact page	√	No problems
Can successfully find the following book title: "My Goodness . . ."	√	Had slight trouble with initiating search
Can find the location of the library	√	
Can download a .PDF from the web site	No	Links broken to .PDFs! Need to fix; relative directory is incorrect
Readability and legibility sufficient (have read aloud)	√	No problems

The Code Test and Comprehensive Testing Procedures

While task-based testing will catch major problems of the web site, you need to ensure that the site will behave correctly in *every* instance and path the user may take. In other words, you want to be sure that there are no major errors or broken links in your site. Similarly, with mission-critical systems, such as e-commerce or transactional systems, you should perform a thorough review of the code to ensure proper calculations. For this, a set of code-testing procedures must be developed. As mentioned earlier, the level to which this needs to occur depends on the nature of the web site you are developing. Mission-critical sites require much more thorough testing than sites designed primarily for entertainment.

There are several methods for code testing that have been established through years of software engineering experience that can be applied to web site design. The following is provided as an overview of the possible methods. You may select the most appropriate for your given needs.

Code Review

Code should be reviewed by another programmer or set of programmers. This means having other programmers actually read through the code line by line to verify that it implements the site's requirements and procedures. This should be an established practice for all mission-critical code. The more eyes that review the code, the more likely it is that you'll catch simple programming mistakes such as one-off errors or rounding errors in calculations. This is essential for any transactional system in order to avoid costly mistakes

Unit Testing

Unit testing refers to taking a functional subset of the system (a unit) and verifying that the outputs are correct—for example, examining a particular subset of a task such as a piece of code that processes an individual form. In unit testing, you want to ensure that a single piece of code can take the proper inputs or parameters and produce the relevant outputs.

Automated Testing

There are several ways to automate the testing of web pages. This is particularly useful for checking links and making sure that they exist and do not surprise the user with a dreaded "404 File Not Found" error.

One method involves writing scripts that behave like a user but send all of the possible paths and elements to the computer. This can be very useful for regression testing. Once a test has been created, it is easy to test updates to the pages because the same script can be run again to ensure that nothing has been broken when making updates.

Another method of automated testing is provided by automated link-testing programs available both in the public domain and on the retail market. These are systems that will automatically check all the links on a given page. Such programs are not perfect, however, and should not replace other forms of testing (see sidebar "Limitations of Automated Testing").

Load Testing

Load testing ensures that you can support a large number of simultaneous users without dropping information in the transfer process. You can load-test the number of concurrent *users* that can view your pages but, more critically, you may want to focus on the number of simultaneous *transactions* that can occur.

Load testing will give you an idea of the number of users or transactions you can expect before experiencing trouble. This will help you understand how your site might handle a spike in traffic, or how well it will stand up to service limitations due to limited back-end or ISP capacity. When performing these tests, you'll want to be sure that the number of users you can handle is sufficiently higher than your average number of users. Estimating such numbers is an art form. At the very least, you should be able to handle spikes of three to four times your normal traffic during peak hours. Again, this also depends on the type of site you have. If you are selling products, then you may expect even larger spikes that coincide with product releases on your web site, and so you may want to set your threshold for much larger spikes (e.g., the spike that comes when a new Harry Potter book is released).

In evaluating what level support you need for various loads, ask yourself the following questions: How critical is it that people can access your site? Do you lose money if people can't get there or perform transactions? What kind of users do you have: a more dynamic user base or a static, consistent user base? (A dynamic user base, one with more turnover in users, may be more highly variable in load, while a more static user base may provide more predictable numbers.) What kind of content do you have? Do you have time-dependent features, such as found on a news site?

Outsourcing

Another approach to testing is to outsource the work. Specialized testing companies can perform a wide variety of tests that are often difficult and expensive to perform in-house. In addition, they often have access to a wide diversity of users and testing environments. For example, they may have several sites around the world that they can use to test global bandwidth or cross-cultural issues. If you require a good deal of testing and don't necessarily have the expertise and equipment in-house, you may want to consider outsourcing as a possible solution.

Severity of Errors

While the severity of an error can be construed as a degree or point along a continuum, it makes sense to rank errors for ease of tracking. A basic software triage categorizes problems into one of three levels of severity: mission-critical errors, moderate errors, and minor errors.

As we mentioned above, you can never eliminate *all* problems, so you'll want to set a target level for declaring that the site is adequately bug-free for launch, called the *test-completion criteria*. A common target is to eliminate all mission-critical problems, most of the moderate problems, and as many minor problems as your budget allows.

Mission-Critical Errors

Mission-critical errors are also known as *fatal errors*. These are the errors you *must* catch or the web site and final product will fail. Mission-critical errors prevent users from achieving their goal. While fatal errors are traditionally thought of as errors that crash the system (or, in this case, the web browser), in web site design this term should be extended. For example, missing a submission button on an order form would be considered a fatal error because a critical task cannot be completed.

Moderate Errors

Moderate errors are those problems that are irritating and may make you look stupid, but don't prevent the users from continuing to do what they need to do. An example of this is a user who is uncertain of how to submit an order request because you've decided to label the button "OK." Moderate problems should be ranked in order of severity and based on the cost involved in making the changes.

Minor Errors

Minor errors are those problems that pose little or no obstacle to the user achieving a task but can be distracting. Typos are often considered minor problems when they appear in the middle of a paragraph of text. Color dithering problems, alignment problems, and duplicate links can all be considered minor problems. They usually do not impede users in performing their tasks but can reflect poorly on the level of professionalism associated with your site.

Types of Errors

In addition to ranking the severity levels of the problems you encounter, it's also important to document and be aware of the *types* of errors that are cropping up. Classifying the type of error will help determine who on the design team needs to make the corrections and also helps to determine the severity and priority of the fix. There are four broad categories of errors.

Cosmetic Errors

Cosmetic errors commonly refer to image-loading problems, alignment flaws, readability and legibility problems, color and palette issues, typos, and basic page layout inconsistencies. These errors are usually only minor disruptions to the user, but you need to be aware that some cosmetic errors can keep the user from achieving desired tasks. For example, a missing graphic might cause navigation problems.

Structural Errors

Structural errors manifest themselves as structural design problems. They are often the result of poor information architecture or overlooked user paths through the web site, for example, a site architecture with a dead-end page requiring the user to hit the browser Back button. Worse yet would be a site that didn't allow a user to get from the product page to the order page. User testing can be extremely useful in identifying structural design errors and should be integrated early in the process to avoid major changes toward the end of the project.

Platform Errors

Platform errors are errors that appear only in specific hardware, operating system, or browser configurations. These appear when testing on multiple platforms. For example, when exploring page layout on different machines, the text may overflow the display area on a PC but not on a Mac (conversely, text that looks fine on a PC may be too small to read on a Mac).

Coding Errors

Coding errors are frequently the most difficult to catch and also the most devastating. Imagine miscalculating a loan or overcharging the user for services (or systematically undercharging)!

Dealing with Errors

Some of the most common problems have to do with layout differences on different platforms. The best way to combat the variations in layouts that occur due to browser differences is to test, test, and retest. You'll want to test early, often, and thoroughly. Knowing of the problems *ahead of time* will keep post-QA testing fixes to a minimum.

Test Completion Criteria

Developing test completion criteria (or *exit criteria*) means setting specific goals that must be met in order to take your web site live. Once the criteria are set, the process consists of running tests repeatedly until you have successfully passed all the listed criteria and then documenting and making the web site live (or moving on to your next phase).

The process includes the following steps:

1. Develop completion criteria.

2. Test.

3. Compare test results with completion criteria.

4. If failed, implement changes and test again. If passed, then move on to the next phase.

Quite often you will base the completion criteria on the type of errors that might occur. For example, you may decide that it is okay for one or two minor errors to remain at the time of launch, but you would not want to allow any major errors that could crash the browser or fail to complete transactions. So when you are creating your completion criteria, be sure to evaluate the level of the error as well.

While it's possible to develop a small site with absolutely no known errors, any reasonably large site will have a few problems, and insisting on zero defects may lead to indefinite delays of your launch date. Establishing a triage system allows you to be pragmatic in accepting some unavoidable problems while showing no tolerance for the worst types of problems.

The following are some example test completion criteria (i.e., criteria that must be met before the site may be launched).

Errors should not exceed: *0 mission-critical errors, 2 moderate errors, 10 minor errors (or break it down further as 2 minor coding errors, 2 minor platform errors, and 6 minor cosmetic errors).*

Unit tests: *All unit tests must complete successfully (no errors).*

Load handling: *Server must not fail with up to 1,000 simultaneous connection requests per second.*

Site uptime: Server must perform at 99.5 percent availability between 8 a.m. and 8 p.m. Server must perform at 98 percent availability outside that time frame.

Reporting the Problems and Fixing the Bugs

Develop a formalized system for recording and making bug fixes. You can either record the errors and changes in a database (for larger projects) or simply keep forms and checklists of the required changes. Whatever you do, you *must* keep a record of the changes. Why? Having a history of the changes you've made and why will keep you from going in circles, making changes and then changing them back. It also provides you with details of who found the problems and who made the corrections. While it may seem like an unnecessary extra effort at the time, you'll appreciate it a year later when you encounter a similar bug. You'll have the error recorded and know who fixed it and how, saving you repeat effort. In addition, documentation will provide you with data that can be used to examine the efficiency of your processes and give you a baseline for measurement and estimation of future projects.

The Problem Report and Resolution Form (Form 11-1; download from *http://www.mkp.com/uew/*) can be used to track problems. While using this detailed form may not be cost-efficient for everyday HTML problems, it is appropriate for complex systems such as database-driven portions of sites. You can also track this information in a database.

The Problem Summary Report (Form 11-2; download from *http://www.mkp .com/uew/*) lists all outstanding problems (any that haven't been resolved) for quick reference. Totals at the bottom allow for quick status checking about the number of problems of each type.

Who Needs to Make the Fixes?

There are a couple of reasons you need to take the bug report back to the person who originally made the mistake. The first reason is to make the person aware of his or her mistakes so similar mistakes will be prevented in the future. Second, that person will have a better idea than anyone else of how the changes may affect the rest of the site.

Problem Report and Resolution Form

Problem report number _____

Problem report date _____

Problem reported by _____

Client name _____

Site _____

Page URL _____

Additional pages _____

Type of error:
☐ Cosmetic ☐ Structural/navigational ☐ Hardware
☐ Coding error ☐ Usability

Severity:
☐ Mission critical ☐ Moderate ☐ Minor

Platform and browsers where problem occurs:
☐ Mac OS ☐ Win 95 / 98 / 2000 / NT ☐ UNIX/Linux
☐ Other _____
☐ Netscape v.____ ☐ IE v. ____ ☐ Other _____

Description of problem and how to reproduce it: _____

_____

Date of problem fix _____

Name of person making fix _____

Problem resolution:
☐ Fixed
☐ Can't be fixed
☐ Fix deferred to later time
☐ Reported problem not a real problem (e.g., designed as specified):

_____

☐ Error not reproducible

Description of problem resolution:

_____

Regression Testing:
☐ Fix tested on all platforms and browsers
☐ Related pages tested

Problem Summary Report

Outstanding Errors (check all that apply):

Problem Report #	Severity of problem			Type of problem					Description
	Mission critical	Moderate	Minor	Cosmetic	Structural	Platform	Coding	Unknown	
17			✔		✔				Site map is missing a link to the copyright policy.
✔						✔			JavaScript code on home page 32 always displays an error when the page loads.
35			✔	✔					Title graphic for About Us page is poorly compressed—showing image degradation.
Total	1		2	1	1		1		

THE FINAL HURDLES BEFORE GOING LIVE

Once you have passed your formal testing procedures and have met all of the predefined exit criteria, you need to verify one last time that everything is in place and ready to go. Checklists are a wonderful way to make sure that you have all of the bases covered. The following worksheets (Forms 11-3, 11-4) provide useful documentation and shortcuts for double-checking that you are indeed ready to go live.

The Postproduction Checklist

A postproduction checklist (Form 11-3; download from *http://www.mkp.com /uew/*) allows you to quickly and decisively test the HTML quality on a page-by-page basis. (We call it *postproduction* rather than *quality assurance* because it includes a set of steps that should be taken before launch but that aren't testing related.)

For large sites (greater than 50 pages or so), testing can be quite a daunting task, and several days (or even weeks) should be scheduled for postproduction. However, on smaller sites, postproduction can usually be completed by a single person in a few hours.

Final Approval for the Launch

In many client relationships, it is critical to get final approval before going live. Review your code testing and postproduction before showing the final site to the client. Quite simply, you want to be sure that *you,* rather than they, find the bugs. This isn't to say that the client won't get a glimpse of the site in its final stages, but you should be sure to complete all your testing before presenting what is considered the final, launchable product. At the same time, you should involve your client in the testing process as appropriate. For example, when testing requires domain knowledge, the client may be able to provide invaluable verification.

It is advisable to have the client sign off on a final approval form. While the client should have already approved the basic look and feel of the site in earlier sign-offs, this is the time for the client to note any errors on the site and to proofread the site. Any major changes requested now by the client may require additional charges. Of course, the client should have agreed earlier to the test completion criteria for quality assurance.

Many design firms use forms like Form 11-4 to secure final approval. (Download from *http://www.mkp.com/uew/*.) This form is not just for external clients; the same one (perhaps slightly modified) can be used internally as well.

Postproduction Checklist

OK	Not OK	N/A	Content
☐	☐	☐	Spelling and grammar
☐	☐	☐	Site includes critical information (e.g., contact info, what the company does, help)
☐	☐	☐	Page titles (the <title> tag), headers, and button labels are correct and consistent
☐	☐	☐	Requirements list has been reviewed and satisfied

Graphics and Layout

OK	Not OK	N/A	
☐	☐	☐	All images are marked with size and <alt> tags (checked by not loading images or mouse-overs)
☐	☐	☐	Download time is acceptable
☐	☐	☐	Image quality is acceptable
☐	☐	☐	Text layout: spacing, typefaces, and font sizes are acceptable
☐	☐	☐	Graphics are aligned properly
☐	☐	☐	Copyright and required logos are present

Browser Compatibility

OK	Not OK	N/A	
☐	☐	☐	Tested on Windows, Mac, Unix, and Linux (color and font problems checked)
☐	☐	☐	Tested on Netscape and IE in all target versions (layout and media problems checked)

User Preference Compatibility

OK	Not OK	N/A	
☐	☐	☐	Layout works at all window sizes
☐	☐	☐	Layout prints acceptably (no cutting off edges)
☐	☐	☐	Layout is reasonable for all typical typefaces and font-size settings

OK	Not OK	N/A	**HTML and Coding**
☐	☐	☐	All links tested on every page (with site up at its final location)
☐	☐	☐	Email links tested by sending mail or clicking and checking the address in mailer
☐	☐	☐	Metatags are present on every page (keywords, description, etc.)
☐	☐	☐	Java and JavaScript code is fully functionally tested (and the HTML contains proper ALT tags)
☐	☐	☐	Mission-critical code has gone through a code review

			Documentation
☐	☐	☐	Fonts and colors are correctly recorded
☐	☐	☐	Client contact info is recorded
☐	☐	☐	File organization and location are recorded
☐	☐	☐	Unusual naming conventions are noted

			Site Submission (once final approval is received)
☐	☐	☐	Yahoo! and *dmoz.org*
☐	☐	☐	Search engines
☐	☐	☐	Market-specific indexes (e.g., local city indexes)

			Wrap-Up
☐	☐	☐	Domain name is working
☐	☐	☐	Account representative and client have been notified
☐	☐	☐	Documentation has been delivered to client (e.g., how to access hit logs)

Form 11-4.

Web Site Final Approval Form.

Web Site Final Approval Form

Project _____

Date _____

Signing this form assures your approval of your web site in its entirety.
Please proofread the accompanying material and return this form to:

Name _____

Address _____

_____

_____

☐ **Your completed web site is located at** _____

☐ Temporary address _____
   Temporary user name _____
   Temporary password _____

☐ Future permanent address _____

Please confirm ☐ This is correct
                ☐ This is not correct

If incorrect, please explain _____

**Please note: Common items requiring your attention are listed below.
Review other areas unique to your job carefully.**

☐ Logos, page titles   ☐ Dates and locations
☐ Names and position titles   ☐ Technical terms
☐ Addresses   ☐ Legal information
☐ Phone, fax, email, etc.   ☐ Recent revisions made correctly
☐ Product names and titles

Comments: _____

I have reviewed the web site and have determined that
☐ It is ready to proceed online
☐ I would like to purchase additional changes

Approved by: _____

Date: _____

In that case, instead of shipping the form to the project leader from your client team, it would be given internally to whomever is in charge of the project. This process protects the designer and ensures that the proper individuals have seen and are satisfied with the project.

TAKING THE SITE UP

During the launch stage, several steps need to be completed. These are as follows:

- Perform final domain name check to ensure DNS routing is working.

- Copy files over from staging area.

- Perform final check of functionality.

- Review postproduction checklist.

- Once the site is online, be sure to get final approval before going public.

- Coordinate with marketing on the expected launch time.

Domain Name Check

It's imperative that you check to make sure the domain name routing to your site is working properly! This should be done *at the very least* a week in advance of taking the site up. Once you have checked to make sure the routing is working properly, you'll want to test it one last time before actually launching the site.

Final Check of Functionality

Once the site is located in its final resting place (i.e., moved over from the staging area), be sure to perform a functionality test before going live. This includes testing any interactivity or events that require back-end processing. Be sure to test email addresses, forms, ordering processes, database interactions, and download time, to ensure adequate responsiveness.

Review Postproduction Checklist

Once the site is up and live, review the postproduction checklist before actually announcing the launch, making sure that everything has been addressed. Review the site to make sure that nothing has been affected by any last-minute moves.

Get Final Approval

Make sure that you have final approval from the primary stakeholders before allowing the web site to be accessed publicly. This will save you from any last-minute embarrassments and will ensure that the site has been reviewed and has received the attention of those who ultimately make the decisions.

Coordinate the Launch with Marketing

Develop a comprehensive marketing schedule for your web site. Tight integration between launching the site and marketing is needed to get the quickest results possible out of your site. A site without marketing will not have users, and marketing without a site gives the users nowhere to go. In addition to luring new customers, marketing your site will help current customers locate your web site. To make this happen smoothly, the last month of development should be tightly coupled with marketing efforts. As is the case in any portion of the development phase, be sure to mention any delays or changes to the initial launch schedule as early as possible. Don't wait until the launch date to inform those in charge of marketing that the site won't be ready for another month!

There are several arenas where you can advertise your web site. Be sure to include the URL in email signature files and in all printed ads and alternative advertising mediums, and incorporate the URL into all other advertising materials. Announce your web site in appropriate newsgroups and mailing lists, purchase banner ads and internet advertising, and arrange for press releases to coincide with the launch.

IMMEDIATELY AFTER THE SITE IS UP

Once your site has made it to the playing field, be sure that it has everything it needs to come out on top. Get your site noticed, keep it up to date and well-maintained, and respond quickly and efficiently to any errors.

Web Site Promotion: Getting the Users to Your Site

Having a highly usable site includes making access simple and straightforward. Even if your site works great—that is, your user tests have shown that users almost always find what they need, the ordering process is easy and intuitive, and the site gets raves from those people who have seen it—users still need to be able to find your site when surfing the Internet. If the site can't be found, it won't be used.

Directories and Search Engines

Users search for sites in several different ways. Occasionally users know exactly what they're looking for; other times they are simply surfing the Web

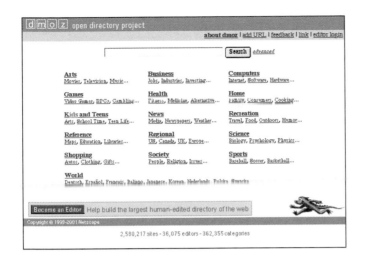

Figure 11-3.

The dmoz.org Open Directory.

dmoz.org is a web directory that is
kept up to date by thousands of volunteers, each maintaining the categories in their areas of interest. This
directory data is available free and is
repackaged and used by many other
web sites.

for something of interest. More commonly, they have a general idea of what
they are looking for, but use the search process itself as a means to clarify and
elaborate their questions. If your goal is to drive traffic to your site, you need
to understand the users' approach to searching.

To make the most out of search engines and directories, consider first how
people use the sites, and second, how the different search engines are structured and respond to queries.

Directory or Categorical Web Indexes

When a user has a good idea of what he or she is looking for, a categorical
index (or directory) is generally a good tool. For example, Yahoo! and *dmoz.org*
(see Figure 11-3) provide structures that facilitate searching by providing pre-
existing categories within a common framework. However, while this is great
for the user, it can make the web site promoter's task more difficult. There are
several things you can do to enhance the prominence of your site. Place your
site at the most detailed level possible. Thoroughly review the possibilities
and place your web site within the most common areas. (The number of categories you can select varies across directories; for instance, Yahoo! allows you
to place a site in two places, whereas *dmoz.org* only allows you to suggest a site
for one category.) Carefully consider where your target audience is most
likely to be looking for sites like yours. What keywords do they use? What
group of sites do they expect to see you among? Describe your site so that it
addresses the information needs your users have as they browse. If you
have appropriately focused subsites, consider submitting different sections
of your site in different search categories. However, if you do this

Figure 11-4.

The Google Search Engine.

Radical simplicity of the Google interface seems to be a significant factor in its success.

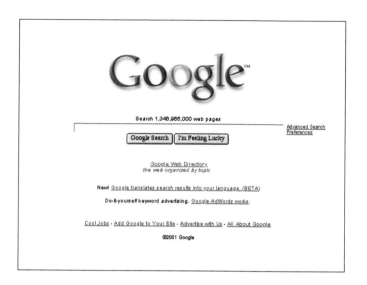

and if the subsites are not sufficiently different, you may end up not being listed at all in the indexing site as a punishment for breaking their rules and regulations (limiting you to only two listings, for instance).

There are many different directories in cyberspace, and there is no way to guarantee you are listed on every single one. In addition, adding your URL to the directories is a labor-intensive task. It's a good thing there are tools to help. However, we still recommend making your own submissions to the major players (e.g., Yahoo!) yourself. This is the only way to ensure that the information is accurate and that you have chosen the right category for your site.

Query-Based Search Engines

Query-based search engines (see Figure 11-4) generally work by comparing a user's query against an index that cross-references web pages. Although each search engine behaves slightly differently behind the scenes, there are some common traits across most systems. Matches are often based on the number of times that a search term appears in your document, weighted by the length of your document (shorter documents with the same number of matches are better) and the overall frequency of the word (rare words are weighted more heavily than common words).

There are several ways to increase the chances that your web site will appear in search listings: be sure that your pages include HTML text, include `<alt>` tags for all your images, include metatags on every page, and follow good writing practice (see Chapter 8, "Writing for the Web").

Make sure your pages include text! Without text, the search engines will have little from which to gauge the content of your page. The only information about your images that crawlers can get is from the names and `<alt>` tags. So be sure to include relevant `<alt>` tags that mention something about the *content* of your images, not just that they are images (e.g., `<alt = "this is a picture">`).

While some people will tell you that it is best to have huge pages full of text in order to receive the best rankings in a search index, this is not always the case. Some indexes divide by the number of words, and thus more words will actually decrease the quality ranking associated with a match.

Responding to Problems

When you find problems with a live site, it is critical that you address these problems right away. Major or minor errors in a live web site lead users to perceive that site as unreliable or unprofessional. Misspellings can damage users' trust in your site as much as broken functionality can. It is imperative that you address all problems as soon as they are noticed.

A quick response to problems should also become part of your quality assurance process. You should be sure to include time immediately after the launch to take care of any potential snags you may have missed in your user testing and earlier quality assurance measures.

A checklist like that in Form 11-5 can augment your quality assurance procedure to allow for rapid verification that a site remains stable as minor updates occur. (Download from *http://www.mkp.com/uew/*.) Of course, when large-scale updates occur, the complete quality assurance procedure should be repeated. And for large, regularly updated sites, a custom checklist can address specific problems that are known to occur as well as include content-specific guidelines and other recurring administrative procedures.

Begin Maintenance Schedule

A regular maintenance schedule should be developed well in advance of your launch, but here is where you put it into action. You should include procedures for regular maintenance and slack time for unexpected maintenance.

Be sure to develop a maintenance schedule that covers the following: updating time-sensitive content (e.g., what's new! items, interest rates, sale prices, submission deadlines, etc.), fixing unexpected or newly found errors and bugs, and running functionality tests of new releases of browsers, server software, and all changes and updates that have been made.

Minimal Maintenance Checklist

Client _____

URL _____

Date _____

Reviewer _____

Verify that the following items are correct and working whenever the web site is updated and before putting the site back online.

OK	Not OK	N/A	
☐	☐	☐	Content verified
☐	☐	☐	Spelling and grammar correct
☐	☐	☐	All links work
☐	☐	☐	Layout is intact
☐	☐	☐	All images load
☐	☐	☐	All HTML, Java, and JavaScript code works
☐	☐	☐	Site works on all supported browser platforms

Plan Major Updates and Revisions

In addition to small changes, bug fixes, and client requests, it's very likely that you'll need to make major updates and revisions at some point. Major updates generally consist of functional changes, major interface revisions, and large-scale redesigns that require the effort of a substantial percentage of the original design team.

Revisions and changes to the web site should be driven by a combination of marketing needs, functionality innovation, and user performance measures from the current site. In other words, a redesign doesn't need to happen just because someone decides the site needs a new look. While this may be the impetus, and indeed where the cash comes from, when you plan updates make sure you have thoroughly investigated current use and problems with the current interface.

Throughout all of your basic maintenance procedures, you should be recording all problems and changes that either are too insignificant to change in the current version or require too much effort to be done on a regular maintenance schedule. These problems can then be addressed when developing an update schedule for your web site. In addition, you should consider major functional changes and large-scale revisions and updates.

POST-LAUNCH TESTING AND ANALYSIS

Once your site has been up for a while, you can begin to investigate the use of the site. Studying the use characteristics of your site will help to inform future design decisions. Use studies differ from user testing in that they are more analytical and look at patterns of use. Also, they represent actual usage characteristics, not simply data generated from a lab setting.

Be cautious when interpreting this data. Without a clear description of use, it can sometimes be misleading to interpret the raw data. For example, suppose you see that a particular page gets 65 percent of your hits. You might think to yourself, "Wow, this page must be the users' favorite; it must be very useful." In reality it may be that your navigational structure forces the majority of the users to go through that page in order to get to the information they are truly searching for. This is a theme that will be repeated throughout this section. It is the relevance that matters, not the raw numbers.

Analyzing Your Hit Logs

An in-depth analysis of your hit logs can reveal a substantial amount of information (see Figure 11-5). The logs can tell you about overall hits, conversion rates, entrance pages, search terms used to reach the site, effects of design changes, general growth over time, peak times, demographics, and system down-time. Each of these is worthy in its own right, but it is the overall picture that the logs provide that is the most informative. A thorough investigation of your hit logs will give you an understanding of how your current site is being used and help suggest a direction for future design.

Overall Hits

It's important to keep in mind that the goal of your site is not overall total hits, but rather relevant hits. For example, if you're selling products, it's much better to have 20,000 hits on your front page and 5,000 hits on your Products page than to have 300,000 hits on your front page and only 1,000 on your Products page. Or, if you are selling parts for a car that is only sold in Europe, and you are getting 80 percent of your hits from people in the U.S., then you aren't attracting the right target audience. While overall hits can be a good indicator of the visibility of your web site, it is very much a mere surface detail; the real meaty information lies in the relevance of those hits.

Figure 11-5.

Example Hit Log Report.

This report shows one month's
worth of hits on the main page
of *usabilityfirst.com*.

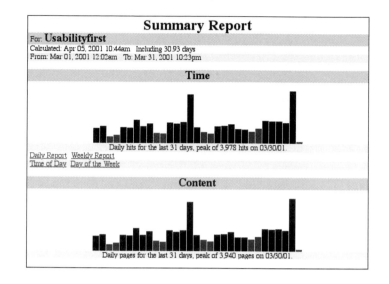

Summary Report
For: **Usabilityfirst**
Calculated: Apr 05, 2001 10:44am Including 30.93 days
From: Mar 01, 2001 12:02am To: Mar 31, 2001 10:23pm

Time

Daily hits for the last 31 days, peak of 3,978 hits on 03/30/01.
Daily Report Weekly Report
Time of Day Day of the Week

Content

Daily pages for the last 31 days, peak of 3,940 pages on 03/30/01.

Conversion Rates

Conversion rates can be very revealing about the quality of your web site. Conversion rates tell you how many people go from one place to another place—in other words, whether users are actually penetrating and moving through your site, or whether they are just looking at one page and leaving for greener pastures at a competing site.

This type of analysis can be particularly useful if you have some sort of linear or sequential operation such as a purchasing system. The example in Table 11-2 demonstrates how you can find potential problems in such a sequence. In this hypothetical purchasing system, which runs across several web pages, note the major drop that occurs after the special offer. This might be telling you something—perhaps that special offer isn't worth it. You'll want to compare the number of people who accept the special offer (page 2) with the number who remain to enter the billing and shipping information (page 3), and then judge whether the extra value of the special offer is worth the loss of up to 4,500 customers. However, the analysis is not that simple, because you still need to compare the results without page 2—perhaps you would lose the same number of people in a different part of the transaction.

Entrance Pages

Hit log analysis can also reveal the pages from which users are entering your site. This is extremely useful information. If 90 percent of your users aren't seeing your home page, then is it really worth spending thousands of dollars to make the home page look nice?

Entrance pages can also tell you what your users find valuable in your site. For example, we have determined that one of our web sites, Usability First (*www.usabilityfirst.com*), has a large proportion of its users entering directly into pages in the Groupware subsection of the site. This tells us that perhaps the subspecialty is more interesting to its specialized market than the overall set of pages is to the rest of the users.

Search Terms Used to Reach the Site

Hit logs can reveal the search terms used by users to reach your site. This can shed light on which keywords are working and which are misleading and can also suggest additional terms that you may not be using. However, this information doesn't tell you who *isn't* finding your site because the search terms didn't lead them to you.

Analyzing users' search terms can demonstrate which of your metatags and description terms users are matching; reveal users' search terms that you don't have in your metatags and description; and suggest new content areas or new pages that might be useful. See Figure 11-6 for a sample search-term analysis.

Analyzing Design Changes

Analyzing your hit logs over time can provide you with information regarding design changes and general growth over time. It can also establish peak times, help estimate spikes, locate orphaned pages, and demonstrate major traffic patterns. To analyze the impact of design changes, you can look at the logs before and after the changes have been implemented to reveal possible ways in which the changes have affected use.

However, you also need to consider other unrelated but simultaneous changes over time. In other words, you can't be sure that it is your design changes that have affected the use. Rather, it could be general changes over time. For example, if you make changes to the home page to include a top-level link for "Usability" and then your Usability page gets twice as many hits over the next six months, you can't necessarily conclude that it was this design change that caused the increase in traffic. Instead, it could just be that the general public has become more interested in the topic and therefore the traffic has increased as a result.

One way to test the impact of a design change is to make the change for a set period of time and then revert to your previous design. If the traffic increases following the change, then decreases again when the change is removed, then you have more reason to believe the traffic increase wasn't due to an external

Table 11-2.

Conversion Rate Example.

| | **Sequential Web Pages** | |
| | Page 1 | Page 2 |
Page Analysis	Purchase Item	Special Offer
Number of hits	10,000	9,000
Percent carryover from previous page	N/A	90%
Percent carryover from start page	N/A	90%

factor. While this tactic is not recommended for any site that survives purely on the basis of increasing traffic, it can provide better evidence that a specific design change has affected the traffic.

A more reasonable way to examine the effect of a design change is to look very closely at the exact time of implementation. If you made the change on Monday at noon, and your traffic tripled at exactly that time (and stayed at three times the previous amount), that should be a good enough indication that the design change is working. However, if your number of hits is small or the degree of change is relatively minor, such as 10 to 20 percent (which is still a nice increase), then it's hard to be certain that the increase really was stimulated by your design change.

Watching General Growth over Time

Log analysis can provide you with basic information about the growth of your site over time. If you have multiple sites to compare, you can get a better idea of how well each is doing. Some sites may grow exponentially, while others may peak and stay at a consistent use level.

In addition to looking at growth rates across sites, you can compare different sections of a single, large site. For example, large corporate sites may compare the differences in use across divisions. Some may grow from month to month, while others may stay static.

Page 3	Page 4	Page 5
Enter Billing and Shipping Information	Make the Purchase	Order Complete
4,500	4,050	4,010
50%	90%	99%
45%	40.5%	40.1%

Establish Peak Times

Hit logs are useful for seeing when your web site is used the most and to establish peak times. There may be trends across the time of day, day of the week, or months of the year. This knowledge can be useful for scheduling maintenance times. It may also be useful for determining when to make revisions.

Peak times may vary tremendously across the time of day. For example, in the United States many sites are fairly inactive in the late evening and early morning (EST). However, the Usability First site has fairly even use throughout the 24 hours (see Figure 11-7). This is most likely because Usability First is used widely outside the U.S.

Finding Orphaned Pages

When analyzing hit logs, you may find a page or two that rarely gets hits. It could be that these pages are just not interesting or important to the users. However, if you think these pages are important, then there may be something else at work. Often you can find orphaned pages, pages that aren't consistently linked to the rest of the site, or links that are hard to find in the page layout.

Finding Extremely Popular Pages

Hit logs may also reveal where your most popular pages are located. These pages can then be used as a measuring stick against the rest of your pages. Better yet, you may use these pages to drive users to other important but less popular areas of your site. You can use them to guide the direction of your site. Hit logs can also help to determine which areas might be candidates for expansion in new popular sections.

Figure 11-6.

Search Terms Used.

This example shows the individual search terms typed by users who found *usabilityfirst.com* (a), and the complete search phrases they used (b). The "Hits" column indicates how many hits resulted from a user using that search term. "Avg. Steps" is the number of pages they looked at after finding the site with that search term.

Search Words

Shows individual search words used to locate this site at the major search engines. The words may have been used alone or have been part of a longer phrase.

For: **Usabilityfirst**

Calculated: Apr 05, 2001 10:44am Including 30.93 days
From: Mar 01, 2001 12:02am To: Mar 31, 2001 10:23pm
Displaying items 1-60 of 962 by hits.

Word	% of Hits	Hits	Avg. Steps
groupware	23.51%	1,669	3.4
usability	6.75%	479	3.7
cscw	5.06%	359	3.2
goms	5.01%	356	4.6
website	2.66%	189	2.7
design	2.24%	159	2.2
of	1.76%	125	2.2
and	1.66%	118	2.9
is	1.20%	85	3.5
what	1.18%	84	3.8
computer	1.10%	78	1.9
web	0.97%	69	2.6
analysis	0.97%	69	2.3
cognitive	0.93%	66	3.2
software	0.83%	59	2.3
mochi	0.79%	56	1.4
walkthrough	0.75%	53	3.5
human	0.72%	51	1.9

(a)

Search Phrases

Shows search phrases used to locate this site at the major search engines.

For: **Usabilityfirst**

Calculated: Apr 05, 2001 10:44am Including 30.93 days
From: Mar 01, 2001 12:02am To: Mar 31, 2001 10:23pm
Displaying items 1-60 of 1216 by hits.

Phrase	% of Hits	Hits	Avg. Steps
groupware	34.29%	1,254	3.5
goms	6.73%	246	5.1
cscw	5.66%	207	3.3
usability	5.50%	201	3.8
mochi	1.31%	48	1.3
what is groupware	1.20%	44	3.5
cognitive walkthrough	1.09%	40	3.9
website design	0.82%	30	1.5
website usability	0.71%	26	3.1
groupware applications	0.68%	25	2.2
goms model	0.46%	17	3.5
groupware products	0.36%	13	3.4
task analysis	0.36%	13	1.9
website design tutorial	0.30%	11	2.4
website design software	0.27%	10	1.1
computer supported cooperative work	0.27%	10	4.1
usability consulting	0.25%	9	3.3
advantages of groupware	0.25%	9	1.5
+"groupware"	0.22%	8	0.9

(b)

Determining the Value of a Page from Hit Logs

Beware not to overvalue the data from your hit logs. As with most data, it is what it is. Taking too much meaning from the data can lead you down the wrong path. Always keep the following in mind:

The Number of Hits Does Not Always Reflect the Value of the Page to a User

You can't automatically assume that because a page gets five times as many hits as the rest of your pages that it is the most valued page on your site. It

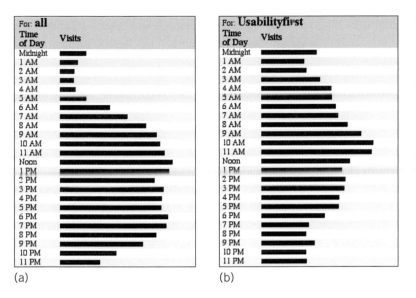

For: **all**		For: **Usabilityfirst**	
Time of Day	Visits	Time of Day	Visits
Midnight		Midnight	
1 AM		1 AM	
2 AM		2 AM	
3 AM		3 AM	
4 AM		4 AM	
5 AM		5 AM	
6 AM		6 AM	
7 AM		7 AM	
8 AM		8 AM	
9 AM		9 AM	
10 AM		10 AM	
11 AM		11 AM	
Noon		Noon	
1 PM		1 PM	
2 PM		2 PM	
3 PM		3 PM	
4 PM		4 PM	
5 PM		5 PM	
6 PM		6 PM	
7 PM		7 PM	
8 PM		8 PM	
9 PM		9 PM	
10 PM		10 PM	
11 PM		11 PM	

(a) (b)

Figure 11-7.

Peak Time Comparison.

Typical traffic patterns for U.S. sites (a) reveal much heavier use during work hours (9 a.m. Eastern Standard Time to 5 p.m. Pacific Standard Time, which is 8 p.m. in this graph because the server is on Eastern Standard Time) compared with the relatively more evenly distributed traffic on *usabilityfirst.com* (b), show-ing visiting hours around the clock, representing international usage.

could be quite the opposite: users may *hate* the page! It could be that your navigation forces them to go through that page in order to get to where they want to go. In this case, you would have an inflated number of hits, and you can't determine the value from that number alone.

Similarly, because a page gets only a few hits doesn't mean its value is low. The page might contain information for emergency data restoration. You would hope this page doesn't get used often, but when it's needed, it's probably the most valuable page on the Internet to the individual using it!

Demographics

Hit logs can provide you with several forms of information about who has visited your site and what type of software they're using—their operating system (PC, Mac, Linux, Unix, Palm, etc.), their browser and version, their IP address, which, like a domain name, can *suggest* their affiliation (*.com* = business; *.edu* = education; *.gov* = government) and country—without really guaranteeing that they fall into a specific demographic (see Figure 11-8).

Beware! You may be missing an entire group of individuals (say, Lynx users) because the users simply aren't out there or aren't interested in the site. However, it may be that they are interested in the site, but it doesn't work well with their browsers.

System Down-Time

Your server logs can also indicate how frequently your server is available, and at what times the server has been down. Your web site can become unavailable for a variety of reasons: system crashes, regular system maintenance, network outages, power outages, incompatible software upgrades, expired security certificates, accidental changes to server settings or file permissions, and so on. A complete list of problems and ways to avoid them is beyond the scope of this book, but the point is that the project manager needs to be aware of the possibilities, make sure the system administrator has adequate contingency plans, and establish standards for system availability.

No one can guarantee 100 percent server uptime or web site availability, but a variety of contingencies are handled by professional hosting companies, such as backup servers, backup network connections, backup power supplies, appropriate software testing platforms, and systematic maintenance procedures. Episodes of server outages should be recorded and tracked by the hosting company in order to continually measure performance and evaluate steps for improvement.

Typically, availability goals for servers are based on a *weighted availability* metric, where outages during peak times are considered more severe than outages in low-traffic times. Thus, regularly scheduled system maintenance should be scheduled for off-peak times.

In summary, there are several keys to analyzing your hit logs: be sure to keep in mind the relevance of each page, look for numbers that are meaningful to the goals of your web site, and beware of making false assumptions.

Email and Other Forms of Feedback from Users

In the first months of your release, you will undoubtedly receive several emails from users of your web site. Kudos, gripes, and bug reports are the most common. These may arrive in several different ways: emails, form data, snail mail, phone calls, feedback through your sales channels and business partners, and press coverage of your site.

Like the quality assurance measures that need to be taken in the development and distribution phases, it is just as critical to establish a method for dealing with user comments. These are extremely informative usability data.

There are several things you should do when dealing with customer feedback: develop a triage for tracking the level of severity, record the type of error, respond promptly (even if it is just responding to the user's query to say you will be working on it later), and track the changes.

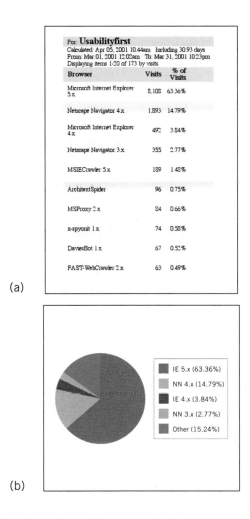

(a)

(b)

Figure 11-8.

Browser Distribution.

This graph shows the percentage of users visiting *usabilityfirst.com* with each type of browser, a useful piece of demographic information. Notice that several of the hits listed in the table (a) come from web crawlers/ spiders, programs that download and index your site for search engines; thus, these hits don't represent actual humans using your system. Also notice the size of the "Other" category (b), showing a large percentage of browsers that are either unidentifiable or obscure.

You should develop a triage of customer feedback similar to that used in your quality assurance process. If your site is large enough, and you are getting a significant amount of communication, you may want to develop a database to help oversee the communication process.

In addition to the level of severity, you should categorize the feedback into the type of problem that it reports, such as typo, content, bug, invoicing, billing/shipping, technical, or customer service.

Knowing the level of severity along with the areas where the problems occur allows you to form action items for each problem. Be sure to prioritize your responses to these incoming problems and establish a method for tracking changes and responding.

Continual and Iterative User Testing

As mentioned earlier, after the site has been up for a while, you will have some data to inform future user testing directions. Log analyses may present questions regarding the use of the site. For example, if a section of your site is rarely being visited, you may want to know if it is because the section is hard to find, or whether the users just aren't interested. Thus, you may want to develop new tests to ferret out this information.

LAUNCH AS A PROCESS

A productive design process needs to be flexible and adaptive. Static methods and procedures do little in the rapidly changing and vast landscape that is the Web. To be successful, you need to be willing to review your procedures occasionally and make changes to your processes. We have provided you with a basis for developing these procedures, but you will need to continually review and change your processes in order to stay on top.

12

EVALUATION

USABILITY EVALUATION

TYPES OF EVALUATION

Most of this book covers methods for *creating* usable designs. This chapter, however, focuses on *evaluating* your designs, measuring how well you've done. To what extent is your design usable, what are the problems with the design, and how can you fix those problems? We'll present three primary approaches: usability inspection, group walkthroughs, and user testing.

Some of the earlier methods (surveys, interviews, focus groups) were introduced as ways to uncover user needs but can also serve as ways to evaluate designs with user feedback. Those techniques work well at capturing users' subjective reactions to designs. We've also covered additional evaluation methods, such as hit logs analysis and gathering user feedback, in Chapter 11. Those methods are ones that gather actual usage data and require a site to be live in order to apply them. This final chapter addresses methods that work well for capturing a number of other usability factors, such as speed, errors, incorrect mental models, and memory limitations.

A *usability inspection* involves a user interface designer sitting down at a desk and evaluating the user interface of a web site based on general design principles or specific lists of guidelines. A group of designers can inspect the site independently and then combine notes to obtain a comprehensive list of problems with the site.

In a *group walkthrough,* a group of stakeholders in the design gets together and walks through common tasks on the web site. At each step of the task, the group identifies any issues in the design and tracks fixes that need to be made. This is very similar to a usability inspection except that it is task-oriented, and it often involves nondesigners (other people might include managers, programmers, writers, client reps, salespeople, marketing specialists, customer support staff, users, and union reps).

User testing involves observing users performing specific activities with your web site to identify what problems they have as they use the site. User testing is one of the most popular of all usability methods because it is relatively inexpensive and it identifies extremely specific problems. Since users are involved and actually performing the task (rather than simply stating opinions), you can have relatively high confidence in the results, and surprising problems are almost always found that wouldn't have been identified by other means.

At times you will choose to use all three forms of evaluation. See the sidebar "Converging Operations" for the rationale behind applying multiple evaluation methods.

CONVERGING OPERATIONS

The principle of *converging operations* says that if you come to the same conclusion from more than one approach to a problem, then that conclusion is more likely to be correct. If you find a problem through a usability inspection and then observe the same problem during user testing, it's likely to be an important problem to fix. If users you've interviewed report that they like the site a lot, and magazine reviews of your site are also favorable, then it's fair to conclude that you have a likable web site. In this sense, if you've observed a problem when using one method, but you feel uncertain about the relevance or severity of the problem (possibly because of weaknesses in the method), then the principle of converging operations suggests testing for the problem in another method for verification.

For instance, in a focus group, users may claim that they find a label incomprehensible, but you may be skeptical because of the subjectivity of their claim or the possibility that groupthink is biasing them. If user testing agrees with their claim, then you need to take it very seriously. But if in user testing you find that everyone is easily able to interpret the label, it is reasonable to conclude that it's a less important concern. Similarly, studies done in a field setting have certain types of problems (such as distractions and biases introduced by each setting), and studies done in the lab have other types of problems (such as lack of realism and different types of stress). If you observe the same problem in both the lab and the field, then that problem is robust and significant. If you don't observe it in both settings, you need to consider what other factors may be involved in whether it occurs.

Patching Things Up

The most important step in any usability evaluation is to go back and fix the problems that were identified. Don't just write up a report and leave it on the shelf—a usability evaluation must first identify the problems and then suggest practical solutions to improve the usability of the site. A report that vaguely states that the navigation is confusing will be worthless. Instead, it needs to state specifically how the navigation might be improved. Then the developers need to return to the code and fix the problem. In some cases, fixing the problem will be simple, and in others it will take considerably more time than the testing itself. For this reason, when you are estimating the budget for usability evaluation, make sure you've included an ample budget for making the fixes.

After you've made the fixes, ideally you want to reevaluate the web site to verify that the fixes actually improved the usability. This type of testing, known as *regression testing*, applies to testing in general, as mentioned in Chapter 11.

In principle, you should continue reevaluating and fixing problems until no major usability problems are identified. In practice, this is usually relatively quick for small, simple web sites. For complex problems, you may only be able to afford to continue iterating until a minimal level of usability is achieved, and may have to postpone further improvements for a later version of the site.

When to Do Usability Evaluation

You can evaluate a web site through usability inspection, walkthroughs, or user testing at almost any point in the design cycle. In the optimal situation, you will evaluate the site periodically during development to verify that the design is staying on track. See Figure 12-1 for a comparison of the advantages and disadvantages of testing at various stages.

USABILITY INSPECTION

Usability inspection is inexpensive, can be completed in as little as a few minutes, and can happen at any stage of design. Inspection is really just looking at a web site to see what problems there might be. Although the inspection can be performed by relying solely on your own expertise at identifying problems, it is usually more effective and more objective if you use a checklist designed for the purpose. Guidelines on a checklist are derived from designer experience, user testing and other user studies, core psychological principles, and problems that crop up again and again.

A usability inspection is sometimes known as an *expert critique,* but that makes it sound harder than necessary. While it's certainly true that an expert evaluator will find more problems and more serious problems than a novice, even a beginner can do a practical, useful inspection. A usability inspection is also sometimes known as a *heuristic evaluation,* where *heuristic* means that the evaluation is based on practical rules of thumb that work well most of the time. However, heuristic evaluation is often interpreted as a specific type of usability inspection with a specific set of 10 guidelines, which we'll review below.

Limitations of Usability Inspection

Usability inspection doesn't actually involve users in the evaluation process. As a result, even if you've identified a problem, you can't be certain that it reflects an actual problem for a user or that your solution won't be worse for

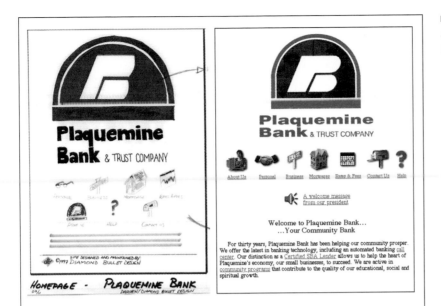

Figure 12-1.

Comparison of Early- versus Late-Stage Evaluation.

Early Evaluation

Early testing can be performed as soon as you have initial page mockups on wireframes.

- Identifies problems *early*, preventing costly redesign.

- Identifies major conceptual issues, such as problems with your overall organization and set of features.

- Detailed problems are not possible to identify because the details haven't been specified yet.

- The user tasks are still somewhat artificial and their behavior is therefore somewhat contrived.

Late Evaluation

Late evaluation can occur when most of the site is completed, or even after it has been launched.

- Finds specific problems.

- Finds problems throughout the site.

- Explores the final task as closely as possible to how it will work when the site goes live.

- When big problems are found, it may be too late to address them within the project budget.

the user. It's good to have the design rationale on hand when you find a problem. The designers may have had to make some difficult design tradeoffs and may already have identified the problem you've spotted. You don't want to reverse their decision and end up making something else worse than they'd already anticipated. In practice, there will be a set of problems you find that will be obviously wrong, and you should make those a high priority. Some other problems will seem to violate a guideline but at the same time seem appropriate in context. In those cases, you should either find a new solution that seems right from every perspective or hold off on the change and mark it as a problem to look for during user testing.

Types of Checklists

A usability inspection is conducted by walking through a checklist of guidelines. Checklists can be short or long, general purpose or special purpose. A short checklist takes less time and, with practice, can substitute single, broad principles for a long list of specific guidelines that all follow the same general principle. For instance, there are many ways in which a web site can be consistent, and if you've learned to check for all the different types of consistency, your checklist only needs to mention "Consistency," rather than a whole list of specific principles like the following:

- Page layouts are consistent throughout the site.

- Page titles are consistent with link names.

- All headers have consistent syntax, capitalization, and punctuation.

- Bullets are the same style throughout the site (e.g., open circles, squares, or diamonds).

- Images receive the same stylistic treatment throughout the site.

- Logos all conform to strict corporate standards without variation.

- Link colors do not vary from page to page.

- Link colors are consistent with web conventions: blue for nonvisited links, green or purple for visited links.

Two good short lists are covered in the following sections: "Ten Web Guidelines" and "Heuristic Evaluation" (see sidebars). These are designed for efficient evaluation of a site, and unlike detailed lists, these help you keep the big picture in mind. A designer or developer can rely on these types of general-purpose checklists as the code is written to quickly verify that the current implementation of the site is on track. An example of a more detailed, general-purpose checklist is shown in Form 12-1, which is useful for spending a little more time to comprehensively review a site. (Download from *http://www.mkp.com/uew/.*) This is just one example of many possible checklists. You should collect a list of guidelines that you find give you insight and record guidelines corresponding to the problems you encounter most often.

This book contains a number of *special-purpose* checklists that can be used to focus on specific aspects of design. For instance, a writer can use writing guidelines. An information architect can use information architecture guidelines. A designer can use a checklist to verify that mockups are designed appropriately.

Ten Web Guidelines

Our short list of general-purpose principles, presented in the sidebar and discussed in this section, is useful for making a quick review of a web site. By reviewing each principle carefully as you work through a web site, you will be able to uncover the vast majority of common problems, provided, of course, that you get experience with the detailed guidelines first and use multiple reviewers for completeness. As you develop expertise, you should be able to work with just the short principles without the detailed descriptions.

TEN WEB GUIDELINES

1. Content and scope
2. Speed
3. Navigation
4. Appropriateness to task
5. Visual design
6. Compatibility
7. Simplicity
8. Consistency and contrast
9. Error handling
10. Respect for the user

Content and Scope

The most important principle is that the web site have the functionality necessary to serve the user's needs. Does the site have the appropriate content? Is the scope broad enough to satisfy the user's requirements? Are the features sufficient? Is the information *useful*?

Form 12-1.

A Detailed, General-Purpose Checklist.

A Detailed, General-Purpose Checklist

Architecture and Navigation
- ☐ Does the structure fit the purpose?
- ☐ Is the navigation scheme clear?
- ☐ Where are you?
- ☐ How do you find what you want?
- ☐ Is there a reasonable number of navbar choices?
- ☐ Are navbar choices logically ordered?
- ☐ Do link names match page names?
- ☐ Are links clearly marked?
- ☐ Is there a clearly marked link back to the home page?
- ☐ Is there an option to search for information?
- ☐ Is there a site map?
- ☐ Does every page make it clear which web site you're in?
- ☐ Does the user have control over navigation?

Layout and Design
- ☐ Does page size exceed window size?
- ☐ Is layout consistent between pages?
- ☐ Is there a clear focal point on each page?
- ☐ Does the layout work visually?
- ☐ Is alignment used effectively?
- ☐ Is grouping used effectively?
- ☐ Is there good contrast?
- ☐ Is the layout cluttered?
- ☐ Is it aesthetically pleasing?

Content
- ☐ Is the text clear and concise?
- ☐ Is text organized in small chunks?
- ☐ Are there spelling or grammar errors?
- ☐ Do pages include introductory text?
- ☐ Do multimedia components support the task?
- ☐ Are units of measure clear and unambiguous for international use?
  - ☐ Date and time? ☐ Phone numbers? ☐ Address and postal codes?

Forms and Interaction
- ☐ Do forms support the task?
- ☐ Do dialogues follow a logical progression?
- ☐ Is it clear where to go next?
- ☐ Are dialogue methods concise and consistent?
- ☐ Are form elements used properly?
- ☐ Are elements grouped properly?
- ☐ Are there clear Submit buttons?

Graphics

- ☐ Is image quality adequate?
- ☐ Do the images include alternate text?
- ☐ Do the images include size information?
- ☐ Do the images use a consistent light source?
- ☐ Are images stored for maximum compression?
- ☐ Is mouse-over feedback provided? Is it useful?
- ☐ Are animations useful? Are there too many? Are they properly compressed?

Color

- ☐ Is the choice of colors appropriate for site?
- ☐ Are too many colors used?
- ☐ Are colors used consistently?
- ☐ Are graphics colors dithered?
- ☐ Do color choices work in grayscale?

Typography

- ☐ Is the text legible?
- ☐ Is the font size large enough?
- ☐ Is the font color appropriate and is there sufficient contrast?
- ☐ Is the text formatted for 10 to 12 words per line?
- ☐ Are there sufficient margins?
- ☐ Are typefaces used properly and consistently?

Error Tolerance

- ☐ Do users need to remember items across pages or sessions?
- ☐ Are confirmations provided before risky or costly actions?
- ☐ Are risky or costly actions reversible?
- ☐ Are entry errors caught locally?
- ☐ Do error pages provide useful information?
- ☐ Do search-error pages provide search broadening tips?
- ☐ Is help available?
- ☐ Is help task-oriented?
- ☐ Is help contextual?

Platform and Implementation

- ☐ Is load-time fast enough? Does it load in 3 to 15 seconds?
- ☐ Do all the links work?
- ☐ Are there broken images?
- ☐ Are pages written to be found by search engines?
- ☐ Does the site work with user's browser?
- ☐ Does the site work with user's hardware platform?
- ☐ Does the site work on high- and low-resolution monitors?
- ☐ Are nonstandard plug-ins required? Are they necessary or useful?

Speed

Slow download time is one of the biggest complaints of users online. While we have to be realistic about what speed is possible, we need to minimize page size and processing time. Use text unless graphics are necessary. Create designs that compress well. Minimize the need to traverse several web pages when one page can do the job.

Navigation

How clear is the organization of the web site? Can users find their way from place to place? Is the navigation bar well organized? Are there any parts missing? Are the relationships between main sections and subsections clear? Do search engines produce useful results? Does the site map give an accurate understanding of the scope and organization of the site?

Appropriateness to Task

What are the user's tasks, and does the site reflect the structure of the tasks? A *detailed* task analysis is also helpful, but you should at least perform a cursory analysis, verifying that the obvious tasks flow well. Make sure users know where they are in a task and that information is automatically carried through from each step to the next.

Visual Design

Does your design have simplicity, consistency, and focus? Does the visual organization structure the task of working with the page, providing emphasis and visual flow? Is it attractive and uncluttered? Does it reinforce the tone and message of the site?

Compatibility

Does the site work with the wide range of users and computers? Does it work well across the wide range of individual differences, linguistic and cultural differences, user preferences, browsers, operating systems, hardware devices, and network access capabilities?

Simplicity

Is everything presented in the simplest, most straightforward way? Is the language simple and direct? Are icons helpful or obscure? Is the text too wordy? Are pages too numerous? Are pages cluttered? Is the site trying to look like more than it is? Follow the principle of minimalism: if anything can be removed, remove it.

EVALUATION

Consistency and Contrast

Similar things should be similar. Different things should be obviously different. Every variation in the design should be deliberate and meaningful. Does the site have internal consistency within the page and between pages? Does it have external consistency with web standards and conventions? Does it have a consistent style and message with the organization's print materials and actual work practices?

Error Handling

In transactional systems especially, does the system prevent the user from entering inappropriate values? Are bad values detected as early as possible? Is error recovery quick and efficient, guiding the user through problem resolution as easily as possible? When users cannot completely resolve a problem (e.g., they don't have a login account or they don't have their credit card), are they able to participate to the maximum extent possible and complete their activities at a later time when the current problems are no longer a factor?

Respect for the User

Are you putting your users' security or privacy at risk? Are you misleading them, wasting their time, or trapping them into a path they don't want to be on? Are you requiring them to opt out of mailing lists that they never wanted to join? While it's tempting to think you want those click-throughs at all costs, do you really want to anger or frustrate users?

Heuristic Evaluation

Jakob Nielsen (1993) created a set of 10 guidelines (see sidebar "Heuristic Evaluation") derived from a factor analysis of a much larger set of guidelines. He demonstrated that using these 10 guidelines will identify the vast majority of problems that can be found with a larger list. Thus, this short list is a more cost-effective approach to finding problems (versus longer lists) if you only need to find the top 80 percent of them. However, this list was created in the early 1990s, before the Web was a major platform for user interface design. Although these principles do apply to web sites, they don't all feel like a good match with the types of issues we normally see. Nevertheless, this list is one of the most carefully constructed and is a useful tool in your collection of design guidelines.

Simple and Natural Dialogue

Keep tasks short and simple. Do the required tasks on the web site match tasks the user is familiar with offline? Follow a principle of minimalism, including only elements necessary to the user's task.

```
┌─────────────────────────────────────────────────────────┐
│ ■  HEURISTIC EVALUATION                                   │
│                                                           │
│      1. Simple and natural dialogue                       │
│                                                           │
│      2. Speak the user's language                         │
│                                                           │
│      3. Minimize the user's memory load                   │
│                                                           │
│      4. Consistency                                       │
│                                                           │
│      5. Feedback                                          │
│                                                           │
│      6. Clearly marked exits                              │
│                                                           │
│      7. Shortcuts                                         │
│                                                           │
│      8. Good error messages                               │
│                                                           │
│      9. Prevent errors                                    │
│                                                           │
│     10. Help and documentation                            │
│                                                           │
└─────────────────────────────────────────────────────────┘
```

Speak the User's Language

Use terminology familiar to the user, not to your organization. Avoid jargon the user would not know. Avoid ambiguity. Accept a wide array of terminology that the user might choose to use.

Minimize the User's Memory Load

Don't require users to remember information, especially between two different pages on your site, and certainly not between two different visits to your site. Show them options and let them recognize the relevant information and choose.

Consistency

Remain consistent within your pages, between pages, and with web standards and conventions. Stick to HTML standards as much as possible.

Feedback

How does the system respond to users' actions? How is the state of the system reflected on-screen? When a user clicks, is the response quick? Are visited links distinguished by color? Does the shopping cart change when items are put into it?

Clearly Marked Exits

Provide ways for users to back out of mistakes they make. Don't create orphan pages with no links back to the home page. Allow operations to be canceled or undone. If users select items for purchase, let them remove those items from their order. Allow users to log out from a system so that another person can log in.

Shortcuts

Make things fast. Minimize the number of steps users need to go through. Provide quick links to important information. Let expert users perform frequent tasks more easily. Save them steps by remembering account information.

Good Error Messages

Help users recognize, diagnose, and recover from errors. Provide clear error messages that explain how the user can correct a problem. Look for errors the user can make that you would never detect. Provide confirmation information and clear feedback to the user's actions so that the user can easily spot when things are not correct.

Prevent Errors

Help the user avoid making errors altogether. If there are only a few valid input options, give the user a drop-down list, not a free-text field. Provide clear instructions to avoid errors of misunderstanding. Watch for navigation confusions. Examine every error condition that is possible on your web site and consider whether it can be entirely avoided.

Help and Documentation

Provide help information, frequently asked questions, and tips. Give instructions. Do users read help information? Not necessarily, but even if only 10 percent of users would like to have help, it will be valuable.

How to Do a Usability Inspection

In its most basic form, performing a usability inspection is as simple as this: find a list of useful guidelines, read down the list and verify that your site conforms to each guideline, write down any problems you identify, and then go back and fix the problems you found. Take, for example, a guideline from Chapter 8, "Writing for the Web": "Italics are avoided except at large font sizes." To apply this legibility guideline, you'd scan through all of your web pages (and your style sheets in this case); and anywhere you found italics used in a regular or small font size, you'd do your best to find a suitable alternative to italics, such as boldface. If you have appropriate editing tools, you may be able to do an automated search for all uses of italics.

As you list the problems, prioritize them to determine which to fix first (some won't be easy fixes, and others may simply be too much work to be practical in your project). Rate how likely the user is to encounter each problem, how much trouble it is likely to cause for the user, and how much work it's going to take to fix it; then determine its priority from these factors.

How long should a usability inspection take? For minor course adjustments, such as checking your status as you put together each web page, a quick review should take only a few minutes. Schedule more careful and detailed reviews at important checkpoints in the design: after your first pass at the design (before any of the design choices have been committed to and before the client has seen your work); after the design is finalized but before the site has been constructed; and as a final quality assurance pass before the site is launched. Depending on the size of your site, these reviews can be performed in anywhere from a few hours to a couple of weeks.

In a more thorough inspection, you'll want to make sure you've found the majority of the problems. How do you ensure this?

Don't Neglect Your First Impressions

Even before beginning to apply the guidelines, if you have a working site, try it out and record your initial impressions and problems. Some problems will be hard to notice after you've used the site once and learned how it works.

Use Several Reviewers

Each person will find a slightly different set of problems, but the overlap is usually sufficient enough that you will probably have found the vast majority of the problems after three to four people have reviewed the site.

Use Internal and External Reviewers

Reviewers who have been involved in the site design may be able to identify deeper problems than other reviewers, but may likewise be blind to certain alternatives. Reviewers who have not been involved in the project will have a fresh perspective and fewer commitments to design choices, but will take much longer to develop a rich enough understanding to spot deeper problems.

Practice

Get experience, especially with long, detailed lists, and share your insights with others. With practice, you'll find a larger number of problems.

EVALUATION

Be Methodical

Don't just glance over the guidelines. Carefully verify each one. For every general principle, such as "consistency," try hard to find at least one problem. In a design that hasn't been refined, it's extraordinarily likely you'll find at least one problem.

Use Automated Tools

Automated tools can check coding standards automatically and can easily spot nonrecommended coding practices, such as the use of a `<blink>` tag, an excessively long page, a missing ALT tag, broken links, and spelling problems.

Expand Your Mind

It's easy to interpret broad principles too narrowly. Consider alternative interpretations of the same principle.

Use Multiple Checklists

Each checklist is organized differently and will tend to find slightly different types of problems. Each will put you in a different frame of mind for identifying a problem that may have slipped by you with a different checklist.

Automatic Usability Evaluation

Several tools exist to help you automatically test whether your site conforms to usability guidelines (a typical example is RetroAccess, *www.retroaccess.com*). These tools vary in the types of usability problems they find (most are focused on quality assurance issues, which we covered in Chapter 11). Their biggest limitation is that there are many items on usability checklists that a computer cannot automatically detect or verify. So, while it is easy to check if images have their ALT tags, it's very difficult to automatically determine if error pages provide useful information. Such a determination requires a human reviewer. Other issues are a matter of degree (such as text legibility) or a difficult design tradeoff (such as page length). Nevertheless, automatic tools are a critical component of overall evaluation because they reduce the overall time needed to spot problems and provide a thorough check of those issues that can be automatically identified.

GROUP WALKTHROUGHS

A group walkthrough brings together several people to review the web site jointly. The group walks through the web site for each major task a user would perform, trying to touch on every page that will be commonly used (see Figure 12-2). For each task, the group steps through every page on a web site

Figure 12-2.

A Group Walkthrough in Progress.

to experience everything that a user would encounter. (A walkthrough of a paper mockup is not quite as thorough as a walkthrough of a live site, but follows the same basic approach.)

A group walkthrough is very similar to conducting a walkthrough in a focus group, except that a group walkthrough emphasizes design *critique,* and the participants include others besides potential users. As you gain experience with all the usability methods, you'll start to see that, like walkthroughs and focus groups, they all relate to one another in a continuum of possible approaches, and you can blend methodologies to attack each specific design problem you encounter. There are several approaches to group walkthroughs. Below are some of the approaches and some suggested possible participants.

Designer Walkthroughs

Informal walkthroughs can be easily organized among the group of designers and developers working on the web site. Such groups can organize spontaneously, discuss design tradeoffs, and immediately incorporate insights back into the design. A team of designers is likely to be able to resolve differences quickly and generate practical design directions.

Pluralistic Walkthroughs

On the other hand, the commonalities among designers and developers that enable them to resolve differences well may also prevent them from considering alternative design considerations. In the *pluralistic walkthrough* approach, the group is deliberately composed of diverse stakeholders in the design. A management or client representative can focus the group on the need for profitability and other business goals. A customer support representative can present common customer complaints and help minimize customer support calls. A sales or marketing representative can help focus the marketing message. A software developer can help the group avoid infeasible software solutions.

Scandinavian Design and User Participation

The Scandinavian design tradition focuses on this diversity of input and also emphasizes participation of the user in the design process. Scandinavian countries have required that employees of companies be involved in the design (or the selection) of software that will be adopted by the company. In the spirit of employee rights, this ensures that employees get software that will be safe and humane and discourages downsizing by automating people out of their jobs. As a result, end users and even union representatives are involved in the design process. In this role, users are not being tested, but are participating as peers on the design team, providing insights from their experience as domain specialists and defending their needs against competing needs of others on the design team. In theory, the user makes the best possible user advocate.

Simulated Roles

In many cases, it's difficult to bring together the full spectrum of stakeholders relevant to the design. Users may not be available and other stakeholders may be distant or otherwise occupied. In this case, members of the design team can be asked to take on the roles of different stakeholders, acting as explicit advocates for their concerns. This helps prevent a group from ignoring points of view and can actually provide a more friendly reception for concerns that might be sensitive if they came from the actual stakeholders (such as management).

Facilitators and Scribes

A walkthrough should usually be conducted with a designated *facilitator*. Since team members can come from all different backgrounds, the facilitator is usually someone with experience in conducting walkthroughs. The facilitator leads the group through the user's tasks, focuses the discussion, and pulls the discussion back on track when it strays too far from relevant design concerns.

Another critical role is that of the *scribe*. The scribe jots down all design concerns and tries to identify what final decisions get made (and asks for a final decision or explicit course of action when none is clear). The scribe writes up design decisions made in the meeting and delivers them to everyone afterward for review. People return corrections and clarifications, and the scribe produces an official document of design changes. Others in the group would do well to take notes on critical issues to provide clarification to the scribe if the review document is not clear on an issue.

Conducting a Walkthrough

Before a walkthrough, you should identify the primary tasks. If your task analysis produced storyboards, these can serve as a basis for an early walkthrough. Walkthroughs can be conducted over the phone when a group is geographically distributed, but some mechanism is needed for coordinating which screen is being viewed. Faxed or emailed mockups can be used, but should be numbered and titled so the groups can coordinate effectively. If the web site is available online, shared browsing tools can allow distant groups to lock their screens together as they browse.

What should be evaluated at each step of the walkthrough? The facilitator may prepare a set of questions to ask the group to consider as they view each screen and perform each action. A simple set of guidelines, such as the usability inspection guidelines presented earlier in this chapter, can help as a review tool to ensure that the review gets good coverage.

Since this approach is task-based, you must always ask how the user would decide what to do next. What is the user hoping to accomplish at each step? What features on the screen are available to accomplish those step-by-step goals? How does the user decide among options? Will the user be able to remember necessary information to perform a task? Will the necessary information be seen and will it be understood correctly?

Be sure to try out mistakes users are likely to make. What will happen if users enter incorrect information? Will they know they've made a mistake? Will they recover from it or get hopelessly lost on the web site?

A walkthrough may be completed in as little as an hour for a small site of 10 to 20 pages, an afternoon for a moderately complex site (such as one with a basic set of e-commerce capabilities), or a couple of weeks for an extremely complex site such as a government site supporting a wide variety of users and

EVALUATION

tasks. A walkthrough can be valuable at many different stages of design, as early as initial tasks are defined up through a final checkup on the web site before launch. Several walkthroughs throughout the development of the site are worth doing, but cost tradeoffs need to be considered carefully since they may involve several people for significant periods of time.

USER TESTING

In user testing, you bring in users, give them tasks to perform, and *watch* what they do. Nothing provides more insight than seeing users actually trying to accomplish something on your site and not succeeding. User testing is popular because it finds practical problems, is persuasive, and is relatively inexpensive. Someone is bound to argue with your analysis when you review a paper design, apply guidelines, or gather opinions from others, but no one argues whether there's a problem when they see users consistently make mistakes on their site.

The overall process of conducting a test follows these steps:

1. Plan the test: Determine the scope of testing and the tasks.

2. Assemble the materials: Prepare the site for testing, and prepare the testing script, consent forms, response sheets, and any other materials you may need.

3. Prepare the location: If testing will happen at your location, prepare the equipment and room.

4. Pilot test: Test one or two co-workers to work out the bugs.

5. Recruit users: Advertise for users, select users, and schedule their testing times.

6. Conduct the test: Welcome the user, get consent, and proceed through each test task, recording user behavior; then debrief the user.

7. Analyze the results: Review the problems found, prioritize problems based on frequency and severity, and identify possible solutions.

8. Fix your site and retest: Make the identified changes and test again to make sure the problem has been solved.

To help in preparation of your user testing, follow a worksheet like the one presented in Form 12-2. (Download from *http://www.mkp.com/uew/*.)

User Testing Preparation Worksheet

User Testing Project _____

Scheduled Dates and Times _____

Location:

    ☐ Usability lab   ☐ On-site testing

    ☐ Other: _____

Testers _____

Observers _____

Required demographic _____

Number of test users _____

Payment (per person) _____

Computer configuration(s):

    Hardware _____

    OS and version _____

    Browser and version _____

    Other software _____

Videotaping and audiotaping: Video / Audio / None

Other equipment:

    ☐ Stopwatch

    ☐ Server logs

    ☐ Event logs (mouse clicks, keystrokes)

    ☐ One-way mirror

    ☐ Other: _____

Preparation

☐ Check when testing location and materials are prepared.

☐ Check when pilot testing has been completed.

☐ Check when sample results have been analyzed.

User Recruiting

Check that each of the following has been prepared:

☐ Recruiting ad

☐ Recruiting sign-up sheet

☐ Recruiting qualifier questions

Materials

Check that you have each of the following, as needed, for your test session:

☐ Testing script

☐ Experimenter notes pages

☐ Consent form

☐ Instruction sheet

☐ Task questionnaires

☐ Post-questionnaire and demographics sheet

☐ Follow-up sheet

Task list

To clarify the goals of this test, list the primary tasks that you'll be testing. The testing script should provide the exact wording for each of these.

1. _____

2. _____

3. _____

4. _____

5. _____

6. _____

7. _____

8. _____

9. _____

10. _____

Planning the Test

Begin your planning by determining who and what to test and what general test procedure to use.

Deciding What to Test

What should be tested? Your task analysis should have identified the most important tasks and goals for the user. These are the minimum you'll want to test. During the design phase, you'll have made a number of design choices that you're not certain of, and you'll want to make sure the tasks you select are ones that will help you determine if your design choices were correct.

Common types of tasks to test include finding specific information ("What is the price of . . ."), finding something you like ("Find an article of interest to you"), comparing items ("Which product is the best value?"), performing a transaction ("Purchase this product"), and entering information ("Fill out the feedback form").

These tasks are targeted and specific. They capture the experience of goal-directed users, which reflects common usage of many business sites. However, many web users browse without explicit goals—looking for something interesting, much like flipping between television channels. In such situations, defining appropriate tasks can be extremely difficult, and open-ended observation of users browsing may be more appropriate. For instance, you can give users a starting point within or close to your own web site and ask them to browse at their leisure for the next hour, after which you can ask them about their experiences with your site. You may even ask them to browse within a specific topic area. In such a case, even the fact that they never come across your web site can be informative to your design. See the sidebar "Diary Studies" for another approach to user testing that provides even greater realism in the tested tasks.

To effectively compare one user with another and to compare one design with another, these tasks need to be unambiguous, such as "How much does a stuffed giraffe cost?" Provided that you only have one stuffed giraffe on the site, you can easily compare people's success rates, times, and error rates in performing the task. However, an alternative approach is to build tasks that allow some degree of user choice, such as "Order a gift you'd like to give someone in your family." This helps ground the task realistically for users. It will often raise their level of motivation and provide a more accurate indication of how people use the site. Its down side, of course, is that each user will be working on a somewhat different task, which makes comparisons more difficult.

Finally, if you know that something doesn't work on your site, don't bother testing it. Fix it. You're wasting precious time with users if you have them simply confirm obvious problems, and since you'll expect to fix the problem anyway, what you really want to know is if people will have trouble using it after you've made the fix. Of course, if there's some debate about whether something is a problem or not, then that's the perfect candidate for testing.

DIARY STUDIES

Another approach to user testing is the *diary study*. In this approach, users are asked to describe their experiences with your web site in a diary whenever they use the web site in their daily work. This works when you have a reasonably high expectation that your site will be visited regularly, such as with subscription services or intranet sites.

Diaries can be simple personal log entries (date, time, description of activity), or you can ask people to fill out a short questionnaire each time they interact with the site. You won't be able to observe what they're doing, so anything you can do to increase the likelihood that people will record all of the information is helpful. If you need information about what is going on around them, give users cameras and ask them to take a picture during each episode of using the site. Ask them to photograph screens or take screen shots when they encounter a problem.

Formulating Questions

Whenever possible, formulate each task as a question requiring a response, such as "How much does a stuffed giraffe cost?" Avoid phrasing tasks as statements (e.g., "Find the price of a stuffed giraffe"). When phrased as a statement, some users will believe they are done as soon as they've found the stuffed giraffe, assuming that a price must be nearby. A question not only forces them to complete the task, but gives you an answer that you can verify. If the user got the answer wrong, you have one more piece of data about problems the user is having.

In addition, when you formulate the questions, be sure to phrase each one in a way that doesn't match your screen design too closely. If you have a Contact button on your site, asking "How would you contact this organization?" will be trivial. People are incredibly good at pattern-matching, so don't hand the pattern right to them. Instead, ask "What is this organization's phone number?" or consider an even more difficult question such as, "You bought a product from this web site and would like to complain that it took several months to get to you. How would you do so?" This more complex question is likely to lead the user to other parts of your site and will help you to see how people solve difficult problems.

In the same spirit, you may also choose a few questions that cannot be answered on the web site. Ask them to find a product that you don't offer. This will give you a lot of information about how people search for information on your site and what their backup strategies are when their first attempt fails. A well-composed site helps people identify that the site doesn't have something they want and supports their secondary strategies. You may want to warn users that such impossible questions may come up—the experience can be extremely frustrating for them.

Expert versus Novice Use

How often will a person be visiting your site? Will they be onetime or infrequent users, or will they be regular users who will become experts at navigating your site? A site targeted at novice and infrequent users can be tested without providing much of an introduction to the test users. However, when testing expert use, a period of training is necessary to understand how experts are likely to approach your site. For applications that will be used extremely frequently, you may need to recruit users who are already familiar with your site, or you may need to provide extensive training.

Assembling the Materials

Most tests will require that you assemble the following materials: a testing script, experimenter notes pages, consent forms, an instruction sheet, task questionnaires, post-questionnaire and demographics sheets, and follow-up sheets.

Testing Script

The testing script should contain everything the tester plans to say. It includes an introduction, explaining how the test will be conducted, and gives the wording for each task. The script helps to ensure consistency among tests and with different testers. You don't need to read the script verbatim (though it can't hurt to do so)—you can simply use it to make sure you haven't forgotten to mention important points. See Form 12-3 for a sample testing script. (Download from *http://www.mkp.com/uew/*.) You'll want to customize the script to suit your own testing needs.

EVALUATION

Typical Testing Script

What the Web Site Is
[Explain what the web site is, but no more than necessary.]

Reading from Notes
I will be reading the following from my notes to make sure I remember to say everything and keep consistent.

Purpose
We're testing this web site to identify strengths and weaknesses in its design.

Anonymity
What you do in this study will be kept completely anonymous.

Video/Audio Recording (optional)
We'll be taping you throughout the session. This tape is used only by our design and testing teams to ensure that we've accurately understood what went on during the session. Please tell us if you would prefer not to be taped.

Voluntary Participation
Your participation in this study is voluntary.
You may choose to skip any of the questions in this study or quit the entire session at any time.

Procedure
This entire session should take about an hour.
We'll be working through several tasks on the web site.
During each task I'll be observing you and taking notes.

If you encounter problems or difficulties, those are exactly the problems with the design that we are trying to identify and improve.
When this happens, I can't give you any help, because we're interested in how you would solve such problems on your own.

After each task, I'll ask you to fill out a brief response sheet.
At the end of the study, I'll ask you to fill out a summary questionnaire, and then we can talk about any remaining issues or concerns you have.

Think Aloud
As you work through the tasks, I would like you to think aloud.
This means saying any thoughts or reactions that come to mind as you work.

However, don't feel that you need to elaborate or explain what you're saying—we'll have an opportunity to discuss it when you've completed each task.
If you remain silent for a while, I may occasionally prompt you to start speaking again.

Do you have any questions?

Experimenter Notes Pages

In most cases, you can simply take notes on plain paper, but you may want to prepare a form for notes beforehand. These forms can help you to remember to look for certain problems and can include spaces to write in information such as Project, User Number, Tester, Date, Time, and Start and End Times for tasks. You may also want to have a site hierarchy (or several) printed for reference. With a site outline, you can jot down problems for each specific page, or you can annotate the outline with the order in which the user browsed through pages (numbering each page as the user goes through). This can save considerable writing time and help you focus on what's happening rather than on your notes.

Consent Form

In many settings, especially companies and universities working on government grants or doing other sensitive human experiments, obtaining explicit consent from participants is legally necessary. Even if you are not required to do so, obtaining consent is a good habit to get into. A consent form usually specifically notes that the study is anonymous. If you have a good reason not to keep it anonymous, be very explicit about that fact on the consent form. For instance, if you plan on videotaping to present the session to clients, include the information about videotaping and your intended use of it. If you don't need to use videotapes for every user, you can present a consent to videotape as a checkbox option. Because you've promised anonymity, make sure you store consent forms in a secure place, and avoid associating users' names with their data. See Form 12-4 for a sample consent form. (Download from *http://www.mkp.com/uew/*.)

Instruction Sheet

If you've read the instructions to the user, an instruction sheet should not be necessary, especially for simple test situations. However, you may choose to have the user read the instructions rather than reading them aloud yourself to ensure consistency and to save the tester time.

Task Questionnaires

You may ask users to fill out questionnaires after each task or set of tasks. These can include asking the users to write the answer to the task question and to describe how well the task was supported and what types of problems they had. Such questionnaires are not strictly necessary but usually gather some useful feedback from the users as well as being a convenient way to assign each task.

EVALUATION

Consent Form

The purpose of this user study is to evaluate the design of web sites we've developed. As a volunteer in this study, your participation will be anonymous. You will fill out some questionnaires while using the web site to work through specific tasks. As you work, you will be observed by an experimenter who may take notes on your activities. The entire study should take no more than an hour. If for any reason you are uncomfortable with the study, you may end it at any time.

I, _____ _____, have read and fully understood the extent of the study and any risks involved. I sign here acknowledging the above information.

Participant Signature _____ _____

Date _____

Tester _____

Project _____

Post-Questionnaire and Demographics Sheet

At the very end of the test, a summary questionnaire can collect general demographic information (to help confirm that the users were sampled correctly and to identify possible biases). The questionnaire can also ask general questions about the user's experience with the web site (an adaptation of the sample survey presented as Form 3-3 in Chapter 3, "User Needs Analysis," works well).

Follow-Up Sheet

While not strictly necessary, it's generally a good idea to provide users with a follow-up sheet that summarizes the purpose of the test and gives them contact information in case they have questions later. This is a good opportunity to give them a low-key promotional message about your site, such as "BuyOurStuff.com is a major e-commerce web site that offers quality products to an international clientele. We value customer feedback and conduct regular studies to continue improving our services." Since this contact information may be used by users with concerns about your study, it's best to keep any other advertising separate, but feel free to separately provide users with brochures and other corporate paraphernalia: buttons, pens, stickers, etc.

Preparing the Location

Where should a user test be conducted? For the most part, you should be flexible. When possible, it's nice to go to the users' workplace where they'd be actually using your site (though, if it's consumer-oriented, you'll want to visit homes, which can be more difficult to arrange). While it's tempting to aim for a quiet environment, if the users' real workplace is noisy, you may as well find out how the noise and interruptions affect their use of the site. In practice, going on-site works best for intranets where all the users are at a few company locations. Otherwise, visiting the users can be tremendously time-consuming, and the advantage of testing in context may not justify the time it takes to get there.

Testing can happen just about anywhere that you have a computer and adequate room for a user and an observer to sit. Other than that, it's preferable to find an environment similar to the one in which the user will be using the web site. For instance, if the user would be browsing from his or her living room, then test in a living room or simulate a living room by providing ambient lighting, couches, and a TV in the background.

In practice, especially early in the design cycle, most problems are so blatant that they aren't very sensitive to the environment in which you're testing. Because of this, you can test at a desk in your office or set up a usability lab for the purpose.

A usability lab can provide convenience and focus for testing. By controlling noise, interruptions, lighting, and so forth, you can avoid the confusion of external environments and get more consistent experiences for each user. Usability labs are a convenient place to organize test materials, make sure the computer environment is set up correctly, and set up other more specialized equipment. Some usability labs are designed with one-way mirrors to allow the tester to observe without bothering the user.

To record the session, a tape recorder or video camera can be permanently set up for optimal audio and video quality, and logging software can be installed on the computers to capture keystrokes and mouse movements. If you are videotaping, it's nice to be able to capture the computer screen, the user's face, and the user's hands all at once, as well as to include time codes with at least 1-second accuracy. Expensive setups will have more than one video camera and will use video mixers to combine these signals. Analyzing videotapes is sufficiently time consuming that it is rarely worth the trouble until you've already fixed the obvious usability problems.

Pilot Testing

Pilot testing means simply that you've pulled in a colleague or two and asked them to go through the user testing. This helps you practice the script, anticipate questions, and get used to the notes you'll need to take. In addition, you will often find obvious problems with the web site that should be fixed before actual users are ever brought in (it's a waste of time to discover that users have problems with something you already knew should be fixed, and those problems may mask other problems). Pilot testing can also help you train multiple testers to ensure a consistent testing style.

Pilot testing can help you determine whether tasks are too easy (and no problems are found) or whether tasks take too long. You typically want your testing to take about an hour. Some users will be slower, and you'll want to stop soon after they've gone over the allocated time, even if they haven't completed all tasks. This by itself is a good indicator that your tasks are not as efficient as they could be. Other users will get the testing done before an hour is up, and you can often use the extra time to have them try out other sites or other tasks. You've paid for the whole hour, so you may as well use it.

As you practice, be sure to go through the whole process of writing up and analyzing the results to make sure you know what you'll do with the results. This may help identify questions that aren't worth asking because you have no idea how to analyze the result, or it may suggest ways to rephrase the questions to make analysis easier.

Recruiting Users

You need to determine who you want to test and how many users to test. Then you need to locate them, verify that the people you find meet your user profile, and bring them in.

Selecting Users to Test

The user profile you put together during requirements analysis identifies the ideal user you would like to have. You'd like to find a range of people within your target audience who represent as broad a sample as possible, making sure you get the most typical user as well as some borderline examples.

Often the first couple of tests will identify some large, obvious problems and won't be too sensitive to the type of user. Therefore, we often start with the most convenient, available users, who may not represent our target population well but can be used to root out the obvious problems. Then, when more subtle problems are sought, it's important to get representative users.

Some types of users are very difficult to find. Many professionals, such as doctors and corporate executives, are simply too busy and too expensive to recruit easily (though they have highly specialized skills and unique viewpoints, so you should get them if you can). Furthermore, some types of users are rare. For instance, if people with color blindness represent about 4 percent of the population, then finding a color-blind doctor for your study will be very difficult. In such cases, you'll want to find acceptable substitutes. While nothing beats the true user, often others with similar training and domain expertise will be useful. For instance, a web site designed for doctors can often be usefully tested on other health-care professionals, including nurses, paramedics, and medical students.

How to Find Users

Developing a list of user volunteers helps to ensure a ready pool of users whenever you're ready to run tests. Such lists need to be maintained regularly or they quickly become outdated as people move or change their minds about participation. Initial lists of people can often be gathered by recruiting them through newspaper ads. For highly specialized target audiences, recruiting may require phone calls to appropriate organizations. Often your client or marketing department can identify appropriate customers who can be contacted for testing.

One of the significant difficulties of testing specialized target audiences is getting to them. For instance, when we wanted to test a project for church staff, we called churches and easily found volunteers. On the other hand, for testing a pharmaceutical web site, we tried calling pharmacies and were mostly ignored. The pharmacists were busy and had no reason to take us seriously. In such circumstances, you may need a referral or letter of reference for such people to consider participation. Your clients may be able to provide this, but it is not uncommon for clients to have serious concerns about letting you talk to their customers (lest you give them the wrong impression) or about bothering their customers (with whom they may already have a fragile relationship). To help in such situations, you can stress the importance of meeting real users, the benefits of having customers feel that their concerns are being addressed in the design process, and the variety of ways such a test can be organized. For instance, user testing can be conducted as part of a plant tour, a training session, or an industry conference.

How Many Users?

With as few as four or five users, you can often find 80 percent of the usability problems with your web site. Thus, quick testing on only a few users can

EVALUATION

be highly productive. In practice, and when your budget allows, we normally suggest testing eight to ten users, often in two phases. First test an initial group of four or five, make some changes to the site, and then test the remaining four or five users. Except for very complex sites, this normally identifies as many problems as you are likely to find at any particular stage of development. Another set of eight to ten users is useful again after major revisions have been made to the design. Iterative testing and evaluation are critical to improvement.

You may hear someone suggest that you test larger numbers of users to get statistically significant results. In fact, depending on the subtlety of the issue you are studying, you may well need many more test users, and statistical significance is an appropriate criterion for any design question that may have important financial implications. However, as any statistician will tell you, you shouldn't avoid a study just because you can't afford enough users for statistical significance. If you can't afford a large number of tests, it's still much better to base your design decisions on experience with *some* users rather than *none*.

In addition, for some very large and complex sites, you can continue to find problems as you explore more and more details of the site. In this case, rather than testing a lot of users, we'd suggest testing a few, identifying the general principles behind the problems you find, and fixing the entire site (even portions you haven't tested yet) based on these principles before testing more. This way you avoid rediscovering the same problems all over a large site.

In the end, the decision of how many users to test rests on three factors: your budget, the degree of confidence you need in the testing results, and the cost of getting the design wrong. In other words, if a design decision will make the difference between earning $500 or $501, you really don't need to be completely confident you've made the right design decision. But if the difference is between $1 million and $2 million, you'd like to have strong confidence that you made the right decision, and you'll be willing to budget quite a bit to know the right answer.

The Recruiting Process

As you prepare to recruit users, you usually need to prepare the following three documents: the recruiting ad, the recruiting sign-up sheet, and recruiting qualifier questions.

The recruiting ad is a rather straightforward announcement saying you are looking for volunteers to test a web site, the amount you're paying, and how to contact you. You may want to indicate that no experience is necessary in order to encourage people who'd otherwise assume that experience was required. You may also need to specify any constraints, such as domain expertise.

When people call or email you to volunteer, keep a list of them. Often, when a spectrum of backgrounds is needed, you won't be able to schedule a test time immediately. So tell your volunteers that a spectrum of users is needed and that you'll call them back when a selection is made and will schedule the test at that time. Then you need to ask them background questions ("qualifier questions") that help you identify who to select. For instance, you generally want an approximate gender balance, so ask them their gender. Also, frequently you'll want a mix of some people with little computer experience and others with more, so ask them how long they've used computers and how much time they spend on the Web.

Some people are "professional volunteers," so you may want to ask them how often they've participated in other user testing, focus groups, and so forth. While it's okay to bring in such people occasionally, you don't want your results to be skewed by them. Similarly, you'll find a lot of extremely experienced people who want to participate, such as other local web designers, software engineers, system administrators, and computer science students. Inviting one or two super users may provide some insight, as they will often easily get past problems that baffle novices and help you identify some more subtle design issues, but make sure you stress that you're interested in how they use the web site, not what their design philosophy is.

Generally you only want to use a volunteer user once. After that, they already know how to use your web site and will be familiar with your design style, although this can be useful if you are trying to examine how easy your site is to learn and use over extended periods of time. Whatever you do, avoid inviting back your favorite or most successful users; you simply won't learn as much from them.

Conducting the Test

At this point, you've prepared all of your materials and written your testing script. After asking users to sign a consent form, you'll introduce them to the study and get them started. The test itself is usually a series of tasks users are asked to perform (see Figure 12-3). As users work, take notes on where they go and what they do. In particular, note when they do anything unexpected, and especially when they appear to be confused or having difficulties. After each task, we often ask users to give some quick feedback on how difficult the

Figure 12-3.

User Testing in Action.

task was and what aspects of the design were helpful or difficult. Finally, at the end of the test, we typically ask users to fill out a post-questionnaire, giving their impressions of the site as a whole. When they're done, ask them for any other general comments or questions. Some people, especially domain experts, will have an enormous number of insights to contribute at this point.

Notetaking

Notetaking skills are crucial during the test, when you want to jot down what the user is saying as well as your observations. Be careful to distinguish between exact quotes and paraphrases (you'll want to quote users later on, and you need to be accurate about how much you are interpreting what they said). Also, if things slow down, you may have time to jot down solutions to problems as they occur to you. However, make sure your notes distinguish between your own ideas and those of the user. This can be as simple as putting your initials in front of any statements or ideas that are yours.

Who Performs the Testing?

Frequently, only a single tester is necessary. This should be someone who's had some practice with user testing and knows how to behave and what to look for. Frequently we invite an observer into a testing session as well, such as a graphic designer, software developer, or client. This is an incredibly revealing experience for anyone involved, and inviting participation by the whole design and development team can increase their receptiveness to the testing results, as well as to the usability process in general. A single observer usually doesn't bother a test user much, but if you have many observers, you may want them to stand outside the room, watching either through a live video connection or through a one-way mirror. Such a large group is rarely necessary and can be intimidating even when the group is in a different room, so let the user know that they're there, but ask the observers to keep a low profile.

Interacting with the User

During the test, encourage users to *think aloud,* saying whatever spontaneously comes to mind. However, if they begin elaborating with detailed design critique, you may remind them that they'll have the opportunity for detailed comments after they've finished the task and that you'd like them to focus on the task and any thoughts that occur spontaneously as they perform the task.

The most common approach is to minimize your own comments, especially avoiding any leading comments. You are trying to see how the user would solve the problem without any outside help. However, except in the most formal studies, it's okay to help out when a user really runs into trouble. If someone really gets stuck, write down where the problem occurred, offer a hint to help the user continue, and write down what you said. You get little value from watching the user sitting stumped for a half hour or letting the person browse off to another web site for a long time without bringing him or her back to the site you intended to test. Keep your comments to a minimum though, and be patient—users can often solve a problem if you give them the opportunity to mull it over.

When a design is incomplete (i.e., when testing simple screen shots or a rough prototype), a second approach is to guide the user through the interface with appropriate questions, following through on any uncertainties the user may have. This gives you the opportunity to fill in details on how the prototype would work in any of its unfinished pieces.

A third approach, known as the *co-discovery method,* involves two users working simultaneously to complete the tasks. This approach is most appropriate when you expect that the end user will rarely be using the web site alone. With two users, you usually can elicit their comments from the conversation between the two of them, so asking them to think aloud is not necessary. In this approach, the users are still likely to mention when they have a problem, but between the two, they'll often find a solution reasonably quickly and avoid the stumped pauses you'll see when they're on their own.

Analyzing the Results

Type up your notes soon after testing to make sure you don't forget anything. A few days later you may not even be able to read your own handwriting. The basic goal of your writeup is to identify what the observed problems were, note how serious each was, and assess what can be done about them. Go through your notes with each user and type up each problem you found. Keep track of how many users had each problem. We rate the severity of a problem as low, medium, or high priority based on a combination of how common the problem was and how serious it is in terms of the user's level of success at the task and the cost of failure.

Some of the problems won't have any obvious solution, and while these should be documented, the focus of your report should be on an action plan that can be taken to address the problems. We like to start a test report with a summary of the top 10 fixes that need to be made to the site, based on how easy they are to fix and how severe the problem is.

Many problems will be easy to identify but complicated to fix. They may interact with a variety of design tradeoffs, in which case you'll need to consult with the initial design team and perform site walkthroughs for major design changes to verify that the proposed changes won't introduce other problems.

Making Modifications to Your Site

After testing, you need to modify your design to reflect what you've learned. There are two extremes in doing so. At one extreme, you can make revisions after testing each user. This allows you to make very rapid improvements to your design and keeps you from having to watch every user repeat a problem whose fix was obvious after the first time, thus making each test more productive. In this approach, you may overreact to a mistake by a single user that really doesn't reflect a common problem. Be especially careful about making changes after your very first user. This person may be unique, and you want to get a feel for whether that's the case by testing at least one more user before you start making changes.

The alternative is to test *all* of your users before making any changes. This ensures that you have a better idea of the frequency of problems before you correct them. Problems that only occur for a single user may be unique to that user or to your testing situation, but problems that occur more frequently are ones that are probably important to fix. If fixing problems doesn't cost anything, your confidence in the problem's significance might not matter, but in practice, fixing problems may involve substantial redesign and may result in creating new problems for other users, so it pays to be conservative.

Both approaches work fine. In practice, you can be flexible: if you observe an *obvious* problem that's easy to fix, you'll probably fix it immediately. If you observe an obscure or expensive-to-fix problem, you should test more users and fix it only if you see a pattern of difficulty for users.

Remote User Testing

A variation of user testing particularly suited to web sites is remote testing—that is, testing people who are at a different location than the tester. Remote testing allows you to test a nonlocal audience conveniently, and the techniques of remote testing help you collect data from a larger number of users at a relatively low cost. When your target audience is global, this may be the only effective way to get input from an appropriate range of users.

In this case, you generally have no means of observing your test users, so you need to collect their data automatically or through users' self-reports. For example, to collect data automatically, ask users to visit your test site and collect hit logs for each visit, from which you can see what pages they visited and when. If your web site is database-driven, you can record more detailed information about data the user enters, types of search queries, and errors in data entry. Other automated techniques involve asking the user to download software that can track keystrokes and mouse clicks, for later analysis.

With the self-report technique, users must actively record what happened in the testing. They can do this by keeping a diary, indicating which pages they went to and problems they encountered. Users can also fill out questionnaires that ask about their experiences with the site. These can be paper questionnaires, email questionnaires, or web-based questionnaires. Of course, if you use a web-based questionnaire, you ought to test the questionnaire with some users to make sure it's usable.

Neither of these approaches elicits the critical information you'd gain from actually observing users. Self-reports often fail to indicate subtle problems that users either don't notice or don't think to report because they blame themselves rather than thinking to attribute the problem to the design. Similarly, server logs can sometimes suggest when someone took a long time to perform a task or got wildly lost on the web site, but guesswork is necessary, and many problems can't be identified. These drawbacks limit the applicability of remote testing to situations where you have relatively specific questions or you have no alternative way to reach the geographically distributed target audience.

Remote testing results often come back to you as data in computerized form, such as hit logs or questionnaire data in an online database. This lends itself well to automated analysis, allowing you to relatively easily summarize data from many users and make live updates to those summaries as more data comes in. In addition, code can be written to track the most common errors and search queries.

EVALUATION THROUGHOUT THE DESIGN PROCESS

Evaluation is a critical component of every phase of design. It raises the quality of your design and keeps costs under control by preventing the design from drifting off track. User testing, in particular, is an extremely informative approach to involving users in design evaluation.

When web sites go live, we want our users' experiences to be successful and happy. This means planning for their success from the beginning of the project and considering the impact on users as each design decision is resolved. While, as designers, we'd love to believe that we can dream up a great design from scratch, most of the best designs are the result of intensive planning, iteration, evaluation, and refinement.

APPENDIX

USABILITY INSPECTION OF WWW.WHITEHOUSE.GOV

As an example of usability inspection, we present a quick inspection of *www.whitehouse.gov* (see Figure A-1). The screen shots will help you understand some of the comments, but an analysis really requires that you navigate the site. (Keep in mind that this site is bound to change over time.) This example reviews how some basic guidelines apply to the site, but a full report would also need to prioritize problems and recommend solutions. You may not agree with how each problem is categorized, but many problems fall into multiple categories (e.g., a problem with inconsistent navigation is a problem both for consistency and navigation), and the point is that each category of guidelines gives you an opportunity to spot a problem. You also may not agree with every criticism. Only multiple reviewers would resolve which concerns are important enough to merit fixing, and issues that remain debatable are good issues to address in user testing.

Content and Scope

- The basic information you'd expect to find is there: about the president, White House news and history, contact information, and basic government information.

- Lengthy text is not always chunked well. For instance, Past First Families within History appears as a long article on multiple pages without paragraph headings and with each page labeled "Page 1," "Page 2," "Page 3," and so on, rather than having meaningful page names (such as chronological dates). (In addition, rather than using "You are here" indicators, links to pages within History disappear when you're on them, creating an unstable navbar.)

- The scope of the site isn't clear (you can discover some interesting and nonobvious gems). A site map would help. Also, navigation below the second level isn't consistent.

- "Appointments" are never really clearly explained (they appear to be a way to apply to have the president appoint you to certain jobs or positions). Are these ordinary jobs? What types of jobs are available? Am I qualified for any of them, or are these jobs only for superhumans and well-connected bureaucrats?

- On the web feedback form, under "Topic," usability is misspelled as "useability"!

- It was a good idea to highlight phrases in boldface in the disabilities section (of Tours), but some of the wrong phrases are highlighted (e.g., "Signing interpretation is also available for **individual visitors** with advance notice" would be more effective if "signing interpretation" were in boldface).

Speed

- The page is fast, with simple graphics, and a text version is available.

- In one case, it's too fast (see Figure A-2): when you follow a link outside the site, a message indicates you are leaving the site, but the message doesn't stay on the screen long enough to read it (only a few seconds).

Navigation

- The home page focuses on news, but it would be nice to see it explain the content of the site. For instance, a brief text explanation (scope notes) of each section of the site would be helpful. The design doesn't lead the viewer into these sections.

- The site contains no metatags, so it won't necessarily be indexed optimally by search engines.

- In the navigation bar, the current page is linked to itself, causing the page to reload when it's clicked.

- On the home page, the link to FirstGov goes to a very useful site, but it looks like an ad and doesn't indicate why you'd go there.

Figure A-2.

Too Fast to Read.

This message appears for only a few seconds.

> ### You are exiting the White House Web Server
>
> Thank you for visiting our site.
>
> You will now access http://access.adobe.com/
>
> We have provided a link to this site because it has information that may be of interest to our users. The White House does not necessarily endorse the views expressed or the facts presented on this site. Further, the White House does not endorse any commercial products that may be advertised or available on this site.
>
> We hope your visit was informative and enjoyable.
>
> *To comment on this service, send feedback to the   Web Development Team*

Figure A-3.

Simplify These Search Results.

The display of search results can be made more succinct, and a less technical format for dates, times, and file names would be helpful.

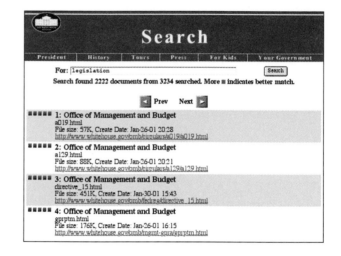

- The search results aren't well crafted (see Figure A-3): file names appear twice (and aren't helpful since files aren't named well); the date and time are in an awkward, nonstandard format; and the search results page is in an inconsistent layout with inconsistent navigation.

- Subnav appears on the bottom left of the page and can be easily missed (e.g., it's easy to miss the fact that there are subpages of the Your Government page). See Figure A-4.

- The Home button is in a strange location in the navbar (the second option in the second group of nav) and disappears on the home page (which would sometimes be okay but is strange in this layout).

Appropriateness to Task

- The search task is confusing and inefficient (see Figure A-5). The search box has the word "Search" inside it, which must be deleted before entering your search term. If not deleted, the word "Search" becomes one of your search terms and usually results in a failed search (no matches).

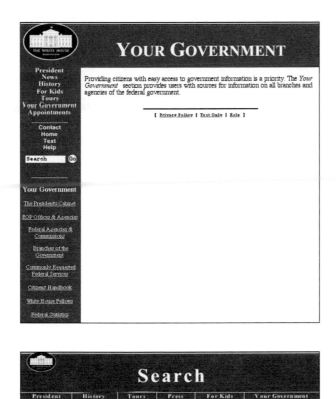

Figure A-4.

This Page Seems to Be Missing Something.

The content of the page should lead readers into the subsections. The subnav at the lower left is easy to overlook.

Figure A-5.

A Reasonable Query That Fails.

It's a bit surprising not to find "bush" on the White House web site. The user must explicitly delete the word "Search" from the search box before entering search terms but may not realize this. Given this design, the word "Search" should probably be one of the *stop words* used by the search engine—that is, one ignored by the search.

Visual Design

- The design is simple, moderately professional, but not especially interesting or impressive.

- Visual focus and flow are pretty good. The main site logo is consistently at top left, page titles are large, and nothing distracts from page content.

- The layout of the left-hand navigation is cluttered. Left alignment of the link labels would help a lot; on the home page, items below the primary nav appear to be thrown in without any planning for how they'd appear.

- Font sizes are generally default font sizes, but occasional small and bold text can be hard to read. For instance, on the home page, "Listen to the President's Remarks" is in a small font that is not very legible, and the Appointments page has a quote that's difficult to read (see Figure A-6).

Compatibility

- Technical compatibility: site appears to work on Netscape and Explorer, Mac and PC, and as small as 640 × 480.

- The JavaScript rollovers sometimes had incorrect highlighting (multiple buttons were highlighted simultaneously). (Observed in IE5 on Mac.)

- An alternate text version enables compatibility with other devices and enables accessibility for screen readers.

Simplicity

- Other than some navigation confusions, the site is very simple and straightforward.

Consistency and Contrast

- Text links are the default blue and work as expected.

- The "For Kids" link in the navigation goes to a "coming soon" web site, with no navigation (all of it is inactive) and no obvious links back to the main site (see Figure A-7).

Error Handling

- "File not found" page is clear and provides adequate navigation.

- When the feedback form is filled out incorrectly, the "Incomplete Correspondence Form" error is adequate but is not worded optimally, doesn't look like the rest of the site, and lacks navigation (see Figure A-8).

Respect for the User

- The site contains a privacy policy and is reasonably clear about it.

- In most cases, domain name issues wouldn't fall under the "Respect for the User" category, but in this site, the domain name problems create serious

Figure A-6.

Legibility Suffers in an Unusual Text Treatment.

This small, bold, right-aligned text can be difficult to read. Long passages of bold text should be avoided anyway.

confusions and even disturbing situations for the user (see Figure A-9). The site should have registered alternate domain names and should consider trying to buy them back. The confusing alternatives are *whitehouse.org* (unclear, broken version of the same site, maybe a spoof), *whitehouse.com* (adult site), and *whitehouse.net* (out-of-date spoof).

Figure A-7.

A Jarring Transition.

Clicking the "For Kids" link takes you to a different site, with no navigation to return you to the main site. This site is "coming soon" and should probably have been kept offline until it was ready and tested.

Incomplete Correspondence Form

Your correspondence was missing certain fields which are required for us to process this form.

- message text

Use your Web browser's **BACK** feature to return to your partially-completed form, or return to the previous White House page and try again.

Figure A-8.

An Imperfect Error Message.

Error messages should be crafted in a style consistent with the rest of the site, with clear-cut explanations. In addition, users have to remember which form field was incorrect. A better design would bring the form back with the required field highlighted.

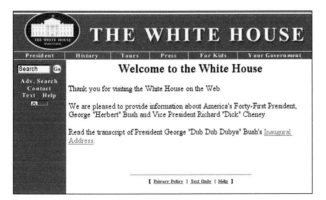

Figure A-9.

Similar Domain Names Have Confusing Content.

www.whitehouse.org is similar to *www.whitehouse.gov* but has broken links and text that doesn't quite make sense. Is this a badly written spoof or an incomplete development version of the site?

REFERENCES

The following presents a select list of readings that may prove useful. Many of these references are *not* referred to in the writing.

Introduction

Gould, J., Boies, S., and Ukelson, J. (1997). How to design usable systems. In M. Helander, T. Landauer, and P. Prabhu (Eds.), *Handbook of human-computer interaction* (pp. 93–121). Amsterdam: North-Holland.

Chapter 1: Usability throughout the Design Process

Borges, J. A., Morales, I., and Rodriguez, N. J. (1996). Guidelines for designing usable World Wide Web pages. In *Proceedings of CHI '96 conference on human factors in computing systems* (pp. 277–278). Vancouver, British Columbia.

Mayhew, D. (1999). *The usability engineering lifecycle.* San Francisco, CA: Morgan Kaufmann.

Olson, J. S., and Moran, T. (1995). Mapping the method muddle: Guidance in using methods for user interface design. In M. Rudisill, C. Lewis, P. Polson, and T. McKay (Eds.), *Human-computer interface design: Success cases, emerging methods and real-world context* (pp. 269–300). San Francisco, CA: Morgan Kaufmann.

Siegel, D. (1997). *Secrets of successful web sites: Project management on the World Wide Web.* Indianapolis, IN: Hayden Books.

Chapter 2: Target Audience and Target Platforms

GVU Center's WWW User Surveys (1998). GVU's Tenth WWW User Survey (October 1998). Retrieved from the World Wide Web: *www.cc.gatech.edu/gvu/user_surveys/*.

Laux, L., McNally, P., Paciello, M., and Vanderheiden, P. (1996). Designing the World Wide Web for people with disabilities: A user centered design approach. In *Proceedings of the second annual ACM conference on assistive technologies* (pp. 94–101). Vancouver, British Columbia.

Chapter 3: User Needs Analysis

Converse, J., and Presser, S. (1986). *Survey questions: Handcrafting the standardized questionnaire.* Beverly Hills, CA: Sage Publications.

Jansen, B. J., Spink, A., and Saracevic, T. (2000). Real life, real users and real needs: A study and analysis of users' queries on the Web. *Information processing and management,* 36 (2), 207–227.

Morgan, D. (1997). *Focus groups as qualitative research.* Thousand Oaks, CA: Sage Publications.

Quay, J. (1994). *Diagnostic interviewing for consultants and auditors: A collaborative approach to problem solving.* Cincinnati, OH: Quay Associates.

Chapter 4: Task Analysis

Beyer, H., and Holtzblatt, K. (1997). *Contextual design: A customer-centered approach to systems design.* San Francisco, CA: Morgan Kaufmann.

Card, S. K., Moran, T. P., and Newell, A. (1983). *The psychology of human-computer interaction.* Hillsdale, NJ: Lawrence Erlbaum.

Diaper, D. (1989). *Task analysis for human computer interaction.* Chichester: Ellis Horwood.

Drury, C. G. (1983). Task analysis methods in industry. *Applied ergonomics,* 14 (1), 19–28.

Jacobson, I. (1992). *Object-oriented software engineering: A use case driven approach.* Reading, MA: Addison-Wesley Publishing Co.

John, B. E. (1995). Why GOMS? *Interactions,* 2, 80–89.

John, B. E., and Kieras, D. E. (1996a). Using GOMS for user interface design and evaluation: Which technique? *ACM transactions on computer-human interaction* 3 (4), 287–319.

———. (1996b). The GOMS family of user interface analysis techniques: Comparison and contrast. *ACM transactions on computer-human interaction* 3 (4), 320–351.

Kieras, D. E. (1999). *A guide to GOMS model usability evaluation using GOMSL and GLEAN3.* Technical report. Ann Arbor: University of Michigan.

———. (1997). A Guide to GOMS model usability evaluation using NGOMSL. In M. Helander, T. Landauer, and P. Prabhu (Eds.), *Handbook of human-computer interaction* (2nd ed.) (pp. 733–766). Amsterdam: North-Holland.

———. (1997). Task analysis and the design of functionality. In A. Tucker (Ed.), *The computer science and engineering handbook*. Boca Raton, FL: CRC Press, Inc.

Kirwan, B., and Ainsworth, L. K. (1992). *A guide to task analysis*. London: Taylor & Francis.

Pressman, R. (2000). *Software engineering: A practitioner's approach* (5th ed.). New York: McGraw-Hill.

Raskin, J. (2000). *The humane interface: New directions for designing interactive systems*. Reading, MA: Addison-Wesley Publishing Co.

Wood, S. (2000). Extending GOMS to human error and applying it to error-tolerant design. Ph.D. dissertation, University of Michigan, Department of Electrical Engineering and Computer Science.

Chapter 5: Information Architecture

Aldenderfer, M., and Blashfield, R. (1984). *Cluster analysis*. Beverly Hills, CA: Sage Publications.

Catledge, L., and Pitkow, J. (1995). Characterizing browsing strategies in the World Wide Web. Retrieved from the World Wide Web: *www.igd.fhg.de/archive/1995_www95/papers/80/userpatterns/UserPatterns.Paper4.formatted.html*.

Fleming, J. (1998). *Web navigation: Designing the user experience*. Sebastopol, CA: O'Reilly.

Golovchinsky, G. (1997). Queries? Links? Is there a difference? In *Proceedings of CHI '97 conference on human factors in computing systems* (pp. 407–414). Atlanta.

Hymes, C., and Olson, G. (1997). Quick but not so dirty web design: Applying empirical conceptual clustering techniques to organise hypertext content. In *Proceedings of the conference on designing interactive systems: Processes, practices, methods, and techniques* (pp. 159–162). The Netherlands.

Kahn, P., and Lenk, K. (2001). *Mapping web sites*. Switzerland: RotoVision.

Larson, K. and Czerwinski, M. (1998). Web page design: Implications of memory, structure and scent for information retrieval. In *Proceedings of CHI '98 conference on human factors in computing systems* (pp. 25–32). Los Angeles, CA.

Nielsen, J. (2000). *Designing Web usability*. Indianapolis, IN: New Riders Publishing.

Rosenfeld, L., and Morville, P. (1998). *Information architecture for the World Wide Web*. Sebastopol, CA: O'Reilly.

Chapter 6: Page Layout

Bertin, J. (1981). *Graphics and graphic information-processing*. Berlin: de Gruyter.

Lynch, P., and Horton, S. (1999). *Web style guide: Basic design principles for creating web sites*. New Haven, CT: Yale University Press.

Mullet, K., and Sano, D. (1995). *Designing visual interfaces: Communication-oriented techniques*. Englewood Cliffs, NJ: SunSoft Press.

Nielsen, J. (2000). *Designing Web usability*. Indianapolis, IN: New Riders Publishing.

Smith, B. (Ed.) (1988). *Foundations of Gestalt theory*. Munich: Philosophia Verlag.

Spool, J. M., Scanlon, T., Schroeder, W., and Snyder, C. (1997). *Web site usability: A designer's guide*. North Andover, MA: User Interface Engineering.

Williams, R. (1994). *The non-designers design book*. Berkeley, CA: Peachpit Press, Inc.

Chapter 7: Envisioning Design

Fuccella, J., and Pizzolato, J. (1999). A divided approach to web design: Separating content and visuals for rapid results. Retrieved from the World Wide Web: *www-106.ibm.com/developerworks/library/wireframe/wireframe.html*.

Levi, M., and Conrad, F. (1997). A heuristic evaluation of a World Wide Web prototype. *Interactions*, 3 (4), 50–61.

Mayhew, D. (1999). *The usability engineering lifecycle*. San Francisco, CA: Morgan Kaufmann.

Nielsen, J. (1993). *Usability engineering*. San Diego, CA: Academic Press.

———. (1990). Paper versus computer implementations as mockup scenarios for heuristic evaluation. In *Proceedings of IFIP INTERACT '90: Human-computer interaction* (pp. 315–320). Cambridge, England.

Virzi, R., Sokolov, J., and Karis, D. (1996). Usability problem identification using both low- and high-fidelity prototypes. In *Proceedings of CHI '96 conference on human factors in computing systems* (pp. 236–243). Vancouver, British Columbia.

Chapter 8: Writing for the Web

Hale, C. (Ed.). (1996). *Wired style: Principles of English usage in the digital age.* San Francisco, CA: HardWired.

Morkes, J., and Nielsen, J. (1998, January 6). Applying writing guidelines to web pages. Retrieved from the World Wide Web: *www.useit.com/papers /webwriting/rewriting.html.*

Spool, J. M., Scanlon, T., Schroeder, W., and Snyder, C. (1997). *Web site usability: A designer's guide.* North Andover, MA: User Interface Engineering.

Strunk, W., and White, E. B. (1979). *Elements of style.* New York: Macmillan.

University of Chicago Press. (1993). *The Chicago manual of style* (14th ed.). Chicago: University of Chicago Press.

Walker, J., and Taylor, T. (1998). *The Columbia guide to online style.* New York: Columbia University Press.

Chapter 9: Design Elements

Albers, J. (1971). *Interaction of color.* New Haven, CT: Yale University Press.

Boyarski, D., Neuwirth, C., Forlizzi, J., and Regli, S. (1998). A study of fonts designed for screen display. In *Proceedings of CHI '98 conference on human factors in computing systems* (pp. 87–94). Los Angeles.

Cavanaugh, S. (1995). *Digital type design guide: The page designer's guide to working with type.* Indianapolis, IN: Hayden Books.

Horton, W. (1994). *The icon book: Visual symbols for computer systems and documentation.* New York: John Wiley & Sons.

Itten, J. (1974). *The art of color: The subjective experience and objective rationale of color.* New York: John Wiley & Sons.

Lynch, P., and Horton, S. (1999). *Web style guide: Basic design principles for creating web sites.* New Haven, CT: Yale University Press.

Moriarty, S. (1977). *The ABC's of typography* (2nd ed.). Glenbrook, CT: Art Direction Book Company, Inc.

Mullet, K., and Sano, D. (1995). *Designing visual interfaces: Communication-oriented techniques.* Englewood Cliffs, NJ: SunSoft Press.

Ohnemus, K. (1997). Web style guides: Who, what, where. In *Proceedings of the 15th annual international conference on computer documentation* (pp. 189–197). Snowbird, UT.

Spool, J. M., Scanlon, T., Schroeder, W., and Snyder, C. (1997). *Web site usability: A designer's guide.* North Andover, MA: User Interface Engineering.

Weinman, L. (1996). *Designing web graphics.* Indianapolis, IN: New Riders Publishing.

Chapter 10: Usability in Software Development

Boehm, B. (1988). A spiral model of software development and enhancement. *IEEE Computer,* 21 (2), 61–72.

Brooks, F. (1975). *The mythical man-month.* Reading, MA: Addison-Wesley Publishing Co.

Conzett, A., Knop, U., and Gupta, S. (2000). *The Front of IBM WebSphere: Building e-business user interfaces.* Raleigh, NC: IBM Publications.

Pressman, R. (1997). *Software engineering: A practitioner's approach.* Boston, MA: McGraw Hill.

Royce, W. (1970). Managing the development of large software systems: Concepts and techniques. *Proceedings of the 9th international conference on software engineering* (pp. 328–38). Monterey, CA.

Sadtler, C., Hilgenberg, F., Kwek, J., Marland, L., Szczeponik, W., Vasudeva, G. (2000). *Patterns for e-business: User-to-business patterns for topology 1 and 2 using WebSphere advanced edition.* Raleigh, NC: IBM Publications.

White, B., Bagwell, D., Galambos, G., Van Winkle, R., Walmsley, A. (1998). *An approach to designing e-business solutions.* Raleigh, NC: IBM Publications.

Chapter 11: Pre-Launch and Post-Launch

Catledge, L., and Pitkow, J. (1995). Characterizing browsing strategies in the World Wide Web. Retrieved from the World Wide Web: *www.igd.fhg.de /archive/1995_www95/papers/80/userpatterns/UserPatterns.Paper4.formatted .html.*

Drott, M. (1998). Using web server logs to improve site design. In *Proceedings of the 16th annual international conference on computer documentation* (pp. 43–50). Quebec, Canada.

Kaner, C., Falk, J., and Nguyen, H. Q. (1993). *Testing computer software* (2nd ed.). Boston, MA: International Thomson Computer Press.

Chapter 12: Usability Evaluation

Kantner, L., and Rosenbaum, S. (1997). Usability studies of WWW sites: Heuristic evaluation vs. laboratory testing. In *Proceedings of the 15th annual international conference on computer documentation* (pp. 153–160). Snowbird, UT.

Nielsen, J. (1993). *Usability engineering.* San Diego, CA: Academic Press.

Rubin, J. (1994). *Handbook of usability testing: How to plan, design, and conduct effective tests.* New York: John Wiley & Sons.

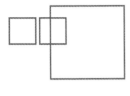

INDEX

→ (arrow) for breadcrumbs, 157
> (greater-than symbol) for breadcrumbs, 157
- (minus sign) with search keywords, 171
+ (plus sign) with search keywords, 171
3-tiered architectures, 345–346
8-bit color monitors, 59

About Us pages, 266–267
accessibility issues, 46–49
   design guidelines, 47
   everyone helped by attention to, 47–49
   for frames, 363
   prevalence of disabilities, 46, 48
   standards for accessibility, 46
   tools for evaluating accessibility, 46
   types of disabilities, 45, 48
accomplished tasks, usability objectives, 70
accuracy in HTML coding, 354–355
action buttons for forms, 323, 325
Active Server Pages (ASPs), 353
active voice, 276
activity-based link labels, 152
actors in use case analysis, 100
administrative interface requirements, 71–72
advertising
   interstitial, 285
   for others, 275
   See also marketing; promotion
age, design issues and, 45, 46
aligning
   form elements, 323, 324, 325
   text, 299
<alt> tags, 391
ALT text for images, 281
alternate spellings in search functions, 172
ambiguity
   in link labels, 5
   in survey questions or responses, 82
   writing style and, 278, 279
animation, 334–336
appropriateness to task, 414, 446–447
arbitrary network site topology, 147, 148
architecture. *See* information
      architecture; 3-tiered architectures

Architecture Review Checklist, 142, 144–145
Arial font, 294, 295
arrow (→) for breadcrumbs, 157
ASPs (Active Server Pages), 353
asset management, 349–350
asset management tools, 351
asymmetrical balance, 188, 189, 190
audience. *See* target audience
automated testing, 375, 376
automatic usability inspection, 419

Back button, 129, 165
Back to Top links, 165
background research, 72–92
   competitive analysis, 83–85
   early use of, 38
   interviews and focus groups, 85–92
   surveys, 72–82
balance in page layout, 188–190
bandwidth, speed differences and, 61
benchmarks, 17
Beyer, H., 102
bias in surveys, avoiding, 80–82
<blink> tag (HTML), 297
Bobby (accessibility evaluation tool), 46
body text, 273
Bookmarks, 129, 362, 363
Boolean searches, 169–170
bottlenecks, 26
bottom-up design of information architec-
      ture, 131–132
brainstorming icons, 315–317
breadcrumbs, 157, 159, 177
brevity, user performance improvements
      from, 112
broad vs. deep structures, 148–149
brochureware, 252
Brooks, Fred, 343
browsers
   compatibility issues, 341
   designing for diversity, 42–45, 49–50,
      56–57, 59–61
   differences among, 59–61
   gaps and gutter sizes, 208–209

browsers *(continued)*
    instrumented, 105
    navigation support in, 129
    platform differences in, 56–57
    screen space used by, 204, 205, 206
    testing, 59–60
    text-only browsing, 243, 281, 282, 283
    user preference settings, 49–50, 286
    See also target platforms
budgets, 21–24
    costs beyond design and building, 24
    evaluation costs, 23–24
    hourly rates, 23
    iterations and slack time in, 23
    iterative design approach and, 17
    planning, 21–22
    projections, 24
    spreadsheet example, 22
    time required, 23
    See also costs (monetary)
bulleted lists, 280
business goals, 68, 69
Business Logic tier, 345, 346

cached pages, database integration issues
    from, 11
capital equipment costs, 21
Card, S. K., 109
card sorting technique, 138, 140–141
    closed card sort, 141
    limitations, 140–141
    open card sort, 138, 140
    similarity matching, 141
    top-down approach, 141
    uses for, 138
cascading menus, 327–328, 329
Census Bureau statistics, 38, 48
CGI programming, 353, 359–360
checkboxes and checklists in surveys, 75
checkboxes in online forms, 323, 325
checklists. *See* forms
clarity, user performance and, 112
client checkpoints, 19
Client Interview/Web Site Information
    Worksheet, 66–67
client-side development, 353, 354–355
client-side programming, 353, 358–359
client-side scripting
    JavaScript for, 50, 353, 357
    overview, 353, 357–358
    Visual Basic for, 353
Client Team, 24–25
clients
    Client Interview/Web Site Information
        Worksheet, 66–67

    communicating with, 29
    Goals Checklist, 68
    graphic design style and, 308
    involving, 215–216
    mockup review process, 232–238
    mockups for client review, 222, 230
    pitfalls of early involvement, 215
closed card sort, 141
co-discovery method in user testing, 438–439
code review, 374–375
code test, 374–377
coding errors, 378
coding HTML. *See* HTML coding; HTML
    tags
coding support tools, 351–352
collecting information for site content, 251,
    252, 255
colors
    accessibility issues, 47
    browser preference settings for links, 49,
        286
    as design element, 309–310
    effective use of, 310
    grayscale and, 309
    of links, 258, 285–288, 289–290
    monitor differences and, 58
    perception of, 4–5, 310
    of static text, 287
columns, multiple, 200
combined functionality for performance
    improvements, 112, 114
communication
    documenting, 30
    during mockup review process, 235
    effective, 29
    writing effectively, 246–256, 257–259, 301
    See also writing for the web
comparison testing for usability, 35
compatibility issues. *See* target platforms
competitive analysis, 83–85
    budget issues, 83
    copyright and patent issues, 83
    example, 84–85
    for usability method selection, 34
    usefulness issues, 85
components, nonscrolling, 362
components of pages
    content considerations, 272–275
    engineering, 353–361
    layout considerations, 182–183
    in mockups, 228–229
    online form elements, 321–323
    See also specific components
Conceptual Design stage
    information architecture, 120–177
    overview, 17–18, 177

scheduling staffing for, 27
selecting usability methods and, 32
task analysis, 96–117
See also information architecture; task
analysis
concise writing, 279
conducting interviews and focus groups,
85–88
confidence level, usability methods and,
32–33
consent form for user testing, 430, 431
consistency
heuristic evaluation, 416
interface, 110–112
link style, 288, 289–290
online forms, 318, 321
page layout, 181, 182, 184, 185, 188
page-width issues, 200–201
usability inspection and, 410
usability inspection for, 415, 448, 449
web page code inconsistency, 341
in writing style, 277
contact information
Contact pages, 153, 268, 269
email links, 292
on every page, 267–268
links, 267
for navigation help, 161
content of sites, 264–275
About Us pages, 266–267
collecting information, 252, 254
contact information, 153, 161, 267–268,
269
copyright policy, 270
delivery formats, 254
elements of pages, 272–275
error pages, 153, 154, 270, 272
graphic design support for, 304
Help pages, 153, 154, 270, 271
home page, 265–266
marketing issues, 264
matching typeface to, 310–311, 312
planning the project, 250–251
privacy policy, 268, 269
Products and Services pages, 267, 268
purchasing, 255
quality of information, 264
site maps, 161, 162, 270, 271
splash pages, 265, 266
style guide for, 251–252, 253–254
types of pages, 265–272
updating for currentness, 264–265
value, providing, 264
www.whitehouse.gov example, 444–445
See also writing for the web
Content Style Guide, 253–254

context-sensitive help pages, 153, 154
contextual inquiry, 102, 105
continual user testing, 402
continuation, good (Gestalt principle), 194,
195
contrast
legibility and, 47, 247, 257, 262
in page layout, 188
in typefaces, 314
usability inspection for, 415, 448, 449
controlled vocabulary for link labels, 164
controls for forms, 322–323, 324–325
converging operations principle, 407
conversion rates, 394, 396–397
cookies, 50, 55
copyright issues, 83, 259, 270
corporate identity on pages, 275
cosmetic errors, 378
costs (mental and time)
information costs approach to navigation,
124
scanning vs. page traversal, 124–125
See also performance
costs (monetary)
beyond design and building, 24
capital equipment, 21
development, 21–22
Evaluation stage, 23–24
maintenance, 22–23, 24, 143
marketing, 22, 24
mockups and prototypes for reducing,
216
operating expenses, 21–23
quality assurance for reducing, 371
of search engines, 171
selecting usability methods and, 30–31,
32
staffing as highest budget cost, 21
See also budgets
country
flags as national identifiers, 51, 53
identifying your location, 51, 52
criterion testing for usability, 34–35
critical path, 26
cross-disciplinary interaction, 26
currencies, international differences in, 52,
54
customer feedback. *See* feedback
customer support
Customer Support pages, 153
live, 163

data sharing, XML and, 357
database integration issues, 9–11
cached web pages, 11

database integration issues *(continued)*
    development, 353, 360–361
    duplicate transactions, 10
    interaction guidelines, 360
    out of sync information, 9, 10
    reloading required, 10
database searches, 171. *See also* search
        functions
dates
    international differences in formats, 53, 55
    last updated date, 274–275
DB2, 361
dead time, 27
deadlines, iterative design approach and, 17
decomposing tasks hierarchically. *See* hierar-
        chical task analysis
deep vs. broad structures, 148–149
demographics
    defining for target audience, 38, 45–49
    hit log analysis for, 399
    surveys for collecting, 73
    user testing and, 431
design change analysis, 395–396
design elements. *See* graphic design
design goals for usability, 2–3
Design Team, 24–25
designer walkthroughs, 420
designing for diversity, 42–45
    deciding who to exclude, 42–43
    general-purpose design, 44
    multipurpose design, 45
    optimization for narrow target, 44
    proliferation of alternatives, 44
    user preference settings, 49–50, 286
    See also diversity; target audience; target
        platforms
Detailed General-Purpose Checklist, 412–413
detecting human errors, 115
developing an information architecture. *See*
        information architecture development
development tools, 350–352
    coding support, 351–352
    project management, 351
    site and asset management, 351
    technology support, 352
DHTML
    accessibility issues, 47
    cascading menus, 327–328, 329
diagramming conventions, 137–138
diagramming information architecture.
        See information architecture
        representations
diary studies, 427
digital mockups
    described, 218–219
    paper mockups vs., 219–220, 221

strengths and weaknesses, 221
    tradeoffs, 219
    See also mockups
digital storyboards, 241, 242. *See also*
        prototypes
direct writing, 279
disabilities, 46–49
    accessibility guidelines, 47
    everyone helped by attention to, 47–49
    prevalence of, 46, 48
    standards for accessibility, 46
    temporary or situational, 48–49
    tools for evaluating accessibility, 46
    types of, 45, 48
diversity
    deciding who to exclude, 42–43
    designing for, 42–45
    international differences, 51–55
    scenarios' usefulness and, 42
    user preference settings, 49–50, 286
    See also target audience; target platforms
dmoz.org web directory, 389
documentation
    heuristic evaluation, 417
    importance of, 30, 342
    of information architecture, 142–143
    of interviews and focus groups, 88, 89
    overview, 30
    of user needs analysis, 64
domain names, 369, 370, 387, 448–449
domain-specific terminology, 173
down-time, determining, 400
drop-down menus
    in forms, 322, 324
    for navigation, 327, 329
Dublin core element set, 176
dynamic font sizes, line spacing and, 109
dynamic request trace, 347–348
dynamic text, 247, 250

ease of learning, 2
ease of remembering, 2
EDI (Electronic Data Interchange), 357
efficiency
    described, 2
    frames and, 363
    See also performance; user performance
        improvements
Electronic Data Interchange (EDI), 357
elements of pages
    content considerations, 272–275
    layout considerations, 182–183
    in mockups, 228–229
    online form components, 321–323
    See also specific elements

email feedback, 400–401
email links, 292
embedded external sites, 362
embedded subnav, 332
emphasis
    in page layout, 181
    squint test for, 312
    of structure, 314
    in writing, 278–279
engineering techniques for web sites,
        343–352
    3-tiered architectures, 345–346
    asset management, 349–350
    choosing web site development tools,
        350–352
    dynamic request trace, 347–348
    mapping control and data flow, 346–348
    need for software engineers, 344
    production servers, 350
    software requirements and specifications,
        343–344
    staging servers, 350
    static design diagrams, 347
    system latency diagrams, 348, 349
    version control, 348–349
engineering web site components, 353–361
    CGI programming, 353, 359–360
    client-side development, 353, 354–355
    client-side programming, 353, 358–359
    database and enterprise integration, 353,
        360–361
    HTML page construction, 353, 354–355
    server-side development, 353
    XML and usability, 356–357
entrance pages, 394–395
entry tunnel, 285
envisioning design, 214–243
    fidelity and, 216
    goals, 214–216
    mockups, 216–238
    prototypes, 238–243
    See also mockups; prototypes
error pages, 153, 154, 270, 272
error tolerance
    aspects of error management, 115
    described, 3
    error recovery example, 116–117
    heuristic evaluation, 417
    human-error-tolerant design, 115–117
    usability objectives, 70
errors
    dealing with, 378–379
    error pages, 153, 154, 270, 272
    good error messages, 417
    reporting, 380, 381–382
    responding to problems, 391

severity of, 377
test completion criteria, 379–380
types of, 378
usability inspection for handling of, 415,
        448, 449
See also quality assurance (QA); testing
essay content example, 249
Evaluation stage, 406–441
    converging operations principle, 407
    costs of, 23–24
    Detailed General-Purpose Checklist,
        412–413
    early for late-stage evaluation, 408
    fixing problems, 407–408
    group walkthroughs, 406, 419–423
    in iterative design approach, 16–17
    overview, 15, 18
    types of evaluation, 406–408
    usability inspection, 406, 408–419
    user testing, 406, 423–441
    See also group walkthroughs; usability
        inspection; user testing
exit criteria, 379–380
exits, clearly marking, 417
expanding outlines (navigation bars),
        158–159
expansion of information architecture,
        142–143
experience level of target audience, 45
experimenter notes pages for user testing,
        430
Extensible Markup Language (XML), 356–357
external links, 165–166

facilitators
    for focus groups, 91
    for group walkthroughs, 421
facilities
    for focus groups, 91
    for user testing, 432
"false bottoms" on pages, 282–284
fatal errors, 377
Favorites, 129
feedback
    dealing with, 400–401
    heuristic evaluation, 416
    methods for quality assurance, 372
file-not-found error pages, 153, 154, 270, 272
Filemaker Pro, 360–361
final approval, 383, 386–387, 388
finding
    orphaned pages, 397
    popular pages, 397
    See also search functions

fixed-width pages, 204–207
    advantages and disadvantages, 200–201
    combining with variable-width, 200–201, 207
    screen space used by browsers, 204, 205, 206
    target resolution safe areas, 204
    using, 205–207
flags as national identifiers, 51, 53
Flash (Macromedia), 336–337, 353, 358
flowcharts
    of information architecture, 133
    task analysis example, 97, 98
Focus Group Preparation Worksheet, 90
focus groups, 85–92
    composition of groups, 92
    conducting, 85–88
    for eliciting user needs and functionality, 87
    facilitator for, 91
    facilities for, 91
    Focus Group Preparation Worksheet, 90
    interviews vs., 85, 86
    for mockup reviews, 87
    notetaking during, 89
    number of groups, 92
    number of people per group, 91
    preparing for, 89–90
    recordings of, 88
    sampling issues, 89
    surveys included with, 86
    for understanding organizations, 88–89
    for understanding tasks, 104
    usefulness issues, 92
    for walkthroughs, 87–88
focus in page layout, 181, 182
follow-up sheet for user testing, 431
fonts
    browser preference settings and, 49
    dynamic font sizes and line spacing, 109
    legibility issues, 47, 247, 257, 262–263
    optimal size, 295, 296
    page layout affected by, 295, 296
    platform differences, 57
    screen fonts, 294–295
    size issues, 295–297
    style sheets, 297
    type effects, 297–298
    typefaces, 294–295
    typography, 310–314
    unpredictability of, 294–297
    See also typography
footers, 274
forcing messages on the user, 285, 286

format tags (HTML), semantic tags vs., 298–299
formatting text, 294–300
    alignment, 299
    grouping chunks, 200
    multiple columns, 200
    semantic vs. format tags, 298–299
    style guide for, 263–264
    style sheets, 297
    type effects, 297–298
    typeface issues, 294–295
    Writing Guidelines Checklist, 257–259
forms
    Architecture Review Checklist, 142, 144–145

    Client Interview/Web Site Information Worksheet, 66–67
    Consent Form, 430, 431
    Content Style Guide, 253–254
    Detailed General-Purpose Checklist, 412–413
    Focus Group Preparation Worksheet, 90
    Form for Brainstorming Icons, 316
    Form for Testing Whether a Set of Icons Maps Uniquely to a Set of Concepts, 320
    Form for Testing Whether an Icon Is Recognizable, 319
    Goals Checklist, 68
    Minimal Maintenance Checklist, 392
    Mockup Checklist, 231
    Mockup Style Review Form, 234–235, 236–237
    Postproduction Checklist, 383, 384–385, 387
    Problem Report and Resolution Form, 380, 381
    Problem Summary Report, 380, 382
    Sample Mockup Development Schedule, 233
    Sample Survey, 76–77
    scenario example, 40–41
    Testing Script, 428–429
    usefulness of, 30
    User Testing Preparation Worksheet, 424–425
    Web Site Final Approval Form, 383, 386–387
    Web Site Materials Request Form, 305, 306–307
    Writing Guidelines Checklist, 257–259
forms, online. See online forms
Forward button, 129, 165

frames
    advantages of, 361–362
    disadvantages of, 362–363
    HTML vs., 364
free response items in surveys, 74
Frequently Asked Questions pages, 153, 270
full mesh site topology, 146, 147
full-text retrieval systems, 171. *See also* search
    functions
functional correctness, 2
functional specifications
    administrative interface, 71–72
    combined functionality for performance
        improvements, 112, 114
    defined, 71
    defining, 70–72
    examples, 71
    final check, 387
    interviews and focus groups for, 87
    scenarios and, 39
functionality test, 387
fuzzy matches in search functions, 171–172

garden paths navigation, 125
gateway pages, 175
gender
    design examples, 46
    survey information about, 73–74
generic applications, scenario usefulness and,
    42
Geneva screen font, 294–295
Gestalt principles, 192–194
    applying, 194, 195
    good continuation, 194, 195
    overview, 192
    pre-attentive processing, 197
    proximity, 192, 195
    similarity, 193, 195
given-new approach to reading, 261–262
Go menu, 129
goals
    design goals for usability, 2–3
    of graphic design, 304
    hierarchical task analysis, 101–102
    of mockups and prototypes, 214–216
    of page layout, 180–182
    of scenarios, 39
    site objectives, 65–72
    supporting user tasks and goals, 246
Goals Checklist, 68
GOMS analysis, 106, 107
good continuation (Gestalt principle), 194,
    195

Google search engine, 390
graphic design, 304–337
    animation, 334–336
    color, 309–310
    content supported by, 304
    establishing parameters, 305–309
    gathering materials, 305, 306–307
    goals of graphic design, 304
    icon design, 314–318, 319–320
    integrating effectively, 337
    interactivity, 336–337
    multimedia, 334–337
    navigation, 325–334
    online forms, 318, 321–323
    style, defining, 305, 308
    tradeoffs, 304
    typography, 310–314
    use-based presentation, 304
    Web Site Materials Request Form, 305,
        306–307
    See also page layout
graphical site maps, 161, 162
graphics
    accessibility issues, 47
    ALT text for, 281
    browser preferences for image-loading,
        49
    delivery formats, 254
    design goals, 304
    legibility and, 262–263
    placement indications in mockups, 226,
        229
    in scenarios, 42
    text-only browsing, 243, 281, 282, 283
grayscale, 309
greater-than symbol (>) for breadcrumbs,
    157
greeking in mockups, 222, 224, 229
grid site topology, 146, 147
group walkthroughs, 419–423
    conducting, 422–423
    designer, 420
    facilitators for, 421
    interviews or focus groups for, 87–88
    overview, 406, 419–420
    pluralistic, 420–421
    Scandinavian design tradition, 421
    scribes for, 422
    simulated roles, 421
    user participation, 421
grouping chunks of text, 200
growth, hit log analysis of, 396
gutter sizes for browsers, 208–209
GVU WWW User Survey, 43, 48

hardware. *See* target platforms
\<head\> tag (HTML), 176
headings, 280
help systems
    help pages, 153, 154, 270, 271
    heuristic evaluation, 417
    for navigation, 161
    in search functions, 174
Helvetica font, 294, 295
heuristic evaluation, 415–417
    clearly marked exits, 417
    consistency, 416
    feedback, 416
    good error messages, 417
    help and documentation, 417
    minimizing user's memory load, 416
    overview, 415, 416
    preventing errors, 417
    shortcuts, 417
    simple and natural dialogue, 415
    speaking the user's language, 416
hidden links, 6
hierarchical task analysis, 101–106
    application-level goals and procedures, 102
    contextual inquiry, 102, 105
    decomposing user tasks, 103, 106
    GOMS analysis, 106, 107
    in hybrid approach, 108–110
    platform-level goals and procedures, 101
    stopping point for task decomposition, 106
    understanding tasks, 102–103, 104–105
    user-level goals and procedures, 101
    for web site design, 103, 106
hierarchy site topology, 146, 147
high-end prototypes, 241, 242, 243
high-end users, low-end users vs., 56
highlighting
    for emphasis, 279
    in mockups, 224, 225
hit log analysis, 393–400
    conversion rates, 394, 396–397
    for demographics, 399
    design change analysis, 395–396
    determining page value, 398–399
    entrance pages, 394–395
    establishing peak times, 397, 399
    finding orphaned pages, 397
    finding popular pages, 397
    overall hits, 393
    report example, 394
    search terms used to reach site, 395, 398
    system down-time, 400
    watching general growth over time, 396

Holtzblatt, K., 102
Home link
    browser button, 129
    buttons for, 164
    on navigation bars, 156–157
home page, 265–266
HON Code of Conduct, 268, 269
horizontal navigation bars, 326, 328
HTML coding
    for accuracy, 354–355
    code review, 374–375
    for maintenance, 355
    for rendering, 354
    for search engines, 355
    for speed, 354
    support tools, 351–352
    text, 251
    unit testing, 375
    See also HTML tags
HTML page construction
    in client-side development, 353
    coding guidelines, 354–355
    coding text, 251
    evolving standards, 355
    graphics-based text vs. HTML text, 311
HTML tags
    \<alt\>, 391
    \<blink\>, 297
    \<head\>, 176
    for margins, 209
    metatags, 175, 176, 258
    semantic vs. format tags, 298–299
    \<title\>, 167, 168, 175, 273
    TITLE parameter for links, 288
    XML vs., 356
human error. *See* error tolerance; errors
human memory issues, 7–9
    accessibility issues, 47
    heuristic evaluation, 416
    increasing memorability, 262
    similarity among items, 7
    time frame too long, 7
    too many items, 7
human perceptual issues, 4–5, 310. *See also* Gestalt principles
hybrid approach to task analysis, 108–110
    determining appropriate technologies, 110
    hierarchical task analysis, 109
    use case analysis, 108–109
hybrid site topologies, 147, 148

icon design, 314–318, 319–320
    brainstorming, 315–317

characteristics of good icons, 315
choosing the best, 317
Form for Brainstorming Icons, 316
Form for Testing Whether a Set of Icons
    Maps Uniquely to a Set of Concepts,
    320
Form for Testing Whether an Icon Is
    Recognizable, 319
limiting options, 317
overview, 314–315
refining with details, 317
testing, 317–318, 319–320
identifying human errors, 115
images. *See* graphics
implementation-based organization,
    150–151
indexes
    for navigation, 161, 162
    promoting web sites and, 389–390
    in search functions, 171, 172
indirect users, 65
information architecture, 120–177
    Architecture Review Checklist, 142,
        144–145
    browser support for navigation, 19
    defined, 120
    development process, 130–142
    garden paths, 125
    Internet framework for site, 175–177
    labeling links, 164–168
    maintenance and expansion, 142–143
    navigation bars, 155–163
    navigation flaws, 5–7
    navigation styles and models, 120–129
    organization schemes, 146–155
    orientation cues, 167–169, 175, 257
    overview, 120
    scanning vs. page traversal costs,
        124–125
    search techniques and search engine
        design, 169–175
    style guide, 142–143
    testing, 131, 141–142
information architecture development,
    130–142
    bottom-up vs. top-down design, 131–132
    card sorting technique, 138, 140–141
    representing the architecture, 132–139
    review checklist, 142, 144–145
    typical process, 130–131
information architecture representations,
    132–139
    diagramming conventions, 137–138
    flowcharts, 133
    outlines, 132, 137

page schematics, 136, 137
sexy diagrams, 135, 137
suiting to roles, 137
tree diagrams, 134, 137
wireframes, 136, 137
information collection for site content, 251,
    252, 255
information costs navigation model, 124,
    127
information foraging navigation model,
    124, 127
information scent (or residue), 121, 123
instruction sheet for user testing, 430
instrumented browsers, 103
integrating design elements, 337
interactivity, 336–337, 360
interbusiness communication, 3
interface consistency, 110–112
international differences in users, 51–55
    country, 51, 52
    currencies, 52, 54
    dates and times, 53, 55
    language, 51, 53
    symbols, 53
    units of measurement, 52, 54
interpreting survey responses, 78
interstitial advertising, 285
interviews, 85–90
    conducting, 85–88
    for content information, 255
    early use of, 38
    for eliciting user needs and functionality,
        87
    focus groups vs., 85, 86
    for mockup reviews, 87
    notetaking during, 89
    preparing for, 89
    recordings of, 88
    sampling issues, 89
    structured vs. unstructured, 86–87
    surveys included with, 86
    for understanding organizations, 88–89
    for understanding tasks, 104
    usefulness issues, 92
    for walkthroughs, 87–88
    See also focus groups
introductory statement for forms, 321, 322
isolating the navigation bar, 334
italics, legibility and, 262–263
iterative design approach
    budgeting for iterations and slack time,
        23
    budgets and deadlines impacting, 17
    overview, 16–17
iterative user testing, 402

Jacobson, Ivar, 99
Java
    accessibility issues, 47
    for client-side development, 353, 358
    Servlet programming, 353
    user preferences and, 50
Java Server Pages (JSPs), 353
JavaScript
    for client-side development, 353, 357
    user preferences and, 50
John, Bonnie, 107
JScript, 357
JSPs (Java Server Pages), 353
just-in-time links, 163

keywords
    in hit log, 395, 398
    padding titles with, 168
    search function syntax, 171

labels for forms, 321, 322–323
labels for links, 164–168
    ambiguous, 5
    controlled vocabulary for, 164
    external links, 165–166
    generating link names, 292
    Home button, 164
    information scent, 121, 123
    labeling systems, 164
    page links, 165
    scope indications, 166–167, 168
    "See also" links, 166
    terminology for, 151–152
    user testing for, 292
    writing text for, 291–292
    "You are here" indicators, 164–165
landmarks for orientation, 169
languages
    accessibility issues, 51, 53
    designing for diversity, 44–45, 46
    flags as national identifiers, 51, 53
large sites, navigation bar design for, 159
last updated date, 274–275
latency diagrams, 348, 349
Launch stage, 368–402
    coordinating with marketing, 388
    domain name check, 387
    final approval, 383, 386–387, 388
    Minimal Maintenance Checklist, 392
    overview, 18
    post-launch tasks, immediate, 388–393
    post-launch testing and analysis, 393–402
    Postproduction Checklist, 383, 384–385,
        387
    pre-launch preparation, 368–369
    as process, 402
    quality assurance (QA) testing, 369–382
    scheduling staffing for, 27
    selecting usability methods and, 32
    taking the site up, 387–388
    See also post-launch tasks; pre-launch
        tasks; quality assurance (QA)
layout. See page layout
leading questions in surveys, 82
learning time
    allocating, 25–26
    selecting usability methods and, 32, 33
    usability objectives, 70
legal expenses, 22
legibility, 47, 247, 257, 262–263
life event organization, 150
Likert scales, 75
line spacing, dynamic font sizes and, 109
linear site topology, 146, 147
links, 285–292
    ambiguous labels for, 5
    Back to Top, 165
    broad vs. deep structures, 148–149
    browser preference settings for colors, 49,
        286
    checklist for, 258
    colors, 258, 285–288, 289–290
    consistent style for, 288, 289–290
    Contact link, 267
    to current page locations, 165
    email, 292
    external, 165–166
    frames and, 362, 363
    garden paths, 125
    hidden or nonstandard, 6
    Home, 156–157, 164
    labels for, 5, 121, 123, 151–152, 164–168,
        291–292
    links pages, 275
    navigation bars, 155–161
    navigation utilities, 161–163
    Next, 157
    nonlinear documents, 285
    Previous, 157
    problems in displaying, 289–290
    to related sites, 175, 177
    "See also" links, 166
    site topologies, 146–149
    standard techniques for indicating, 6
    TITLE parameter for, 288
    types, distinguishing, 288

underlined, 285–286, 287, 288, 289
  See also labels for links; organization
    schemes for web sites
links pages, 275
Linux systems. *See* target platforms
lists, bulleted, 280
literacy, 261
live customer support, 163
load testing, 375–376
lookup tables, perceptual problems for, 4–5
low-end users, high-end users vs., 56

Macromedia Flash, 336–337, 353, 358
Macs. *See* target platforms
maintenance
  costs, 22–23, 24
  frames and, 362
  HTML coding for, 355
  of information architecture, 142–143
  Minimal Maintenance Checklist, 392
  schedule, 391–392
mapping control and data flow, 346–348
  dynamic request trace, 347–348
  static design diagrams, 347
  system latency diagrams, 348, 349
margins, HTML tags for, 209
market segment of target audience, 45
marketing
  background research and, 72
  content and, 264
  costs, 22, 24
  launch coordination with, 388
  resources for user statistics, 38
  scenarios' usefulness and, 42
  See also advertising; promotion
materials
  for graphic design, 305, 306–307
  training materials as resources, 104
  for user testing, 428–431
  Web Site Materials Request Form, 305,
    306–307
matrix site topology, 146, 147
memorability, increasing, 262
memory, human. *See* human memory issues
mental maps navigation model, 123, 125,
    126, 128
metaphors. *See* visual metaphors
metatags, 175, 176, 258
metatext, 258
Microsoft Access, 360–361
milestones
  defined, 26
  documenting, 30
  in typical project schedule, 19

minesweeping navigation, 125
Minimal Maintenance Checklist, 392
mining for usability problems, 34
minor errors, 377
minus sign (-) with search keywords, 171
mission-critical errors, 377
mitigating error consequences, 115
Mockup Checklist, 231
mockup review process, 232–238
  achieving closure, 234
  communicating about, 235
  development schedule sample, 223
  Mockup Style Review Form, 234–235,
    236–237
  multiple draft system for, 232–234
  procedures needed for, 232, 234
  sign-off, 234, 238
  tips, 235, 238
Mockup Style Review Form, 234–235,
    236–237
mockups, 216–238
  bad alternatives, leaving out, 235
  checking for missing requirements, 230,
    231
  for client review, 222, 230
  creation process, 220–231
  digital mockups, 218–219
  for early stages, 220, 223
  for early user testing, 215–217
  fidelity of, 216
  focus groups for reviews, 87
  goals of, 214–216
  greeking in, 222, 224, 229
  highlighting in, 224, 225
  idea generation, 217
  for internal use, 222
  for later stages, 220, 223
  Mockup Checklist, 231
  outlining in, 224, 225
  overview, 216–220
  page boundaries, 228
  for page structure exploration, 214, 215
  paper mockups, 218
  paper vs. digital mockups, 219–220, 221
  photo placement indications, 226, 229
  pitfalls of early client involvement, 215
  realistic quality for, 235
  refining with details, 229–230
  review process, 232–238
  roughing the basic elements and struc-
    ture, 228
  selecting pages to mock up, 220, 222, 223
  shadows in, 224, 225
  sketches in, 224–225, 226
  sketching in major elements, 228–229

mockups *(continued)*
  step-by-step example, 227–230
  techniques, 222, 224–226
  thumbnail sketches, 217
  thumbnails for, 227
Mockups and Prototypes stage
  envisioning design, 214–243
  fidelity and, 216
  focus groups for reviewing, 87
  goals, 180–181, 214–216
  mockups, 216–238
  overview, 18
  page layout, 180–210
  prototypes, 238–243
  scheduling staffing for, 27
  selecting usability methods and, 32
  See also mockups; page layout; prototypes
modem speed differences, 61
moderate errors, 377
monitors
  frames and, 363
  reading on a screen, 262–263
  screen resolutions, 55, 57, 59, 60,
    204–205
Moran, T. P., 107
Morkes, J., 256
mouse-over events, 358
multimedia, 334–337
  animation, 334–336
  interactive, 336–337
  Macromedia Flash, 336–337
multipage search results, 174
multiple choice items in surveys, 75
multiple columns, 200
multiple navigation areas, 333
multiple pages, 284–285
multiple projects, scheduling, 28
multipurpose design, diversity issues, 45
mystery meat navigation, 125
Mythical Man-Month, 343

names for links. *See* labels for links
narrow path approach, 155
navigation bars, 155–161
  alternative utilities, 161–163
  breadcrumbs, 157, 159, 177
  deciding which links to show, 156–160
  expanding outlines, 158–159
  frames and, 363
  Home link on, 156–157
  horizontal, 326, 328
  isolating, 334
  layout, 326–330
  minimal forms, 156–157
  order of options on, 152

Previous and Next links on, 157
  as primary browsing mechanism,
    155–156
  progress bars, 159, 160
  redundant, 160–161
  screen real estate limitations and,
    326–328
  for standalone subsites, 160
  subnav design, 331–332, 333
  subpages on, 156
  top-level categories on, 157–158
  vertical, 326, 327, 328
  for very large sites, 159
navigation design, 325–334
  cascading menus, 327–328, 329
  combined approaches, 330
  drop-down menus, 327, 329
  grouping navigation items, 333
  horizontal navigation bars, 326, 328
  isolating the navigation bar, 334
  multiple navigation areas, 333
  navigation bar layout, 326–330
  presentation, 325–326
  screen real estate limitations and,
    326–328
  scrolling lists, 330
  sideways text, 329
  subnav design, 331–332, 333
  tabs, 330
  usability inspection for, 414, 445–446
  vertical navigation bars, 326, 327, 328
  visual metaphors, 325–326, 327
  See also information architecture
navigation flaws, 5–7
  ambiguous links, 5
  hidden links, 6
  lack of context, 6–7
  nonstandard navigation elements, 6
  poor site identification, 7, 8
navigation (router) pages, 153
navigation styles and models, 120–129
  assumptions about users, 126–127
  browser support for navigation, 129
  design implications of, 126–127
  garden paths, 125
  information costs model, 124, 127
  information foraging model, 124, 127
  information scent and, 121, 123
  mental maps model, 123, 125, 126, 128
  minesweeping, 125
  mystery meat navigation, 125
  omniscience model, 121, 126
  optimal rationality model, 121, 126
  rote memorization model, 123–124, 127
  satisficing model, 121–122, 126
  scanning vs. page traversal costs, 124–125

sense-making, 125, 128
tasks and navigation styles, 121
navigation utilities
contact information, 161
help systems, 161
indexes, 161, 162
just-in-time links, 163
live customer support, 163
navigation area, 273
navigation bars, 155–161
site maps, 161, 162
tables of contents, 161, 162
negative questions in surveys, 81
network speed differences, 43, 61
newbies. *See* novice users
Newell, A., 107
news and information articles, example, 248
Next link, 157
Nielsen, J., 256, 415
non-body text, 281
nonlinear documents, 285
notetaking
for interviews or focus groups, 89
for user testing, 437
novice users
designing for, 56
scrolling neglected by, 199
user testing and, 428

objective writing, 279
objectives for the site, 65–72
business goals, 69
Client Interview/Web Site Information
Worksheet, 66–67
functional specifications, 70–72
Goals Checklist, 68
informed vs. presumed, 93
stakeholders, 65
usability objectives, 69–70
user goals, 69
objectives of envisioning design, 214–216
cut costs, 216
explore and define the design space, 215
get everyone involved, 214–215
increase quality, 216
providing for early user testing, 215–216
reduce errors, 216
objectives of page layout, 180–181
aesthetics, 180
consistency, 181, 182, 184, 185, 188
focus, 181, 182
rationale for, 181–182
simplicity, 180, 182, 184, 185–187
observation, for understanding tasks, 104
omniscience navigation model, 121, 126

online forms
action buttons, 323, 325
checkboxes, 323, 325
checklist for, 258
controls, 322–323, 324–325
designing, 318, 321–325
drop down menus, 322, 324
elements of, 321–323
example, 249
identifying required fields, 321
introductory statement, 321, 323
keeping short, 321
labels, 321, 323–324
layout, 323–325
radio buttons, 322, 325
scripting for validation, 358
scrolling lists, 322, 324
style guide for, 318, 321
text fields, 322, 324
open card sort, 138, 140
operating expenses
development costs, 21–22
maintenance costs, 22–23, 24
operating procedures, understanding tasks
from, 104
operating systems, 56–57, 58–59. *See also* target platforms
optimal rationality navigation model, 121, 126
Oracle, 361
order of options on navigation bars, 152
org chart approach to structure, 150
org chart-based link labels, 152
organization schemes for web sites, 146–155
broad vs. deep structures, 148–149
order of options on navigation bars, 152
paths or trails, 155
semantics, 149–151
support pages, 152–154
terminology influences, 151–152
topologies, 146–148
organizational roles, understanding, 88–89
orientation cues, 167–169, 175, 257
orphaned pages, finding, 397
outlines
of information architecture, 132, 137
navigation bar style, 158–159
subnav design, 331
outlining in mockups, 224, 225
outsourcing testing, 376–377

page layout, 180–210
aesthetics, 180
balance, 188–190
basic layout, 182–183
breaking the rules, 194, 196–197

page layout *(continued)*
   breaking up text, 279
   bulleted lists, 280
   common page structures, 183–184
   common problems, 109–110
   consistency, 181, 182, 184, 185, 188
   constraints, pitfalls, and solutions,
      197–210
   contrast, 188
   dynamic font sizes and line spacing, 109
   "false bottoms," 282–284
   focus, 181, 182
   font size and, 295, 296
   form layout, 323–325
   gaps and gutter sizes, 208–209
   Gestalt principles, 192–194, 195, 197
   goals, 180–182
   headings, 280
   landmarks, 169
   less is better, 183
   margins, HTML tags for, 209
   navigation bar layout, 326–330
   orientation cues, 167–169, 175, 257
   page components, 182–183, 272–275
   paper-based vs. web-based documents,
      197–198
   pop-out effect, 195, 196, 197
   reducing attention-grabbing items, 185,
      187
   reducing visual vertical lines, 185, 186
   repetition, 190–192
   resolution and page-width restrictions,
      199–210
   scrolling and, 282–284
   simplicity, 180, 182, 184, 185–187
   "sweet spot," 198–199, 207–208
   techniques, 184–197
   templates, 184–185
   titles, 167–168, 273
   usability and, 210
   white space, 210
   Writing Guidelines Checklist, 257–259
   See also page-width restrictions
page links, 165
page schematics, of information architecture,
   136, 137
page structure exploration. *See* mockups; prototypes
page titles, 167–168, 273
page-tracking spreadsheet, 350
page traversal vs. scanning costs, 124–125
page-width restrictions, 199–210
   combination approach, 200–201, 207
   common problems, 109–110
   fixed-width approach, 200–201, 204–207
   problems from, 199, 202

   screen space used by browsers, 204, 205,
      206
   "sweet spot," 198–199, 207–208
   variable-width approach, 200–201,
      203–204
pagination, 258
paper-based vs. web-based documents,
   197–198
paper mockups
   described, 218
   digital mockups vs., 219–220, 221
   strengths and weaknesses, 221
   thumbnails vs., 218
   See also mockups
paper storyboards, 239–240, 242. *See also* prototypes
parametric searches, 170
passive voice, 276
patent issues, 83
paths or trails, 155
PCs. *See* target platforms
PDAs, 282
PDF (Portable Document Format), 293
peak times, establishing, 397, 399
perceptual issues, 4–5, 310. *See also* Gestalt
   principles.
performance
   download time, 61
   frames and, 362
   HTML coding for, 354
   network speed differences, 43, 61
   poor response times, 340–341
   web guidelines, 414
   www.whitehouse.gov example, 445
   See also user performance improvements
person (writing style), 276
pervasive usability, 11, 14, 35
Pervasive Usability Process
   as ideal model, 16
   illustrated, 15
   iterative design in, 16–17
   overview, 15–16
   project schedule, 19
   stages, 17
   See also specific stages
photos
   placement indications in mockups, 226,
      229
   in scenarios, 42
   See also graphics
PHP, 353
pictures. *See* graphics
pilot testing, 433
platforms. *See* target platforms
plug-ins
   guidelines for using, 50

user preferences and, 49, 56
pluralistic walkthroughs, 420–421
plus sign (+) with search keywords, 171
Policies page, 268, 269
pop-out effect, 195, 196, 197
popular pages, in hit log, 397
Portable Document Format (PDF), 293
post-launch tasks
    customer feedback, dealing with, 400–401
    hit log analysis, 393–400
    immediate, 388–393
    maintenance schedule, 391–392
    Minimal Maintenance Checklist, 392
    planning updates and revisions, 392–393
    promotion, 388–391
    responding to problems, 391
    testing and analysis, 393–402
post-questionnaire and demographics sheet,
    431
Postproduction Checklist, 383, 384–385, 387
pre-attentive processing, 197
pre-launch tasks
    domain name check, 387
    domain name registration, 369, 370
    final approval, 383, 386–387, 388
    functionality test, 387
    planning, 368–369
    Postproduction Checklist, 383, 384–385,
        387
    quality assurance (QA) testing, 369–382
    schedule development, 368
    See also quality assurance (QA)
precise search results, 172
preference settings of users, 49–50, 286
Presentation tier, 345, 346
Pressman, R., 343
preventing human errors, 115
Previous link, 157
print writing vs. web writing, 281–293
    forcing messages on the user, 285, 286
    links, 285–292
    multiple pages, 284–285
    non-body text, 281
    PDF documents, 293
    scrolling, 282–284
    supporting screen readers, 282, 283, 298
    text-only browsing, 281, 282, 283
printing, frames and, 362
privacy
    HON Code of Conduct, 268, 269
    Policies page, 268, 269
    target audience and, 38
Problem Report and Resolution Form, 380,
    381
Problem Summary Report, 380, 382
processing levels in reading, 262

production servers, 350
Production stage
    color, 309–310
    content supported by graphics, 304
    design elements, 304–337
    establishing parameters, 305–309
    gathering materials, 305, 306–307
    icon design, 314–318, 319–320
    interactivity and multimedia, 334–337
    navigation design, 325–334
    online forms, 318, 321–325
    overview, 18
    scheduling staffing for, 27
    selecting usability methods and, 32
    typography, 310–314
    usability in software development,
        340–364
    writing for the web, 246–301
    See also graphic design; software develop-
        ment; writing for the web
productivity, technology and increase in, 4
Products and Services pages, 267, 268
programming
    client-side, 353, 358–359
    code review, 374–375
    coding errors, 378
    server-side, 353, 359–360
progress bars, 159, 160
project management
    documentation, 30
    effective communication, 29
    elements of, 20
    forms for, 30
    overview, 20–21
    stakeholders, 21
    standardizing your process, 29
    techniques for succeeding at, 29–30
    tools, 351
    tradeoffs, 20–21
project schedule
    Client Interview/Web Site Information
        Worksheet, 66–67
    learning time, 25–26
    maintenance, 391–392
    mockup development schedule sample,
        233
    for multiple projects, 28
    overview, 19
    pre-launch, 368
    scheduling staffing by project stage,
        27–28
    terminology, 26–27
    typical example, 19
promotion, 388–391
    for directories and search engines,
        388–389

promotion *(continued)*
  for directory or categorical web indexes, 389–390
  for query-based search engines, 390–391
  See also advertising; marketing
prose fiction content example, 249
prototypes, 238–243
  for early user testing, 215–216
  fidelity of, 216
  goals of, 214–216
  high-end, 241, 242, 243
  methods compared, 242
  overview, 238
  for page and site structure exploration, 214, 215
  pitfalls of early client involvement, 215
  redesigning tip, 241
  storyboards, 238–241
  text-only site versions from wireframes, 243
  wireframes, 136, 137, 241, 242, 243
proximity (Gestalt principle), 192, 195
pull quotes, 273, 274
punctuation, 277

quality assurance (QA), 369–382
  automated testing, 375, 376
  challenge of, 369–372
  code review, 374–375
  comprehensive testing procedures, 374–377
  as continuous process, 369
  dealing with errors, 378–379
  feedback methods, 372
  fixing bugs, 380
  integrating into process, 371–372
  load testing, 375–376
  Minimal Maintenance Checklist, 391, 392
  outsourcing testing, 376–377
  Problem Report and Resolution Form, 380, 381
  Problem Summary Report, 380, 382
  purposes of, 370–371
  regression testing, 372, 408
  reporting problems, 380, 381–382
  severity of errors, 377
  task-based testing, 373–374
  test completion criteria, 379–380
  types of errors, 378
  usability as subset of, 14
  See also testing
quality of content, 264
question skipping in surveys, 81
quotes, pull, 273, 274

radio buttons in forms, 322, 325
range bias in survey questions, 82
readability, 247, 257
reading considerations
  given-new approach, 261–262
  levels of processing, 262
  literacy and, 261
  scanning the page, 256, 260–261
  on screen, 262–263
  screen readers, 282, 298
  task-orientation and, 256
  topic-comment approach, 261–262
recall (search results), 172–173
recovery from human errors
  defined, 115
  example, 116–117
  See also error tolerance; errors
reducing human errors, 115
redundant navigation bars, 160–161
reference information, example, 248
Reference pages, 153
registering your domain name, 369, 370
regression testing, 372, 408
relevance, search functions and, 171, 173
remote user testing, 440–441
rendering, HTML coding for, 354
repetition in page layout, 190–192
required tasks, usability methods and, 31, 32
Requirements Analysis stage
  background research, 72–92
  competitive analysis, 83–85
  overview, 17
  scenarios, 39–42
  scheduling staffing for, 27
  selecting usability methods and, 31, 32, 34
  setting web site objectives, 65–72
  surveys, 72–82
  target audience, 38–55
  target platforms, 55–61
  user needs analysis, 64–93
  See also target audience; target platforms
resolution, screen, 55, 57, 59, 60, 204–205.
      See also page-width restrictions
resources
  critical, 21
  money (budget), 21–24
  staff, 24–26
  time (scheduling), 26–28
respect for the user, 415, 448–449
response order for surveys, 81
response rates to survey items, 75, 78
response time, poor, 340–341
RetroAccess (accessibility evaluation tool), 46
return rate for surveys, 78–79

reuse, XML and, 356
reviews
    code review, 374–375
    group walkthroughs, 406, 419–423
    information architecture development,
       142, 144–145
    mockup review process, 232–238
    usability inspection, 406, 408–419
    Writing Guidelines Checklist, 257–259
    of written text, 251, 256
    See also testing
revisions, planning for, 392–393
revisits as usability objective, 70
role-based link labels, 152
rollovers, 358
rote answers in surveys, 81
rote memorization navigation model,
    123–124, 127
router pages, 153

sampling issues
    for interviews and focus groups, 89
    for surveys, 78–80
satisficing navigation model, 121–122, 126
scalability of sites, 308–309
Scandinavian design tradition, 421
scannability, 257
scanning the page (by readers), 256, 260–261
scanning vs. page traversal costs, 124–125
scenarios for target audience, 39–42
    example, 40–41
    goal of, 39
    number needed, 39
    schedule and interaction episode in,
       41–42
    sketch or photo in, 42
    usefulness issues, 42
    user profile in, 41–42
    uses of, 39
    validating, 39
scenarios for use case analysis, 108–109
schedule and interaction episode in scenar-
    ios, 41–42
scheduling. *See* project schedule
scope
    indications for links, 166–167
    scope notes, 166–168
    of sites, 166, 308–309
    www.whitehouse.gov example, 444
screen
    fonts, 294–295
    frames and, 363
    reading on, 262–263
    real estate limitations and navigation

    design, 326–328
    resolutions, 55, 57, 59, 60, 204–205
    space used by browsers, 204, 205, 206
    See also page-width restrictions
screen fonts, 294–295
screen readers, 282, 298
screen space used by browsers, 204, 205, 206
scribes for group walkthroughs, 422
scripting. *See* client-side scripting
scrolling
    frames and, 362, 363
    novice users' neglect of, 199
    usability issues, 202–204
scrolling lists
    in forms, 322, 324
    for navigation, 330
Search button, 129
search functions
    Boolean searches, 169–170
    database interaction guidelines, 360
    desirable capabilities, 171–172
    displaying results, 173–175
    domain-specific terminology, 173
    frames and, 363
    full-text retrieval systems, 171
    helping users, 174
    HTML coding for, 355
    multipage results, 174
    need for, 169
    no matches, help after, 174
    obtaining search engines, 171
    parametric searches, 170
    precision in results, 172
    promotion for search engines and
       directories, 388–391
    quality of results, 172–173
    recall, 172–173
    relevance of results, 171, 173
    repeating the query, 172
    search engine design, 171–175
    similar documents, help for finding, 174
    sorting result listings, 175
    specifying number of results, 172
    style guide for search engines, 254
    syntax for searches, 171
    title and description for results, 174
    too many results, 174
    traditional database searches, 171
    users' search techniques, 169–171
    XML for, 357
search terms used to reach site, 395, 398
section-oriented subnav, 332
security
    target audience and, 38
    user preferences and, 50

selecting survey recipients, 79–80
self-selection issues for surveys, 80
semantic tags (HTML), format tags vs.,
   298–299
semantics-based organization, 149–151
   implementation approach, 150–151
   life event approach, 150
   org chart approach, 150
   purity of approaches, 151
   systematic approach in absence of
      semantic relationships, 151
   task-based approach, 149–150
   topical approach, 150
   user type approach, 150
sense-making navigation, 125, 128
sentence fragments, 277–278
server-side development, 353
service marks, 275
Services pages, 267, 268
Services tier, 345–346
sexy diagrams, 135, 137
shadows
   legibility and, 263
   in mockups, 224, 225
shipping, design issues for, 65
shortcuts, 417
sidebars, 273
sideways text for navigation, 329
similarity (Gestalt principle), 193, 195
similarity matching (card sorting technique),
   141
simplicity
   heuristic evaluation of, 415
   in page layout, 180, 182, 184, 185–187
   web guidelines, 414
site management tools, 351
site maps, 161, 162, 270, 271
site structure exploration. *See* prototypes
situational disabilities, 48–49
sketches
   in mockups, 224–225, 226
   in scenarios, 42
slack time, 23, 26
software development, 340–364
   3-tiered architectures, 345–346
   asset management, 349–350
   choosing web site development tools,
      350–352
   engineering web site components,
      353–361
   mapping control and data flow, 346–348
   need for software engineers, 344
   principled, 364
   production servers, 350
   requirements and specifications, 343–344

staging servers, 350
   usability of web technologies, 361–364
   usability problems, 340–342
   version control, 348–349
   web site engineering techniques, 343–352
Software Engineering, 343
software engineering. *See* software development
software usability problems, 340–342
   platform incompatibilities, 341
   poor product documentation, 342
   poor response time, 340–341
   poor use of technology, 342
   web page code inconsistency, 341
software, user. *See* browsers; target platforms
sorting search result listings, 175
specific writing, 279
speech synthesizers (screen readers), 282, 298
speed. *See* performance
spelling
   domain name alternates, 369, 370
   spell-correction in search functions, 172
   style guide for, 254
Spiral engineering method, 343
splash pages, 265, 266
squint test for emphasis use, 312
staffing
   challenges, 24
   Client Team, 24–25
   cross-disciplinary interaction, 26
   Design Team, 24–25
   as highest budget cost, 21
   learning on the job, 25–26
   scheduling by project stage, 27–28
staging servers, 350
stakeholders
   Client Interview/Web Site Information
      Worksheet, 66–67
   communicating with, 29
   Goals Checklist, 68
   identifying, 65, 68
   indirect users, 65
   overview, 21
standalone subsites, 160
standardizing processes, 29
standards
   for accessibility, 46
   link indications, 6
   for writing style, 259, 277
static design diagrams, 347
stem words, search functions and, 172
stop words, search functions and, 172
storyboards
   digital, 241, 242
   digital vs. paper, 242

overview, 238–239
paper, 239–240, 242
strengths and weaknesses, 242
See also prototypes
structural errors, 378
style guides
for graphic design, 305, 308
for information architecture, 142–143
for online forms, 318, 321
for site content, 251–252, 253–254
style sheets, 297
subjectively pleasing design, 3, 70
subnav design, 331–332, 333
subsites, standalone, 160
support pages, 152–154
error pages, 153, 154
help pages, 153, 154
router pages, 153
surveys, 72–82
ambiguous questions or responses in, 82
bias, avoiding, 80–82
checkboxes and checklists, 75
of demographic information, 73
design impact of questions, 73–74
early use of, 38
by email, 80
form example, 76–77
free response items, 74
information to seek, 72–74
interpreting responses, 78
with interviews or focus groups, 86
leading questions in, 82
Likert scales in, 75
multiple choice items, 75
negative questions in, 81
pretesting questions, 81
question skipping in, 81
range bias in questions, 82
response order for, 81
response rates to items, 75, 78
return rate for, 78–79
rote answers in, 81
sampling issues, 78–80
selecting recipients, 79–80
self-selection issues, 80
structuring responses to, 74–75, 78
usefulness issues, 82
of user needs and preferences, 73
"sweet spot" for page layout, 198–199,
207–208
symbols, international differences in, 53
symmetrical balance, 188, 189, 190
synonyms, search functions and, 169, 172
system down-time, 400
system latency diagrams, 348, 349

tables of contents, for navigation, 161, 162
tabs for navigation, 330
tags. *See* HTML tags
target audience, 38–55
deciding who to exclude, 42–43
demographics of, 38, 45–49
designing for diversity, 42–45
differences in user preference settings,
49–50, 286
disabilities and, 45–49
experience level of, 45
individual differences, 45–49
international differences, 51–55
low-end vs. high-end users, 56
market segment of, 45
mockup review process, 232–238
novice users, 56
resources for user statistics, 38
scenarios, 39–42
surveys and interviews with, 38
See also user needs analysis
target platforms, 55–61
browsers, 59–61
compatibility issues, 341
defined, 38
designing for diversity, 42–45
differences in user preference settings,
49–50, 286
fixed-width pages and, 201–202, 204–207
gutter sizes for browsers, 208–209
hardware and operating systems, 56–57,
58–59
monitors, 55, 57, 59, 60
network speed differences, 43, 61
non-optimal systems, 55–56
platform errors, 378
screen resolutions, 55, 57, 59, 204
screen space used by browsers, 204, 205,
206
typefaces and, 294–295
usability inspection for, 414, 448
XML and, 356
See also browsers
task analysis, 96–117
defined, 96
as design road map, 99
flowchart example, 97, 98
GOMS analysis, 106, 107
hierarchical, 101–106, 107
human-error-tolerant design, 115–117
hybrid approach, 108–110
inefficient task example, 114–115
levels to consider, 99
overview, 96–99
performance improvements, 110–115

task analysis *(continued)*
    task defined, 96
    use case analysis, 99–101
    user goals and, 96
    for web site design, 99
    See also hierarchical task analysis; use
        case analysis
task-based link labels, 152
task-based organization approach, 149–150
task questionnaires for user testing, 430
tasks
    defined, 96
    navigation styles and, 121
technology support tools, 352
templates for page layout, 184–185
temporary disabilities, 48
terminology
    domain-specific, 173
    influences on organization, 151–152
test completion criteria, 379–380
testing
    automated, 375, 376
    on browser varieties, 59–60
    code test, 374–377
    colors in grayscale, 309
    diary studies, 427
    domain name check, 387
    fixing problems, 407–408
    functionality test, 387
    hit log analysis, 393–400
    icons, 317–318, 319–320
    information architecture, 131, 141–142
    link names, 292
    load testing, 375–376
    outsourcing, 376–377
    pilot testing, 433
    post-launch testing and analysis, 393–402
    providing for early user testing, 215–217
    quality assurance (QA) testing, 369–382
    regression testing, 372, 408
    squint test for emphasis use, 312
    survey questions, 81
    test completion criteria, 379–380
    user testing, 402, 406, 423–441
    in writing process, 251, 256
    See also post-launch tasks; quality assur-
        ance (QA); user testing
Testing Script, 428–429
tethered subnav, 332
text
    ALT text for images, 281
    body text, 273
    breaking up, 279, 284–285
    brochureware, 252
    colors, 258, 285–288

delivery formats, 254
dynamic, 247, 250
formatting, 253–254, 294–300
graphics-based vs. HTML, 311
greeking, 222, 224, 229
legibility, 47, 247, 257, 262–263
for links, 291–292
non-body, 281
readability, 247, 257
scannability, 257
search engines' need for, 391
static, colors for, 287
text-only browsing, 243, 281, 282, 283
underlined, 285–286, 287, 288, 289
See also fonts; formatting text; labels for
    links; typography; writing for the web
text fields in forms, 322, 324
text-only browsing, 243, 281, 282, 283
think-aloud protocol, 105
three-click rule, 70
thumbnail sketches
    described, 217
    paper mockups vs., 218
    starting mockups from, 227
    See also mockups
tiered subnav, 333
time formats, international differences in, 53,
    55
time to perform, selecting usability methods
    and, 31, 32
Times fonts, 294
TITLE parameter for links, 288
<title> tag (HTML), 167–168, 175, 273
titles
    ambiguous, 278, 279
    for pages, 167–168, 273, 281
    for search results, 174
tone of writing, 276–277
top-down approach
    to card sorting, 141
    to information architecture design,
        131–132
top-level categories on navigation bars,
    157–158
topic-based link labels, 152
topic-comment approach to reading, 261–262
topical organization, 150
topologies of sites, 146–148
    arbitrary network, 147, 148
    full mesh, 146, 147
    hierarchy or tree, 146, 147
    hybrid, 147, 148
    linear, 146, 147
    matrix or grid, 146, 147
total quality management (TQM), 14

trademarks
    checklist for, 259
    overview, 275
    style guide for, 254
tradeoffs
    digital mockups, 219
    with Flash, 336
    in graphic design, 304
    inevitability of, 20
    key principles for making, 20–21
    overview, 20–21
    page width issues, 200–201
    scanning vs. page traversal costs, 124–125
    setting objectives and, 65
trails or paths, 155
training materials, understanding tasks from, 104
tree diagrams of information architecture, 134, 137
tree site topology, 146, 147
type effects, 297–298
typefaces. *See* fonts; typography
typography, 310–314
    contrasting typefaces, 314
    emphasizing structure, 314
    graphics-based text vs. HTML text, 311
    knowing your typefaces, 311
    matching typeface to content, 310–311, 312
    not going overboard, 311–312
    squint test for emphasis use, 312
    unpredictability of typefaces, 294–295
    variations on a single typeface, 312–313

underlined links, 285–286, 287, 288, 289
units of measurement, international differences in, 52, 54
Unix systems. *See* target platforms
updating
    content for currency, 264–265
    last updated date, 274–275
    planning for, 392–393
usability
    defined, 2
    design goals, 2–3
    example of poor usability, 2
    of frames, 361–364
    importance of, 3–4
    page layout and, 210
    software engineers as critical for, 344
    software problems, 340–342
    stakeholder priorities and, 21
    types of, 34–35
    of web technologies, 361–364
    See also Pervasive Usability Process

usability evaluation, 406–441
    converging operations principle, 407
    early vs. late, 409
    fixing problems, 407–408
    group walkthroughs, 406, 419–423
    throughout the design process, 441
    timing for, 408, 409
    types of, 406–408
    usability inspection, 406, 408–419
    user testing, 406, 423–441
    See also group walkthroughs; usability inspection; user testing
usability inspection, 408–419
    automatic, 419
    checklists, 410–411, 412–413
    Detailed General-Purpose Checklist, 412–413
    heuristic evaluation, 415–417
    limitations of, 408–410
    overview, 406
    performing, 417–419
    web guidelines, 411, 414–415
    www.whitehouse.gov example, 444–449
usability methods
    cost analysis for, 30–31
    deciding upon, 34–35
    defined, 14–15
    estimating in user's absence, 15
    framework for contrasting, 32–33
    real data from real users, 15
    selection criteria for, 31–34
    user study approaches and, 34–35
usability objectives
    defining, 69–70
    examples, 70
    Goals Checklist, 68
    three-click rule and, 70
usability problems
    database integration, 9–11
    human memory, 7–9
    human perception, 4–5
    navigation, 5–7
use case analysis, 99–101
    example diagram, 101
    example specification, 100
    in hybrid approach, 108–109
    overview, 99–100
    weaknesses of, 100–101
user goals
    defining, 69
    Goals Checklist, 68
    task analysis and, 96
user needs analysis, 64–93
    background research, 72–92
    Client Interview/Web Site Information Worksheet, 66–67

user needs analysis *(continued)*
    competitive analysis, 83–85
    Goals Checklist, 68
    objectives of, 64–65, 93
    primary activities in, 64
    surveys, 72–82
    target audience, 38–55
    web site objectives, 65–72
user performance improvements, 110–115
    brevity for, 112
    clarity for, 112
    combined functionality for, 112, 114
    inefficient task example, 114–115
    interface consistency for, 110–112
user platforms. *See* target platforms
user profiles
    for target audience, 4
    in use case analysis, 108–109
user studies
    comparison testing, 35
    criterion testing, 34–35
    mining for problems, 34
user testing, 423–441
    analyzing results, 439
    assembling materials, 428–431
    co-discovery method, 438–439
    conducting the test, 436–439
    Consent Form, 430, 431
    continual, 402
    deciding what to test, 426–427
    diary studies, 427
    experimenter notes pages, 430
    expert vs. novice use, 428
    finding users to test, 434
    follow-up sheet, 431
    instruction sheet, 430
    interacting with users, 438–439
    iterative, 402
    location preparation, 432
    modifying design after, 439–440
    notetaking, 437
    number of users to test, 434–435
    overview, 406, 423
    pilot testing, 433
    planning the test, 426–428
    post-questionnaire and demographics
        sheet, 431
    process of, 423
    question formulation, 427–428
    recruiting process for users, 435–436
    remote, 440–441
    selecting users to test, 433–434
    task questionnaires, 430
    tester for, 437–438
    testing script, 428–429

User Testing Preparation Worksheet,
    424–425
user type organization, 150
users, target. *See* target audience

validating
    scenarios for target audience, 39
    scripting for, 358
variable-width pages
    advantages, 200, 203
    combining with fixed-width, 200–201, 207
    disadvantages, 201, 203–204
    using, 203–204
vendors. *See* stakeholders
Verdana screen font, 294–295
version control, 348–349
vertical navigation bars, 326, 327, 328
Visual Basic scripting, 353
visual design, usability inspection for, 414,
    447, 448
visual metaphors for navigation, 325–326, 327
vocabulary, controlled, for link labels, 164

walkthroughs. *See* group walkthroughs
Waterfall engineering method, 343
web-based vs. paper-based documents,
    197–198
web browsers. *See* browsers
web guidelines, 411
    appropriateness to task, 414, 446–447
    compatibility, 414, 448
    consistency and contrast, 415, 448, 449
    content and scope, 411, 444–445
    error handling, 415, 448, 449
    navigation, 414, 445–446, 447
    respect for the user, 415, 448–449
    simplicity, 414, 448
    speed, 414, 445
    visual design, 414, 447, 448
    www.whitehouse.gov example, 444–449
Web Site Final Approval Form, 383, 386–387
Web Site Materials Request Form, 305,
    306–307
Web Site Usability: A Designer's Guide, 283
white space, 210
White House site usability inspection.
        See *www.whitehouse.gov* usability
        inspection
Windows PCs. *See* target platforms
wireframes
    of information architecture, 136, 137
    prototypes, 241, 242, 243
    for text-only browsers, 243

worksheets. *See* forms
writing for print. *See* print writing vs. web
  writing
writing for the web, 246–301
  brochureware, 252
  coding text into HTML, 251
  collecting information, 251, 252, 255
  composition, 251, 255
  content considerations, 250–252, 264–275
  effective communication, 246–256,
    257–259, 301
  forcing messages on the user, 285, 286
  formatting text, 291–293
  how people read, 256, 260–263
  legibility of, 47, 247, 257, 262–263
  links, 285–292
  multiple pages, 284–285
  non-body text, 281
  PDF documents, 293
  planning the project, 250–251
  print writing vs. web writing, 281–293
  process of, 247, 250–256
  readability of, 247, 257
  reviewing, testing, and rewriting, 251, 256
  scrolling and, 282–284
  style considerations, 276–280
  style guide for, 251–252, 253–254
  supporting screen readers, 282, 283
  supporting user tasks and goals, 246
  text-only browsing and, 281, 282, 283
  types of writing, 247, 248–250
  Writing Guidelines Checklist, 257–259
  See also content of sites; formatting text;
    labels for links
Writing Guidelines Checklist, 257–259
writing process, 247, 250–256
  coding text into HTML, 251

  collecting information, 251, 252, 255
  composition, 251, 255
  concise summary, 251
  defining a style guide, 251–252, 253–254
  overview, 247, 250
  planning the project, 250–251
  reviewing, testing, and rewriting, 251, 256
writing style
  basics (grammar, spelling, capitalization,
    punctuation), 276–278
  person, 276
  style guide, 251–252, 253–254
  tone, 276–277
  usage guidelines, 278–280
  voice, 276
  Writing Guidelines Checklist, 257–259
www. in domain names, 370
www.whitehouse.gov usability inspection,
    444–449
  appropriateness to task, 446–447
  compatibility, 448
  consistency and contrast, 448, 449
  content and scope, 444–445
  domain name issues, 448–449
  error handling, 448, 449
  navigation, 445–446, 447
  respect for the user, 448–449
  simplicity, 448
  speed, 445
  visual design, 447, 448

XML (Extensible Markup Language),
    356–357

"You are here" indicators, 164–165

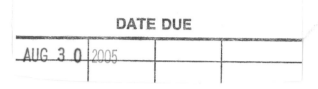
ABOUT THE AUTHORS

Tom Brinck is Chief Usability Officer at Diamond Bullet Design, a firm specializing in web site design and usability consulting. Tom has master's degrees in computer science and cognitive psychology from Stanford University and the University of Michigan, respectively. He's done user interface research at Apple Computer, Toshiba, and Bellcore. He is currently an adjunct faculty member at the University of Michigan's School of Information.

Darren Gergle is a doctoral student in human-computer interaction at Carnegie Mellon University. He has a master's degree in human-computer interaction from the University of Michigan's School of Information, where he performed research at the Collaboratory for Research on Electronic Work. He also received undergraduate degrees in psychology and fine arts from the University of Michigan. Prior to beginning his graduate work, he was the lead designer at Diamond Bullet Design.

Scott D. Wood is a Senior Scientist at Soar Technology, a research and development company focusing on cognitive modeling, artificial intelligence, and information visualization. He has over ten years of research and industry experience in the areas of software development, e-business consulting, cognitive modeling, and human-computer interaction. He earned a B.S. in computer science from Tulane University and an M.S. and Ph.D. in computer science and engineering from the University of Michigan, Ann Arbor.